THE

POETICAL WORKS

OF

J O H N S K E L T O N:

PRINCIPALLY ACCORDING TO THE EDITION

OF THE

REV. ALEXANDER DYCE.

IN THREE VOLUMES.

VOLUME III.

———————

BOSTON:
LITTLE, BROWN AND COMPANY
NEW YORK: BLAKEMAN AND MASON.
CINCINNATI: RICKEY AND CARROLL.
M.DCCC.LXIV.

CAMBRIDGE:

STEREOTYPED BY H. O. HOUGHTON.

Presswork by John Wilson & Son, Boston.

NOTES TO VOLUME I.

OF THE DEATH OF THE NOBLE PRINCE, KYNGE EDWARDE THE FORTH.

Page 3. Edward the Fourth died April 9th, 1483, in the 41st year of his age and the 23d of his reign: see Sir H. Nicolas's *Chron. of Hist.* pp. 325, 349, sec. ed. These lines were probably composed soon after the king's death—*per Skeltonidem laureatum* having been subsequently added to the title.

Page 4. v. 8. *lykynge*] i. e. joy, pleasure.

* v. 22. *a cheryfayre*] Cherry-fairs are still held in some parts of England on Sunday evenings, in the cherry orchards. They are the resort of the gay and thoughtless, and as such afforded frequent metaphors to our early writers for the vanity of worldly things.

> See Brand's *Antiquities*, by Sir H. Ellis, vol. ii. p. 457.—Halliwell's *Dict.* in v.

> " For all is but *a cherie feire*,
> This worldes good, so as thei tell."
> Gower's *Conf. Am.*, Prol., fol. 3. ed. 1554.

" And that endureth but a throwe,
      Right as it were a *cherie feste."*
                        Id. Ib. B. vi. fol. cxxxiii. ed. 1554.

" This worlde ys but *a chyrye feyre,* whan ȝe be
      heyest ȝe mowe aslake."
            Lydgate's verses entitled *Make Amendes,—*
                        MS. Cott. Calig. A ii. fol. 67.

" Reůoluyng als this liif *a chere fayre,*
  To loke how sone she deyde the fayrist wight."
            Poems by C. Duke of Orleans,—*MS. Harl.*
                        682. fol. 42.

" Thys werld hyt turnys euyn as a whele,
      All day be day hyt wyl enpayre,
      And so, sone, thys worldys wele,
      Hyt faryth but as *a chery fare."*
            How the wise man taught his son,—Pieces of
                  An. Pop. Poetry, p. 90. ed. Ritson.

Page 4. v. 28. *to contribute Fraunce*] i. e. to take
tribute of France.   In 1475, Edward withdrew from
France with his army on condition that Louis should
pay him immediately 75 thousand crowns, settle on
him an annuity for life of 50 thousand more, &c.   See
Lingard's *Hist. of Engl.* v. 303. ed. 8vo.

Page 5. v. 35. *as who sayth*] A not unfrequent ex-
pression in our early poetry, equivalent to—as one
may say, as the saying is.

  v. 37. *I se wyll, they leve that doble my ȝeris*] i. e. I
see well, that they live that double my years.

  v. 38. *This dealid this world*] i. e. Thus dealed this
world.   Skelton elsewhere, like many of our old poets,
uses *this* for *thus;* as in his *Ware the Hauke;*

      " Where Christis precious blode

Dayly offred is,
To be poluted *this*." v. 179. vol. i. 179.

Page 5. v. 40. *Had I wyst*] i. e. Had I known,—the exclamation of one who repents of a thing done unadvisedly. It is very common in our early poetry. In *The Paradyse of daynty deuises*, 1576, the second copy of verses is entitled *Beware of had I wyst*.

v. 52. *occupy*] i. e. possess,—or, rather, use: "Surgyons *occupy* oyntmentes, &c., Vulnarii medici *vtuntur*," &c. Hormanni *Vulgaria*, sig. I. vi. ed. 1530.

v. 53. *I made the Tower stronge*] "Edward iv. ... . fortified the Tower, and *made it strong*." Stow's *Survey*, B. i. 79. ed. 1720.

v. 54. *I purchased Tetersall*] I have not found elsewhere any mention of Edward the Fourth having possessed Tattershall Castle in Lincolnshire. "It does not appear into whose hands the Tattershall estate fell after the death of the Lord Treasurer Cromwell [in 1455], until the year 1487, when Henry VII. granted the manor to his mother Margaret Countess of Richmond," &c. *Hist. of the County of Lincoln*, ii. 73.

v. 55. *I amendid Douer*] "K. Edw. iv., by the advice of Lord Cobham, expended 10,000*l.* in repairing and fortifying the several works, and beautifying the apartments in it [Dover Castle]." Hasted's *Hist. of Kent*, iv. 63.

Page 6. v. 56. *And London I prouoked to fortify the wall*]—*prouoked*, i. e. incited, caused.—"In the Seventeenth of Edward iv., Ralph Josceline, Maior, caused part of the Wall about the City to be repaired, to wit, between Aldgate and Aldersgate," &c. Stow's *Survey*, B. I. 10. ed. 1720.

v. 57. *I made Notingam a place full royall*] Leland,

describing Nottingham Castle, says; " But the moste bewtifullest Part and gallant Building for lodgyng is on the Northe side, wher Edward the 4. began a right sumptuus pece of Stone Work, of the which he clerely finichid one excellent goodly Toure of 3. Hightes yn Building, and brought up the other Part likewise from the Foundation with Stone and mervelus fair cumpacid Windoes to layyng of the first soyle for Chambers and ther lefte." *Itin.* i. 107. ed. 1770.

Page 6. v. 58. *Wyndsore*] " The present magnificent fabrick [St. George's Chapel at Windsor], which exhibits one of the most beautiful specimens in this or any other kingdom, of that richly ornamented species of architecture, which prevailed towards the close of the fifteenth and the commencement of the 16th century, was begun by King Edward IV., who having found it necessary to take down the old chapel on account of its decayed state, resolved to build another on the same site, upon a larger scale, and committed the superintendence of the building to Richard Beauchamp, bishop of Salisbury. The work was not completed till the reign of King Henry VIII.," &c. Lysons's *Berkshire*, p. 424: see too p. 468 of the same volume.—An account of the manors, &c., granted by Edward to Windsor College, will be found in Pote's *Hist. of Wind. Castle*, p. 107.

—— *Eltam*] " K. Edw. iv. repaired this house [Eltham Palace] with much cost, and inclosed Horne-Park," &c. Hasted's *Hist. of Kent*, i. 51.

v. 64. *solas*] i. e. sport, amusement.

v. 66. *Lady Bes*] Edward married, May 1st, 1464, the Lady Elizabeth Grey, widow of Sir John Grey, and daughter of Wydevile Lord Rivers by Jacquetta (or Jacqueline) Duchess of Bedford.

Page 6. v. 70. *But Windsore alone,* **now** *I haue no mo*]—*mo,* i. e. more.—"He [Edward **IV.**] lies buried at Windsor, in the new Chappel (whose Foundation himself had laid, being all the Works of Piety by him left) under a Monument of Steel, polish'd and gilt, [iron gilt—see Lysons's *Berkshire,* p. 210.], representing a Pair of Gates, betwixt Two Towers, all of curious transparent Workmanship after the Gothick Manner, which is placed in the North-Arch, faced through with Touch-Stone, near to the High-Altar." Sandford's *Geneal. Hist.* p. 413. ed. 1707.

v. 73. *Why should a man be proude or presume hye?*
   Sainct Bernard therof nobly doth trete,
   Seyth a man is but a sacke of stercorry,
      And shall returne vnto wormis mete.
   Why, what cam of Alexander the greate?
   Or els of stronge Sampson, who can tell?
      Were not wormes ordeyned theyr flesh to frete?
   And of Salomon, that was of wyt the well?
   Absolon profferyd his heare for to sell,
      Yet for al his bewte wormys ete him also]

stercorry, i. e. dung: *frete,* i. e. eat, devour: *heare,* i. e. hair.

In cap. iii. of *Meditationes piissimæ de cognitione humanæ conditionis,* a piece attributed to Saint Bernard, we find, " *Nihil aliud est homo, quam* sperma fœtidum, *saccus stercorum, cibus vermium . . . . Cur ergo superbis homo . . . . Quid superbis* pulvis et cinis," &c. Bernardi *Opp.* ii. 335-36. ed. 1719. In a *Rythmus de contemptu mundi,* attributed to the same saint, are these lines;

   " Dic *ubi Salomon,* olim tam nobilis ?
   Vel *ubi Samson* est, dux invincibilis ?

Vel *pulcher Absalon, vultu mirabilis?*

.   .   .   .

O esca vermium! O massa pulveris!
O roris vanitas, *cur sic extolleris ?* ”

Opp. ii. 913-14. ed. 1719.

(This *Rythmus* is printed by Mr. Wright among *The
Latin Poems attributed to Walter Mapes*, p. 147.)   So
also Lydgate in a poem on the mutability of human
affairs ;

   “ And *wher is Salomon* moost soueryn of konnynge,
   Richest of bildyng, of tresour incomparable ?
   Face of *Absolon* moost fair, moost amyable ?

   .   .   .   .

   And *wher is Alisaundir* that conqueryd al ? ”

MS. Harl. 2255. fol. 4, 5.

Page 7. v. 85. *I haue played my pageyond*] i. e. I
have played my pageant,—my part on the stage of
life.   Compare

     “ Theyr *pageandes* are past,
     And ours wasteth fast,
     Nothynge dothe aye last
       But the grace of God.”

Feylde’s *Contrav. bytwene a louer
and a Iaye,* sig. B iii. n. d. 4to.

The word *pageant* was originally applied to the tem-
porary erections (sometimes placed upon wheels) on
which miracle-plays were exhibited, afterwards to the
exhibition itself.   See Sharp’s *Diss. on Coventry Pag.
and Myst.* p. 2 ; Collier’s *Hist. of Engl. Dram. Poet.*
ii. 151.

   v. 86. *yeld*] i. e. eld, age.

   v. 87. *This*] i. e. Thus: see note on v. 38.

SKELTON LAUREATUS LIBELLUM SUUM, &C.

* Page 8. v. 3. *leonis*] Alluding to his crest and supporters. See v. 109 of the poem following.

VPON THE DOULOUR[U]S DETHE AND MUCHE LA-
MENTABLE CHAUNCE OF THE MOST HONORABLE
ERLE OF NORTHUMBERLANDE.

This elegy must have been written soon after the earl's murder: see v. 162.—"The subject of this poem . . . is the death of Henry Percy, fourth earl of Northumberland, who fell a victim to the avarice of Henry vii. In 1489, the parliament had granted the king a subsidy for carrying on the war in Bretagne. This tax was found so heavy in the North, that the whole country was in a flame. The E. of Northumberland, then lord lieutenant for Yorkshire, wrote to inform the king of the discontent, and praying an abatement. But nothing is so unrelenting as avarice : the king wrote back that not a penny should be abated. This message being delivered by the earl with too little caution, the populace rose, and, supposing him to be the promoter of their calamity, broke into his house, and murdered him, with several of his attendants, who yet are charged by Skelton with being backward in their duty on this occasion. This melancholy event happened at the earl's seat at Cocklodge, near Thirske, in Yorkshire, April 28, 1489. See Lord Bacon, &c. If the reader does not find much poetical merit in this old poem (which yet is one of Skelton's best [?]), he will see a striking picture of the state and magnificence kept up by our ancient nobility

during the feudal times. This great earl is described
here as having, among his menial servants, KNIGHTS,
SQUIRES, and even BARONS: see v. 32, 183, &c.,
which, however different from modern manners, was
formerly not unusual with our greater Barons, whose
castles had all the splendour and offices of a royal
court, before the Laws against Retainers abridged and
limited the number of their attendants." PERCY.

Page 8. v. 4. *Of the bloud royall descending nobelly*]
" The mother of Henry, first Earl of Northumberland,
was Mary daughter to Henry E. of Lancaster, whose
father Edmond was second son of K. Henry iii. The
mother and wife of the second Earl of Northumber-
land were both lineal descendants of K. Edward iii.
The Percys also were lineally descended from the
Emperour Charlemagne and the ancient Kings of
France, by his ancestor Josceline de Lovain (son of
Godfrey Duke of Brabant), who took the name of
Percy on marrying the heiress of that house in the
reign of Hen. ii. Vid. Camdeni Britan., Edmondson,
&c." PERCY.

Page 9. v. 6. *again*] i. e. against.

v. 14. *Elyconys*] i. e. Helicon's.

v. 16. *astate*] i. e. estate, high rank.

v. 20. *nobles*] i. e. nobless, nobleness.

v. 21. *dites*] i. e. ditties.

* v. 24. *hastarddis*] " i. e. perhaps, hasty, rash fel-
lows." PERCY.—Jamieson gives "*Hastard*. Irascible.
But compare *haskardis*, rough, rude fellows, p. 319,
v. 607.

—— *tene*] i. e. wrath.

v. 26. *Confetered*] i. e. Confederated.

v. 27. *slee*] i. e. slay.

v. 30. *ken*] i. e. know.

Page 10. v. 34. *karlis of kind*] i. e. churls by nature.

v. 35. *slo*] i. e. slay.

v. 40. *bode*] i. e. abode.

.v. 43. *redouted*] i. e. dreaded.

v. 45. *great estates*] i. e. persons of great estate or rank.

—— *lowted*] i. e. bowed, made obeisance.

v. 46. *mayny*] i. e. train, company, set.

v. 48. *paues*] i. e. shield (properly a large shield covering the body).

v. 49. *mot*] i. e. may.

Page 11. v. 51. *fyll*] i. e. fell.

v. 53. *agayne*] i. e. against.

v. 59. *worshyp*] i. e. honour, respectability.

Page 12. v. 71 *fals packing*] i. e. false dealing (*packing* is—iniquitous combination, collusion, for evil purposes, for deceiving, &c.).

v. 73. *occupied*] i. e. used : see note p. 3. v. 52.

—— *shilde*] i. e. shield.

v. 78. *renyed*] i. e. refused.

v. 81. *buskt them*] "i. e. prepared themselves, made themselves ready." PERCY. Rather,—hied.

v. 81. *bushment*] i. e. ambushment.

—— *baile*] i. e. sorrow, trouble.

v. 82. *wring*] "i. e. contend with violence." PERCY.

v. 84. *forsed*] i. e. regarded.

v. 87. *Presed*] i. e. Pressed.

v. 88. *faught them agayne*] i. e. fought against them.

Page 13. v. 96. *whose*] i. e. whoso.

v. 98. *sort*] i. e. set, band.

v. 100. *wode*] i. e. frantic, wild.

v. 102. *gode*] i. e. good.

v. 106. *spylt*] i. e. destroyed.

Page 13. v. 109. *The myghty lyon*] " Alluding to his crest and supporters." PERCY.

—— *doutted*] i. e. dreaded.

Page 14. v. 115. *shoke*] i. e. shook.

v. 118. *mysuryd*] " i. e. misused, applied to a bad purpose." PERCY.

v. 125. *enharpit of mortall drede*] " i. e. hooked, or edged with mortal dread." PERCY.

v. 126. *kit*] i. e. cut.

v. 128. *aureat*] i. e. golden, excellent.

—— *ellumynynge*] i. e. embellishing.

v. 131. *fuyson*] i. e. abundance.

v. 134. *Paregall*] i. e. Equal (thoroughly equal).

v. 135. *Surmountinge*] i. e. Surpassing.

v. 136. *reporte me*] i. e. refer.

Page 15. v. 142. *enkankered*] i. e. corroded.

v. 143. *worshiply*] i. e. honourably.

v. 145. *supprised*] i. e. overpowered, smitten.

—— *lust*] i. e. liking, desire.

v. 151. *Tretory*] i. e. Traitory, treachery.

v. 155. *hole quere*] i. e. whole quire.

v. 160. *holy*] i. e. wholly.

Page 16. v. 162. *yonge lyon*] See note on v. 109 The fifth Earl of Northumbèrland was only eleven years old at his father's death.

v. 172. *faytors*] " i. e. deceivers, dissemblers." PER-CY.—" *Faytowre.* Fictor, Simulator." *Prompt. Parv.* ed. WAY.

v. 176. *chere*] i. e. countenance, or (as it may mean here) spirit.

v. 179. *Algife*] i. e. Although.

—— *thorow saught*] i. e. sought through.

v. 181. *complayne*] i. e. lament for.

Page 17. v. 186. *worshyply*] i. e. honourably.

v. 195. *finaunce*] i. e. fine, forfeiture.

v. 199. *eterminable*] i. e. interminable.

Page 18. v. 212. *hole sorte*] i. e. whole company.

v. 213. *mot*] i. e. may.

—— *ad magistrum Rukshaw*] The person here addressed was perhaps " William Rowkshaw, priest," by whom a letter, dated from the Gilbertine priory of Watton in the east riding of Yorkshire, is printed among the *Plumpton Correspondence*, p. 82. Camd. Soc. ed.

AGAYNSTE A COMELY COYSTROWNE, THAT CURY-OWSLY CHAWNTYD, AND CURRYSHLY COWNTRED, &c.

* Page 19. *Coystrowne* (which Skelton uses again in his poem *Howe the douty Duke of Albany*, &c., v. 171. vol. ii. 327., and has Latinized in his *Speke, Parot*, v. 125. vol. ii. 251.) is written by Chaucer *quistron;*

> " This God of Loue of his fashion
> Was like no knaue ne *quistron*,
> [*Ne resembloit pas un garçon*]."
>   *Rom. of the Rose*, fol. 113,—*Workes*,
>   ed. 1602.

Coystrowne (*questron, quoitron, coestron*) is—bastard, (from quæstuaria, quæ quæstu corporis vivit). " *Chetif, coquin, truant, Questron, bastart.*" Ducange, ed. Henschel, in v. QUÆSTUARIUS.

In *Prompt. Parv.* we find " *Cowntryn* in songe. Occento." ed. 1499. To *counter* is properly—to sing an extemporaneous part upon the plain chant. Skelton uses the word in. other places, and perhaps not always in its strict sense.

Page 19. v. 4.

> *In peuyshnes yet they snapper and fall,*
> *Which men the viii dedly syn call*]

Snapper is commonly explained—stumble; but Palsgrave makes a distinction between the words : " I *Snapper*, as a horse dothe that tryppeth, *Je trippette.* My horse dyd nat *stumble*, he dyd but *snapper* a lytell, *Mon cheual ne choppyt poynt, il ne fit que trippetter vng petit.*" Palsgrave,* p. 723. Compare the following lines ;

> · " Not say y this but wel parcas that y
>   In *pevisshe synne* myght happe me ī aseven,
>   Which is the viii *synne* to synnes vii."
>
> > *Poems* by C. Duke of Orleans,—
> > *MS. Harl.* 682. fol. 145.

v. 6. *prendergest*] A word (probably the origin of the surname *Prendergast*) which I am unable to explain.

v. 8. *bayardys bun*] i. e. horse-loaf, a sort of bread formerly much used for feeding horses : *bayard* is, properly, a bay horse.

v. 9. *sumdele*] i. e. somewhat.

v. 11. *maunchet*] Properly, a small loaf of fine white bread.

—— *morell*] Properly, a dark-coloured, a black horse.

---

* L'Éclaircissement de la Langue Française, par Jean Palsgrave, ed. F. Génin. Paris, 1852.

Page 19. v. 13. *carp*] Which generally means—speak, talk,—is sometimes found applied to music, and here, perhaps, is equivalent to—make a noise.

v. 14. *Lo, Jak wold be a jentylman !*] So in Heywood's *Dialogue ;*

"*Iacke would be a gentleman*, if he could speake
French."

Sig. D 2,—*Workes*, ed. 1598.

See also Ray's *Proverbs*, p. 124. ed. 1768.

Page 20. v. 15.

Wyth, Hey, troly, loly, lo, whip here, Jak,
Alumbek sodyldym syllorym ben !
Curyowsly he can both counter and knak
Of Martyn Swart and all hys mery men]

Hey, troly, loly, Ritson observes, is a chorus or burden " of vast antiquity ; " see *Anc. Songs*, ii. 8. ed. 1829 : *counter ;* see note on title of the poem : *knak,* i. e. triflingly, or affectedly shew off his skill in singing about, &c. In *A very mery and Pythie Commedie, called The longer thou liuest, the more foole thou art,* &c. *Newly compiled by W. Wager,* 4to. n. d. (written in the early part of Elizabeth's reign), Moros sings, among other fragments of songs,

" *Martin swart and his man, sodledum, sodledum,*
Martin swart and his man, sodledum bell."

Sig. A 3.

and in a comparatively recent drama we find ;

" The Beare, the Boare, and Talbot with his tuskish
white,
Oh so sore that he would bite,·
The Talbot with his Tuskish white,
Soudledum Soudledum ;

The Talbot with his Tuskish white, *Soudledum bell.*
The Talbott with his Tuskish white,
Oh so sore that he would bite,
Orebecke soudledum, sing orum bell."

> *The Varietie* (by the Duke of Newcastle),
> 1649. 12mo. p. 41.

Martin Swart, " a noble man in Germany, and in marciall feactes verye expert," (Hall's *Chron.* (*Henry VII.*) fol. ix. ed. 1548), headed the auxiliaries sent by the Duchess of Burgundy with Lambert Simnel, and fell, fighting with great valour, at the battle of Stoke.

Page 20. v. 19. *pohen*] i. e. pea-hen.

v. 21. *An holy water clarke*] *Aquæbajulus;* an office generally mentioned with contempt.

v. 23. *solfyth to haute*] i. e. solfas too haughtily,—highly.

v. 25. *to sharp is hys my*] " The syllable Mi used in solmisation." Hawkins's *Hist. of Music,* iii. 41.

v. 26. *pyrdewy*] Compare *Hycke Scorner;*

> " Than into loues daunce we were brought,
> That we played *the pyrdewy.*"

> > Sig. A v. ed. W. de Worde.

and *Colkelbie Sow;*

> " Sum *Perdowy,* sum Trolly lolly."

> > v. 303. Laing's *Early Pop. Poet. of*
> > *Scotland.*

v. 27. *besy*] i. e. busy.

v. 29. *a lewde lewte*] i. e. a vile lute.

—— *Roty bully joyse*] " The initial words of some old song." Hawkins's *Hist. of Music,* iii. 41.—In our author's *Magnyfycence,* Courtly Abusyon exclaims,

> " *Rutty bully,* ioly rutterkyn, heyda ! "

> > v. 757, vol. ii. 36.

Perhaps the same air is alluded to in *Colkelbie Sow;*

" Sum *Rusty bully* with a bek."

v. 320.—Laing's *Early Pop. Poet. of Scotland.*

Page 20. v. 33. *and he wyst*] i. e. if he knew.

v. 34. *sped*] i. e. versed.

—— *tauellys*] " *Tauell,* an instrument for a sylke woman to worke with." Palsgrave, p. 279.

v. 36. *a payre of clauycordys*] i. e. a clavichord (so, formerly, an organ was called *a pair of organs*) ; of which see an engraving in Hawkins's *Hist. of Music,* ii. 443.

Page 21. v. 43. *jet*] Is explained in modern dictionaries—strut.—" I *Get,* I vse a proude countenaunce and pace in my goyng, *Je braggue.*" Palsgrave, p. 563.

v. 47. *dumpys*] i. e. dumps.

v. 48. *prycke songe*] i. e. music *pricked* or noted down ; when opposed (see v. 54) to *plain song,* it meant counter-point, as distinguished from mere melody.

v. 49. *a larg and a long*] Characters in old music : one *large* contained two *longs,* one *long* two breves, &c.

v. 50. *iape*] i. e. jest, joke.

v. 51. *solayne*] i. e. sullen.

v. 53. *fayne*] Palsgrave gives, " *I feyne* in syngyng, *Je chante a basse voyx.* We maye nat synge out, we are to nere my lorde, but lette vs *fayne* this songe," &c., p. 548. But here, I apprehend, *fayne* can only mean—sing in falsetto. Our author, in *The Bowge of Courte,* has

" His throte was clere, and lustely coude *fayne.*"

v. 233. vol. i. 47.

Page 21. v. 55. *Thys docter Deuyas commensyd in a cart*] So again Skelton in his *Colyn Cloute*,

"Auaunt, syr *doctour Deuyas !*"

v. 1159. vol. ii. 165.

Compare a much later writer : "What, a graue Doctor, a base Iohn Doleta the Almanack-maker, *Doctor Deuse-ace* and Doctor Merryman ?" Nash's *Haue with you to Saffron-Walden*, 1596. sig. L 3.—*commensyd*, i. e. who took his degree.

v. 60. *ne*] i. e. nor.

v. 61. *wark*] i. e. work, business.

v. 62. *walk, and be nought !*] Equivalent to—away, and a mischief on you!

* Page 22. v. 68. *Take thys in worth*] To take in *worth*, or in *gree*, is to accept favorably, be satisfied with.

* v. 69. *Wryten at Croydon by Crowland in the Clay*] To G. Steinman Steinman, Esq., author of the *Hist. of Croydon*, I am indebted for the following observations: "The passage has been a puzzle to me. The distance is very great between Crowland and Croydon in Cambridgeshire ; and in Croydon in Surrey there is no such place as Crowland, though I can point out to you 'the Clays' there. The manor of Crou*ham* is in the Surrey Croydon, but far away from 'the Clays.'" [Perhaps two distant places are purposely brought together for grotesque effect. This would be in the same humor as the confusion of times in the next line,

"Candelmas euyn, the Kalendas of May: "

which expression, it may be observed, occurs also in the Interlude of *Thersytes*, obviously written in imitation of Skelton.

" Wrytinge at my house on *Candelmasse daye,*
Mydsomer moneth, *the Calenders of Maye.*]

Page 22. *Qd*] i. e. Quod, quoth.

VPPON A DEEDMANS HED, &C.

couenable, i. e. befitting : *sentence,* i. e. sense, mean-
ing.

v. 13. *shyderyd*] i. e. split, splintered.

v. 18. *fell*] i. e. skin.

Page 24. v. 24. *mell*] i. e. meddle.

v. 29.   *Oure days be datyd,*
                 To be chekmatyd
                 With drawttys of deth]

Checkmate, the term at chess when the king is made
prisoner, and the game consequently finished, is often
used figuratively by our early writers. With the
present lines compare the following passages :

        " *Wyth a draght* he was *chek mate.*"
                Kyng Roberd of Cysylle,—MS. Harl.
                        1701. fol. 93.

" But she had taken suche cold for the defaute of
helpe that depe *draughtes of deth* toke her, that nedes
she must dye," &c. *Morte d'Arthur,* B. viii. c. i. vol. i.
247. ed. Southey.

v. 36. *brynnyng*] i. e. burning.

v. 40. *rew*] i. e. have pity.

v. 43. *shylde*] i. e. shield.

v. 45. *dyne*] i. e. dun, dark.

v. 46. *boteles bale*] i. e. remediless sorrow.

v. 48. *fendys blake*] i. e. fiends black.

Page 25. v. 54. *solace*] i. e. pleasure.

"WOMANHOD, WANTON, YE WANT," &C.

Page. 25. v. 4. *recheles*] i. e. reckless.

v. 6. *draffe*] i. e. refuse: in our author's *Elynour Rummyng*, v. 171. vol. i. 115, it means hog-wash,—the coarse liquor, or brewers' grains, with which swine are fed.

v. 13. *pohen*] i. e. peahen.

Page 26. v. 18. *auayle*] i. e. advantage, profit.

v. 19. *shayle*] Is several times used by Skelton. "*Schayler*, that gothe awrie with his fete, *boytevx*." Palsgrave, p. 266. "I *Shayle*, as a man or horse dothe that gothe croked with his legges: *Je vas eschays.* p. 700.

* v. 20. *pyggysny*] i. e. pigsney, little pig, a term of endearment.

v. 21. *quyte*] i. e. requite.

v. 26. *doute*] i. e. fear.

v. 28. *all beshrewde*] i. e. altogether cursed.

v. 29. *that farly swete*] i. e. that strange sweet one.

v. 30. *wonnes*] i. e. dwells.

—— *Temmys strete*] i. e. Thames' street.

DYUERS BALETTYS AND DYTIES, &C.

solacyous] i. e. pleasant, amusing.

Page 27. v. 2. *quod*] i. e. quoth.

v. 4. *hardely*] i. e. boldly, with confidence.

v. 7. *kepe*] i. e. heed, regard, care.

v. 8. *With ba, ba, ba, and bas, bas, bas,*
    She cheryshed hym both cheke and chyn]

i. e. With kissings,—with, kiss me.

" Come ner my spouse, and let me *ba* thy cheke."
   Chaucer's *Wif of Bathes Prol.* v. 6015. ed. Tyr.
" I wald him chuk, *cheik and chyn*, and *cheris* him so
    mekill."
    Dunbar's tale of *The Tua Maryit Wemen and*
    the Wedo,—Poems, i. 71. ed. Laing.

Page 27. v. 11. *He had forgoten all dedely syn*] Compare our author's *Phyllyp Sparowe,* v. 1081. vol. i. 98.

Page 28. v. 15. *rowth*] i. e. rough.

—— *waters wan*] Many passages of our early poetry might be cited where this epithet is applied to water: see note on *Why come ye nat to Courte,* v. 887, where a wrong reading has misled H. Tooke and Richardson.

v. 18. *halsyd*] i. e. embraced (round the neck).

v. 19. *cought*] i. e. caught.

v. 20. *lefe*] i. e. dear.

—— *rowtyth*] i. e. snoreth.

v. 21. *I wys*] i. e. truly, certainly (*i-wis*, adv.).

* v. 23. *lust and lykyng*] i. e. pleasure and delight. This somewhat pleonastic expression (used again more than once by Skelton) is not uncommon in our old writers : " Allas ! my swete sones, thenne she sayd, for your sakes I shalle lese my *lykynge and lust.*" *Morte d'Arthur,* B. xi. c. x. vol. ii. 174. ed. Southey. Nay, in the interlude of *The Worlde and the Chylde,* 1522, one of the characters bears the name of *Lust and Lykynge.*

* v. 24. *blowboll*] i. e. drunkard.

" To *blowe in a bowle,* and for to pill a platter," &c.
   Barclay's *First Egloge,* sig. A iiii. ed. 1570.

" Farewell ! Peter *blowbowle* I may wel call thee."
   Enterlude of Kyng Daryus, 1565. sig. B.

Page 28. v. 25. *luggard*] i. e. heavy fellow, sluggard.

v. 28. *powle hachet*] So again in our author's *Gar-lande of Laurell;*

" *Powle hatchettis,* that prate wyll at euery ale pole."
v. 613. vol. ii. 197.

—— *bleryd thyne I*] (I—eye) i. e. imposed on, put a cheat on you.

v. 4. *pastaunce*] i. e. pastime.

v. 7. *corage*] i. e. heart.

Page 29. v. 8. *fauorable*] i. e. well-favoured, beautiful.

* v. 11. *Menolope*] In a " ballade" entitled *The IX. Ladies Woorthie,* printed among Chaucer's *Workes,* the writer, after celebrating the eighth, " Quene Semiramys," concludes thus ;

" Also the ladie *Menalip* thy sister deere,
    Whose marcial power no man coud withstand,
    Through the worlde was not found her pere,
    The famous duke Thes[e]us she had in hand,
    She chastised hym and [conquered] all his land,
    The proude Greekes mightely she did assaile,
    Ouercame and vanquished them in battaile."
fol. 324. ed. 1602.

[Menalippe was a sister of Antiope, queen of the Amazons, and was so far from subduing Theseus that she taken prisoner by Hercules. *Penelope* is a more probable reading.]

v. 16. *curtoyl*] i. e. curtal.

—— *set nowght by*] i. e. set no value, or regard, on.

* v. 17.   *Gup, morell, gup,*
              With jayst ye——]

morell ; see note, p. 12. v. 11.—*Gup* [go up?] and

jayst [stand still ?] are exclamations applied to horses; compare our author's *Elynour Rummyng*, v. 390. vol. i. 123., and his third *Poem against Garnesche*, v. 13. vol. i. 139. So too in *Camelles Rejoindre* to Church-yarde (fol. broadside);

"Then *gip* fellowe asse, then *jost* fellowe lurden."

Page 29. v. 19. *corage*] i. e. heart, affection, inclination.

—— *haggys*] I know not in what sense Skelton uses this word: [Qy. youth, hero, gallant?] so again in his *Colyn Cloute;*

> "I purpose to shake oute
> All my connyng bagge,
> Lyke a clerkely *hagge.*"
>
> v. 50. vol. ii. 127.

and in his poem *Howe the douty Duke of Albany*, &c.;

> "For thou can not but brag,
> Lyke a Scottyshe *hag.*"
>
> v. 294. vol. ii. 331.

v. 20. *Haue in sergeaunt ferrour*] i. e. Bring in sergeant farrier. The title *sergeant* belongs properly to certain of the king's servants: so in an unpublished *Liber Excerpt. Temp. Hen. vii. et Hen. viii.* in the Chapter-house, Westminster;

(xix. of   "Item payd to the *sergeant* plum-
Hen. vii.)   mer and
           bartram upon their indentures } xx*li.*"
           for grenewiche

* v. 23. *kalkyns*] i. e. calkins, the parts of a horse-shoe which are turned up to prevent slipping.

* *keylyth*] i. e. cales, gambols, moves irregularly.

* v. 24. *hewyth*] i. e. knocks the ankles together.

Page 29. v. 24. *neuer a dele*] i. e. not a bit.

Page 30. v. 30. *dyntes*] i. e. blows.

v. 31. *He bresyth theyr braynpannys*] i. e. He bruiseth, breaketh their skulls, heads.

v. 32. *all to-brokyn*] A writer in the new ed. of Boucher's *Gloss.* (in v. *All*) justly observes that it is a mistake to suppose that in such expressions *all* is coupled with *to*, and that it becomes equivalent to *omnino* from being thus conjoined. The augmentative *to* is connected with the following word as a prefix, and often occurs without being preceded by *all:* so in our author's *Bowge of Courte*,

" A rusty gallande, *to-ragged* and *to-rente*."—
v. 345. vol. i. 52.

—— *clappys*] i. e. strokes.

v. 33. *to lepe the hach*] i. e. to run away :—(*hatch*— the fastened half or part of the door, the half-door).

" I pretende [i. e. intend] therefore *to leape ouer the hatche*."
The Triall of Treasure, 1567, sig. E ii.

* v. 34. *conusaunce*] i. e. acquaintance, experience : *py* is magpie.

v. 36. *It can be no counsell that is cryed at the cros*] i. e. It can be no secret that is proclaimed at the market-place.

* Page 31. v. 3. *Corage wyth lust*] Affection with desire.

v. 7. *surmountyng*] i. e. surpassing.

v. 8. *Allectuary*] i. e. Electuary.

* —— *arrectyd*] i. e. appointed.

—— *redres*] i. e. relieve, remedy.

* v. 9. *axys*] i. e. (access) fits, paroxysms.

Page 31. v. 10. *Of thoughtfull hertys plungyd in dys-tres*] Skelton borrowed this line from Lydgate, whose *Lyf of our Lady* begins

"O *thoughtful herte plungyd in distresse.*"

Thoughtfull is anxious, heavy, sad.

* v. 13. *Herber*] i. e. arbour.

v. 16. *ruddys*] i. e. ruddy tints of the cheek, complexion.

v. 17. *Saphyre of sadnes*]—*sadnes*, i. e. steadiness, constancy :

"For hit is write and seide how *the safere*
Doth token trowthe.*"

> *Poems* by C. Duke of Orleans,—
> *MS. Harl.* 682. fol. 44.

—— *enuayned with indy blew*] *enuayned*, i. e. en-veined. "*Inde.* Fr., Azure-coloured." Tyrwhitt's *Gloss. to Chaucer's Cant. Tales.* "Inde, *ynde :* couleur de bleu foncé, d'azur, *indicum.*" Roquefort's *Gloss. de la Lang. Rom.* So again our author in his *Magnyfy-cence ;*

"The streynes of her vaynes as asure *inde blewe.*"

> v. 1571. vol. ii. 73.

See too his *Garlande of Laurell,* v. 478. vol. ii. 191., and Nevil, son of Lord Latimer, in a poem of great rarity ;

"On the gates two scryptures I aspyed,
Theym for to rede my mynd than I applyed,
Wryten in gold and *indye blewe* for folkes forther-aunce.*"

> *The Castell of pleasure,* sig. A v. 1518.

Sir John Mandeville says that the beak of the Phœnix

" is coloured blew as *ynde*." *Voiage and Travaile*, &c., p. 58. ed. 1725.

Page 31. v. 20. *Geyne*] i. e. Against.

——   ——— *the emeraud comendable;*
Relucent smaragd]

Emeraud (emerald) and *smaragd* are generally considered as synonymous; but here Skelton makes a distinction between them. So too Drayton in his *Muses Elizium*, 1630. p. 78; and Chamberlayne in his *Pharonnida*, 1659. B. ii. c. 4. p. 150. And so R. Holme: " The *Emrauld* is green."—" The *Smaradge* is of an excellent fresh green, far passing any Leaf." *Ac. of Armory*, 1688. B. ii. pp. 39, 41.

v. 22. *perspectyue*] Which generally signifies a glass to look through, seems here, from the context, to mean some sort of reflecting glass.

v. 23. *Illumynyd*] i. e. Adorned.

Page 32. v. 29. *Remorse*] Means commonly in early writers,—pity; but that sense is unsuited to the present passage: it seems to be used here for—[a painful] recollection.

—— *most goodlyhod*] i. e. perfect goodness.

v. 33. *praty*] i. e. pretty.

v. 40. *mastres*] i. e. mistress.

v. 41. *nys*] i. e. ne is—is not.

v. 43. *more desyrous*] i. e. more desirable.

Page 33. v. 11. *rede*] i. e. advise.

v. 12. *fals poynt*] " This *fals poynt* . . . Hæc *fraus*." Hormanni *Vulgaria*, sig. s viii. ed. 1530.

v. 13. *fell*] i. e. skin.

v. 15. *lesard*] In the Latin above, the corresponding word is *anguis*: long after Skelton's time, the poor harmless lizard was reckoned venomous; so in Shakespeare's *Third Part of Henry VI.*, act ii. sc. 2., " *liz-ards'* dreadful stings."

Page 33. v. 1. *rasyd*] i. e. torn, wounded.

v. 3. *vaynys*] i. e. veins.

—— *blo*] i. e. livid. " *Blo*, blewe and grene col-oured, as ones body is after a drie stroke, *jaunastre*." Palsgrave, p. 306.

Page 34. v. 5. *ouerthwart*] i. e. cross, perverse, ad-verse.

v. 7. *dyscure*] i. e. discover.

* v. 10. *dysease*] i. e. disquiet.

MANERLY MARGERY MYLK AND ALE.

Skelton mentions this piece among his works, in the *Garlande of Laurell*, v. 1198. vol. ii. 223. Sir John Hawkins, who printed it together with the music, says that it "appears to have been set by William Cornish of the Chapel Royal in the reign of Henry vii." *Hist. of Music*, iii. 2.

Page 35. v. 1. *besherewe yow*] i. e. curse you,—con-found you!

—— *be my fay*] i. e. by my faith.

v. 2. *This wanton clarkes be nyse all way*] i. e. These wanton scholars be always foolish, inclined to folly, to toyish tricks: compare our author's *Phyllyp Sparowe;*

> " Phyllyp, though he were *nyse*,
> In him it was no *vyse*," &c.
> > v. 173. vol. i. 67.

v. 3. *Avent*] i. e. Avaunt.

—— *popagay*] i. e. parrot.

Page 35. v. 5. *Tully valy*] Or *Tilly vally*—an exclamation of contempt, the origin of which is doubtful.

v. 6. *Gup*] See note, p. 20. v. 17.

—— *Cristian Clowte*] Compare our author's *Colyn Cloute ;*

> " He coud not syng himselfe therout
> But by the helpe of *Christyan Clout.*"
> > v. 880. vol. ii. 155.

—— *Jak of the vale*] [The hero of some popular ditty.] So our author in his *Magnyfycence ;* " some iangelynge *Jacke of the vale*," v. 260. vol. ii. 14. Compare two pieces of a much later date ;

> " I am not now to tell a tale
> Of George a Greene, or *Jacke a Vale.*"
> > *The Odcombian Banquet,* 1611. sig. C 3.

> " And they had leauer printen *Jacke a vale*
> Or Clim o Clough," &c.
> > J. Davies,—*Other Eglogues* annexed to
> > *The Shepheards Pipe,* 1614. sig. G 4.

v. 8. *Be*] i. e. By.

—— *praty pode*]—*praty,* i. e. pretty: *pode,* i. e., perhaps, toad. Compare Roy's satire, *Rede me, and be nott wrothe,* &c. ;

> " A littell, *pratye,* foolysshe *poade.*"
> > *Harl. Miscell.* ix. 19. ed. Park.

* v. 10. *Strawe, Jamys foder, ye play the fode*] i. e. apparently, nonsense ! James Fodder, you play the child, or fool.

v. 12. *bole*] i. e. (I suppose) bull.

Page 36. v. 15. *I wiss*] i. e. truly, certainly (*i-wis,* adv.).

* v. 17. *piggesnye*] darling.

Page 36. v. 19. *Be*] i. e. By.

—— *hardely*] i. e. assuredly.

* v. 20. *japed*] i. e. sported with, etc. See Putten-
ham's *Arte of English Poesie,* ed. Haslewood, p. 212.

* v. 25. *best chepe*] i. e. cheapest.

v. 27. *thought*] i. e. sadness, grief: see note, p. 23.
v. 10.

THE BOWGE OF COURTE.

* "It is a *bouge of courte. Ceremonia aulica* est."
Hormanni *Vulgaria,* sig. s iii. ed. 1530. "*Bouche à
Court. Budge-a-Court,* diet allowed at Court." Cot-
grave's *Dict.* "The Kings Archers . . . . had *Bouch
of Court* (to wit, Meat and Drink) and great Wages
of six Pence by the Day." Stow's *Survey,* B. vi. 49.
ed. 1720. [Probably from old French, *bouge,* kitchen.]

"The poem called the BOUGE OF COURT, or the
Rewards of a Court, is in the manner of a pageaunt,
consisting of seven personifications. Here our author,
in adopting the more grave and stately movement of
the seven lined stanza, has shewn himself not always
incapable of exhibiting allegorical imagery with spirit
and dignity. But his comic vein predominates." War-
ton's *Hist. of E. P.,* ii. 347. ed. 4to.

"*Bouge of Court,* a corruption of *bouche,* Fr. An
allowance of meat and drink for the tables of the in-
ferior officers, and others who were occasionally called
to serve and entertain the court. Skelton has a kind
of little drama called *Bouge of Court,* from the name
of the *ship* in which the dialogue takes place. It is a
very severe satire, full of strong painting, and excel-
lent poetry. The courtiers of Harry must have winced
at it." Gifford, note on Ben Jonson's *Works,* vii. 428.

Page 37. v. 7. *to werre hym dyde dres*] i. e. did address, apply himself to war.

Page 38. v. 15. *rede*] i. e. conceive, consider.

v. 17. *aforce*] i. e. attempt.

v. 18. *dyscure*] i. e. discover.

v. 20. *illumyne*] i. e. embellish a subject.

v. 21. *Auysynge*] i. e. Advising.

v. 22. *he so*] i. e. who so.

v. 23. *connynge*] i. e. knowledge.

v. 30. *ne wyste*] i. e. knew not.

v. 31. *sore enwered*]—*enwered* means simply—wearied. Richardson (*Dict.* in v. *En*) observes that "Skelton appears to have wantoned in such compounds."

v. 33. *I me dreste*] i. e. I addressed, applied myself.

v. 36. *Methoughte I sawe a shyppe, goodly of sayle,*
Come saylynge forth into that hauen brood,
Her takelynge ryche and of hye apparayle]
Of this passage Mr. Wordsworth has a recollection in one of his noble Sonnets;

"*A goodly Vessel* did I then espy
Come like a giant from a *haven broad;*
And lustily along the bay she strode,
Her tackling rich, and of apparel high."

Works, iii. 34. ed. 1836.

v. 39. *kyste*] i. e. cast.

v. 40. *what she had lode*] i. e. what she had been freighted with.

Page 39. v. 44. *prece*] i. e. press,—the throng.

v. 49. *hyghte*] i. e. is called.

v. 50. *estate*] i. e. high rank, dignity.

v. 54. *chaffre*] i. e. merchandise.

v. 58. *traues*] Means here a sort of low curtain or

screen.—Hall, describing the preparations for combat between the Dukes of Hereford and Norfolk, tells us that the former, having entered the lists, " set hym doune in a chayer of grene veluet whiche was set in a *trauers* of grene and blewe veluet," &c.; and that the latter " satte doune in his chayer whiche was Crimosen Veluet, *cortened* [curtained] aboute with white and redde Damaske." *Chron.* (*Henry IV.*) fol. iii. ed. 1548.—At a later period, curtains, which were used on the stage as substitutes for scenes, were called *traverses.* See also Singer's note on Cavendish's *Life of Wolsey,* p. 167. ed. 1827, and Sir H. Nicolas's note on *Privy Purse Expenses of Elizabeth of York,* p. 259.

Page 39. v. 60. *trone*] i. e. throne.

v. 61. *spere*] i. e. sphere.

Page 40. v. 72. *she trowed that I had eten sause*] Compare our author's *Magnyfycence;*

'' Ye haue *eten sauce, I trowe,* at the Taylors Hall."
v. 1421. vol. ii. 66.

v. 78. *quod*] i. e. quoth.

v. 80. *glome*] i. e. glum,—sullen look, frown.

v. 82. *daynnously*] i. e. disdainfully.

—— *fro me she dyde fare*] i. e. from me she did go.

v. 83. *mased*] i. e. amazed, confounded.

v. 87. *hardely*] i. e. confidently.

v. 90. *I auyse you to speke, for ony drede*] i. e. I advise you to speak, notwithstanding any dread you may feel.

Page 41. v. 94. *And this an other*] i. e. And this is another reason.

v. 95. *not worth a bene*] *Bene* (bean) is frequently used by our early poets to express any thing worthless:

" I yeue not of her harme *a bene.*"

Chaucer's *Rom. of the Rose,*— *Workes,*
fol. 137. ed. 1602.

Page 41. v. 96. *lene*] i. e. lend, furnish with.

v. 100. *cheuysaunce*] i. e. achievement,—profit, gain.

v. 101. *nys*] i. e. ne is,—is not.

v. 106. *werne*] i. e. warn.

v. 107. *styreth*] i. e. steereth, directeth.

* v. 114. *luste*] i. e. desire.

Page 42. v. 117. *casseth*] " *Casser* . . . . to *casse,*
cassere, discharge, turne out of service, deprive of
entertainment." Cotgrave's *Dict.*

v. 120. *route*] i. e. company, crowd.

v. 122. *thronge*] i. e. thronged.

* Page 43. v. 134. *Fauell*] i. e. Flattery, Cajolery.

v. 137. *Mysdempte*] i. e. Misdeemed.

* v. 138. *Haruy Hafter*] [i. e. Sharper] Eds., as
already noticed, have " *Haruy* Haster ; " and in the
fourth of Skelton's *Poems against Garnesche,* v. 164.
vol. i. 152, the MS. gives the name with the same
error. Compare our author's *Why come ye nat to
Courte ;*

" Hauell and Haruy *Hafter.*"

v. 94. vol. ii. 280.

and his *Magnyfycence ;*

" Nowe, *benedicite,* ye wene I were some *hafter.*"

v. 259. vol. ii. 14.

" Craftynge and *haftynge* contryued is by me."

v. 707. vol. ii. 34.

" For to vse suche *haftynge* and crafty wayes."

v. 1698. vol. ii. 79.

" And from crafters and *hafters* I you forfende."

v. 2485. vol. ii. 119.

Page 43. v. 138. *male*] i. e. bag, wallet, pouch.

v. 144. *solace*] i. e. sport.

* v. 150. *Deynte to haue with vs suche one in store*] [*Deynte* means often—pleasant, "nice."] But both in the present passage, and in a subsequent stanza of the same poem—

" Trowest thou, dreuyll, I saye, thou gawdy knaue,
  That I haue *deynte* to see thé cherysshed thus ? "

v. 337—

" deynte " seems to be equivalent to—pleasure : compare

" Bycause that he hath ioye and great *deintye*
  To reade in bokes of olde antiquitye."

Lydgate's *Warres of Troy* (*Prologue*),
sig. B i. ed. 1555.

"Adew, dolour, adew ! my *daynte* now begynis."

Dunbar's tale of *The Tua Maryit Wemen and
the Wedo,—Poems*, i. 76. ed. Laing.

v..154. *it is surmountynge*] i. e. it is surpassing, it excels.

Page 44. v. 155. *ony*] i. e. any.

v. 173. *lewde cok wattes*]—*lewde*, i. e. ignorant, vile. Compare our author's third copy of verses *Against venomous tongues ;*

" Than ye may commaunde me to gentil *Cok wat*."

vol. i. 155.

and his *Magnyfycence ;*

" What canest thou do but play *cocke wat ?* "

v. 1206. vol. ii. 56.

Is *cock wat* only another form of *cockward*, i. e. cuckold ? See *Arthur and the King of Cornwall*, p. 279,— *Syr Gawayne*, &c., edited by Sir F. Madden.

Page 44. v. 174. *hardely*] i. e. assuredly.

v. 175. *but no worde that I sayde*] i. e. but mention not a word that I said.

Page 45. v. 180. *reboke*] i. e. belch, cast up.

"As grunting and drinking, *reboking* vp agayne."
          Barclay's *Ship of Fooles*, fol. 229. ed. 1570.

v. 181. *at a brayde*] i. e. at a start, at a turn, on a sudden, forthwith.

v. 184. *lete*] i. e. hinder.

v. 186. *Twyst*] i. e. Tush.

—— *ne reke*] i. e. reck not.

* v. 187. *a soleyne freke*] i. e. a sullen fellow.

v. 189. *Ye*] i. e. Yea.

v. 191. *whom and ha*] i. e. hum and ha.

v. 193. *quoke*] i. e. quaked.

Page 46. v. 198. *commaunde*] i. e. communed, conversed.

—— *party space*] May mean—a short space; but (as I have noticed *ad loc.*) "*party*" is probably a misprint for "*praty*" (pretty).

v. 199. *auowe*] i. e. vow.

"That hyr *auowe* maad of chastyte."
          Lydgate's *Lyf of our Lady*, sig. b i.

v. 215. *shryue me*] i. e. confess myself, tell my mind.

Page 47. v. 216. *plenarely*] i. e. fully.

v. 219. *dyscure*] i. e. discover.

v. 221. *with all my besy cure*] i. e. with all my busy care,—a common expression in our early poetry.

v. 226. *all and some*] Another expression frequently used by our early poets. "All and some: *Tout entierement.*" Palsgrave, p. 847.

Page 47. v. 228. *he wolde be come*] i. e. he would go.

* v. 231. *lyghte as lynde*] So in *Annunciacio;*

> " A, what, I am *light as lynde !* "
>
> *Towneley Myst.* p. 80.

and in Chaucer's *Clerkes Tale;*

> " Be ay of chere *as light as* lefe on *linde.*"
>
> v. 9087. ed. Tyr.

Lynde is the linden or lime-tree.

v. 232. *a versynge boxe*] Does it mean—a dice-box ?

v. 233. *fayne*] i. e. sing in falsetto. See note, p. 15. v. 53.

v. 234. *foxe*] i. e. fox-skin.

v. 235. *Sythe I am no thynge playne*] i. e. Since I, &c.—the commencement of some song.

v. 236. *pykynge*] i. e. picking, stealing.

—— *payne*] i. e. difficulty.

Page 48. v. 239. *sadde*] i. e. grave, serious.

v. 252. *Heue and how rombelow*] A chorus of high antiquity, (sung chiefly, it would seem, by sailors) :

> " They sprede theyr sayles as voyde of sorowe,
> Forthe they rowed, saynt George to borowe,
> For ioye theyr trumpettes dyde they blowe,
> And some songe *heue and howe rombelowe.*"
>
> *Cocke Lorelles bote,* sig. C 1.

> ." They rowede hard, and sungge thertoo,
> With *heuelow and rumbeloo.*"
>
> *Richard Coer de Lion,*—Weber's *Met. Rom.* ii. 99.

> " Maydens of Englande sore may ye morne
> For your lemmans ye haue loste at Bannockys
>   borne,
> Wyth *heue a lowe.*

What weneth the king of England
So soone to haue wone Scotland,
    Wyth *rumbylowe*."
        Scottish Song on the Battle of Bannock-
          burn,—Fabyan's *Chron.*, vol. ii. fol.
              169. ed. 1559.

   " Your maryners shall synge arowe
    Hey how and rumby lowe."
          The Squyr of Lowe Degre,—Ritson's
           Met. Rom. iii. 179.

" I saw three ladies fair, singing *hey and how*,
    Upon yon ley land, hey :
  I saw three mariners, singing *rumbelow*,
    Upon yon sea-strand, hey."
          Song quoted *ibid.*, iii. 353.

    Page 48. v. 252. *row the bote, Norman, rowe !*] A frag-
ment of an old song, the origin of which is thus recorded
by Fabyan : " In this. xxxii. yere [of King Henry the
Sixth] Jhon Norman foresaid, vpon the morowe of
Simon and Judes daie, thaccustomed day when the
newe Maior vsed yerely to ride with greate pompe
vnto westminster to take his charge, this Maior firste
of all Maiors brake that auncient and olde continued
custome, and was rowed thither by water, for the
whiche ye Watermen made of hym a roundell or song
to his greate praise, the whiche began : *Rowe the bote,
Norman, rowe* to thy lemman, and so forth with a
long processe." *Chron.* vul. ii. fol. 457. ed. 1559.

    v. 253. *Prynces of youghte can ye synye by rote ?*]
The meaning of this line seems to be—Can you sing
by rote the song beginning, *Princess of youth ?* Skel-
ton, in his *Garlande of Laurell*, calls Lady Anne
Dakers

"*Princes of ȝowth*, and flowre of goodly porte."
v. 897, vol. ii. 210.

Page 48. v. 254. *Or shall I sayle wyth you a felashyp assaye*] i. e., I suppose,—Or try, of good fellowship, (or, perhaps, together with me,) the song which commences *Shall I sail with you?* Compare the quotation from *The Complaynt of Scotland* in preceding page.

"Nowe, *of good felowshyp*, let me by thy dogge."
Skelton's *Magnyfycence*, v. 1095. vol. ii. 51.

"*Yng.* But yf thou wylt haue a song that is good,
I haue one of robynhode,
The best that euer was made.
Hu. Then *a feleshyp* let vs here it."
Interlude of the iiii Elementes, n. d.
Sig. E vii.

v. 259. *bobbe me on the noll*] i. e. beat me on the head.

Page 49. v. 262. *gete*] i. e. got.

v. 275. *vnneth*] i. e. scarcely, not without difficulty.

v. 276. *But I requyre you no worde that I saye*] i. e. But I beg you not to mention a word of what I say.

v. 278. *wetynge*] i. e. knowledge, intelligence.

v. 283. *wonderly besene*] i. e. of strange appearance, or array.

v. 284. *hawte*] i. e. haughty.

v. 285. *scornnys*] i. e. scorns.

Page 50. v. 287. *by Cockes blode*] i. e. by God's blood (*Cock* a corruption of *God*).

v. 288. *bote*] i. e. bit.

v. 289. *His face was belymmed, as byes had him stounge*] i. e. His face was disfigured, as if bees had stung him.

Page 50. v. 290. *jape*] i. e. jest, joke.

v. 294. *this comerous crabes hyghte*] i. e. (I suppose)
this troublesome crab was called.

v. 298. *euyll apayed*] i. e. ill satisfied, ill pleased.

v. 301. *Dawes*] Equivalent to—simpleton; the *daw*
being reckoned a silly bird: so again, in the next line
but one, " doctour *Dawcocke*."

v. 302. *in conceyte*] i. e. in the good opinion, favour
of our Lady Fortune: compare v. 270.

v. 304. *sleyte*] i. e. sleight, artful contrivance.

Page 51. v. 311. *layne*] i. e. conceal.

v. 312. *beyte*] i. e. bait.

v. 315. *And soo outface hym with a carde of ten*]
" A common phrase," says Nares, " which we may
suppose to have been derived from some game, (pos-
sibly *primero*), wherein the standing boldly upon a *ten*
was often successful. *A card of ten* meant a tenth
card, a ten. . . . . I conceive the force of the phrase
to have expressed originally the confidence or impu-
dence of one who with a ten, as at brag, *faced*, or
outfaced one who had really a faced card against him.
To face meant, as it still does, to bully, to attack by
impudence of face." *Gloss.* in v. *Face it*, &c. " The
phrase of *a card of ten* was possibly derived, by a joc-
ular allusion, from that of *a hart of ten*, in hunting,
which meant a full grown deer, one past six years of
age." *Ibid.* in v. *Card of ten*.

v. 317. *meuyd all in moode*] i. e. moved all in anger.

v. 320. *I wende he had be woode*] i. e. I thought he
had been mad.

* v. 327. *hayne*] i. e. (perhaps) hind, slave, peasant:
[more probably—mean fellow, Ang. Sax. *hean*.]

v. 329. *suche maysters to playe*] i. e. to play such

pranks of assumed superiority. Compare v. 341. See Jamieson's *Et. Dict. of Scot. Lang.* in v. *Maistryss.*

Page 51. v. 330. *I am of countenaunce*] i. e. per- haps, I am a person of credit, good means, consequence (see Gifford's note on B. Jonson's *Works,* ii. 111).

Page 52. v. 334. *no force*] i. e. no matter.

v. 337. *dreuyll*] i. e. drudge, low fellow.

* v. 338. *deynte*] i. e. pleasure. See note on v. 150. p. 31.

v. 340. *Well, ones thou shalte be chermed, I wus*] i. e. Well, one time or other thou shalt be charmed (quelled, as if by a charm), certainly (*I wus—i-wis,* adv.).

v. 344. *Ryotte*] "Is forcibly and humorously pic- tured." Warton, *Hist. of E. P.* ii. 348. ed. 4to.

v. 345. *A rusty gallande, to-ragged and to-rente*] i. e. A shabby gallant, utterly ragged and tattered: see note on v. 32. p. 22.

v. 346. *bones*] i. e. dice.

v. 348. *by saynte Thomas of Kente*] i. e. by saint Thomas a Becket:

"Thought I, *By saint Thomas of Kent,*" &c.
Chaucer's *House of Fame,—Workes,* fol. 267.
ed. 1602.

The picture of Ryotte in the present passage and in v. 389 sqq. gave birth no doubt to the following lines in a poem called *Syrs spare your good;*

"No, by my faith, he saide incontinente,
But by saint Thomas of Kente
I woulde haue at the hasarde a cast or two,
For to learne to caste the dyce to and fro;
And if here be any body that wyll for money playe,
I haue yet in my purse money and pledges gaye:

Some be nobles, some be crownes of Fraunce;
Haue at all who wyll of this daunce.
One of them answered with that worde,
And caste a bale of dyce on the borde," &c.

I quote from *Brit. Bibliog.* ii. 371, where are extracts
from an ed. of the poem printed by Kytson, n. d.: it
originally appeared from the press of W. de Worde;
see *Cens. Liter.* i. 55. sec. ed.

Page 52. v. 349. *kyst I wote nere what*] i. e. cast I
know never (not) what.

v. 350. *His here was growen thorowe oute his hat*]
i. e. His hair, &c.   Compare Barclay's *Argument of
the first Egloge;*

" At diuers holes *his heare grewe through his hode*."

Sig. A i. ed. **1570.**

and Heywood's *Dialogue;*

" There is a nest of chickens which he doth brood
   That will sure *make his hayre growe through his
         hood*."

Sig. G 2.,—*Workes*, ed. 1598.

Ray gives, " *His hair grows through his hood.*   He is
very poor, his hood is full of holes."   *Proverbs*, p. 57.
ed. 1768.

v. 351. *how he dysgysed was*] i. e. what a wretched
plight he was in:

" Ragged and torne, *disguised* in array."

Chaucer's *Court of Loue*, fol. 329,—
Workes, ed. 1602.

v. 352. *watchynge ouer nyghte*] i. e. over-night's de-
bauch:

v. 355. *he wente so all for somer lyghte*]—*somer*, i. e.
summer.   Compare;

" It semed that he caried litel array,
   Al light for sommer rode this worthy man."
                Chaucer's *Chanones Yemannes Prol.*
                v. 16035. ed. Tyr.

See too Bale's *Kyng Iohan*, p. 34. ed. Camd. Soc.; and
our author's *Phyllyp Sparowe*, v. 719. vol. i. 85.

Page 52. v. 356. *His hose was garded wyth a lyste of
grene*] i. e. his breeches were faced, trimmed with, &c.
" There was an affectation of smartness in the trimming
of his hose." Warton, note on *Hist. of E. P.* ii. 348.
ed. 4to.

Page 53. v. 359. *Of Kyrkeby Kendall was his shorte
demye*] Kendal, or Kirkby in Kendal, was early famous
for the manufacture of cloth of various colours, par-
ticularly green.   Here the word " Kendall " seems
equivalent to—green : so too in Hall's *Chronicle*, where
we are told that Henry the Eighth, with a party of
noblemen, "came sodainly in a mornyng into the
Quenes Chambre, all appareled in shorte cotes of
Kentishe *Kendal* . . . like outlawes, or Robyn Hodes
men." (*Henry viii.*) fol. vi. ed. 1548.—*demye ;* i. e.,
says Warton, note on *Hist. of E. P.* ii. 348. ed. 4to.,
" doublet, jacket : " rather, I believe, some sort of close
vest,—his " cote " having been mentioned in the pre-
ceding line.

v. 360. *In fayth, decon thou crewe*] The commence-
ment of some song ; quoted again by our author in
A deuoute trentale for old Iohn Clarke, v. 44. vol. i.
190, and in *Why come ye nat to Courte*, v. 63. vol. ii
279.

v. 361. *he ware his gere so nye*] i. e., I suppose, he
wore his clothes so near, so thoroughly.   But Warton
explains it " his coat-sleeve was so short." Note on
Hist. of E. P. ii. 348. ed. 4to.

Page 53. v. 363. *whynarde*] i. e. a sort of hanger, sword.

———————————————————— *his pouche,*
The deuyll myghte daunce therin for ony crowche]
—*ony crowche*, i. e. any piece of money,—many coins being marked with a *cross* on one side. "The devil might dance in his purse without meeting with a single sixpence." Warton, note on *Hist. of E. P.* ii. 348. ed. 4to. So in Massinger's *Bashful Lover;*

> " The devil sleeps in my pocket; *I have no cross*
>   *To drive him from it."*
>   *Works* (by Gifford), iv. 398. ed. 1813.

v. 365. *Counter he coude O lux vpon a potte*]— *Counter;* see note, p. 11 :—i. e. he could sing *O lux*, playing an accompaniment to his voice on a drinking-pot. *O lux beata Trinitas* was an ancient hymn, " which," says Hawkins, " seems to have been a very popular melody before the time of King Henry viii." *Hist. of Music*, ii. 354. In a comedy by the Duke of Newcastle is a somewhat similar passage : " I danced a Jig, while Tom Brutish whistled and *play'd upon the head of a pint pot." The Humorous Lovers*, 1677, act i. sc. 1. p. 5.

v. 366. *eestryche fedder*] i. e. ostrich-feather.

v. 367. *fresshely*] i. e. smartly.

v. 368. *What, reuell route*] Here, as below, " route " is a verb—What, let revel roar ! Compare ;

> " And euer be mery lett *reuell rought."*
>   *A Morality,—Anc. Mysteries from the*
>   *Digby MSS.* p. 187. ed. Abbotsf.

Page 53. v. 370. *Felyce fetewse*]—*Felyce*, i. e. Phillis : *fetewse*, i. e. feateous ; " *Fetyce* and prety. Paruiculus. Elegantulus." *Prompt. Parv.* ed. 1499.

* v. 731. *klycked gate*] *klycked* is clicket, latch. " *Cliquetus*, pessulus versatilis ; " French, *Loquet ;* from *Clingere* — clinch. See Ducange, in v. In Chaucer's *Marchantes Tale*, v. 9991. ed. Tyr., " *clicket* " means a latch-key.

v. 372. *rebaudrye*] i. e. ribaldry.

v. 375. *in the deuylles date*] An exclamation several times used by Skelton.—In *Pierce Plowman*, a charter, which is read at the proposed marriage of Mede, is sealed " *in the date of the deuil*," sig. C i. ed. 1561.

v. 380. *done*] i. e. do.

Page 54. v. 386. *Plucke vp thyne herte vpon a mery pyne*] The expression occurs often in our early poetry ; and is found even in one of Wycherley's comedies.

* v. 387. *And lete vs laugh a placke or tweyne at nale*]—" plucke," as I have observed *ad loc.*, seems to be the right reading, though the word occurs in the preceding line : compare *Thersytes*, n. d.

" Darest thou trye maystries with me a *plucke*."

p. 60. Rox. ed.

and a song quoted in the note on our author's *Magnyfycence*, v. 757 ;

" A stoupe of bere vp at *a pluk*."

at nale, (*atten ale*, *at then ale ;* see Price's note, Warton's *Hist. of E. P.* ii. 501. ed. 1824), i. e. at the alehouse. [*Plack*, however, is provincial for " a portion or piece of anything." See Halliwell's *Dict.*]

Page 54. v. 389. *of dyce a bale*] i. e. a pair of dice.

* v. 390. *A brydelynge caste*] An expression which I am unable to explain. [Qy. a *parting* cast? Halliwell.] It occurs (but applied to drinking) in Beaumont and Fletcher's *Scornful Lady ;*

> " Let's have *a bridling cast* before you go.
> Fill's a new stoop." act ii. sc. 2.

—— *male*] i. e. bag, wallet, pouch.

v. 391. *burde*] i. e. board.

v. 393. *the dosen browne*] Is used sometimes to signify thirteen; as in a rare piece entitled *A Brown Dozen of Drunkards*, &c., 1648. 4to., who are *thirteen* in number. But in our text "the dosen browne" seems merely to mean the full dozen: so in a tract (*Letter from a Spy at Oxford*) cited by Grey in his notes on *Hudibras*, vol. ii. 375 ; " and this was the twelfth Conquest, which made up the Conqueror's *brown Dozen* in Number, compared to the twelve Labours of Hercules."

v. 394. *pas*] Seems here to be equivalent to—stake; but I have not found *pass* used with that meaning in any works on gaming. See *The Compleat Gamester*, p. 119. ed. 1680.

v. 398. *The armes of Calyce*] In our author's *Magnyfycence* is the same exclamation ;

> " By *the armes of Calys*, well conceyued ! "
>
> v. 685. vol. ii. 33.

Whether Calais in France, or Cales (Cadiz) be alluded to, I know not.

v. 399. *renne*] i. e. run.

v. 401. *To wete yf Malkyn, my lemman, haue gete oughte*] i. e. To know if Malkin, my mistress, has got aught.

Page 54. v. 406. *Bordews*] i. e. Bordeaux.

Page 55. v. 411. *curtel*] i. e. curtal.

v. 412. *lege*] i. e. allege.

* v. 413. *haue*] i. e. take.

v. 414. *rybaude*] i. e. ribald.

v. 418. *kyste*] i. e. cast.

v. 420. *sadde*] i. e. serious, earnest.

v. 423. *stede*] i. e. place.

v. 425. *Me passynge sore myne herte than gan agryse*] For the reading of all the eds. " aryse," I have ventured to substitute " agryse," i. e. cause to shudder. Compare ;

" *Sore* might *hir agrise.*"
> *Arthour and Merlin*, p. 34. ed. Abbotsf.

" Of his sweuen *sore hin agros.*"
> *Marie Maudelein*, p. 226,—Turnbull's *Legendæ Catholicæ* (from the Auchinleck MS.).

" The kinges *herte* of pitee *gan agrise.*"
> Chaucer's *Man of Lawes Tale*, v. 5034. ed. Tyr.

" Swiche peines, that your *hertes* might *agrise.*"
> Chaucer's *Frères Tale*, v. 7231. ed. Tyr.

v. 426. *I dempte and drede*] i. e. I deemed and dreaded.

Page 56. v. 428. *Than in his hode, &c.*]—*hode*, i. e. hood.—This passage is quoted by Warton, who observes, " There is also merit in the delineation of DISSIMULATION . . . . and it is not unlike Ariosto's manner in imagining these allegorical personages." *Hist. of E. P.* ii. 349. ed. 4to.

v. 431. *coost*] i. e. coast, approach.

v. 436. *spone*] i. e. spoon.

v. 437. *to preue a dawe*] i. e. to prove, try a simpleton : see note on v. 301. p. 36.—Warton, who gives the other reading, " to *preye* a dawe," explains it—to catch a silly bird.   Note on *Hist. of E. P.* ii. 349. ed. 4to.

Page 56. v. 438. *wrete*] i. e. writ.

v. 440. *His hode was syde, his cope was roset graye*] i. e. His hood was long (or full), his cope was russet grey.

v. 445. *a connynge man ne dwelle maye*] i. e. a wise, a learned man may not dwell.

v. 448. *that nought can*] i. e. that knows nothing.

Page 57. v. 454. *clerke*] i. e. scholar.

v. 455. *in the deuylles date*] See note on v. 375. p. 41.

v. 456. *longe*] i. e. belong.

v. 457. *lewde*] i. e. wicked.

v. 460. *herte brennynge*] i. e. heart-burning.

v. 464. *It is a worlde*] Equivalent to—It is a matter of wonder.

v. 466. *A man can not wote where to be come*] i. e A man cannot know whither to go : compare v. 228

v. 467. *I wys*] i. e. truly, certainly (*i-wis*, adv.).

—— *home*] i. e. hum.

v. 476. *shall wene be hanged by the throte*] i. e. (I suppose) shall think themselves hanged, &c.

v. 477. *a stoppynye oyster*] Compare Heywood ;
" Herewithall his wife to make vp my mouth,
  Not onely her husbands taunting tale auouth,
  But thereto deuiseth to cast in my teeth
  Checks and *choking oysters.*"
              Dialogue, sig. E,— *Workes*, ed. 1598.

v. 477. *poke*] i. e. pouch.

v. 484. *teder*] i. e. toder, t'other.

* Page 57. v. 486. *dreuyll*] drudge, knave.

Page 58. v. 488. *on flote*] i. e. flowing, full.

v. 491. *but what this is ynowe*] i. e. but that this is enough.

v. 502. *Sterte*] i. e. Started.

Page 59. v. 504. *nobles*] i. e. the gold coins so called.

v. 508. *His hode all pounsed and garded*]—*hode*, i. e. hood : *pounsed*, i. e. perforated, having small holes stamped or worked in it, by way of ornament—*garded*, i. e. adorned with *gards*, facings.

v. 513. *rounde*] i. e. whisper,—or, rather, mutter, for Skelton (*Garlande of Laurell*, v. 250. vol. ii. 181) and other poets make a distinction between *whisper* and *round:*

> " Me lyste not now whysper *nether rowne.*"
> Lydgate's *Storye of Thebes, Pars Prima,*
> sig. b vii. ed. 4to. n. d.

> " Whisper *and rounde* thinges ymagined falsly."
> Barclay's *Ship of Fooles*, fol. 208. ed. 1570

> " They 're here with me already, whispering, *rounding.*"
> Shakespeare's *Winter's Tale*, act i. sc. 2.

* v. 521. *hafte*] i. e. cheat, trick.

v. 522. *payne*] i. e. difficulty.

v. 525. *shrewes*] i. e. wicked, worthless fellows.

Page 60. v. 527. *confetryd*] i. e. confederated.

v. 528. *lewde*] i. e. vile, rascally.

v. 530. *hente*] i. e. seized.

v. 536. *Syth*] i. e. Since.

PHYLLYP SPAROWE

Must have been written before the end of 1508; for
it is mentioned with contempt in the concluding lines
of Barclay's *Ship of Fooles*, which was finished in that
year: see *Account of Skelton and his Writings*.

The *Luctus in morte Passeris* of Catullus no doubt
suggested the present production to Skelton, who,
when he calls on "all maner of byrdes" (v. 387) to
join in lamenting Philip Sparow, seems also to have
had an eye to Ovid's elegy *In mortem Psittaci, Amor.*
ii. 6. Another piece of the kind is extant among the
compositions of antiquity,—the *Psittacus Atedii Melioris* of Statius, *Silv.* ii. 4. In the *Amphitheatrum Sapientiæ Socraticæ Joco-seriæ*, &c., of Dornavius, i. 460
sqq. may be found various Latin poems on the deaths,
&c. of sparrows by writers posterior to the time of
Skelton. See too Herrick's lines *Upon the death of
his Sparrow, an Elegie, Hesperides*, 1648. p. 117; and
the verses entitled *Phyllis on the death of her Sparrow*,
attributed to Drummond, *Works*, 1711. p. 50.

"Old Skelton's 'Philip Sparrow,' an exquisite and
original poem." Coleridge's *Remains*, ii. 163.

Page 61. v. 1. *Pla ce bo, &c.*] Skelton is not the
only writer that has taken liberties with the Romish
service-book. In Chaucer's *Court of Loue*, parts of it
are sung by various birds; *Domine, labia* by the nightingale, *Venite* by the eagle, &c., *Workes*, fol. 333. ed.
1602: in a short poem by Lydgate "dyuerse foules"
are introduced singing different hymns. *MS. Harl.*
2251. fol. 37: and see too a poem (attributed, without
any authority, to Skelton) called *Armony of Byrdes*,
n. d., reprinted (inaccurately) in *Tyqog. Antiq.* iv. 380.

ed. Dibdin ; and Sir D. Lyndsay's *Complaynt of the Papingo, Works,* i. 325. ed. Chalmers. In *Reynard the Fox,* we are told that at the burial of " coppe, chanteklers doughter,"—" Tho begonne they *placebo domino,* with the verses that to longen," &c. Sig. a 8. ed. 1481. Compare also the mock *Requiem* printed (somewhat incorrectly) from *MS. Cott. Vesp.* B. 16. in Ritson's *Antient Songs,* i. 118. ed. 1829 ; Dunbar's *Dirige to the King at Stirling, Poems,* i. 86. ed. Laing ; and the following lines of a rare tract entitled *A Commemoration or Dirige of Boner,* &c., by Lemeke Auale, 1569,—

" *Placebo.* Bo. Bo. Bo. Bo. Bo.
Heu me, beware the bugge, out quod Boner alas,
De profundis clamaui, how is this matter come to passe.
Lœvaui oculos meos from a darke depe place," &c.
sig. A viii.

Other pieces of the kind might be pointed out.

Page 61. v. 7. *Philip Sparowe*] *Philip,* or *Phip,* was a familiar name given to a sparrow from its note being supposed to resemble that sound.

v. 8. *Carowe*] Was a nunnery in the suburbs of Norwich. " Here [at Norwich]," says Tanner, " was an ancient hospital or nunnery dedicated to St. Mary and St. John ; to which K. Stephen having given lands and meadows without the south gate, Seyna and Leftelina two of the sisters, A. D. 1146, began the foundation of a new monastery called Kairo, Carow, or Carhou, which was dedicated to the blessed Virgin Mary, and consisted of a prioress and nine Benedictine nuns." *Not. Mon.* p. 347. ed. 1744. In 1273, Pope Gregory the Tenth inhibited the Prioress and

convent from receiving more nuns than their income
would maintain, upon their representation that the
English nobility, whom they could not resist, had
obliged them to take in so many sisters that they were
unable to support them. At the Dissolution, the num-
ber of nuns was twelve. The site of the nunnery,
within the walls, contained about ten acres. It was
granted, with its chief revenues, in the 30th Henry
viii. to Sir John Shelton, knight, who fitted up the
parlour and hall, which were noble rooms, when he
came to reside there, not long after the Dissolution.
It continued in the Shelton family for several genera-
tions.

This nunnery was during many ages a place of edu-
cation for the young ladies of the chief families in the
diocese of Norwich, who boarded with and were taught
by the nuns. The fair Jane or Johanna Scroupe of
the present poem was, perhaps, a boarder at Carow.

See more concerning Carow in Dugdale's *Monast.*
(new ed.) iv. 68 sqq., and Blomefield's *Hist. of Nor-
folk*, ii. 862 sqq. ed. fol.

Page 61. v. 9. *Nones Blake*] i. e. Black Nuns,—
Benedictines.

v. 12. *bederolles*] i. e. lists of those to be prayed for.

Page 62. v. 24. *The tearys downe hayled*] So Hawes ;

" That euermore the salte *teres downe hayled*."

   The Pastime of pleasure, sig. Q viii. ed. 1555.

v. 27. *Gyb our cat*] *Gib*, a contraction of *Gilbert*,
was a name formerly given to a male cat :

" *Gibbe our Cat*,
That awaiteth Mice and Rattes to killen."

   Romaunt of the Rose,—Chaucer's *Workes*,
    fol. 136. ed. 1602.

Page 62. v. 29. *Worrowyd her on that*] So Dunbar;
" He that dois *on* dry breid *wirry*."
Poems, i. 108. ed. Laing.

v. 34. *stounde*] i. e. moment, time.

v. 35. *sounde*] i. e. swoon.

v. 37. *Vnneth I kest myne eyes*] i. e. Scarcely, not without difficulty, I cast, &c.

v. 42. *Haue rewed*] i. e. Have had compassion.

v. 46, *senaws*] i. e. sinews.

Page 63. v. 58. *frete*] i. e. eat, gnaw.

v. 69. *marees*] i. e. waters.

v. 70. *Acherontes well*] i. e. Acheron's well. So,—after the fashion of our early poets,—Skelton writes *Zenophontes* for *Xenophon*, *Eneidos* for *Eneis*, *Achilliedos* for *Achilleis*, &c.

v. 76. *mare*] i. e. hag.—" *Mare* or witche." *Prompt. Parv.* ed. 1499.

v. 78. *edders*] i. e. adders.

* v. 87. *outraye*] i. e. vanquish, overcome : and so in the following passages.

" Whom Hercules most strong and coragious,
Sumtime *outraid*, and slewe hym with his hand."
Lydgate's *Fall of Prynces*, B. i. leaf **xxvii.**
ed. Wayland.

" Al be that Cresus faught long in hys defence,
He finally by Cyrus was *outrayed*,
And depriued by knyghtly vyolence,
Take in the felde," &c.
Id. B. ii. leaf lviii.

" But it may fall, a dwerye [i. e. dwarf] in his right,
To *outray* a gyaunt for all his gret might."
Id. B. iii. leaf lxvii.

Page 64. v. 98. *Zenophontes*] i. e. Xenophon : see note on v. 70, preceding page.

* v. 107. *thought*] i. e. sorrow.

Page 65. v. 114. *go*] i. e. gone.

v. 115. *fole*] i. e. fool.

v. 117. *scole*] i. e. school, instruction.

v. 118.   *For to kepe his cut,*
            Wyth, Phyllyp, kepe your cut !]

Compare Sir Philip Sidney in a sonnet;

" Good brother Philip, I haue borne you long,
    I was content you should in fauour creepe,
    While craftily you seem'd your *cut to keepe*,
As though that faire soft hand did you great wrong."
                Astrophel and Stella, p. 548. ed. 1613.

Brome in *The Northern Lasse*, 1632 ;

" A bonny bonny Bird I had
    A bird that was my Marroe :
A bird whose pastime made me glad,
    And Phillip twas my Sparrow.
A pretty Play-fere : Chirp it would,
    And hop, and fly to fist,
Keepe cut, as 'twere a Vsurers Gold,
    And bill me when I list."

                        Act iii. sc. 2. sig. G 2.

and in *The New Academy ;* " But look how she turnes
and *keeps cut like my Sparrow.* She will be my back
Sweet-heart still I see, and love me behind." Act iv.
sc. 1. p. 72. (*Five New Playes*, 1659).

v. 125.   *Betwene my brestes softe*
            It wolde lye and rest]

So Catullus, in the beginning of his verses *Ad Pas-*

serem Lesbiæ, (a distinct poem from that mentioned at p. 46) ;

> " Passer, deliciæ meæ puellæ,
> Quicum ludere, *quem in sinu tenere,*" &c.

Page 65. v. 127. *It was propre and prest*] Compare v. 264, " As *prety* and as *prest,*" where " prety " answers to " propre " in the present line. " *Proper* or feate. *coint, godin, gentil, mignot.*" Palsgrave, p. 312 :—*prest,* which generally means—ready, seems here to be nearly synonymous with *propre ;* and so in a passage of Tusser,—" more handsome, and *prest,*"— cited by Todd (*Johnson's Dict.* in v.), who explains it " neat, tight."

v. 137. *gressop*] i. e. grasshopper.—" *Cicada* . . . anglice *a gresse hoppe.*" *Ortus Vocab.*, fol. ed. W. de Worde, n. d.

Page 66. v. 141. *slo*] i. e. slay.

v. 147. *dome*] i. e. judgment, thinking.

v. 148. *Sulpicia*] Lived in the age of Domitian. Her satire *De corrupto statu reipub. temporibus Domitiani, præsertim cum edicto Philosophos urbe exegisset,* may be found in Wernsdorf's ed. of *Poetæ Latini Minores,* iii. 83.

v. 151. *pas*] i. e. pass, excel.

v. 154. *pretende*] i. e. attempt.

Page 67. v. 171. *perde*] i. e. *par dieu,* verily.

v. 173. *nyse*] i. e. foolish, inclined to folly, to toyish tricks: compare our author's *Manerly Margery, &c.,* v. 2. vol. i. 35.

v. 176. *too*] i. e. toe.

* v. 186. *ryde and go*] A sort of pleonastic expression which repeatedly occurs in our early writers. [It means ride and *walk.*]

Page 67. v. 192. *Pargame*] i. e. Pergamus.

Page 68. v. 198. *wete*] i. e. know.

v. 205. *be quycke*] i. e. be made alive.

v. 211. *the nones*] i. e. the occasion.

v. 213. *My sparow whyte as mylke*] Compare Sir P
Sidney;

> " They saw a maid who thitherward did runne,
>   To catch her sparrow which from her did swerue,
>   As shee a black-silke Cappe on him begunne
>   To sett, for foile of his *milke-white* to serue."
>   *Arcadia*, lib. i. p. 85. ed. 1613.

v. 216. *importe*] i. e. impart.

v. 218. *solas*] i. e. amusement.

Page 69. v. 230. *kest*] i. e. cast.

v. 242. *bederoule*] i. e. list of persons to be prayed
for.

v. 244. *Cam, and Sem*] i. e. Ham, and Shem.

v. 247. *the hylles of Armony*]—*Armony*, i. e. Arme-
nia.—So in *Processus Noe* ;

> " What grownd may this be ?
> *Noe. The hyllys of Armonye.*"
>   *Townley Myst.* p. 32.

v. 248.   *Wherfore the birdes yet cry*
>   *Of your fathers bote*]

The reading of Kele's ed., " bordes," (as I have already
observed *ad loc.*) is perhaps the true one ;—(compare
Pierce Plowman ;

> " And [God] came to Noe anone, and bad him not let
> Swyth go shape a shype of shydes and of *bordes.*"
>   Pass. Non. sig. M ii. ed. 1561.)—

and qy. did Skelton write,—

> " *Whereon* the *bordes* yet *lye ?* "

Page 70. v. 264. *prest*] i. e. neat. See note on v. 127, p. 51.

v. 272. *hardely*] i. e. assuredly.

v. 281. *Carowe*] See note on v. 8. p. 47.

v. 282. *carlyshe kynde*] i. e. churlish nature.

v. 284. *vntwynde*] i. e. tore to pieces, destroyed: so again in our author's *Garlande of Laurell;*

" This goodly flowre with stormis was *vntwynde.*"

v. 1445. vol. ii. 234.

Page 71. v. 290. *Lybany*] i. e. Libya.

v. 294. *mantycors*] " Another maner of bestes ther is in ynde that ben callyd *manticora*, and hath visage of a man, and thre huge grete teeth in his throte, he hath eyen lyke a ghoot and body of a lyon, tayll of a Scorpyon and voys of a serpente in suche wyse that by his swete songe he draweth to hym the peple and deuoureth them And is more delyuerer to goo than is a fowle to flee." Caxton's *Mirrour of the world*, 1480. sig. e vii. See also R. Holme's *Ac. of Armory*, 1688. B. ii. p. 212.—This fabulous account is derived from Pliny.

v. 296. *Melanchates, that hounde, &c.*] See the story of Actæon in Ovid's *Metam.;*

" Prima *Melanchœtes* in tergo vulnera fecit."

iii. 232.

v. 305.   *That his owne lord bote,*
      Myght byte asondre thy throte !]

—*bote*, i. e. bit.—So in *Syr Tryamoure;*

" He toke the stuarde by the *throte*,
  And *asonder* he it *botte.*"

Early Pop. Poetry (by Utterson), i. 28.

v. 307. *grypes*] i. e. griffins.

Page 71. v. 311. *The wylde wolfe Lycaon*] See Ovid's *Metam.* i. 163 sqq. for an account of Lycaon, king of Arcadia, being transformed into a wolf. I ought to add, that he figures in a work well known to the readers of Skelton's time—*The Recuyel of the Historyes of Troy.*

Page 72. v. 325. *corage*] i. e. heart, mind, disposition.

v. 329. *departed*] i. e. parted. So in our old marriage-service; "till death us *depart*."

v. 336. *rew*] i. e. have compassion.

* v. 345. *And go in at my spayre,*
          And crepe in at my gore
          Of my gowne before]

"*Sparre* of a gowne, *fente de la robe.*" Palsgrave, p. 273. "That parte of weemens claiths, sik as of their gowne or petticot, quhilk vnder the belt and before is open, commonly is called the *spare.*" Skene, quoted by Jamieson, *Et. Dict. of Scot. Lang.* in v. *Spare*. *Gore*, a triangular piece of cloth inserted at the bottom of a shirt or shift, to give breadth to the lower part of it.

Page 73. v. 361. *kusse*] i. e. kiss.

    " And if he maie no more do,
      Yet woll he stele a *cusse* or two."
                    Gower's *Conf. Am.* lib. v. fol. cxix.
                              ed. 1554.

v. 362. *musse*] i. e. muzzle,—mouth.

v. 366. *this*] i. e. thus.

Page 74. v. 387.

    To wepe with me loke that ye come,
    All maner of byrdes in your kynd, &c.]

—*loke*, i. e. look. Compare Ovid (see note on title of this poem, p. 46) ;

> " Psittacus, Eois imitatrix ales ab Indis,
>   Occidit: exequias ite frequenter, aves.
> Ite, piæ volucres, et plangite pectora pennis,
>   Et rigido teneras ungue notate genas.
> Horrida pro mœstis lanietur pluma capillis,
>   Pro longa resonent carmina vestra tuba."
> > > *Amor.* lib. ii. El. vi. 5. 1.

Page 74. v. 396. *ianglynge*] i. e. babbling, chattering—an epithet generally applied to the jay by our old poets.

Page 75. v. 403. *the red sparow*] i. e. the reed-sparrow.

> " The *Red-sparrow*, the Nope, the Red-breast, and
> > the Wren."
> > > Drayton's *Polyolbion*, Song xiii. p. 215.
> > > > ed. 1622.

" The *Red Sparrow*, or Reed Sparrow." R. Holme's *Ac. of Armory*, 1688. B. ii. p. 246.

v. 406. *to*] i. e. toe.

v. 407. *The spynke*] i. e. The chaffinch. In the *Countrie Farme*, the " spinke " is frequently mentioned (see pp. 886, 890, 891, 898, 900. ed. 1600) ; and in the French work by Estienne and Liebault, from which it is translated, the corresponding word is " pinçon : " in Cotgrave's *Dict.* is " Pinson. *A Spink, Chaffinch*, or Sheldaple ; " and in Moor's *Suffolk Words*, " *Spinx. The chaffinch.*"

v. 409. *The doterell, that folyshe pek*] The dotterel is said to allow itself to be caught, while it imitates the gestures of the fowler : *pek*, or *peke*, seems here to be used by Skelton in the sense of—contemptible fellow; so in his *Collyn Cloute;*

> " Of suche *Pater-noster pekes*
> All the worlde spekes."

v. 264. vol. ii. 134.

And see Todd's Johnson's *Dict.*, and Richardson's *Dict.* in v. *Peak.*

Page 75. v. 411. *toote*] i. e. pry, peep, search.

v. 412. *the snyte*] i. e. the snipe.

v. 415. *His playne songe to solfe*] See note, p. 15, v. 48 : *solfe*, i. e. solfa.

v. 418. *The woodhacke, that syngeth chur*
Horsly, as he had the mur]
—*woodhacke*, i. e. woodpecker : *mur*, i. e. a severe cold with hoarseness. Compare Lydgate ;

> " And at his feete lay a prykeryd curre ;
> He rateled in the throte *as he had the murre.*"

Le Assemble de dyeus, sig. b i. n. d. 4to.

v. 421. *The popyngay*] i. e. The parrot.

v. 422. *toteth*] Or *tooteth ;* see note on v. 411.

v. 424. *The mauys*] Is properly the song-thrush, as distinguished from the missel-thrush : see note on v. 460, p. 58.

v. 425. *the pystell*] i. e. the Epistle.

v. 426. *a large and a longe*] See note, p. 15. v. 49.

v. 427. *To kepe iust playne songe,*
Our chaunters shalbe the cuckoue]
See note, p. 15. v. 48. So Shakespeare mentions " *the plain-song cuckoo* gray." *Mids. Night's Dream*, act iii. sc. 1.

v. 430. *puwyt the lapwyng*] In some parts of England, the lapwing is called *pewit* from its peculiar cry.

Page 76. v. 432. *The bitter with his bumpe*] "The *Bitter*, or Bitterne, *Bumpeth*, when he puts his Bill in the reeds." R. Holme's *Ac. of Armory*, 1688. B. ii. p. 310.

v. 434. *Menander*] Means here *Mœander:* but I have not altered the text; because our early poets took great liberties with classical names; because all the eds. of Skelton's *Speke, Parrot*, have

" Alexander, a gander of *Menanders* pole."

v. 178. vol. ii. 254.

and because the following passage occurs in a poem by some imitator of Skelton, which is appended to the present edition;

" Wotes not wher to wander,
Whether to *Meander*,
Or vnto *Menander*."

The Image of Ipocrisy, Part Third.

v. 437. *wake*] i. e. watching of the dead body during the night.

v. 441. *He shall syng the grayle*]—*grayle*, says Warton (correcting an explanation he had formerly given), signifies here " *Graduale*, or the *Responsorium*, or *Antiphonarium*, in the Romish service . . . . He shall sing that part of the service which is called the *Grayle*, or *graduale*." *Obs. on the F. Queen*, ii. 244. ed. 1762.

v. 442. *The owle, that is so foule*]—*foule*, i. e. ugly. The Houlate, (in the poem so called, by Holland), says,

" Thus all the foulis, for my *filth*, hes me at feid."

Pinkerton's *Scot. Poems*, iii. 149.

v. 444. *gaunce*] i. e. gaunt.

v. 445. *the cormoraunce*] i. e. the cormorant.

* Page 76. v. 447. *the gaglynge gaunte*]—*gaglynge* is cackling: Our author in his *Elynour Rummyng* has—

> " In came another dant,
> Wyth a gose and a *gant*."

v. 515. vol. i. 127.

where *gant* is plainly used for gander. In the present passage, however, *gaunte* must have a different signification (" The gose and the *gander*" being mentioned v. 435), and means, I apprehend,—wild goose. [Rather gannet, solan goose, as explained by Way, *Promptor. Parvul.* vol. i. p. 186.]

v. 449. *The route and the kowgh*] The Rev. J. Mitford suggests that the right reading is " The *knout* and the *rowgh*,"—i. e. the knot and the ruff.

v. 450. *The barnacle*] i. e. The goose-barnacle,— concerning the production of which the most absurd fables were told and credited : some asserted that it was originally the shell-fish called barnacle, others that it grew on trees, &c.

v. 451. *the wilde mallarde*] i. e. the wild-drake.

v. 452. *The dyuendop*] i. e. The dabchick or did-apper.

v. 454. *The puffin*] A water-fowl with a singular bill.

v. 455. *Money they shall dele, &c.*] According to the ancient custom at funerals.

v. 460. *The threstyl*] Or *throstle*, is properly the missel-thrush : see note on v. 424.

v. 461. *brablyng*] i. e. clamour, noise—properly, quarrel, squabble.

Page 77. v. 462. —————————— *the ospraye*
                    That putteth fysshes to a fraye]
—*fraye*, i. e. fright.   It was said that when the osprey,
which feeds on fish, hovered over the water, they be-
came fascinated and turned up their bellies.

  v. 468. *The countrynge of the coe*]—*countrynge;*
see note p. 11 : *coe*, i. e. jack-daw.

  v. 469.   *The storke also,*
                That maketh his nest
                In chimneyes to rest;
                Within those walles
                No broken galles
                May there abyde
                Of cokoldry syde]
The stork breeds in chimney-tops, and was fabled to
forsake the place, if the man or wife of the house
committed adultery.   The following lines of Lydgate
will illustrate the rest of the passage :
                " a certaine knight,
    Gyges called, thinge shameful to be tolde,
    To speke plaine englishe, made him [i. e. Can-
                daules] cokolde.
    Alas! I was not auised wel beforne,
        Vnkonnyngly to speake such langage :
    I should haue sayde how that he had an horne,
        Or sought some terme wyth a fayre vysage,
        To excuse my rudenesse of thys gret outrage :
    And in some land Cornodo men do them cal,
    And some affirme that *such folke haue no gal.*"
                Fall of Prynces, B. ii. leaf lvi. ed Wayland.

  v. 478.   *The estryge, that wyll eate*
                An horshowe so great]

—*estryge*, i. e. ostrich : *horshowe*, i. e. horse-shoe.—In *Struthiocamelus*, a portion of that strange book *Philomythie*, &c., by Tho. Scot., 1616, a merchant seeing an ostrich, in the desert, eating iron, asks—

" What nourishment can from those mettals grow ?
  The Ostrich answers ; Sir, I do not eate
  This iron, as you thinke I do, for meate.
  I only keepe it, lay it vp in store,
  To helpe my needy friends, the friendlesse poore.
  I often meete (as farre and neere I goe)
  Many a fowndred horse that wants a shooe,
  Seruing a Master that is moneylesse :
  Such I releiue and helpe in their distresse."

Sig. E 7.

Page 77. v. 482. *freat*] i. e. gnaw, devour.

v. 485. *at a brayde*] Has occurred before in our author's *Bowge of Courte;* see note, p. 32. v. 181 ; but here it seems to have a somewhat different meaning, and to signify—at an effort, at a push. " *At a brayde, Faysant mon effort, ton effort, son effort,* &c." Palsgrave, p. 831. This expression is used here in connection with singing : [?] and in one of the *Christmas Carols*, printed for the Percy Society, p. 51, we find,

" Wherefor syng we alle *atte a brayde,*
nowell."

v. 487. *To solfe aboue ela*]—*solfe*, i. e. solfa : *ela*, i. e. the highest note in the scale of music.

v. 488. *lorell*] i. e. good-for-nothing fellow (see Tyrwhitt's *Gloss.* to Chaucer's *Cant. Tales*) : used here as a sportive term of reproach.

Page 78. v. 491. *The best that we can,*
 To make hym our belman,
 And let hym ryng the bellys ;
 He can do nothyng ellys]

" *Sit campanista, qui non vult esse sophista,* Let him bee a bell-ringer, that will bee no good Singer." Withals's *Dict.* p. 178. ed. 1634.

v. 495.   *Chaunteclere, our coke,*

. . . . .

 By the astrology
 That he hath naturally, &c.]

So Chaucer ;

" But when *the cocke,* commune *Astrologer,*
 Gan on his brest to beate," &c.
 Troilus and Creseide, B. iii. fol. 164.—
 Workes, ed. 1602.

See also Lydgate's *Warres of Troy,* B. i. sig. D v. ed. 1555; and his copy of verses (entitled in the Catalogue *Advices for people to keep a guard over their tongues*), *MS. Harl.* 2255. fol. 132.

v. 501. *Albumazer*] A famous Arabian, of the ninth century.

v. 505. *Haly*] Another famous Arabian : " claruit circa A. C. 1100." Fabr. *Bibl. Gr.* xiii. 17.

v. 507. *tydes*] i. e. times, seasons.

v. 509. *Partlot his hen*] So in Chaucer's *Nonnes Preestes Tale ;* Lydgate's copy of verses (entitled in the Catalogue *Advices for people to keep a guard over their tongues*), *MS. Harl.* 2255. fol. 132; and G. Douglas's Prol. to the xii Booke of his *Eneados,* p. 401. l. 54. ed. Ruddiman, who conjectures that the name was applied to a hen in reference to the ruff (the *partlet*), or ring of feathers about her neck.

Page 79. v. 522. *thurifycation*] i. e. burning incense.

v. 524. *reflary*] As I have already noticed, should probably be " reflayre,"—i. e. odour. See Roquefort's *Gloss. de la Lang. Rom.* in v. *Flareur*, and *Suppl.* in v. *Fleror;* and Cotgrave's *Dict.* in v. *Reflairer.* In *The Garlande of Laurell*, our author calls a lady " *reflaring* rosabell.*" v. 977. vol. ii. 213.

v. 525. *eyre*] i. e. air, scent.

> ". Strowed wyth floures, of all goodly *ayre*."
>> Hawes's *Pastime of pleasure*, sig. D iiii.
>>> ed. 1555.

See too *The Pistill of Susan*, st. viii.—Laing's *Early Pop. Poetry of Scot.*

* v. 526. *sence*] i. e. incense.

v. 534. *bemole*] i. e. in B molle, soft or flat. So in the last stanza of a poem by W. Cornishe, printed in Marshe's ed. of Skelton's *Workes*, 1568 ;

> " I kepe be rounde and he by square
> The one is *bemole* and the other bequare."

v. 536.   *Plinni sheweth all*
            In his story naturall]

See *Historia Naturalis*, lib. x. sect. 2.

v. 545. *corage*] i. e. heart,—feelings.

* Page 80. v. 552. *the sedeane*] Does it mean subdean, or subdeacon ? [*Sedekine*, sub-deacon. Halliwell, *Dict.*]

v. 553. *The quere to demeane*] i. e. to conduct, direct the choir.

v. 555. *ordynall*] i. e. ritual.

v. 556. *the noble fawcon*] " There are seuen kinds of Falcons, and among them all for her *noblenesse* and hardy courage, and withal the francknes of her mettell, I may, and doe meane to place the Falcon gentle in chiefe." Turbervile's *Booke of Falconrie*, &c. p. 25. ed. 1611.

Page 80. v. 557. *the gerfawcon*] " Is a gallant Hawke to behold, more huge then any other kinde of Falcon, &c." *Id.* p. 42.

v. 558. *The tarsell gentyll*] Is properly the male of the gosshawk; but Skelton probably did not use the term in its exact meaning, for in the fifth line after this he mentions " the goshauke." It is commonly said (see Steevens's note on *Romeo and Juliet*, act ii. sc. 2.) to be called *tiercel* because it is a *tierce* or third less than the female. But, according to Turbervile, " he is termed a *Tyercelet*, for that there are most commonly disclosed three birds in one selfe eyree, two Hawkes and one Tiercell." *Booke of Falconrie*, &c. p. 59. ed. 1611.

v. 560. *amysse*] i. e. amice—properly the first of the six vestments common to the bishop and presby-ters. " Fyrst do on the *amys*, than the albe, than the gyrdell, than the manyple, than the stoole, than the chesyble." Hormanni *Vulgaria*, sig. E iiii. ed. 1530.

v. 561. *The sacre*] A hawk " much like the Falcon Gentle for largenesse, and the Haggart for hardines." Turbervile's *Booke of Falconrie*, &c. p. 45. ed. 1611.

v. 563. *role*] i. e. roll.

v. 565. *The lanners*] " They are more blancke Hawkes then any other, they haue lesse beakes then the rest, and are lesse armed and pounced then other Falcons be." Turbervile's *Booke of Falconrie*, &c. p. 47. ed. 1611.

—— *the marlyons*] Or *merlins*,—the smallest of the hawks used by falconers.

v. 566. *morning gounes*] i. e. mourning-gowns.

Page 80. v. 567. *The hobby*] " Of all birdes of prey
that belong to the Falconers vse, I know none lesse
then the Hobby, unles it be the Merlyn." Turber-
vile's *Booke of Falconrie*, &c. p. 53. ed. 1611.

—— *the muskette*] i. e. the male sparrow-hawk.
" You must note, that all these kind of hawkes haue
their male birdes and cockes of euerie sort and gender,
as the Eagle his Earne . . . . . . and the Sparrow-
hawke his *Musket.*" *Id.* p. 3. " The male sparrow
hawke is called a *musket.*" *The Countrie Farme*, p.
877. ed. 1600.

v. 568. *fet*] i. e. fetch.

v. 569. *The kestrell*] A sort of base-bred hawk.

—— *warke*] i. e. work, business.

v. 570. *holy water clarke*] See note, p. 14. v. 21.

Page 81. v. 590. *And wrapt in a maidenes smocke*]
Spenser seems to have recollected this passage: he
says, that when Cupid was stung by a bee, Venus

—— " tooke him streight full pitiously lamenting,
  And wrapt him in her smock."

See a little poem in his *Works*, viii. 185. ed. Todd.

v. 595. *Lenger*] i. e. Longer.

v. 600.   —— *the prety wren,*
  That is our Ladyes hen]

So in a poem (attributed, on no authority, to Skelton)
entitled *Armony of Byrdes*, n. d., and reprinted entire
in *Typogr. Antiq.* iv. 380. ed. Dibdin;

  " Than sayd *the wren,*
  I am called *the hen*
    Of our lady most cumly." p. 382.

Wilbraham, in his *Cheshire Gloss.* p. 105, gives the
following metrical adage as common in that county;

"The Robin and *the Wren*
Are *God's* cock and *hen,*
The Martin and the Swallow
Are God's mate and marrow."

In the *Ballad of Kynd Kittok*, attributed to Dunbar, we are told that after death she " wes *our Ledyis hen-wyfe,*" *Poems,* ii. 36. ed. Laing.—An Elysium, very different from that described in the somewhat profane passage of our text, is assigned by the delicate fancy of Ovid to the parrot of his mistress, in the poem to which (as I have before observed, p. 46,) Skelton seems to have had an eye;

" *Colle sub Elysio nigra nemus illice frondens,*" &c.

Amor. ii. 6. 49.

Page 82. v. 609. *asayde*] i. e. tried—tasted:

v. 619. *scath*] i. e. harm, mischief.

v. 629. *Of Gawen*] Son of King Lot and nephew of King Arthur. Concerning him, see the *Morte d'Arthur* (of which some account is given in note on v. 634),—*Syr Gawayn and the Grene Kny3t,* in *MS. Cott. Nero* A. x. fol. 91,—*Ywaine and Gawin,* in Ritson's *Met. Rom.* vol. i.,—the fragment of *The Marriage of Sir Gawaine,* at the end of Percy's *Rel. of A. E. P.,*—*The Awntyrs of Arthure at the Terne Wathelyn,* in Laing's *Early Pop. Poetry of Scot.,* (the same romance, from a different MS., under the title of *Sir Gawan and Sir Galaron of Galloway,* in Pinkerton's *Scot. Poems,* vol. iii.),—*The Knightly Tale of Golagrus and Gawane,* reprinted at Edinburgh in 1827 from the ed. of 1508, (the same romance, under the title of *Gawan and Gologras,* in Pinkerton's *Scot. Poems,* vol. iii.),—and the romance of *Arthour and Merlin,* from the Auchinleck MS., published by the Abbotsford Club, 1838.

I had written the above note before the appearance of a valuable volume put forth by the Bannatyne Club, entitled *Syr Gawayne ; A collection of Ancient Romance-Poems, by Scotish and English Authors, relating to that celebrated Knight of the Round Table, with an Introduction, &c., by Sir F. Madden*, 1839.

Page 82. v. 629. *syr Guy*] In *The Rime of Sire Thopas*, Chaucer mentions " *Sire Guy* " as one of the " romaunces of pris." For an account of, extracts from, and an analysis of, the English romance on the subject of this renowned hero of Warwick, see Ritson's *Met. Rom.* (*Dissert.*) i. xcii., Warton's *Hist. of E. P.* i. 169. ed. 4to., and *Ellis's Spec. of Met. Rom.* ii. I must also refer the reader to a volume, issued by the Abbotsford Club, entitled *The Romances of Sir Guy of Warwick, and Rembrun his son. Now first edited from the Auchinleck MS.* 1840.

v. 631. —— *the Golden Flece,*
         How Jason it wan]
A boke of the hoole lyf of Jason was printed by Caxton in folio, n. d. (about 1475), being a translation by that venerable typographer from the French of Raoul le Fevre. A copy of it (now before me) in the King's Library, though apparently perfect, has no title of any sort. Specimens of this prose-romance, which is not without merit, may be found in Dibdin's *Biblioth. Spenc.* iv. 199.—The story of Jason is also told by Chaucer, *Legend of Hipsiphile and Medea ;* by Gower, *Conf Am.* Lib. v.; and, at considerable length, by Lydgate. *Warres of Troy*, B. i.

Page 82. v. 634.

> *Of Arturs rounde table,*
> *With his knightes commendable,*
> *And dame Gaynour, his quene,*
> *Was somwhat wanton, I wene;*
> *How syr Launcelote de Lake*
> *Many a spere brake*
> *For his ladyes sake;*
> *Of Trystram, and kynge Marke,*
> *And al the hole warke*
> *Of Bele Isold his wyfe*]

—*warke*, i. e. work, affair.—Concerning the various romances on the subject of Arthur, Lancelot, Tristram, &c. see Sir F. Madden's Introduction to the volume already mentioned, *Syr Gawayne, &c.*—In this passage, however, Skelton seems to allude more particularly to a celebrated compilation from the French— the prose romance of *The Byrth, Lyf, and Actes of Kyng Arthur*, &c., commonly known by the name of *Morte d'Arthur.* At the conclusion of the first edition printed in folio by Caxton (and reprinted in 1817 with an Introd. and Notes by Southey) we are told " *this booke was ended the ix. yere of the reygne of kyng Edward the Fourth by syr Thomas Maleore, knyght*" . . . . " *Whiche booke was reduced in to Englysshe by Syr Thomas Malory knyght as afore is sayd and by me* [Caxton] *deuyded in to xxi bookes chaptyred and emprynted and fynysshed in thabbey Westmestre the last day of July the yere of our lord* MCCCCLXXXV."

In the *Morte d'Arthur*, the gallant and courteous Sir Launcelot du Lake, son of King Ban of Benwyck, figures as the devoted lover of Arthur's queen, Gueneuer (Skelton's " *Gaynour*"), daughter of King Lode-

greans of Camelard.   On several occasions, Gueneuer
after being condemned to be burnt, is saved by the
valour of her knight.   But their criminal intercourse
proves in the end the destruction of Arthur and of the
fellowship of the Round Table.   Gueneuer becomes
a nun, Launcelot a priest.   The last meeting of the
guilty pair,—the interment of Gueneuer's body by
her paramour,—and the death of Launcelot, are re-
lated with no ordinary pathos and simplicity.

The same work treats fully of the loves of Sir Trys-
tram, son of King Melyodas of Lyones, and La Beale
Isoud (Skelton's " *Bele Isold* "), daughter of King
Anguysshe of Ireland, and wife of King Marke of
Cornwall, Trystram's uncle.—(Trystram's wife, Isoud
La Blaunche Maynys, was daughter of King Howel
of Bretagne).—The excuse for the intrigue between
Trystram and his uncle's spouse is, that their mutual
passion was the consequence of a love-potion, which
they both drank without being aware of its nature.

" In our forefathers time," observes Ascham, some-
what severely, " when Papistrie, as a standing poole,
couered and ouerflowed all England, fewe bookes were
red in our tonge, sauing certayne bookes of Chiualrie,
as they sayd for pastime and pleasure, which, as some
say, were made in Monasteries, by idle Monkes, or
wanton Chanons : as one for example *Morte Arthur :*
the whole pleasure of which booke standeth in two
speciall pointes, in open mans slaughter, and bolde
bawdrye : in which booke, those bee counted the noblest
knights, that doe kill most men without any quarell,
and commit fowlest aduoulteries by sutlest shifts : as
Sir Launcelote, with the wife of king Arthure his
maister : Sir Tristram, with the wife of King Marke

his uncle : Syr Lamerocke, with the wife of king Lote, that was his own aunte. This is good stuffe, for wise men to laugh at, or honest men to take pleasure at. Yet I knowe, when Gods Bible was banished the Court, and *Morte Arthure* receaued into the Princes chamber." *The Schole Master*, fol. 27. ed. 1571.

Page 83. v. 649. —— *of syr Lybius,*
                            Named Dysconius]

See the romance of *Lybeaus Disconus* (*Le beau des-connu*), in Ritson's *Met. Rom.* ii. ; also Sir F. Madden's note in the volume entitled *Syr Gawayne*, &c. p. 346.

v. 651.   *Of Quater Fylz Amund,*

    .   .   .   .   .   .

        . . *how they rode eche one*
        On Bayarde Mountalbon ;
        Men se hym now and then
        In the forest of Arden]

The English prose romance on the subject of these worthies came originally from the press of Caxton, an imperfect copy of his edition n. d. folio, being in Lord Spencer's library; see Dibdin's *Ædes Althorp.* ii. 298 : and that it was also translated from the French by Caxton himself, there is every reason to believe; see Dibdin's *Bibliog. Decam.* ii. 438. According to the colophon of Copland's ed., this romance was reprinted in 1504 by Wynkyn de Worde; see *Typ. Antiq.* ii. 116. ed. Dibdin. Copland's edition has the following title : *The right pleasaunt and goodly Historie of the foure sonnes of Aimon the which for the excellent en-dytyng of it, and for the notable Prowes and great ver-tues that were in them : is no les pleasaunt to rede, then worthy to be knowen of all estates bothe hyghe and lowe,* M.CCCCC.LIIII. folio.

The names of the brothers were " Reynawde, Alarde, Guycharde, and Rycharde, that were wonderfull fayre, wytty, great, mightye, and valyaunte, specyally Reynawde whiche was the greatest and the tallest manne that was founde at that tyme in al the worlde. For he had xvi. feete of length and more." fol. i. ed. Copl. The father of this hopeful family was Duke of Ardeyne.

Bayarde—(properly a bay horse, but used for a horse in general)—" was suche a horse, that neuer was his like in all the world nor neuer shall be except Busifal the horse of the great Kinge Alexander. For as for to haue ronne. xxx. myle together he wolde neuer haue sweted. The sayd Bayard thys horse was growen in the Isle of Boruscan, and Mawgys the sonne of the duke Benes of Aygremount had gyuen to his cosin Reynawde, that after made the Kynge Charlemayne full wrothe and sory." fol. v. Reynawde had a castle in Gascoigne called Mountawban ; hence Skelton's expression, " *Bayarde Mountalbon.*" A woodcut on the title-page represents the four brothers riding " *eche one* " upon the poor animal. " I," says Reynawde, relating a certain adventure, " mounted vpon Bayarde and my brethern I made to mount also thone before and the two other behynde me, and thus rode we al foure vpon my horse bayarde." fol. lxxxii.

Charlemagne, we are told, made peace with Reynawde on condition that he should go as a pilgrim, poorly clothed and begging his bread, to the holy land, and that he should deliver up Bayard to him. When Charlemagne had got possession of the horse,—" Ha Bayarde, bayarde," said he, " thou hast often angred me, but I am come to the poynt, god gramercy, for to

auenge me ; " and accordingly he caused Bayarde to
be thrown from a bridge into the river Meuse, with a
great millstone fastened to his neck. " Now ye ought
to know that after that bayarde was caste in the riuer
of meuze : he wente vnto the botom as ye haue herde,
and might not come vp for bicause of the great stone
that was at his necke whiche was horryble heuye, and
whan bayarde sawe he myghte none otherwise scape :
he smote so longe and so harde with his feete vpon
the mylle stone : that he brast it, and came agayne
aboue the water and began to swym, so that he passed
it all ouer at the other syde, and whan he was come
to londe : he shaked hymselfe for to make falle the
water fro him and began to crie hie, and made a mer-
ueyllous noyse, and after beganne to renne so swyftlye
as the tempest had borne him awaie, and entred in to
the great forest of Ardeyn . . . . . and wit it for very
certayn that the folke of the countrey saien, that he
is yet alyue within the wood of Ardeyn. But wyt
it whan he seeth man or woman : he renneth anon
awaye, so that no bodye maye come neere hym." fol.
cxlv.

Page 83. v. 661. *Of Judas Machabeus*] " Gaultier
de Belleperche Arbalestrier, ou Gaultier Arbalestrier
de Belleperche, commença *le Romans de Judas Mach-
abee*, qu'il poursuiuit jusques à sa mort . . . . Pierre
du Riez le continua jusques à la fin." Fauchet's *Rec-
veil de l'origine de la langue et poesie Françoise*, &c.,
p. 197.

v. 662. —*of Cesar Julious*] In the prologue to an
ancient MS. poem, *The boke of Stories called Cursor
Mundi*, translated from the French, mention is made
of the *romance*

" Of *Julius Cesar* the emperour."

Warton's *Hist. of E. P.*, i. 123, note, ed. 4to.

Page 83. v. 663. —— *of the loue betwene Paris and Vyene*]

This prose romance was printed by Caxton in folio: *Here begynneth thystorye of the noble ryght valyaunt and worthy knyght Parys, and of the fayr Vyēne the daulphyns doughter of Vyennoys, the whyche suffred many aduersytees bycause of theyr true loue or they coude enioye the effect therof of eche other.* Colophon: *Thus endeth thystorye of the noble*, &c. &c., *translated out of frensshe in to englysshe by Wylliam Caxton at Westmestre fynysshed the last day of August the yere of our lord* MCCCCLXXXV, *and enprynted the xix day of decembre the same yere, and the fyrst yere of the regne of kyng Harry the seuenth.*

Gawin Douglas tells us in his *Palice of Honour*, that, among the attendants on Venus,

" Of France I saw thair *Paris and Veane.*"

p. 16. Bann. ed.

v. 665. *duke Hannyball*]—*duke*, i. e. leader, lord.— So Lydgate;

" Which brother was vnto *duke Haniball.*"

Fall of Prynces, B. ii. leaf xlv. ed.

Wayland;

and in a copy of verses entitled *Thonke God of alle*, he applies the word to our Saviour;

" The dereworth *duke* that deme vs shalle."

MS. Cott. Calig. A ii. fol. 66.

v. 667. *Fordrede*] i. e. utterly, much afraid.

" To wretthe the king thai were *for dred* [*sic*]."
>> *Seynt Katerine*, p. 170,—Turnbull's *Legendæ*
>> *Catholicæ* (from the Auchinleck MS.).

Page 83. v. 668. *wake*] i. e. watch,—besiege.

Page 84. v. 673. *Of Hector of Troye,*
>> *That was all theyr ioye*]

See the *Warres of Troy* by Lydgate, a paraphrastical translation of Guido de Colonna's *Historia Trojana:* it was first printed in 1513. See too the *Recuyel of the Historyes of Troy.* Compare Hawes;

" Of the worthy *Hector that was all theyr ioye."*
>> *The Pastime of pleasure*, sig. P iii. ed. 1555.

v. 677. —— *of the loue so hote*
>> *That made Troylus to dote*
>> *Vpon fayre Cressyde, &c.*]

See Chaucer's *Troilus and Creseide.*

v. 682. *Pandaer*] Or *Pandare* as Chaucer occasionally calls Pandarus.

—— *bylles*] i. e. letters: see Chaucer's *Troilus and Creseide.*

* v. 686. *An ouche*] [i. e. a buckle, clasp, brooch; or any other ornament.]—Concerning *ouche*, a word whose etymology and primary signification are uncertain, see Tyrwhitt's *Gloss.* to Chaucer's *Cant. Tales*, v. *Nouches*, and Richardson's *Dict.* in v. *Ouch.*—Here, perhaps, it means a brooch: for in the third book of Chaucer's *Troilus and Creseide*, Cressid proposes that Pandarus should bear a " blew ring" from her to Troilus; and (*ibid.*) afterwards the lovers

" enterchaungeden her *ringes,*
Of which I can not tellen no scripture,
But well I wot, a *broche* of gold and azure,

In which a Rubbie set was like an herte,
Creseide him yaue, and stacke it on his sherte."
Chaucer's *Workes*, fol. 164. ed. 1602.

After Cressid becomes acquainted with Diomede, she gives him *a brooch*, which she had received from Troilus on the day of her departure from Troy. *Id.* fols. 179, 181.

* Page 85. v. 700. *That made the male to wryng*] So Skelton elsewhere;

" That ye can not espye
Howe the *male* dothe *wrye*."
Colyn Cloute, v. 687. vol. ii. 149.

" The countrynge at Cales
Wrang vs on the *males*."
Why come ye nat to Courte, v. 74.
vol. ii. 279.

and so Lydgate;

" Now al so mot I thryue and the, saide he than,
I can nat se for alle wittes and espyes,
And craft and kunnyng, but that *the male so wryes*
That no kunnyng may preuayl and appere
Ayens a womans wytt and hir answere."
The prohemy of a mariage, &c.,—*MS. Harl.*
372. fol. 50.

I do not understand the expression. [Mail sometimes signifies that part of a clasp which receives the spring into it. (Halliwell.) Might not the expression here mean, there was something that " made the catch to swerve," prevented the lovers from coming together ?]

v. 702. *The song of louers lay*]—*lay* seems here to mean—law.[?]

" Of *louers lawe* he toke no cure."

Harpalus (from pieces by uncertain authors printed with the poems of Surrey),—Percy's *Rel. of A. E. P* ii. 68. ed. 1794.

　　* Page 85. v. 716. *kys the post*] [i. e. to be baffled, fail of one's object.]　So Barclay ;

" Yet from beginning absent if thou be,
Eyther shalt thou lose thy meat and *kisse the post*," &c.
　　　　　　　　　　Egloge ii. sig. B iiii. ed. 1570.
The expression is found in much later writers : see, for instance, Heywood's *Woman Kilde with Kindnesse*, sig. E 2. ed. 1617.

　　v. 717. *Pandara*] So in Chaucer (according to some copies) ;

" Aha (quod *Pandara*) here beginneth game."
　　　　　　Troilus and Creseide, B. i. fol. 147,
　　　　　　　　　　　　Workes, ed. 1602.

　　v. 719. *But lyght for somer grene*] See note, p. 38. v. 355.

　　v. 727. *ne knew*] i. e. knew not.

　　v. 728. *on lyue*] i. e. alive.

　　Page 86. v. 732. *make*] i. e. mate.

　　v. 735. *proces*] i. e. story, account.　So again in this poem " *relation* " and " *prosses* " are used as synonymous, vv. 961, 969.　The 15th chap. of the first book of Lydgate's *Fall of Prynces* is headed " A *processe* of Narcissus, Byblis, Myrra," &c.

　　v. 736. — *of Anteocus*] Whom Chaucer calls " the cursed king Antiochus." *The Man of Lawes Prol.* v. 4502. ed. Tyr.　His story may be found in Gower's *Confessio Amantis*, lib. viii. fol. clxxv. sqq. ed. 1554.

　　v. 739.　　　——— *of Mardocheus,*
　　　　　　And of great Assuerus, &c.]

" Even scripture-history was turned into romance. The story of Esther and Ahasuerus, or of Amon or Hamon, and Mardocheus or Mordecai, was formed into a fabulous poem." Warton, note on *Hist. of E. P.* ii. 178. (where some lines of the romance are quoted from a MS.) ed. 4to.

Page 86. v. 741. *Vesca*] i. e. Vashti.

v. 742. *teene*] i. e. wrath : see the book of *Esther.*

v. 745. *Of kyng Alexander*] See Weber's *Introduction*, p. xx. sqq., and the romance of *Kyng Alisaunder* in his *Met. Rom.* i.; also *The Buik of the most noble and vailȝeand Conquerour Alexander the · Great*, reprinted by the Bannatyne Club, 1831.

v. 746. — *of kyng Euander*] As the lady declares (v. 756) that she was slightly acquainted with Virgil, we may suppose that her knowledge of this personage was derived from *The Recuyel of the Historyes of Troy*, and Caxton's *Boke of Eneydos.*

v. 751. *historious*] i. e. historical.

v. 752. *bougets and males*] i. e. budgets and bags.

v. 754. *sped*] i. e. versed in.

Page 87. v. 760. *mo*] i. e. more.

v. 766. *Phorocides*] i. e. Pherecydes.

v. 767. *auncyente*] i. e. antiquity.

v. 768. *to diffuse for me*] i. e. too difficult for me to understand. "*Dyffuse*, harde to be vnderstande, *diffuse.*" Palsgrave, p. 310.

" But oft yet by it [logick] a thing playne, bright and
         pure,
Is made *diffuse*, vnknowen, harde and obscure."
                Barclay's *Ship of Fooles*, fol. 53. ed. 1570.

v. 775. *enneude*] " I *Ennewe*, I set the laste and fresshest coloure vpon a thyng, as paynters do whan their worke shall remayne to declare their connyng, *Je renouuelle.* Your ymage is in maner done ; so sone as I haue *ennewed* it I wyl sende it you home," &c. Palsgrave, p. 536.

> " Ylike *enewed* with quickenes of coloure,
> Both of the rose and the lyly floure."
> > Lydgate's *Warres of Troy*, B. ii.
> > sig. I ii. ed. 1555.

Page 87. v. 776. *pullysshed*] i. e. polished.

—— *lusty*] i. e. pleasant, beautiful.

v. 779. *frowardes*] i. e. frowardness.

v. 788. *sped*] i. e. versed.

Page 88. v. 791. *Solacious*] i. e. affording amusement.

v. 792. *alowed*] i. e. approved.

* v. 793. *enprowed*] In the Glossary to Fry's *Pieces of Ancient Poetry*, 1814, where a portion of the present poem is given, *enprowed* is rendered " profited of."

v. 799. *warke*] i. e. work.

v. 804.   —— *Johnn Lydgate*
          Wryteth after an hyer rate]

Lydgate, however, disclaims all elevation of style: see his *Fall of Prynces*, Prol. sig. A iii. ed. Wayland ; his *Warres of Troy*, B. ii. sigs. F ii, K ii, B. v. sigs. E e i. ii. iii. ed. 1555.

v. 806. *dyffuse*] i. e. difficult : see note on v. 768, *supra.*

v. 807. *sentence*] i. e. meaning.

v. 809. *No man that can amend*, &c.] So Hawes, speaking of the works of Chaucer, Gower, and Lydgate ;

> " Whose famous draughtes *no man can amende.*"
> > *The Pastime of pleasure,* sig. G iiii. ed. 1555.

Page 88. v. 812. *to haute*] i. e. too high, too loftily.

* v. 817. *In worth*] i. e. kindly.

v. 841. .*Joanna*] See note p. 48.

Page 90. v. 860. *If Arethusa wyll send*
                        Me enfluence to endyte]

Skelton recollected that Virgil had invoked this nymph
as a Muse;

" Extremum hunc, *Arethusa*, mihi concede laborem."
                                        Ecl. x. 1.

v. 869. *lust*] i. e. pleasure.

v. 872. *enbybed*] i. e. made wet.

Page 91. v. 875. *Thagus*] i. e. Tagus.

v. 882. *remes*] i. e. realms.

v. 886. *Perce and Mede*] i. e. Persia and Media.

v. 896.   *She floryssheth new and new*
                    In bewte and vertew]

So Lydgate:

" And euer encrecyng *in vertue new and newe*."
                    The Temple of Glas., sig. b vii. n. d. 4to.

Page 92. v. 903. *askry*] i. e. call out against, raise a
shout against: see note on v. 1358.

v. 905. *odyous Enui, &c.*] Here Skelton has an eye
to Ovid's picture of Envy:

" Pallor in ore sedet; macies in corpore toto:
    Nusquam recta acies: livent rubigine dentes:
    Pectora felle virent: lingua est suffusa veneno.
    Risus abest, nisi quem visi movere dolores.
    Nec fruitur somno, vigilacibus excita curis:
    Sed videt ingratos, intabescitque videndo,
    Successus hominum: carpitque et carpitur una:
    Suppliciumque suum est."   *Met.* ii. 775

See too the description of Envy in *Pierce Plowman*, sig. F ii. ed. 1561.

Page 92. v. 908. *ledder*] i. e. leather, leathern.

v. 912. *crake*] i. e. creak.

v. 913. *Leane as a rake*] From Chaucer.

> " As *lene* was his hors *as is a rake*."
>> *Prol. to Cant. Tales*, v. 289. ed. Tyr.

v. 915. *vnlusty*] i. e. unpleasant, unseemly.

v. 919. *wronge*] i. e. wrung.

* v. 930. *bete*] i. e. agitated; or bitten.

v. 931. *frete*] i. e. eaten, gnawed.

Page 93. v. 936. *semblaunt*] i. e. semblance, appearance.

v. 947. *slo*] i. e. slay.

v. 963. *agayne*] i. e. against.

Page 94. v. 968. *dres*] i. e. address, apply.

v. 969. *prosses*] i. e. relation, story. See note, p. 75.

v. 970. *ken*] i. e. instruct.

v. 973. *As hym best lyst*] i. e. As best pleases him.

* v. 980. *bedell*] i. e. servitor.

* v. 987. *Compyle*] i. e. compose.

Page 95. v. 999. *sort*] i. e. set, assemblage.

v. 1002. *fauour*] i. e. appearance, look—or, perhaps, beauty,—in which sense the word occurs v. 1048.

v. 1003. *Ennewed*] See note on v. 775.

* v. 1014. *stepe*] i. e. deep sunk in the head. [?]

v. 1016.   .   .   .   .   .

> *With her browes bent*]

—*bent*, i. e. arched.   Compare Hawes;

> " Her forehead *stepe with* fayre *browes ybent*,
>> *Her eyen gray*."
>>> *The Pastime of pleasure*, sig. S i. ed. 1555

I may just observe that these passages (and many others which might be cited) shew how unnecessarily Ritson substituted " brent " for " bent " in *The Squyr of Lowe Degre;* see his note, *Met. Rom.* iii. 351.

Page 95. v. 1019. *Polexene*] i. e. Polyxena, the daughter of Priam,—celebrated by Lydgate in his *Warres of Troy*, and by others.

Page 96. v. 1031. *The Indy saphyre blew*] *Indy* may perhaps be used here for—Indian ; but I believe the expression is equivalent to—the azure blue sapphire (Skelton in his *Garlande of Laurell* has "*saphiris indy blew*," v. 478, vol. ii. 191) ; see note, p. 23. v. 17.

* v. 1032. *ennew*] give a finish to, embellish. See note on v. 775. p. 76.

v. 1034. *lere*] i. e. skin.

v. 1035. *lusty*] i. e. pleasant, beautiful.

—— *ruddes*] i. e. ruddy tints of the cheek, complexion.

v. 1048. *with fauour fret*]—*fauour*, i. e. beauty ; so Skelton has " feturs *fauorable*," in the second of his *Balettys*, v. 8. vol. i. 29 : *fret*, I believe, does not here mean fraught (see Tyrwhitt's *Gloss.* to Chaucer's *Cant. Tales*), but is equivalent to—wrought, adorned,— in allusion to fret-work ; so in our author's *Garlande of Laurell*,—

" *Fret* all with orient perlys of Garnate."

v. 485. vol. ii. 191.

Page 97. v. 1052. *The columbine commendable,*
The ielofer amyable]

Ielofer is perhaps what we now call gillyflower ; but it was formerly the name for the whole class of carnations, pinks, and sweetwilliams. So Graunde Amoure terms La Bell Pucell ;

" The gentyll *gyllofer*, the goodly *columbyne*."
Hawes's *Pastime of pleasure*, sig. N i. ed. 1555.

Page 97. v. 1065. *denayd*] i. e. denied.

v. 1069. *conuenyently*] i. e. fittingly, suitably.

* Page 98. v. 1077. *sker*] i. e. scar, meaning the wart.

v. 1078. *Enhached*] i. e. Inlaid : our author has the word again in his *Garlande of Laurell* ;

" *Enhachyde* with perle and stones preciously."
v. 40. vol. ii. 172.

v. 1081. *To forget deadly syn*] Compare the first of our author's *Balettys*, v. 11. vol. i. 27.

v. 1096. *pastaunce*] i. e. pastime.

v. 1097. *So sad and so demure*]—*sad*, i. e. serious, grave, sober: so afterwards, " *Sobre*, demure Dyane."
v. 1224.

v. 1100. *make to the lure*] A metaphor from falconry: " *Lure* is that whereto Faulconers call their young Hawks, by casting it up in the aire, being made of feathers and leather, in such wise that in the motion it looks not unlike a fowl." Latham's *Faulconry* (*Explan. of Words of Art*), 1658.

Page 99. v. 1105. *crased*] i. e. crushed, enfeebled.

v. 1106. *dased*] i. e. dazzled.

* v. 1116.   *And to amende her tale,*
               Whan she lyst to auale]

—*auale* is generally—to let down, to lower : [condescended to show me some favor ?] but I know not how to explain the present passage, which appears to be defective.

Page 99. v. 1118.

> And with her fyngers smale,
> And handes soft as sylke,
> Whyter than the mylke,
> That are so quyckely vayned]

—*quyckely vayned*, i. e. lively veined.   Compare Hawes;

> " By her propre *hande, soft as any sylke*."
> > *The Pastime of pleasure*, sig. H iiii. ed. 1555.

> " *Her fingers small*, and therto right longe,
> *White as the milke, with blew vaynes* among."
> > *Id.* sig. S i.

v. 1124. *Vnneth*] i. e. Scarcely, not without difficulty.   Here again the text seems to be defective.

v. 1125. *reclaymed*] A metaphor from falconry. " *Reclaiming* is to tame, make gentle, or to bring a Hawk to familiarity with the man." Latham's *Faulconry (Explan. of Words of Art)*, 1658.

Page 100. v. 1146. *tote*] i. e. look, gaze.

v. 1147. *fote*] i. e. foot.

v. 1148. *hert rote*] i. e. heart-root.

* v. 1151.   She is playnly expresse
> Egeria, the goddesse,
> And lyke to her image,
> Emportured with corage,
> A louers pilgrimage]

I must leave the reader to form his own idea of the meaning of the last two lines, which are beyond my comprehension. [Perhaps—made to bear herself (or else, simply portrayed) with courage (feeling) ; a fit object for lovers to make pilgrimages to.]

v. 1157. *Ne*] i. e. Nor.

Page 100. v. 1157. *wood*] i. e. mad, furious.

Page 101. v. 1170.

> *So goodly as she dresses,*
> *So properly she presses*
> *The bryght golden tresses*
> *Of her heer so fyne,*
> *Lyke Phebus beames shyne.*
> *Wherto shuld I disclose*
> *The garterynge of her hose?*]

—*Phebus beames shyne,* i. e. the shine of Phœbus' beams.   Compare Hawes;

> " *Her shining here so properly she dresses*
> Alofe her forehed with fayre *golden tresses*
>
> .   .   .   .
>
> Her fete proper, she *gartered well her hose.*"
>
> *The Pastime of pleasure,* sig. S i. ed. 1555

v. 1177. *to suppose*] i. e. to be supposed.

v. 1178. *were*] i. e. wear.

v. 1179. *gere*] i. e. dress, clothes.

v. 1180. *fresshe*] i. e. gay.

Page 102. v. 1194. *kyrtell*] " *Kyrtell,* a garment, *corpset, surcot, cotelle.*" Palsgrave, p. 236.   It has been variously explained (see notes on *Henry IV.* Part ii. act ii. sc. 4, *Shakespeare* by Malone and Boswell, xvii. 98, 99, Todd's *Johnson's Dict.,* and Nares's *Gloss.*), petticoat,—safe-guard or riding-hood,—long cloak,—long mantle, reaching to the ground, with a head to it that entirely covered the face, and usually red,—apron,—jacket,—and loose gown !!!   The following note by Gifford on *Cynthia's Revels* (Jonson's *Works,* ii. 260) gives the most satisfactory account of a kirtle : " Few words have occasioned such controversy among the commentators on our old plays as this; and all for want of knowing that it is used in a twofold sense, sometimes for the jacket merely, and sometimes for the train or upper petticoat attached to it. A full kirtle was always a jacket and petticoat, a half kirtle (a term which frequently occurs) was either the one er the other: but our ancestors, who wrote when this article of dress was everywhere in use, and when there was little danger of being misunderstood, most commonly contented themselves with the simple term (kirtle), leaving the sense to be gathered from the context."

Page 102. v. 1199. *let*] i. e. hinder.

v. 1205. *pullysshed*] i. e. polished.

v. 1223. *Jane*] See note, p. 48.

Page 103. v. 1242. *saynt Jamys*] i. e. Saint James of Compostella : see note on *Elynour Rummyng*, v. 354.

v. 1243. *pranys*] i. e. prawns.

v. 1244. *cranys*] i. e. cranes.

v. 1250. *sadly*] i. e. seriously, soberly.

v. 1251. *gyse*] i. e. guise, fashion.

Page 104. —— *an adicyon*] Though found in all the eds. of *Phyllyp Sparowe* which I have seen, it was not, I apprehend, originally published with the poem. It is inserted (and perhaps first appeared) in our author's *Garlande of Laurell*, v. 1261. vol. ii. 226, where he tells us that some persons " take greuaunce, and grudge with frownyng countenaunce," at his poem on Philip Sparrow,—alluding probably more particularly to Barclay ; see note, p. 46, and *Account of Skelton and his Writings.*

v. 1269. *ianglynge iayes*] See note on v. 396, p. 55.

v. 1274. *depraue*] i. e. vilify, defame. " Thus was

syr Arthur *depraued* and euyl sayd of." *Morte d'Arthur*, B. xxi. c. i. vol. ii. 433. ed. Southey.

Page 105. v. 1289. *estate*] i. e. high rank, dignity.

v. 1291. *Hercules that hell dyd harow*]—*harow*, i. e. lay waste, plunder, spoil,—overpower, subdue,—Hercules having carried away from it his friends Theseus and Pirithous, as well as the dog Cerberus. The *harrowing of hell* was an expression properly and constantly applied to our Lord's descent into hell, as related in the Gospel of Nicodemus. There were several early miracle-plays on this favourite subject; and Lydgate strangely enough says that Christ

" Took out of helle soulys many a peyre,
Mawgre Cerberus and al his cruelte."
Testamentum,—MS. Harl. 2255. fol. 49.

I may add, that Warner, speaking of Hercules, uses the words "harrowed hell." *Albion's England*, p. 23. ed. 1612.

v. 1293. *Slew of the Epidaures, &c.*] Qy. is not the text corrupted here?

v. 1295. *Onocentaures*] i. e. Centaurs, half human, half asses. See Ælian *De Nat. Anim.* lib. xvii. c. 9. ed. Gron., and Phile *De Anim. Prop.* c. 44. ed. Pauw. Both these writers describe the onocentaur as having the bosom of a woman. R. Holme says it " is a Monster, being the Head and Breasts of a Woman set upon the Shoulders of a Bull." *Ac. of Armory*, 1688. B. ii. p. 208.

v. 1296. *Hipocentaures*] i. e. Centaurs, half human, half horses.

v. 1302. *Of Hesperides withhold*] i. e. Withheld by the Hesperides.

Page 106. v. 1314. *rounses*] i. e. common hackney-

horses (though the word is frequently used for horses
in general).

Page 106. v. 1318.

> *He plucked the bull*
> *By the horned skull,*
> *And offred to Cornucopia*]

The "bull" means Achelous, who, during his combat
with Hercules, assumed that shape:

> "rigidum fera dextera cornu
>
> Dum tenet, infregit; truncaque a fronte revellit.
> Näides hoc, pomis et odoro flore repletum,
> Sacrarunt; divesque meo bona Copia cornu est."
>
> > Ovid. *Met.* ix. 85.

v. 1322. *Ecates*] i. e. Hecate's.

v. 1326.   —— *the venemous serpent,*
> *That in hell is neuer brent*]

—*brent*, i. e. burned.   A somewhat profane allusion to
the scriptural expression " the worm dieth not; "—
(*worm* and *serpent* were formerly synonymous).

v. 1332. *infernall posty*]—*posty*, i. e. power.   So
Lydgate ;

> " Of heuene and erthe and *infernal pooste.*"
> > *Testamentum,*—*MS. Harl.* 2255. fol. 47

v. 1333. *rosty*] i. e. roast.

v. 1335. *wood*] i. e. mad, wild.

Page 107. v. 1340. *frounsid*] i. e. wrinkled.

v. 1344. *Primo Regum*] i. e. *The First Book of
Kings*, or, as it is now called, *The First Book of Sam-
uel*, chap. xxviii.

> " *Primo regum* as ye may playnly reade."
> > Lydgate's *Fall of Prynces*, B. ii. leaf xxxix.
> > > ed. Wayland.

Page 107. v. 1345.

> *He bad the Phitonesse*
>
> .   .   .   .   .
>
> *But whether it were so,*
> *He were idem in numero,*
> *The selfe same Samuell, &c.*]

—*Phitonesse*, i. e. Pythoness, witch,—the witch of Endor.

> " And speke as renably, and faire, and wel,
>   As to the *Phitonesse* did Samuel :
> And yet wol som men say it was not he," &c.
>   Chaucer's *Freres Tale*, v. 7091. ed. Tyr.

> " And secretelye this Saule is forth gone
> To a woman that should him rede and wisse,
> In Israell called a *phytonesse*.
>
> .   .   .   .
>
> To diuines this matter I commit,
>
> .   .   .   .
>
> *Whether it was the soule of Samuell,*" &c.
>   Lydgate's *Fall of Prynces*, B. ii. leaf xl.
>   ed. Wayland.

See also Gower's *Conf. Am.* B. iv. fol. lxxiii. ed. 1554 ;
Barbour's *Bruce*, B. iii. v. 982. ed. Jam.; G. Doug-
las's Preface to his Virgil's *Æneados*, p. 6, l. 51. ed.
Rudd. ; and Sir D. Lyndsay's *Monarchie*, B. iv.
Works, iii. 151. ed. Chalmers.

v. 1346. *dresse*] i. e. address, apply.

v. 1351. *condityons*] i. e. qualities. But in our au-
thor's *Garlande of Laurell*, where this "adicyon" is
given, the passage according to Fake's ed., and rightly
perhaps (compare the preceding lines), stands thus ;

" And by her supersticiouns
        Of wonderfull condiciouns."

                        v. 1343. vol. ii. 229.

Page 107. v. 1352. *stede*] i. e. place.

* v. 1358. *ascry*] i. e. to assail (with a shout). In Langtoft's *Chronicle* we find,

    " Edward was hardie, the Londres gan he *ascrie.*"

                        p. 217. ed. Hearne,—

(who in Gloss. renders " *ascrie* "—cry to). The original French has,

    " Sir Eduuard fiz le rays, les loundrays *escrye.*"

                        MS. Cott. Jul. A v. fol. 122.

Roquefort gives " *Escrier :* Faire entendre son cri d'armes dans une bataille . . . marcher à l'ennemi, l'attaquer," &c. *Gloss. de la Lang. Rom. (Sup.)* : [crier, attaquer, poursuivre avec des cris. Duconge. *Suppl.*]

v. 1360. *my selfe dyscharge*] i. e. unburden myself,—open my mind.

v. 1365. *shene*] i. e. shine.

Page 108. v. 1371. *Scroupe pulchra Joanna*] See note p. 48.

ELYNOUR RUMMYNGE.

On the title-page, and also on the last leaf of Rand's edition of this poem, 1624, 4to, (reprinted, not with perfect accuracy, in the *Harleian Miscellany ;* see vol. i. 415. ed. Park,) is an imaginary portrait, of which the subjoined is a fac-simile :

"When Skelton wore the Laurell Crowne,
My Ale put all the Ale-wiues downe."

George Steevens having heard that a copy of Rand's edition was in the Library of Lincoln Cathedral, prevailed on the Dean to bring it to London; and having made a drawing of the title-page, gave it to Richardson the printseller, who engraved and published it. Steevens, soon after, contributed to the *European Magazine* for May, 1794, vol. xxv. 334,—

" Verses meant to have been subjoined (with the following Motto) to a Copy from a scarce Portrait of Elinour Rumming, lately published by Mr. Richardson, of Castle-street, Leicester-square.

Ne sit ancillæ tibi amor pudori
Xanthia Phoceu! prius insolentem
Serva Briseis niveo colere
   Movit Achillem.

Movit Ajacem Telamone natum
Forma captivæ dominum Tecmessæ;
Arsit Atrides medio in triumpho
   Virgine rapta.

       HORACE.

  " Eleonora Rediviva.

To seek this nymph among the glorious dead,
Tir'd with his search on earth, is Gulston fled :—
Still for these charms enamour'd Musgrave sighs;
To clasp these beauties ardent Bindley dies ;—
For these (while yet unstag'd to public view)
Impatient Brand o'er half the kingdom flew ;—
These, while their bright ideas round him play,
From classic Weston force the Roman lay :—
Oft too, my Storer ! heaven has heard thee swear,
Not Gallia's murder'd Queen was half so fair :—
' A new Europa !' cries the exulting Bull,
' My Granger now (I thank the gods) is full : '—
Even Cracherode's self, whom passions rarely move,
At this soft shrine has deign'd to whisper love.—
Haste then, ye swains, who Rumming's form adore,
Possess your Elinour, and sigh no more.

       W. R."

The Marquis of Bute told Dallaway that he gave
twenty guineas for the original engraving of Elinour:
see Dallaway's *Letheræum*, 1821, p. 6.

Rand's edition opens with the following lines, which,
I need hardly observe, are by some rhymer of the day :

" *Skeltons Ghost.*

To all tapsters and tiplers,
And all ale house vitlers,
Inne-keepers and cookes,
That for pot-sale lookes,
And will not giue measure,
But at your owne pleasure,
Contrary to law,
Scant measure will draw
In pot and in canne,
To cozen a man
Of his full quart a penny,
Of you there's to many :
For in King Harry's time,
When I made this rime
Of Elynor Rumming
With her good ale tunning,
Our pots were full quarted,
We were not thus thwarted
With froth-canne and nick-pot
And such nimble quick shot,
That a dowzen will score
For twelue pints and no more.
Full Winchester gage
We had in that age ;
The Dutchmans strong beere
Was not hopt ouer heere,
To vs t'was unknowne :
Bare ale of our owne

In a bowle we might bring
To welcome the king,
And his grace to beseech,
With, *Wassall my Leigh.*[1]
Nor did that time know
To puffe and to blow
In a peece of white clay,
As you doe at this day,
With fier and coale,
And a leafe in a hole;
As my ghost hath late seene,
As I walked betweene
Westminster Hall
And the church of Saint Paul,
And so thorow the citie,
Where I saw and did pitty
My countrymen's cases,
With fiery-smoke faces,
Sucking and drinking
A filthie weede stinking,
Was ne're knowne before
Till the deuill and the More
In th' Indies did meete,
And each other there greete
With a health they desire
Of stinke, smoake, and fier.
But who e're doth abhorre it,
The citie smoakes for it;
Now full of fier-shops
And fowle spitting chops,
So neesing and coughing,
That my ghost fell to scoffing,

1 *Leigh*] Meant for " Liege."

And to myselfe said,
Here's fylthie fumes made;
Good physicke of force
To cure a sicke horse.
Nor had we such slops,
And shagge-haire on our tops:
At wearing long haire
King Harry would sweare,
And gaue a command
With speede out of hand
All heads should be powl'd,
As well young as old,
And his owne was first so,
Good ensample to show.
Y'are so out of fashion,
I know not our nation;
Your ruffes and your bands,
And your cuffes at your hands,
Your pipes and your smokes,
And your short curtall clokes;
Scarfes, feathers, and swerds,
And thin bodkin beards;
Your wastes a span long,
Your knees with points hung,
Like morrice-daunce bels;
And many toyes els,
Which much I distaste:
But Skelton's in haste.
My masters, farewell;
Reade ouer my Nell,
And tell what you thinke
Of her and her drinke:

> If shee had brew'd amisse,
> I had neuer wrote this."

At the end of the poem is, from the same hand,

" *Skelton's Ghost to the Reader.*[1]

> Thus, countrymen kinde,
> I pray let me finde,
> For this merry glee,
> No hard censure to be.
> King Henry the Eight
> Had a good conceit
> Of my merry vaine,
> Though duncicall plaine
> It now nothing fits
> The time's nimble wits :
> My lawrell and I
> Are both wither'd dry,
> And you flourish greene
> In your workes daily seene,
> That come from the presse,
> Well writ I confesse ;
> But time will devouer
> Your poets as our,
> And make them as dull
> As my empty scull."

---

[1] *Skelton's Ghost to the Reader*, &c.] I give these lines from the *Harl. Miscel.*, the copy of Rand's ed. which was lent to me by Mr. Heber, wanting the last leaf.

Concerning Elynour Rummyng and the poem by which Skelton has rendered her famous, Dallaway has the following remarks,—*his account of the circumstances which introduced Skelton to her acquaintance being a mere hypothesis! !* " When the Court of Henry viii was frequently kept at the palace of Nonsuch (about six miles distant), the laureate, with other courtiers, sometimes came to Leatherhead for the amusement of fishing, in the river Mole ; and were made welcome at the *cabaret* of Elinor Rummyng, whom Skelton celebrated in an equivocal encomium, in a short [?—it consists of 623 lines—] poem, remarkable only for a very coarse jest, after a manner peculiar to the author and the times in which he lived, but which has been more frequently reprinted than his other works. The gist or point of this satire had a noble origin, or there must be an extraordinary coincidence of thought in the *Beoni,* or Topers, a ludicrous effusion of the great Lorenzo de Medici, when a young man.* . . . . . . Her domicile, near the bridge, still exists. The annexed etching was made from a drawing taken previously to late repairs, but it still retains its first distinction as an ale-house."

* Dallaway was led to this remark by the following passage in Spence's *Anecdotes,* &c.; " Skelton's poems are all low and bad: there's nothing in them that's worth reading.— P. [Mr. Cleland, who was by, added, that the Tunning of Ellinor Rummin, in that author's works, was taken from a poem of Lorenzo de'Medici's]." p. 173, ed. 1820.—" *I Beoni,*" observes Mr. D'Israeli, referring to Roscoe's *Life of Lorenzo de'Medici,* i. 290, " was printed by the Giunti in 1568, and therefore this burlesque piece could never have been known to Skelton." *Amen. of Lit.* ii. 79.

" Some of her descendants occur in the parish register in the early part of the last century." *Lethe-ræum*, 1821, pp. 4-6.

The Tunnyng of Elynour Rummyng] Whan *tonne* you and God wyll : *Quant brasserez vous,*" &c. Palsgrave, p. 759. and here *Tunnyng* means—Brewing.

Page 109. v. 1.

> *Tell you I chyll,*
> *If that ye wyll*
> *A whyle be styll*]

—*I chyll*, i. e. Ich wyll, I will. Compare *Syr Gawayn and the Grene Knyʒt ;*

" *And ȝe wyl a whyle be stylle,*
  I schal telle yow how thay wroȝt."

p. 74. Bann. ed

and the Prol. to *Kyng Alisaunder;*

" *Yeſ ye wolen sitte stille,*
  Ful feole *Y wol yow telle.*"

Weber's *Met. Rom.* i. 5.

Page 109. v. 4. *gyll*] Equivalent here to girl—a familiar name for a female ; as in the proverb, " Every Jack must have his *Gill :* " supposed by some etymologists to be an abbreviation of *Julia, Juliana,* or *Gillian ;* by Richardson (*Dict.* in v.) to be a corruption of *giglot.*

v. 6. *gryll*] " Grymm, *gryl* and horryble : horribilis." *Prompt. Parv.* [ed. Way.] The word is of frequent occurrence ; but its exact meaning here seems to be doubtful.

v. 12. *lere*] i. e. complexion, skin.

v. 14. *chere*] i. e. look, countenance.

v. 17. *bowsy*] i. e. bloated by drinking.

Page 110. v. 21. *here*] i. e. hair.

v. 22. *lewde*] i. e. vile, nasty.

v. 23. *sayne*] i. e. say.

v. 27. ·   *Her nose somdele hoked,*
              And camously croked]

—*somdele hoked,* i. e. somewhat hooked. " *Cammyd,* or schort nosyd. Simus." *Prompt. Parv.* [ed. Way.] " A *Camoise* nose, that is to saie crooked vpward as the Morians [Moors]." Baret's *Alvearie.* " *Camuse.* Flat." Tyrwhitt's *Gloss.* to Chaucer's *Cant. Tales.* " *Camused.* Flat, broad and crooked ; as applied to a nose, what we popularly call a *snub-nose.*" Nares's

Gloss. Todd, quoting this passage of Skelton, explains *camously*, awry. *Johnson's Dict.* in v.

* Page 110. v. 34. *gowndy*] i. e. sore running eyes. So Lydgate ;

> " A *goundy* eye is deceyued soone,
> That any colour cheseth by the moone."
>> *Warres of Troy*, B. ii. sig. H iii. ed. 1555.

v. 35 *vnsowndy*] i. e. unsound.

v. 38. *jetty*] i. e. that part of a building which projects beyond the rest.

v. 40.   —— *how she is gumbed,*
         Fyngered and thumbed]

i. e. what gums, fingers, and thumbs she has.

v. 45. *huckels*] i. e. hips.

Page 111. v. 49. *Foted*] i. e. Footed.

v. 51. *iet*] i. e. strut.

v. 52. *fet*] Means, perhaps, *feat*,—neat, handsome one.

v. 53. *flocket*] " Is described as a loose garment with large sleeves : " see Strutt's *Dress and Habits*, &c. ii. 373.

v. 54. *rocket*] i. e. a garment, worn often without, and sometimes with sleeves ; sometimes it was made to reach the ground, and sometimes much shorter and open at the sides. See *Id. Ibid.*

v. 55. *Wyth symper the cocket*] So Heywood in his *Dialogue* ;

> " Vpright as a candell standth in a socket,
> Stoode she that day, so *simper decocket*."
>> Sig. F,—*Workes*, ed. 1598.

and Jonson in his Masque, *The Gipsies Metamorphosed ;*

" Lay by your wimbles,
    Your boring for thimbles,
    Or using your nimbles,
    In diving the pockets,
    And sounding the sockets
    Of *simper-the-cockets.*"

Works (by Gifford), vii. 376.
In a note on the latter passage, Whalley quotes from
Cotgrave's *Dict.:* " *Coquine,* a beggar-woman, also a
cockney, *simper de cockit,* nice thing." Gifford (*ibid.*)
remarks, " *Cocket* was a fine species of bread, as dis-
tinguished from common bread; hence, perhaps, the
name was given to an overstrained affectation of deli-
cacy. To *simper* at, or over, a thing, is to touch it *as
in scorn.*" Nares (*Gloss.* in v.) doubts (justly, I think)
the connexion of *simper-the-cocket* with *cocket* bread,
and explains it, " quasi simpering coquette," observing,
that " one of Cotgrave's words in rendering ' coquette '
is *cocket.*" I may add, that in *Gloss. of Prov. and Loc.
Words* by Grose and Pegge, ed. 1839, is, " *Cocket,*
brisk, apish, pert," and " *Simper,* to mince one's words."
[" An affected mealy-mouthed girl." *Cotgrave.* " A
simper-de-cocket, *coquine, fantastica.* Howell, 1660.
Halliwell.]

Page 111. v. 56.

> Her *huke of Lyncole grene,*
> *It had ben hers, I wene,*
> *More then fourty yere*]

" Huke, *surquanie, froc.*" Palsgrave, p. 233. " A
loose kind of garment, of the cloak or mantle kind."
Strutt's *Dress and Habits,* &c. ii. 364. " *Lyncolne* an-
ciently dyed *the best greene* of England." Marg. note

in Drayton's *Polyolbion*, Song 25. p. 111. ed. 1622.—
Compare a celebrated ballad ;

> " My *cloake* it was a verry good cloake,
> Itt hath been always true to the weare,
> But now it is not worth a groat ;
> I have had it *four and forty yeere.*"
>
>> *Take thy old cloak about thee,*—Percy's
>> *Rel. of A. E. P.* i. 206. ed. 1794.

Page 111. v. 63. *woll*] i. e. wool.

v. 68. *gytes*] i. e. clothes.   *Gite* is properly a gown :

> " And she came after in a *gite* of red."
>
>> Chaucer's *Reves Tale*, v. 3952. ed. Tyr.

v. 69. *pranked with pletes*]—*pletes*, i. e. plaits.   " I
Pranke ones gowne, I set the *plyghtes* in order." Pals-
grave, p. 664.

v. 70. *Her kyrtel Brystow red*]—*kyrtel ;* see note
p. 83. v. 1194.

> " London hath scarlet, and *Bristowe* pleasaunt red."
>
>> Barclay's *Fourth Egloge*, sig. C iiii. ed. 1570.

" At *Brystowe* is the best water to *dye reed.*"   Hor-
manni *Vulgaria*, sig. V ii. ed. 1530.

* v. 72. *sowe* of led] i. e. as we say, a pig, about
250 lbs.

* v. 73. *wrythen*] i. e. twisted.

v. 74. *gyse*] i. e. guise, fashion.

v. 75. *whym wham*] i. e. something whimsically, fan-
tastically devised.   The word is frequently applied to
articles of female finery by our early dramatists.   In
Ane Interlude of the Laying of a Gaist, we are told
that the Gaist (ghost)

> " stall fra peteouss Abrahame
> An quhorle and *ane quhum quhame.*"
>
>> —Laing's *An. Pop. Poetry of Scotland.*

Whim-wham is used by Gray, *Works*, iii. 123. ed. Mit-ford, and by Lamb, *Prose Works*, ii. 142.

Page 111. v. 76. *trym tram*] i. e. some trim, neat ornament, or pretty trifle.   In Weaver's *Lusty Juuentus*, Hipocrisie, after enumerating a variety of popish trumpery, adds

> " And a hundred *trim trams* mo."
>
> Sig. B iiii. ed. Çopland.

v. 77. *brayne pan*] i. e. skull, head.

v. 78. *Egyptian*] i. e. gipsy.

Page 112. v. 85. *gose*] i. e. goose.

v. 88. *shone*] i. e. shoes.

v. 90. *baudeth*] i. e. fouls.   " I *Baudy*, or fyle or soyle with any filthe, *Je souylle*."   Palsgrave, p. 444. " The auter clothes, and the vestementes shulde be very clene, not *baudy*, nor torne," &c.   Hormanni *Vulgaria*, sig. E iiii.

v. 94. *wonnynge*] i. e. dwelling.

v. 96. *Sothray*] i. e. Surrey.

v. 97. *stede*] i. e. place.

v. 98. *Lederhede*] i. e. Leatherhead; see p. 95.

v. 99. *tonnysh gyb*] The epithet *tonnysh* is perhaps derived from her occupation of *tunning* (see note, p. 96), or perhaps it may allude to her shape: *gyb* is properly a male cat (see note, p. 48. v. 27); but the term, as here, is sometimes applied to a woman;

> " And give a thousand by-words to my name,
>   And call me Beldam, *Gib*, Witch, Night-mare,
>   Trot."
>
> Drayton's *Epistle from Elinor Cobham
>   to Duke Humphrey,—Poems*, p. 175.
>   ed. 1619. fol.

Page 112. v. 100. *syb*] i. e. related, akin.

v. 102. *noppy*] i. e. nappy.

Page 113. v. 103. *port sale*] If the right reading, must be used here for—sale in general. " Port-sale, The Sale of Fish as soon as it is brought into the Harbour ; also an Out-cry or Publick Sale of any Commodity." Kersey's *Dict.*

v. 105. *To sweters, to swynkers*] i. e. to those who sweat and labour hard, — to labourers of various kinds.

> " For we can neyther *swyncke nor sweate*."
> > *Pierce Plowman*, sig. I ii. ed. 1561.

v. 110. *Now away the mare*] Skelton has the same expression in his *Magnyfycence*, v. 1342. vol. ii. 62. Compare *The Frere and the Boye ;*

> " Of no man he had no care,
> But sung, hey howe, *awaye the mare*."
> > Ritson's *An. Pop. Poetry*, p. 37.

and *Jyl of Braintfords Testament*, n. d.;

> " Ah sira, mary *away the mare*,
> The deuil giue thee sorow and care."
> > sig. B ii.

and *A new Commodye* &c. *of the bewte & good propertes of women*, &c. n. d.

> " Tush, syr, be mery, let pas *awey the mare*."
> > Sig. A ii.

The words are doubtless a portion of some song or ballad. In Ravenscroft's *Melismata, Mvsicall Phansies*, &c. 1611, is a song (No. 6) supposed to be sung by " Seruants out of Seruice " who " are going to the Citie to looke for new ; "

" Heigh ho, *away the Mare*,
  Let vs set aside all care,
  If any man be disposed to trie,
  Loe here comes a lustie crew,
  That are enforced to crie
  A new Master, a new," &c.

Page 113. v. 111. *sley*] i. e. slay.

v. 115. *Wyth, Fyll the cup, fyll*] So in *The Hye Way to the Spyttell Hous*, by Copland, n. d. ;

" *With, Fyll the pot, fyll*, and go fyll me the can."
          Utterson's *Early Pop. Poet.* ii. **15.**

v. 122. *Hardely*] i. e. Assuredly.

v. 123. *heles dagged*] In *Prompt. Parv.* ed. 1499. is " *Daggyd*, Fractillosus,"—a sense in which Skelton certainly has the word elsewhere (*Garlande of Laurell*, v. 630. vol. ii. 198) ; but here perhaps *dagged* may mean—be-mired : " I Daggyll or I *dagge* a thing with myer." Palsgrave, p. 506.

v. 124. *all to-iagged*] See note, p. 22. v. 32.

Page 114. v. 130. *tunnynge*] i. e. brewing ; see note, p. 96.

v. 131. *leneth . . . on*] i. e. lendeth, furnisheth . . of: compare v. 491.

v. 139. *sorte*] i. e. set, company.

* v. 142. *skewed*] Does it mean—distorted ? **or** walking obliquely ? or squinting ? see Todd's Johnson's *Dict.* in v. *Skew.* A friend suggests that this epithet, as well as that in the preceding line, may be applied to colour, [piebald]—the words being still used as terms of the stable.

v. 143. *sho clout*] i. e. shoe-cloth.

v. 145. *herelace*] i. e. hair-band.

Page 114. v. 147. *tresses vntrust*] So Lydgate ;—
" With *heyr vntrussed." Warres of Troy*, B. iii. sig.
S i. ed. 1555.

v. 148. *vnlust*] i. e. unpleasantness, unseemliness.

*v. 149.   *Some loke strawry,*
                Some cawry mawry]

—*loke,* i. e. look : *strawry* [newly come from the
straw ?] I do not remember to have met with else-
where : *cawry mawry* (as a substantive) occurs in
Pierce Plowman;

" [Envy] was as pale as a pellet; in the palsey he
        semed
And clothed in *Caurymaury,*" &c.

                        sig. F ii. ed. 1561.

v. 151. *tegges*] A term found again in our author's
first poem *Against Garnesche;*

" Your wynde schakyn shankkes, your longe lothy
        legges

.   .   .   .

Bryngges yow out of fauyr with alle femall *teggys."*
                        v. 29. vol. i. 134.

In what sense Skelton uses *tegge*, I cannot pretend to
determine. In Warwickshire and Leicestershire, a
teg means a sheep of a year old ; and Ray gives, " A
Tagge, a Sheep of the first Year, *Suss." Coll. of
Words,* &c., p. 88, appended to *Proverbs,* ed. 1768.
[Palsgrave (p. 279) applies the term to a young deer :
" *tegge,* a pricket saillant ; " properly the doe in its
second year. Halliwell.]

v. 152. *Lyke rotten egges*] Lydgate in a satirical de-
scription of a lady has—

" Colowryd *lyche a rotyn eey* [i. e. egg]."
MS. Harl. 2255. fol. 156.

Page 114. v. 153. *lewde sorte*] i. e. vile set, low rabble.

v. 155. *tyde*] i. e. time, season.

Page 115. y. 161. *commy*] i. e. come.

* v. 163. *shreud aray*]—*shreud*, i. e. evil, bad : *aray*, i. e. case, plight, situation, condition.

v. 171. *draffe*] i. e. hog-wash — either the coarse liquor, or brewers' grains, with which swine are fed.

v. 173. *swyllynge tubbe*] i. e. tub in which *swillings* (hog-wash) are preserved for swine.

* v. 174. *For, be there neuer so much prese*
These swyne go to the hye dese]
—*prese*, i. e. press, throng : *dese*, or *dais*, a word of doubtful etymology, generally means — a table of estate,—the upper table raised on a platform more elevated than the others. See Tyrwhitt's note on *Cant. Tales*, v. 372 ; and Richardson's *Dict.* in v. *Dais*. It sometimes signifies a long bench (see Jamieson's *Et. Dict. of Scot. Lang.* in v. *Deis*) ; and such seems to be its meaning here, as in the fourth line after this " the hye benche " is mentioned.—Roy in his satire against Wolsey, *Rede me, and be nott wrothe*, &c., has imitated the present passage of Skelton ;

" *For, be there never so grett prease,*
They are set up at the hy dease."
Harl. Miscell. ix. 51. ed. Park.
[To *go to the hye dese* seems here to mean only to take the best place].

Page 116. v. 185.
God gyue it yll preuynge
Clenly as yuell cheuynge]
—*preuynge*, i. e. proving; *clenly*, i. e. wholly.

" And prechest on thy benche, *with evil prefe ;* "   (i. e.
    evil may it prove !)
        Chaucer's *Wif of Bathes Prol.* v. 5829. ed. Tyr.
—*yuell cheuynge,* i. e. evil ending, bad success.

        " *God geve it yvell chevynge.*"
    Roy's *Rede me,* &c., *Harl. Miscell.* ix. 79. ed. Park.

See also *Cocke Lorelles bote,* sig. B i., *Towneley Myst.*
p. 108, and Chaucer's *Chanones Yemannes Tale,* v
16693. ed. Tyr.

    Page 116. v. 189. *patch*] I know not how to ex-
plain.

    v. 190. *ron*] i. e. run.

    v. 192. *ioust*] i. e. joist.

    v. 196. *bolle*] i. e. bowl.

    v. 198. *skommeth*] i. e. skimmeth.

    v. 199. *Whereas*] i. e. Where.

    v. 201. *blennes*] i. e. blends.

    v. 212. *And ye may it broke*] i. e. If you may
brook it.

    v. 213. *loke*] i. e. look.

    Page 117. v. 218. *ble*] i. e. colour, complexion.

    v. 219. *Ich am*] i. e. I am.

    v. 222. *In lust and in lykyng*] See note, p. 19. v. 23.

    v. 223. *whytyng*] So in our early dramas, *whiting-
mop* (young whiting) is a cant term for a nice young
woman, a tender creature : see Puttenham's *Arte of
E. P.,* 1589. p. 184., and note in my ed. of Webster's
Works, iii. 37.

    v. 224. *mullyng*] This term of endearment occurs in
the *Coventry Mysteries,* applied by one of the shepherds
to the infant Saviour ;

" Thow I be the last that take my leve,
ȝit fayre *mullynge* take it nat at no greve."

MS. Cott. Vesp. D viii. fol. 91.

Compare also Hormanni *Vulgaria :* " This is a fayre
and swete *mullynge.* Blandus est *puerulus* insigni fes-
tiuitate." Sig. dd vii. ed. 1530.

—— *mytyng*] In the *Towneley Mysteries,* one of the
shepherds says to the infant Saviour,

" Haylle, so as I can, haylle, praty *mytyng !* " p. 96.

and Jamieson gives *myting* as a fondling designation
for a child, *Et. Dict. of Scot. Lang.*—In our author's
third poem *Against Garnesche,* v. 115. vol. i. 143,
" myteyng "—(but used as a term of contempt)—is, as
here, the rhyme to " wyteyng."

Since writing the above note, I have met with a
passage in the comedy called *Wily Beguilde,* which
might be adduced in support of the reading, " nytyng ; "
but I still think that " mytyng " is the true one : the
dramatist evidently recollected Skelton's poem, in the
ed. of which he had found " nytyng," " nittinge," or
" nittine : "—" Comely Pegge, my *nutting,* my sweet-
ing, my Loue, my doue, my honnie, my bonnie, my
ducke, my deare and my deareling." Sig. C 4. ed. 1606.

Page 117. v. 225. *His nobbes and his conny*] So in
a song in *The Triall of Treasure,* 1567 ;

" My mouse, my *nobs,* and *cony* swete." Sig. E.

conny, i. e. rabbit.

v. 227. *Bas*] i. e. Kiss.

—— *bonny*] i. e. precious one (rather than—beauti-
ful one,—for it has the epithet " prety ").

v. 229. *This make I my falyre fonny*] This, i. e.
Thus ; it has been suggested that *falyre* means fellow ;

which I doubt: *fonny* i. e. to be foolishly amorous
compare—

> " As freshly then thou shalt begin to *fonne*
> And dote in loue."

Chaucer's *Court of Loue,—Workes*, fol. 329. ed. 1602.

Page 117. v. 230. *dronny*] i. e. drone.

v. 232. *rout*] i. e. snore.

Page 118. v. 247. *a salt*] i. e. a salt-cellar.

v. 251.   *Some fyll theyr pot full*
           Of good Lemster woll]

The meaning is—in the pot which was to hold the ale
they brought wool " instede of monny " (v. 244).

v. 254. *athrust*] i. e. a-thirst.

v. 258. *slaty or slyder*] i. e. miry or slippery.

Page 119. v. 266. *renne*] i. e. run.

v. 269. *byrle*] The word *birl*—to pour out, furnish
for, or part drink among guests—(see Jamieson's *Et.
Dict. of Scot. Lang.* in v., and Leyden's Gloss. to *The
Comp. of Scotland* in v. *Beir*)—is not very common in
English literature: " the olde God of wyne called
Baccus *birlying* the wyne." Hall's *Chronicle*, (*Hen.
viii.*) fol. lxxiii. ed. 1548.

v. 271. *She swered by the rode of rest*]— *rode*, i. e.
rood,—cross: see note on *Ware the Hauke*, v. 69.

> " That is hardly saide, man, *by the roode of rest.*"
>   Barclay's *First Egloge*, sig. A iii. ed. 1570.

* v. 274. *By and by*] i. e. straightway.

v. 280. *haruest gyrdle*] i. e. perhaps, a girdle worn
at the feast after the gathering in of the corn.

* v. 283. *Some*] i. e. one.

v. 286. *To offer to the ale tap*] So in *Jak Hare*, a
poem attributed to Lydgate;

" And with his wynnynges he *makith his offrynge*
  At the ale stakis."

MS. Harl. 2251. fol. 14.

* Page 119. v. 288. *sowre dowe*] i. e. leaven.

v. 289. *howe*] i. e. ho.

v. 292. *And pype tyrly tyrlowe*] Compare a Song belonging to the Tailors' and Shearmen's Pageant;

" Thé sange *terly terlow.*"

Sharp's *Diss. on Coventry Pag. and Myst.*, p. 114.

Page 120. v. 295. *hekell*] i. e. comb for dressing flax.

v. 296. *rocke*] i. e. distaff.—In a poem entitled *Cryste Crosse me Spede. A. B. C. Imprynted at London in Fletestrete at the sygne of the Sonne, by me Wynkyn de Worde*, 4to. (which I know only from the account of it in *Typog. Antiq.* ii. 367. ed. Dibdin) are the following lines;

" A grete company of gossyps, gadred on a route,
  Went to besyege an ale hous rounde aboute;
  Some brought a distaffe & some a rele,
  Some brought a shouell & some a pele,
  Some brought drynke & some a tankarde,
  And a galon potte faste they drewe thederward," &c.

Though no edition of *Elynour Rummyng* has come down to us printed anterior to *Cryste Crosse me Spede*, the evident imitation of the former in the passage just quoted, shews that it must have existed.

v. 298. *wharrowe*] i. e. whirl, or wharve, for a spindle. " A spyndell with a *wharowe*——fusus cum *spondulo, siue verticillo siue harpage.*" Hormanni *Vulg.* sig. t i. ed. 1530.

* Page 120. v. 299. *rybskyn*] In *Prompt. Parv., MS. Harl.* 221, is " *Rybbe skynn.* Melotula." In a MS. *Catholicon in Lingua materna*, dated 1483, I find " *Rybbynge skyn.* nebrida. pellicudia."—Does it mean (as Albert Way, Esq. has obligingly suggested to me) a leather apron, used during the operation of flax-dressing ? [" ' *Pellicula*, Anglice a rybschyn ; *nebrida*, idem est.' Nominale MS." Halliwell's *Dict.* See also the same, in v. Trip-skin : " a piece of leather, worn on the right-hand side of the petticoat by spinners with the rock, on which the spindle plays, and the yarn is pressed by the hand of the spinner.— Forby."]

v. 303. *thrust*] i. e. thirst.

v. 305.   *But drynke, styll drynke,*
          And let the cat wynke]

So in *The Worlde and the Chylde*, 1522 ;

" *Manhode.* Now *let vs drynke* at this comnaunt,
             For that is curtesy.

Folye.   Mary, mayster, ye shall haue in hast :
             A ha, syrs, *let the catte wyncke*," &c.
                                        Sig. C ii.

See also three epigrams by Heywood *Of the winking Cat,—Workes*, sig. P 4. ed. 1598.

v. 314. *chaffer*] i. e. merchandise.

v. 319. *in all the hast*] Compare :

    " Bulwarkes were made *in all the haste.*"
              Hormanni *Vulgaria*, sig. z iii. ed. 1530.

                    " the ryght way
To London they tooke *in all the haste.*"
        Smith's *xii Mery Jests of the wyddow Edyth,*
              ed. 1573. sig. H iiii.

Page 120. v. 320. *vnlast*] i. e. unlaced.

Page 121. v. 323. *all hallow*] i. e. all saints,—perhaps, All-saints' day.

> v. 324. *It was a stale to take*
> *The deuyll in a brake*]

For " *stare*," which is the reading of all the eds., I have substituted " *stale*"—i. e. lure, decoy. So in Marmyon's *Hollands Leaguer*, 1632;

> " And if my skill not failes me, her I'll make
> *A Stale, to take* this Courtier *in a brake*."
>
> Act ii. sc. 1. sig. D 3.

Compare too an epigram by Heywood;

> " Take time when time commeth : are we set time to take ?
> Beware time, in meane time, *take* not vs *in brake*."
>
> *Workes*, sig. Q 3. ed. 1598.

and Cavendish's *Life of Wolsey ;* " At last, as ye have heard here before, how divers of the great estates and lords of the council lay in a-wait with my Lady Anne Boleyn, to espy a convenient time and occasion *to take* the cardinal *in a brake*." p. 147. ed. 1827.—In our text, and in the passages just quoted, *brake* seems to be used for trap: among its various significations, it means a strong wooden frame for confining the feet of horses, preparatory to their being shod; see Gifford's note on Jonson's *Works*, iii. 463.

v. 327. *gambone*] i. e. gammon.

v. 328. *resty*] i. e. reasty, rancid.

v. 330. *Angry as a waspy*]—*waspy*, i. e. wasp. So Heywood;

> " Now mery as a cricket, and by and by,
> *Angry as a waspe*."
>
> *Dialogue*, sig. C 4,— *Workes*, ed. 1598.

* Page 121. v. 331. *yane*] i. e. yawn, gape.

—— *gaspy*] i. e. gasp.

* v. 332. *go bet*] [apparently an old hunting cry, " go better," i. e. faster.] Compare ;

> " Arondel, queth Beues tho,
> For me loue *go bet*, go."
>> *Sir Beues of Hamtoun*, p. 129.
>> Maitl. ed.

> " *Go bet*, quod he, and axe redily,
> What corps is this," &c.
>> Chaucer's *Pardoneres Tale*, v. 12601.
>> ed. Tyrwhitt,—

who observes that in the following lines of Chaucer's *Legend of Dido* (288), *go bet* seems to be a term of the chase ;

> " The herd of hartes founden is anon,
> With hey, *go bet*, pricke thou, let gon, let gon."

> " He hath made me daunce, maugre my hede,
> Amonge the thornes, hey *go bette*."
>> *The Frere and the Boye*,—*An. Pop. Poetry*,
>> p. 46. ed. Ritson,—

who supposes the words to be the name of some old dance.

v. 333. *met*] i. e. measure.

v. 334. *fet*] i. e. fetched.

* v. 335. *spycke*] i. e. bacon.

v. 336. *flycke*] i. e. flitch.

v. 339. *stut*] i. e. stutter.

v. 343. *sayne*] i. e. says.

—— *a fyest*] So Hawes ;

> " She let no ferte nor yet *fyste* truelye."
>> *The Pastime of pleasure*, sig. Q viii. ed. 1555.

" *A fiest*, Tacitus flatus."

Withals's *Dict.* p. 343. ed. 1634.

Page 121. v. 346. *wyth shamfull deth*] Equivalent to—may you die with a shameful death! see Tyrwhitt's *Gloss.* to Chaucer's *Cant. Tales*, in v. *With.*

v. 347. *callettes*] i. e. trulls, drabs, jades.

v. 348. *I shall breake your palettes*]—*palettes*, i. e. crowns, pates. So in a poem by Sir R. Maitland;

" For your rewarde now *I sall brek your pallat.*"

Anc. Scot. Poems from Maitl. MSS.,
ii. 317. ed. Pinkerton,—

who in the Gloss., wrongly explains it " cut your throat."

v. 350. *And so was made the peace*] In confirmation of the reading which I have given, compare *Reynard the Fox;*

" Thus was *the pees made* by fyrapel the lupaerd frendly and wel."

Sig. e 5. ed. 1481 ;

and see note on v. 319. p. 110.

Page 122. v. 354. *sainct James in Gales*] The body of Saint James the Great having, according to the legend, been buried at Compostella in Galicia (*Gales*), a church was built over it. Pilgrims flocked to the spot; several popes having granted the same indulgences to those who repaired to Compostella, as to those who visited Jerusalem. In *The foure P. P.* by Heywood, the Palmer informs us that he has been

" At saynt Cornelys, at *saynt James in Gales*,
And at saynt Wynefrydes well in Walles," &c.

Sig. A ii. ed. n. d.

v. 355. *Portyngales*] i. e. Portuguese.

Page 122. v. 356. *I wys*] i. e. truly, certainly (*i-wis*, adv.).

v. 360. *the Crosse in Chepe*] Was originally erected in 1290 by Edward I. at one of the resting places of the body of his beloved Eleanor, in its progress from Herdeby, where she died, to Westminster Abbey, where she was buried; and was adorned with her image and arms. Of its being afterwards rebuilt,— of the conduits that were added to it, &c. &c. an account will be found in Stow's *Survey*, B. iii. 35. ed. 1720, and *Sup. to Gent. Mag.* for 1764, vol. 34. 607. This structure was barbarously demolished in 1643, as a monument of Popish superstition.

v. 362. *route*] i. e. disorderly crowd.

v. 364.   *Sneuelyng in her nose,*
          As thoughe she had the pose]
—*pose*, i. e. a rheum in the head. So Chaucer;

              " *he speketh in his nose,*
     And sneseth fast, and eke *he hath the pose.*"
              The Manciples Prol. v. 17010. ed. Tyr.
See also *Reves Tale*, v. 4149.

v. 371. *fyll*] i. e. fell.

* v. 372. *barlyhood*] Or *barlikhood*, is said to mean a fit of obstinacy or violent ill-humour produced by drunkenness: see Jamieson's *Et. Dict. of Scot. Lang.* and *Supp.* in v.; also Stevenson's addition to Boucher's *Gloss.* in v. *Barlic.* [Here, more probably, simple intoxication.]

v. 378. *newe ale in cornes*] So in *Thersytes*, n. d.;

" I will make the drincke worse than good *ale in the cornes.*"
                              p. 56. Rox. ed.

" *New ale in cornes.   Ceruisia cum recrementis* "
Baret's *Alvearie*, in v. *Ale.*

Page 123. v. 386. *fabell*] i. e. talking.

v. 388.   ——————— *folys fylly*
That had a fole wyth wylly]

Whether *folys fylly* means a foolish young jade (a
filly,—compare what follows), or foolish Philly (*Phil-
lis,*—compare our author's *Bowge of Court,* v. 370.
vol. i. 53) ; and whether or not *wylly* is meant for a
proper name (as it is given in the comparatively recent
ed. of Rand), let the reader judge.

v. 390. *Iast you, and, gup, gylly*] See note, p. 20.
v. 17. " What, *gyppe, gyll* with a galde backe, begynne
you to kycke nowe : *Hey, de par le diable, gilotte,*" &c.
Palsgrave, p. 598.   So Dunbar uses *gillot* for a young
mare ; see his *Poems,* i. 65, ii. 459 (note), ed. Laing.

v. 394. *sennet*] i. e. sennight, week.

v. 395. *pay*] i. e. satisfaction, content.

v. 397. *Of thyne ale let vs assay*]—*assay,* i. e. try,
taste.

v. 398. *pylche*] i. e. cloak of skins.

v. 399. *conny*] i. e. rabbit.

* v. 400. *donny*] Richardson, *Dict.* in vv. *Dun,
Dunny,* cites this line as containing an example of the
latter word,—rightly, perhaps, for *donne* (dun) occurs
in Skelton's *Magnyfycence,* v. 1002. vol. ii. 47.—The
common people of Ireland, employ *donny* in the sense
of—poor, mean-looking, as " a *donny* creature ; " also
in the sense of—poorly, [so in Lancashire,] as " How
are you to-day ? "—" Och ! but *donny,* very *donny.*"
For this information I am indebted to the kindness of
Miss Edgeworth, who has used the word in one of her
excellent tales.

Page 123. v. 407. *blommer*] i. e. perhaps, noise, up-roar.

v. 408. *a skommer*] i. e. a skimmer.

* Page 124. v. 409. *a slyce*] ["An instrument of the kitchen to turne meate that is fried," Elyot, in v. *Spatha*, ed. 1569.   Halliwell, *Dict.*]

v. 412. *sterte*] i. e. started, rushed.

v. 414. *somdele seke*] i. e. somewhat sick.

v. 415. *a peny cheke*] Does it mean—a puny chick ?

v. 418. *Margery Mylkeducke*] So again in our au-thor's *Magnyfycence;*

"What, *Margery Mylke Ducke*, mermoset !"

v. 462. vol. ii. 23.

Compare one of the *Coventry Mysteries ;*

"Malkyn *Mylkedoke* and fayre Mabyle."

MS. Cott. Vesp. D viii. fol. 74.

v. 419.   *Her kyrtell she did vptucke*
               An ynche aboue her kne]

So in our old ballad poetry ;

" Then you must cut your gowne of greene,
     An inch above your knee."

Child Waters,—Percy's *Rel. of A. E. P.*
iii. 56. ed. 1794.

v. 422. *stubbed*] i. e. short and thick.

v. 423. *pestels*] i. e. legs,—so called, perhaps, be-cause the leg-bone resembles a *pestle* used in a mortar. The expression " *pestle* of pork " frequently occurs in our early writers; as in the following passage con-cerning the tremendous appetite of Charlemagne; " Whan he took hys repaast he was contente wyth lytel brede, but as touchyng the pytaunce, he ete at his repaast a quarter of moton, or ii hennes, or a grete ghoos, or a grete *pestel* of porke, or a pecok, or a crane, or an hare all hool." Caxton's *Lyf of Charles the Grete*, &c., 1485. sig. b iii.

Page 124. v. 423. *clubbed*] i. e. like clubs.

v. 426. *foule*] i. e. ugly.

v. 429. *cantell*] i. e. corner, piece, fragment.

v. 431. *quycke*] i. e. live.

v. 435. *punyete*] i. e. pungent.

v. 436. *sorte*] i. e. set, company.

Page 125. v. 441. *I wote nere*] i. e. I know never, not.

* v. 443. *podynges and lynkes*] " *Links*, a kind of Pudding, the skin being filled with Pork Flesh, and seasoned with diverse Spices, minced, and tied up at distances." (R. Holme's *Ac. of Armory*, 1688. B. iii. p. 83.) [Strings of sausages.]

v. 450. *keke*] i. e. kick.

v. 451. *the vertue of an vnset leke*] " *Vnsette lekes* be of more *vertue* than they that be sette . . . . . *præstant in medicina.*" Hormanni *Vulgaria*, sig. f ii. ed. 1530.

v. 452. *breke*] i. e. breeches.

v. 453. *feders*] i. e. feathers.

v. 460. *noughty froslynges*] i. e. worthless things, stunted by frost. In Suffolk, *froslin* is applied to any thing—a lamb, a *goslin*, a chicken, an apple, &c., nipped, or pinched, or injured by frost: see Moor's *Suffolk Words, Appendix*.

v. 462. *callet*] i. e. trull, drab, jade.

* v. 465. *wretchockes*] " The famous imp yet grew a *wretchock ;* and though for seven years together he was carefully carried at his mother's back, rocked in a cradle of Welsh cheese, like a maggot, and there fed

with broken beer, and blown wine of the best daily,
yet looks as if he never saw his *quinquennium.*" Jon·
son's Masque, *The Gipsies Metamorphosed,*— *Workes,*
vii. 371. ed. Gifford, who thus comments on the pas-
sage in his authoritative style: "i. e. pined away,
instead of thriving. Whalley appears to have puzzled
himself sorely in this page, about a matter of very
little difficulty. In every large breed of domestic
fowls, there is usually a miserable little stunted crea-
ture, that forms a perfect contrast to the growth and
vivacity of the rest. This unfortunate abortive, the
goodwives, with whom it is an object of tenderness,
call a *wrethcock;* and this is all the mystery. Was
Whalley ignorant that what we now term chick, was
once chocke and *chooke?* " The fol. ed. of the *Masque
of Gipsies* has " *wretch-cock,*" which Nares, who does
not know what to make of the word, observes " would
admit of an easy derivation from *wretch* and *cock,*
meaning a poor wretched fowl." *Gloss.* in v. [Per-
haps *wretchock* is merely a diminution of *wretch.*]

Page 125. v. 466. *shyre shakyng nought*] i. e. sheer
worthless. So again our author in his *Magnyfycence;*

" From *qui fuit aliquid* to shyre shakynge nought."

v. 1319. vol. ii. 61.

Page 126. v. 475. *fall*] i. e. fallen.

* v. 483. *foggy*] i. e. bloated.

v. 489. *craw*] i. e. crop, stomach.

v. 491. *on*] i. e. of: compare v. 131.

v. 492. *an old rybibe*] Chaucer, in *The Freres Tale,*
says,

" This Sompnour, waiting ever on his pray,
Rode forth to sompne a widewe, *an olde ribibe.*"

v. 6958. ed. Tyrwhitt,—

who says he cannot guess how this musical instrument came to be put for an old woman, " unless perhaps from its shrillness." The word so applied occurs also in Jonson's *Devil is an Ass*, act i. sc. 1, where Gifford observes, " *Ribibe*, together with its synonym *rebeck*, is merely a cant expression for an old woman. A ribibe, the reader knows, is a rude kind of fiddle, and the allusion is probably to the inharmonious nature of its sounds." *Works*, v. 8.

Page 126. v. 493. *She halted of a kybe*] i. e. She limped from a chap in the heel. The following remedy is seriously proposed in *The Countrie Farme*, and was no doubt applied by our ancestors : " *For kibes on the heeles*, make powder of old shooe soles burned, and of them with oile of roses annoint the kibes ; or else lay vnto the kibes the rinde of a pomegranat boiled in wine." p. 83. ed. 1600.

v. 498. *wroken*] i. e. wreaked.

* Page 127. v. 501. *on Gods halfe*] [i. e. for God's sake : *halfe*, like *halben* in German.]

v. 503. *beshrew*] i. e. curse.

v. 506. *lampatrams*] A word which I am unable to explain.

v. 507. *shap*] i. e. pudendum.

v. 512. *stert*] i. e. started.

v. 515. *dant*] In Kilian's *Dict*. is " *Dante. Ambubaia, mulier ignaua.*" ed. 1605 ; and in *Gloss. to West. and Cumb. Dialect*, " *Dannet*, a . . . woman of disreputable character :" but, for aught I know, the word in the text may have some very different signification.

v. 516. *a gose and a gant*] Must mean here,—a goose and a gander : yet Skelton in *Phyllyp Sparowe* mentions first " the gose and the *gander*," and afterwards " the gaglynge *gaunte* :" see note, p. 58. v. 447.

Page 127. v. 517. *wesant*] i. e. weasand.

v. 519. *olyfant*] i. e. elephant.

* **v.** 520. *bullyfant*] [A mock derivation from bull, in imitation of elephant.]

v. 522. *hedes*] i. e. heads.

v. 525. *ale pole*] i. e. pole, or stake, set up before an ale-house by way of sign.

Page 128. v. 535. *A strawe, sayde Bele, stande vtter*] —*stande vtter*, i. e. stand more out, back.

" *Straw,* quod the thridde, ye ben lewed and nice."
> Chaucer's *Chanones Yemannes Tale*, v. 16393.
> ed. Tyr.

" *Stonde vtter,* felowe! where doest thou thy curtesy preue?"
> *The Worlde and the Chylde,* 1522.
> sig. B iv.

v. 538. *sterte*] i. e. started.

—— *fysgygge*] " *Trotiere :* A raumpe, *fisgig,* fisking huswife, raunging damsell, gadding or wandring flirt." Cotgrave's *Dict.* " *Fiz-gig,* a wild flirting wench." *Dialect of Craven,* &c.

v. 550. *bybyll*] i. e. drink, tipple.

v. 553. *Wheywormed*] i. e. covered with *wheyworms,*—pimples from which a whey-like moisture exudes.

Page 129. v. 555. *puscull*] i. e. pustule.

v. 556. *muscull*] i. e. muscle,—the shell of which is frequently " scabbyd."

v. 557. *noppy*] i. e. nappy.

v. 558. *soppy*] i. e. sop.

v. 560. *mote I hoppy*] i. e. may I hop. " *Hoppy,* to hop or caper. Exm." Grose's *Prov. Gloss.* ed. 1839

Page 129. v. 561. *coleth*] i. e. cooleth.

—— *croppy.*] i. e. crop, stomach.

* v. 563. *Haue*] i. e. Take.

v. 573. *defoyled*] i. e. defiled.

v. 575. *sorte*] i. e. set, company.

v. 582. *a pryckemedenty*] i. e. one affectedly nice, finical.

> v. 583.   *Sat lyke a seynty,*
> *And began to paynty*
> *As thoughe she would faynty*]

—*seynty*, i. e. saint : *paynty*, (p. 130,) i. e. paint,—feign : *faynty*, i. e. faint.   Compare our author's *Colyn Cloute* ;

> " That counterfaytes and *payntes*
> As they were very *sayntes*."
>
>> v. 922. vol. ii. 157.

Page 130. v. 587. *a lege de moy*] So again in our author's *Colyn Cloute* ;

> " And howe Parys of Troy
> Daunced a *lege de moy*,
> Made lusty sporte and ioy
> With dame Helyn the quene."
>
>> v. 952. vol. ii. 158.

I have not found elsewhere the term *lege de moy*. Mace, in his *Musick's Monument*, 1676, mentions a *Tattle de Moy*,—" a New Fashion'd Thing, much like a Seraband ; only It has more of Conceit in It, as (in a manner) speaking the word (Tattle de Moy)," &c. p. 129.

v. 594. *I wys*] i. e. truly, certainly (*i-wis*, adv.).

* Page 130. v. 598. *spence*] i. e. store-room, for drink, or victuals ; pantry, cupboard, &c.

v. 609. *awne*] i. e. own.

v. 610. *Neyther gelt nor pawne*] i. e. Neither money nor pledge.

Page 131. v. 615. *balke*] i. e. beam, post : " *Balke* of an house, *pouste*." Palsgrave, p. 196.

v. 616. *tayle*] i. e. tally.

v. 617. *yll hayle*] i. e. ill health,—ill luck,—a common imprecation in our old poetry ;

> " *Ill haile*, Alein, by God thou is a fonne."
>
> Chaucer's *Reves Tale*, v. 4087. ed. Tyr.

See too *Chester Mysteries* (*De Del. Noe*), p. 27. Roxb. ed.

v. 619. *to mytche*] i. e. too much.

v. 620. *mummynge*] i. e. frolicking, merriment.

v. 622. *gest*] i. e. story.

v. 623. *this worthy fest*] So in the *Coventry Mysteries ;*

> " At *wurthy festys* riche men woll bene."
>
> *MS. Cott. Vesp.* D viii. fol. 32.

and in Cavendish's *Life of Wolsey*, " It is not to be doubted but that the king was privy of all *this worthy feast*." p. 199. ed. 1827.

POEMS AGAINST GARNESCHE.

All the particulars concerning Garnesche which I have been able to discover, will be found in the *Account of Skelton and his Writings*. (vol. i. pp. xli, lxvii.)

Page 132. v. 1. *Sithe*] i. e. Since.

Page 132. v. 4. *Syr Tyrmagant*]—or *Termagant*,—
a very furious deity, whom the Crusaders and ro-
mance-writers charged the Saracens with worshipping,
though there was certainly no such Saracenic divinity.
Concerning the name, see Gifford's note on Massin-
ger's *Works*, ii. 125. ed. 1813, and Nares's *Gloss*. in v.—
So in *The Flyting of Dunbar and Kennedy*, which in
various minute particulars bears a strong resemblance
to the present pieces *Against Garnesche ;*

" *Termygantis* temptis and Vespasius thy eme."
                    Dunbar's *Poems*, ii. 85. ed. Laing.

—— *tyrnyd*] i. e. tourneyed, encountered.

v. 5. *Syr Frollo de Franko*] Was a Roman knight,
governor of Gaul, slain by King Arthur : see *Geoffrey
of Mon.* l. ix. cap. ii., *The Legend of King Arthur*,
Percy's *Rel. of A. E. P.* iii. 39. ed. 1794, &c. &c.

—— *talle*] i. e. valiant.

v. 6. *Syr Satrapas*] Neither with this, nor with the
personage mentioned in the next line, have I any
acquaintance.

v. 8. *haue ye kythyd yow a knyght*]—*kythyd*, i. e.
made known, shewn.

" It *kythit* be his cognisance *ane knight* that he wes."
         Golagros and Gawane, p. 137, *Syr Gawayne*, &c.
                         ed. Bann.

Garnesche had the dignity of knighthood ; see *Account
of Skelton and his Writings*. In the heading, and first
line, of this poem, he is called *Master ;* but knights
were frequently so addressed. In Cavendish's *Life of
Wolsey* mention is made of " Sir William Fitzwilliams,
a knight," who is presently called " *Master* Fitzwil-
liams," pp. 310, 311. ed. 1827, and of " Sir Walter

Walshe, *knight,*" who is immediately after termed
" *Master* Walshe," pp. 339, 340, and of " that wor-
shipful *knight Master* Kingston," p. 374.

Page 132. v. 8. *Syr Dugles the dowty*] " The high
courage of Dowglasse wan him that addition of *Doughty
Dowglasse,* which after grew to a Prouerbe." Marg.
Note on the description of the Battle of Shrewsbury,
in Drayton's *Polyolbion,* Song 22. p. 37. ed. 1622

v. 9. *currysly*] i. e. currishly.

Page 133. v. 10. *stowty*] i. e. stout.

v. 11. *Barabas*] The robber mentioned in Scrip-
ture.

―― *Syr Terry of Trace*]―*Trace,* i. e. Thrace : but
I do not recollect any romance or history in which a
Sir Terry of that country is mentioned.

v. 12. *gyrne*] i. e. grin.

―― *gomys*] i. e. gums.

v. 15. *Syr Ferumbras the ffreke*]―*ffreke* (common
in romance-poetry in the sense of―man, warrior) is
here, as the context shews, equivalent to furious fellow :
we have had the word before, see p. 32. v. 187.   Con-
sult the analysis of the romance of *Sir Ferumbras* in
Ellis's *Spec. of Met. Rom.* ii. 356, and Caxton's *Lyf of
Charles the Grete,* &c., 1485, for much about this Sar-
acen, called in the latter *Fyerabras,*―" a meruayllous
geaunte,"―" whyche was vaynquysshed by Olyuer,
and at the laste baptysed, *and was after a Saynt in
heuen.*" Sig. b viii.

v. 16. *Syr capten of Catywade, catacumbas of Cayre*]
Cayre is Cairo ; but I am unable to explain the line.
In the opening of Heywood's *Four P. P.,* the Palmer
says, he has been at " the graet God of Katewade,"
alluding, as O. Gilchrist thinks, to Catwadebridge in

Sampford hundred in Suffolk, where there may have
been a famous chapel and rood; see Dodsley's *Old
Plays*, i. 61. last ed.

Page 133. v. 17. *Thcw*] i. e. Though.

—— *Syr Lybyus*] See note, p. 69. v. 649.

v. 18. *contenons oncomly*] i. e. countenance un-
comely.

v. 19. *apayere*] i. e. impair—become less.

v. 22. *Of Mantryble the Bryge, Malchus the mur-
ryon*]—*murryon*, i. e. Moor; so in the third of these
poems, Skelton calls Garnesche "Thou *murrionn*, thou
mawment," v. 170. vol. i. 145; so too in the Scottish
Treasurer's Accounts for 1501, "Peter the *Moryen*,"
Dunbar's *Poems*, ii. 306. ed. Laing; and in a folio
broadside, *M. Harry Whobals mon to M. Camell*, &c.
(among the "flytings" of Churchyard and Camell),
" Some *morryon* boye to hold ye vp." If the present
passage means that the Bridge was guarded by a Moor
called Malchus, I know not what authority Skelton
followed. Concerning the Bridge of Mantryble see
the analysis of the romance of *Sir Ferumbras*, Ellis's
Spec. of Met. Rom. ii. 389; and Caxton's *Lyf of Charles
the Grete*, &c., 1485, " Of the meruayllous bridge of
Mantryble, of the trybute there payed for to passe
ouer," &c., sig. e viii., and how " the strong brydge of
mantryble was wonne not wythoute grete payne," sig.
h viii.: it was kept by a giant, named Algolufre in the
former, and Galafre in the latter, who was slain by the
Frenchmen when the Bridge was won. In *The Bruce*
of Barbour, the hero reads to his followers " Romanys
off worthi Ferambrace " and how Charlemagne " wan
Mantrybill and passit Flagot." B. ii. v. 832 sqq. ed.
Jam. " The tail of *the brig of the mantribil* " is men-

tioned in *The Complaynt of Scotland*, p. 98. ed. Ley-
den. Compare also *Don Quixote;* " nor that [history]
of Fierabras, with the *Bridge of Mant[r]ible*, which
befell in Charlemaines time, and is, I sweare, as true,
as that it is day at this instant." P. i. B. iv. c. xxii. p.
546., Shelton's trans., 1612.

Page 133. v. 23. *blake Baltazar with hys basnet routh
as a bere*] Does *blake Baltazar* mean one of the Magi,
or, as they were commonly called, the Three Kings of
Cologne ? " the third, Balthasar, a black or Moor,
with a large spreading beard," &c. *Festa Anglo-Ro-
mana*, p. 7, cited in Brand's *Pop. Ant.* i. 19 (note), ed.
1813 : *with his basnet routh as a bere*, i. e. with his cap
(not helmet, it would seem,) rough as a bear.

v. 24. *Lycon, that lothly luske*]—*Lycon* is probably
Lycaon ; see note, p. 54. v. 311. " Here is a great
knaue i. a great lyther *luske*, or a stout ydell lubbar."
Palsgrave's *Acolastus*, 1540. sig. X ii. " *Luske*, a vyle
parsone, *ribavlt, esclaue, lovrdavlt.*" Palsgrave, *Lesclar
de la Lang. Fr.* p. 241. The word is often used as a
term of reproach in general.

v. 25. *brymly*] i. e. fiercely, ruggedly.

—— *here*] i. e. hair.

v. 26. *bake*] i. e. back.

—— *gere*] i. e. dress.

Page 134. v. 30. *a camoke*] Is explained—a crooked
stick, or tree ; a crooked beam, or knee of timber.

v. 31. *teggys*] See note, p. 104. v. 151.

v. 33. *Orwelle hyr hauyn*] By Harwich.

v. 36. *Sarson*] i. e. Saracen. So in *The Flyting of
Dunbar and Kennedy* (see note, p. 123. v. 4), " *Sara-
zene*, syphareit," &c. Dunbar's *Poems*, ii. 75. ed.
Laing.

Page 134. v. 36. *ble*] i. e. colour, complexion.

v. 37. *As a glede glowynge*] i. e. glowing like a burning coal :—but qy. did Skelton write " as a glede *glowrynge ?* " i. e. staring like a kite. He uses *glede* in this latter sense in *Magnyfycence*, v. 1059. vol. i. p. 50 : and in *The Flyting of Dunbar and Kennedy* (see note, p. 123. v. 4) we find,—

> " hungry *gled.*"

. . . .

> " Lyke to ane stark theif *glowrand* in ane tedder."
> > Dunbar's *Poems*, ii. 70, 72. ed. Laing.

—— *ien*] i. e. eyne, eyes.

v. 39. *passe*] i. e. excel.

v. 40. *Howkyd as an hawkys beke, lyke Syr Topyas*] i. e. Hooked, &c. The allusion is to Chaucer's *Sire Thopas*, who " had a semely nose." v. 13659. ed. Tyr.

v. 41. *buske*] i. e. prepare, or rather, perhaps, hie. *Be*] i. e. By.

Page 135. *gorbelyd*] i. e. big-bellied.

Godfrey] Concerning this person, who assisted Garnesche in his compositions, and is afterwards called his *scribe*, I can give the reader no information.

v. 2. [*Your*] *gronynge, ʒour grontynge, your groinynge lyke a swyne*] Skelton has elsewhere ;

> " Hoyning like hogges that *groynis* and wrotes."
> > *Against venemous tongues*, vol. i. 154.

> " The Gruntyng and the *groynninge* of the gronnyng swyne."
> > *Garlande of Laurell*, v. 1376. vol. ii. 230.

To *groin* is explained to groan, to grunt, to growl ; but perhaps our author may have used it like the

French "*Groigner*. To nuzle, or to root with the snout." Cotgrave's *Dict.*

Page 135. v. 3. *alle to peuiche*] See note, p. 22. v. 32.

v. 4. *mantycore*] See note, p. 53. v. 294.

—— *maltaperte*] i. e. malapert, (perhaps an error of the transcriber).

v. 5. *lere*] i. e. complexion, skin.

—— *gresyd bote*] i. e. greased boot.

v. 6.

Ye cappyd Cayface copious, your paltoke on your pate,
Thow ye prate lyke prowde Pylate, be ware yet of chek
mate]—

Cayface, i. e. Caiaphas : *copious* is perhaps an allusion to some sort of cope, in which that personage might have figured on the stage. The usual explanations of *paltock* ("*Paltok*. Baltheus," *Prompt. Parv.*; "a short garment of the doublet kind," Strutt's *Dress and Habits*, &c. ii. 352) do not seem to suit the present passage. In Palsgrave, p. 251, we find "*Paltocke*, a patche, *palleteau;*" and see what immediately follows in this poem: *Thow*, i. e. Though: *chek mate;* see note, p. 17. v. 29.

Compare *The Flyting of Dunbar and Kennedy* (see note, p. 123. v. 4)

"Thow irefull attircop, *Pylat* appostata."

. . . .

. . . "*Cayphass* thy fectour."

Dunbar's *Poems*, ii. 85, 86. ed. Laing.

v. 8. *Hole*] i. e. Whole, healed.

—— *Deu[ra]ndall*] Was the celebrated sword of Roland : see (among other works which might be referred to) Caxton's *Lyf of Charles the Grete*, &c., 1485, " How Rolland deyed holyly after many martyres and orysons made to god ful deuoutely, and of the complaynte maad for *hys swerde durandal.*" Sig. m i.

Page 135. v. 8. *awne*] i. e. own.

Page 136. v. 11. *Ye countyr vmwhyle to capcyously, and ar ye be dysiryd*]—*countyr;* see note, p. 11 : *vmwhyle,* i. e. some time : *to,* i. e. too : *ar,* i. e. ere.

v. 12. *all to-myryd*] meaning, I suppose, all befouled.

v. 15. *Gabionyte of Gabyone*] So in his *Replycacion agaynst certayne yong scolers,* &c. Skelton calls them " *Gabaonitæ,*" vol. i. 244.

* —— *gane*] i. e. gape, yawn.

* v. 16. *Huf a galante*] [Huff seems to mean a swaggering, bullying fellow.] Compare ;

" *Hof hof hof a* frysch *galaunt.*"
Mary Magdalene,—An. Mysteries from the Digby MSS. p. 85. ed. Abbotsf.

" Make rome syrs and let vs be mery,
With *huffa galand,* synge tyrll on the bery."
Interlude of the iiii Elementes, n. d.
sig. B ii.

In some *Glossary,* to which I have lost the reference, is " *Huff,* a gallant."

—— *loke*] i. e. look.

v. 17. *Lusty*] See note on title of the next poem, p 131.

—— *jaspe*] Does it mean—wasp ?

v. 19. *that of your chalennge makyth so lytyll fors*] i. e. that maketh (make) so little matter of your challenge.

Page 136. v.˙22. *Syr Gy, Syr Gawen, Syr Cayus, for and Syr Olyuere*] Concerning the first two see notes, p. 65, 66. v. 629 : *Cayus*, or Kay, was the foster-brother of King Arthur; see the *Morte d'Arthur*, &c. &c. : *for and* [and eke] is an expression occasionally found in much later writers; see Middleton's *Fair Quarrel*, act v. sc. 1., *Works*, iii. 544. ed. Dyce; and Beaumont and Fletcher's *Knight of the Burning Pestle,*—

"*For and* the Squire of Damsels, as I take it."

Act ii. sc. 2. [sc. 3.],—

a passage which the modern editors have most absurdly altered : *Olyuere* was one of the twelve peers of France.

v. 23. *Priamus*] Perhaps the personage so named, who fought with Gawayne, and was afterwards made a knight of the Round Table; see *Morte d'Arthur*, B. v. ch. x. xii. vol. i. 148 sqq. ed. Southey.

v. 24. *Arturys auncyent actys*] An allusion, perhaps, more particularly to the *Morte d'Arthur;* see its other title in note, p. 67. v. 634.

Page 137. v. 25. *fysnamy*] i. e. physiognomy. So in *The Flyting of Dunbar and Kennedy.*

" —— thy frawart phisnomy."

Dunbar's *Poems*, ii. 68. ed. Laing.

v. 26. *to hawte*] i. e. too haughty.

—— *I wys*] i. e. truly, certainly (*i-wis*, adv.).

v. 29. *Godfrey*] See note on title of this poem, p. 127.

—— *gargons*] i. e. Gorgon's.

v. 30. *Syr Olifranke*] Qy. a mistake of the transcriber for *Syr Olifaunte*, the giant mentioned in Chaucer's *Sire Thopas ?*

Page 137. v. 30. *splay*] i. e. display.

v. 31. *Baile*] Seems to mean—howl, cry. "I *Balle*, as a curre dogge doth, *Ie hurle*." Palsgrave, p. 443.

—— *folys*] i. e. fools.

v. 32. *ȝe*] i. e. ye.

v. 36. *Gup*] See note, p. 20. v. 17.

—— *gorbellyd*] i. e. big-bellied.

v. 37. *turney*] i. e. tourney, contend.

—— *to fare to seke*] i. e. too far at a loss, inexperienced,—unable.

* v. 38. *whypslovens*] [A general term of abuse which explains itself.]

—— *a coke stole*] i. e. a cucking-stool, a chair or stool fixed at the end of a long pole, used for the punishment of scolds and brawlers by plunging them in the water.

Page 138. v. 39. *mantycore*] See note, p. 53. v. 294 : *marmoset*, a kind of ape, or monkey.

v. 40. *wraw*] i. e. peevish, angry.

* Page 139. —— *lusty Garnyche, welle be seyn Crysteouyr*] Both these epithets allude to his dress : " *Lusty* or fresshe in apparayle, *frisque*." Palsgrave, p. 318 ; *welle be seyn*, [well looking.]—Compare Dunbar ;

> " Gife I be *lusty in array*,
> Than luve I paramouris thay say
>
> . . . .
>
> Gife I be nocht *weill als besene*," &c.
>
> *Poems*, i. 185. ed. Laing.

v. 1. *lewde*] i. e. ignorant, vile.

v. 3. *skrybe*] Means Godfrey, see note on title of the preceding poem, p. 127, and compare v. 90 of the present.

Page 139. v. 6. *I caste me*] i. e. I project, design.

v. 9. *fauyr*] i. e. appearance, look.

v. 11. *cousshons*] i. e. cushions.

v. 12. *condycyonns*] i. e. qualities, dispositions, habits.

v. 13. *Gup, marmeset, jast ye, morelle*] See notes, p. 12. v. 11. p. 20. v. 17, and preceding page, v. 39.

v. 14. *lorelle*] i. e. good-for-nothing fellow.

* v. 15. *Lewdely*] i. e. [ill, maliciously ;] but in v. 19 it is to be understood in its more original meaning—ignorantly.

v. 20. *ȝe*] i. e. ye.

* Page 140. v. 26. *dryvyll*] i. e. menial.

v. 27. *your nose dedde sneuylle*] So in *The Flytyng of Dunbar and Kennedy* (see note, p. 123. v. 4) ;

" Out! out! I schowt, upon *that snout that snevillis.*"
                    Dunbar's *Poems*, ii. 86. ed. Laing.

v. 30. *fonne*] i. e. fool.

v. 31. *A gose with the fete vponne*] i. e. a goose with its feet on.

v. 32. *slufferd vp*] i. e. slabbered up.

—— *sowse*] " Succiduum. anglice. *sowce.*" *Ortus Vocab.* fol. ed. W. de Worde, n. d. (and so *Prompt. Parv.* ed. 1499). " *Souce, trippes.*" Palsgrave, p. 273.

v. 34. *xulde*] i. e. should : a provincialism (see, for instance, the *Coventry Mysteries* passim), to be attributed not to Skelton, but to the transcriber.

v. 36. *bawdy*] i. e. foul ; see note, p. 101. v. 90.

* v. 38. *haftynge*] i. e. cheating.

—— *polleynge*] i. e. plundering.

v. 40. *Gynys*] i. e. Guines.

v. 41. *spere*] i. e. spire, shoot,—stripling.

Page 140. **v.** 42. *lewdly*] i. e. vilely, meanly.

—— *gere*] i. e. apparel.

* v. 46. *dud frese*] i. e. coarse frieze : [a *dudd* was also a coarse wrapper or dread-nought. Rags, or poor clothes in general, are still called duds. See Way's *Prompt. Parv.*]

Page 141. v. 52. ჳe] i. e. ye.

v. 53. *warde*] i. e. wardrobe.

v. 54. *kyst a shepys ie*] i. e. cast a sheep's eye.

v. 56. *gonge*] i. e. privy.

v. 62. *bassyd*] i. e. kissed.

* v. 68. *pyllyd garleke*] [i. e. scalled—*pylled* is peeled.] Compare the next poem *Against Garnesche ;*

" Thow callyst me *scallyd*, thou callyst me mad :
Thow thou be *pyllyd*, thow ar nat sade."

v. 116. vol. i. 151.

Pilled-garlick was a term applied to a person whose hair had fallen off by disease; see Todd's *Johnson's Dict.* in v.

v. 69. *hocupy there no stede*] i. e. occupy there no place, stand in no stead,—avail nothing.

v. 70. *Syr Gy of Gaunt*] So our author again, in his *Colyn Cloute ;*

" Auaunt, *syr Guy of Gaunt.*"

v. 1157. vol. ii. 165.

In *The Flyting of Dunbar and Kennedy* (which, as already shewn, strongly resembles the present pieces *Against Garnesche* in several minute particulars) we find—

" thow *spreit of Gy.*"

Dunbar's *Poems*, ii. 72. ed. Laing.

and at p. 37 of the same vol., in *The Droichis Part of the Play*, attributed to Dunbar,—

" I wait I am *the spreit of Gy.*"

So too Sir D. Lyndsay in his *Epistill to the Kingis Grace* before his *Dreme,*—

" And sumtyme, lyke *the grislie gaist of Gy.*"
Works, i. 187. ed. Chalmers,—

who explains it " the well-known Sir Guy of romance." But both Dunbar and Lyndsay allude to a story concerning the ghost of a person called Guy, an inhabitant of Alost. There is a Latin tract on the subject, entitled *De spiritu Guuidonis,* of which various translations into English are extant in MS. One of these is now before me, in verse, and consisting of 16 closely written 4to pages: *Here begynnyth a notabyll matere and a gret myracule don be oure lord ihesus cryst and shewyd In the ʒeer of his incarnacion* MCCCXXIII. [printed Latin tract now before me has MCCCXXIIII.] *and in the xvi day of decembyr in the Cete of Aleste. Whiche myracule ys of a certeyn man that was callyd Gy. and deyde and aftyr viii days he apperyd to his wyf aftyr the comaundment of god. of whiche apperyng she was aferd and oftyn tyme rauysshid. Than she toke conseyl and went to the ffreris of the same cete and tolde the Pryor ffrere Iohnn goly of this mater, &c.* As *Gaunt* is the old name of Ghent, and as Alost is about thirteen miles from that city, perhaps the reader may be inclined to think,—what I should greatly doubt,— that Skelton also alludes to the same story.

Page 141. v. 71. *olyfaunt*] i. e. elephant.

v. 72. *pykes*] i. e. pickaxe. " *Pykeys.* Ligo. Marra." *Prompt. Parv.* ed. 1499.

—— *twybyll*] " *Twybyll,* writis instrument. Bisacuta. Biceps." *Prompt. Parv.* ed. 1499. " Twybill or mactok. Marra. Ligo." *Ibid.* " Bipennis . . . . a *twyble* or axe, a twall." *Ortus Vocab.* ed. 1514. (in the earlier ed. fol. n. d. W. de Worde, the English explanation is less full).

* Page 141. v. 75.· *wary*] [i. e. abuse, speak evil of ; often, to curse ; but here, possibly, war, contend, warray.]

Page 142. v. 79. *eldyr steke*] i. e. elder-stick.

v. 87. *sowtters*] i. e. shoemakers, cobblers.

v. 88. *seche a nody polle*] i. e. such a silly head, ninny.

v. 89. *pryste*] i. e. priest.

v. 90. *your scrybys nolle*] i. e. your scribe's head,— Godfrey's ; see note on title of the preceding poem, p. 127.

v. 91. *fonde*] i. e. foolish.

v. 93. *make*] i. e. compose verses.

v. 94. *dawpate*] i. e. simple pate, simpleton ; see note, p. 36. v. 301.

v. 101. *Bolde bayarde*] The proverbial expression, " as bold as blind bayard,"—(*bayard*, properly a bay horse, but used for a horse in general),—is very ancient, and of very frequent occurrence in our early literature ; its origin is not known :

" For *blynde bayarde* caste peryll of nothynge,
    Tyll that he stumblyng fall amydde the lake."
                            Lydgate's *Warres of Troy*, B. v.
                                sig. E e ii. ed. 1555.

v. 102. *kynde*] i. e. nature.
Page 143. v. 108.

>   *Ye wolde be callyd a maker,*
>   *And make moche lyke Jake Raker*]

i. e. You would be called a composer of verses, or
poet, and you compose much in the style of Jack
Raker. So again our author ;

> " Set *sophia* asyde, for euery *Jack Raker*
> And euery mad medler must now be a maker."
>
> <p align="right"><i>Speke, Parrot</i>, v. 165. vol. ii. 253.</p>

> " He maketh vs *Jacke Rakers ;*
> He sayes we ar but crakers," &c.
>
> <p align="right"><i>Why come ye nat to Courte</i>, v. 270. vol. ii. 285.</p>

So too in the comedy by Nicholas Udall, entitled
Ralph Royster Doyster ;

> " Of Songs and Balades also he is a maker,
> And that can he as finely doe as *Jacke Raker*."
>
> Act ii. sc. 1. p. 27. (reprint.)

Mr. Collier (*Hist. of Engl. Dram. Poet.* ii. 448) speaks
of Jack Raker as if he really had existed : I rather
think that he was an imaginary person, whose name
had become proverbial.

Page 143. v. 110. *crakar*] i. e. vaunter, big talker.

v. 114. *despyghtyng*] i. e. grudging, malice.

v. 115. *nat worthe a myteyng*]—*myteyng* (which
occurs in our author's *Elynour Rummyng* as a term of
endearment, v. 224. vol i. 117) is here perhaps equiv-
alent to " *Myte*, the leest coyne that is." Palsgrave,
p. 245.

v. 117. *scole*] i. e. school.

v. 118. *occupyed no better your tole*] i. e. used no
better your tool, pen :

v. 119. *Ye xulde haue kowththyd me a fole*] i. e. You
should have made me known for, shewn me to be, a
fool.

v. 121. *wyse*] i. e. think, intend.

Page 143. v. 122. *xall*] i. e. shall.

v. 123. *Thow*] i. e. Though.

—— *Sarsens*] i. e. Saracen's.

v. 124. *Row*] i. e. Rough.

—— *here*] i. e. hair.

v. 125. *heuery*] i. e. every.

v. 127. *peson*] i. e. pease.

v. 129. *geson*] i. e. scarce, scanty.

* v. 131. *Your skyn scabbyd and scuruy,*
        Tawny, tannyd, and shuruy, &c.]

—*shuruy,* i. e., perhaps, "*shrovy,* squalid." Forby's
Vocab. of East Anglia: [probably only a softened
form of *scurvy.*] With this passage compare *The Fly-
ting of Dunbar and Kennedy* (see note, p. 127. v. 4) ;

" Fy ! skolderit skyn, thow art bot skyre and skrum-
        ple."

.   .   .   .

" Ane crabbit, *skabbit,* evill facit messane tyk."

.   .   .   .

" Thow lukis *lowsy.*"

                Dunbar's *Poems,* ii. 70, 84, 72. ed. Laing.

Page 144. v. 139. *Xall kyt both wyght and grene*] i. e.
Shall cut both white and green,—an allusion to the
dress which our author appears to have worn as Lau-
reat ; see *Account of Skelton and his Writings.*

v. 140. *to grett*] i. e. too great.

v. 143. *puauntely*] i. e. stinkingly, strongly.

v. 155. *crawes*] i. e. crops, stomachs.

v. 157. *perke*] i. e. perch.

v. 158. *gummys*] i. e. gums.

* v. 159. *serpentins*] [i. e. a kind of cannon.] " His
campe was enuironed with artilerie, as fawcones, *ser-*

pentynes, cast hagbushes," &c. Hall's *Chronicle* (Henry viii.), fol. xxviii. ed. 1548.

Page 144. v. 160. *bynde*] i. e. bend; so in the next poem we find "*wyll*" for "*well*," and "*spynt*" for "*spent*," peculiarities to be attributed to the transcriber, not to Skelton.

v. 162. *scorpyone*] So in *The Flyting of Dunbar and Kennedy* "*scorpion* vennemous." Dunbar's *Poems*, ii. 75. ed. Laing.

v. 163. *bawdy babyone*] i. e. filthy baboon; see note, p. 101. v. 90.

v. 165. *mantycore*] See note, p. 53. v. 294.

Page 145. v. 168. *gresly gargone*] i. e. grisly Gorgon.

—— *glaymy*] i. e., I suppose, slimy, clammy.

v. 169. *seymy*] i. e. greasy.

v. 170. *murrionn*-] i. e. Moor; see note, p. 125. v. 22.

—— *mawment*] "*Mawment*. Idolum. Simulacrum." *Prompt. Parv.* ed. 1499. "*Maument, marmoset, poupee*." Palsgrave, p. 244. "*Mawment*, a puppet." Brockett's *Gloss. of North Country Words.*—(*Mawmet*, i. e. Mahomet.)

v. 172. *marmoset*] A sort of ape or monkey.

v. 173. *I wyll nat dy in they det*]—*they*, i. e. thy; as in the next poem.—Compare *Cocke Lorelles Bote*;

" Yf he call her calat, she calleth hym knaue agayne;
She *shyll not dye in his dette*."   Sig. B i.

v. 175. *xulddst*] i. e. shouldst.

v. 176. *xall*] i. e. shall.

v. 177. *hole*] i. e. whole.

v. 178. *Soche pelfry thou hast pachchyd*] I do not

understand this line: *pelfry* is, perhaps, pilfery; but does it not rather mean—petty goods,—which Garnesche had *pachchyd*, fraudulently got together? "Muche of theyr fishe they do barter with English men, for mele, lases, and shoes, and other *pelfery*." Borde's *Boke of knowledge*, sig. I, reprint. "Owt of whyche countre the sayd Scottys fled, and left mych corne, butters, and other *pylfre*, behinde theim, whyche the ost hade." Letter from Gray to Crumwell, *State Papers*, iii. 155,—the Vocabulary to which renders *pylfre*, pillage—wrongly, I believe. Dekker, describing "The Blacke Arte" (or "Picking of Lockes"), tells us that "The gaines gotten is *Pelfry*." *The Belman of London*, &c. sig. F 4. ed. 1608.

Page 145. v. 179. *houyr wachyd*] i. e. over watched.

v. 180. *thou xuldyst be rachchyd*] i. e. thou shouldest be stretched—have thy neck stretched. So in *The Flyting of Dunbar and Kennedy*;

"For substance and geir thow hes *a widdy* teuch
       On Mont Falcone, about *thy craig to rax*."
                                   Dunbar's *Poems*, ii. 79. ed. Laing.

v. 182. *be bedawyd*] Does it mean—be daunted? or, be called simple fellow? see note, p. 36. v. 301.

v. 183. *fole*] i. e. fool.

v. 184. *gronde*] i. e. ground.

v. 186. *Syr Dalyrag*] So our author elsewhere;

"Let syr Wrigwrag wrastell with *syr Delarag*."
                          Speke, Parrot, v. 91. vol. ii. 250.

"Adue nowe, sir Wrig wrag,
   Adue, *sir Dalyrag!*"
                   Howe the douty Duke of Albany, &c.
                          v. 297. vol. ii. 331.

Page 145. v. 187. *brag*] i. e. proud, insolent.

v. 189. *kyt . . . to large*] i. e. cut . . . too large.

v. 190. *Suche pollyng paiaunttis ye pley*] i. e. Such plundering pageants, thievish pranks, you play. The expression to " play a pageant "—to play a part,—has before occurred, see note, p. 6. v. 85. With the present passage compare: " This one *pageant* hath stayned al other honest dedes . . . . *flagitium*." Hormanni *Vulgaria*, sig. N v. ed. 1530. " That was a wyly *pageaunt . . . commentum*." *Id.* sig. N vi. " Thou gatest no worshyp by this *pageant . . facinore*." *Id.* sig. P v. " He had thought to playe me a *pagent: Il me cuyda donner le bont*." Palsgrave, p. 658. " A felowe which had renued many of Robin Hodes *Pagentes*." Fabyan's *Chron.* vol. ii. fol. 533. ed. 1559. " After he had *plaied* all his troublesome *pageants*," &c. Holinshed's *Chron.* (Hen. viii.) vol. iii. 830. ed. 1587.

v. 191. *poynt*] i. e. appoint, equip.

—— *fresche*] i. e. smart.

v. 192. *he*] i. e. Godfrey; see note on title of the second of these poems, p. 127.

v. 193. *rowllys*] i. e. rolls.

v. 194. *sowllys*] i. e. souls.

Page 146. v. 197.

> *That byrd ys nat honest*
> *That fylythe hys owne nest*]

—*fylythe*, i. e. defileth. This proverb occurs in *The Owl and the Nightingale* (a poem of the 12th century), p. 4. Rox. ed.

v. 199. *wyst what sum wotte*] i. e. knew what some know.

v. 204. *Jake a thrum*] In his *Magnyfycence*, our

author mentions " *Jacke a thrommys* bybyll," v. 1444. vol. ii. 67 (also in his *Garlande of Laurell,* v. 209. vol. ii. 179) ; and in his *Colyn Cloute* he uses the expression,—

" As wyse as *Tom a thrum.*"

v. 284. vol. ii. 134.

where the MS. has " *Jacke* athrum."—Compare : " And therto acordes too worthi prechers, *Jacke a Throme* and Ione Brest Bale." *Burlesques,—Reliquiæ Antiquæ* (by Wright and Halliwell), i. 84.

* *goliardum*] Equivalent, probably, to buffoon, or ridiculous rhymer. [" The *goliardi,* in the original sense of the word, appear to have been in the clerical order somewhat the same class as the jongleurs and minstrels among the laity, riotous and unthrifty scholars, who attended on the tables of the richer ecclesiastics, and gained their living and clothing by practising the profession of buffoons and jesters. The name appears to have originated towards the end of the twelfth century ; and, in the documents of that time and of the next century, is always connected with the clerical order." Wright, Poems of Walter Mapes, p. x.] See Du Cange's *Gloss.* in v., Tyrwhitt's note on Chaucer's *Cant. Tales,* v. 562, and Roquefort's *Gloss.* in v. *Goliard.*

lusty Garnyshe well beseen Crystofer] See note on title of the third of these poems, p. 131.

Page 146. v. 1. *gargone*] i. e. Gorgon.

v. 3. *Thowthe ye kan skylle of large and longe*] i. e. Though you be skilled in large and long ; see note, p. 15. v. 49.

Page 146. v. 4.

> *Ye syng allway the kukkowe songe :*
>
> . . . .
>
> *Your chorlyshe chauntyng ys al o lay*]

—*o lay*, i. e. one strain.   So Lydgate ;

> " *The cokkowe syng can* than *but oon lay.*"
>
>   *The Chorle and the Bird,—MS. Harl.*
>   116. fol. 151.

Page 147. v. 12. *Cicero with hys tong of golde*] So
Dunbar speaking of Homer and *Tully ;*

> " Your *aureate tongis* both bene all to lyte," &c.
>
>   *Poems,* i. 13. ed. Laing.

v. 17. *xalte*] i. e. shalt.

——— *warse*] i. e. worse.

v. 18. *They*] i. e. Thy ; as in the preceding poem.

v. 23. *lest good kan*] i. e. that knows the least good.

v. 25. *wylage*] i. e. village.

v. 28. *Lothsum as Lucifer*] So in *The Flyting of
Dunbar and Kennedy,* " *Luciferis* laid." Dunbar's
Poems, ii. 75. ed. Laing.

v. 29. *gasy*] i. e. gaze, look proudly.

v. 30. *Syr Pers de Brasy*] i. e. Pierre de Brézé,
grand-seneschal of Anjou, Poitou, and Normandy, and
a distinguished warrior during the reigns of Charles
vii. and Lewis xi. : he fell at the battle of Montlhéry
in 1465.

Page 148. v. 31. *caytyvys carkes*] i. e. caitiff's car-
cass.

v. 32. *blasy*] i. e. blaze, set forth.

v. 33. *Gorge Hardyson*] Perhaps the " George
Ardeson " who is several times mentioned in the un-

published *Bokis of Kyngis Paymentis Temp. Hen.* vii. *and* viii., preserved in the Chapter-House, Westminster : one entry concerning him is as follows ;

" [xxiii. of *George Ardeson* and Dollen. vii.] mynicke Sall er bounden in an obligacion to pay for the lycence of cccl buttes of malvesey vi^s viii^d for euery but within iii monethes next after they shalbe layde vpon lande $\Big\}$ cxvi^{li} xiii^s."

Page 148. v. 34. *habarion*] i. e. habergeon. " *Haburion.* Lorica." *Prompt. Parv.* ed. 1499.

v. 35. *the Januay*] i. e. the Geneose. " The *ianuays* . . . . Genuenses." Hormanni *Vulgaria,* sig. k iii. ed. 1530.

v. 36. *trysyd hys trowle away*] i. e. (I suppose) enticed away his trull.

v. 37. *paiantes*] i. e. tricks.   See note, p. 140. v. 190.

v. 39. *gate*] i. e. got.

* —— *gaudry*] i. e., perhaps, trickery, [from gaud, a trick.   The word often occurs in other poets in the sense of finery.]

v. 41. *Fanchyrche strete*] i. e. Fenchurch Street.

v. 42. *lemmanns*] i. e. mistresses.

v. 43. *Bas*] i. e. Kiss.

* —— *buttyng*] A term of endearment, which I do not understand. [The same as " bunting " (Qy. bantling ?) in the nursery song, " Bylo (balow), baby bunting."]

—— *praty*] i. e. pretty.

Page 148. v. 47. *Bowgy row*] i. e. Budge Row: " This Ward [Cordwainers Street Ward] beginneth in the East, on the West side of Walbrooke, and runneth West, thorow *Budge Row* (a street so called of the Budge Furr, and of Skinners dwelling there)," &c. Stow's *Survey*, B. iii. 15. ed. 1720.

v. 50. *mow*] i. e. mouth,—mock.

* v. 54. *lust*] i. e. desire.

v. 55. *broke*] i. e. badger.

* v. 56. *Gup, Syr Gy*] See notes, p. 20. v. 17. p. 133. v. 70 : *moke*, i. e. mock.

v. 57. *xulde*] i. e. should.

v. 59. *herey*] i. e. hairy.

* v. 60. *on Goddes halfe*] for God's sake.

Page 149. v. 61. *pray*] i. e. prey.

v. 63. *auncetry*] i. e. ancestry.

v. 66. *askry*] i. e. assail with a shout. See note, p. 78. v. 903.

v. 68. *Haroldis*] i. e. Heralds.

v. 69. *Thow*] i. e. Though.

v. 73. *brothells*] i. e. harlots. " Brothell, *pailliarde, putayn.*" Palsgrave, p. 201.

v. 75. *Betweyn the tappett and the walle*] A line which occurs again in our author's *Magnyfycence*, v. 1249. vol. ii. 58 ; *tappett*, i. e. tapestry, hangings.

v. 76. *Fusty bawdyas*] An expression used again by Skelton in his *Garlande of Laurell ;*

" Foo, *foisty bawdias !* sum smellid of the smoke."
v. 639. vol. ii. 198.

It occurs in the metrical tale *The Kyng and the Hermyt ;*

" When the coppe comys into the plas,
  Canst thou sey *fusty bandyas,* [*baudyas*]

And think it in your thouht ?
And you schall here a totted frere
Sey *stryke pantnere,*
And in ye [the] cope leve ryht nouht."

Brit. Bibliogr. iv. 90.

and several times after, in the same poem.

* Page 149. v. 77. *harres*] Equivalent to—collection. " *Haras*, a race ; horses and mares kept only for breed." Cotg. Way's *Prompt. Parv.*

v. 78. *clothe of Arres*] i. e. tapestry ; so called from Arras in Artois, where the chief manufacture of such hangings was.

v. 79. *eylythe*] i. e. aileth.

—— *rebawde*] i. e. ribald.

v. 82. *Auaunsid*] i. e. Advanced.

v. 83. *hole*] i. e. whole.

* v. 85. *lorell*] good-for-nothing, worthless fellow. See note, p. 132. v. 14.

—— *to lewde*] i. e. too ignorant, vile.

v. 86. *Lythe and lystyn*] i. e. Attend and listen—a sort of pleonastic expression common in our earliest poetry.

* —— *all bechrewde*] all accursed.

v. 88. *pointyd*] i. e. appointed.

v. 89. *semyth*] i. e. beseemeth.

* —— *pyllyd*] i. e. scalled.

Page 150. v. 91. *scryue*] i. e. write.

v. 92. *cumys*] i. e. becomes.

v. 93. *tumrelle*] i. e. tumbrel.

v. 94. *melle*] i. e. meddle.

v. 95. *The honor of Englande*] i. e. Henry the Eighth.

v. 97. *wyl*] i. e. well ; as afterwards in this poem.

Page 150. v. 97. *parcele*] i. e. part, portion.

v. 98. *yaue*] i. e. gave.

v. 99. *Eliconys*] i. e. Helicon's.

v. 101. *commyth*] i. e. becometh.

—— *remorde*] Fr. "*Remordre*. To bite again; also, to carpe at, or find fault with." Cotgrave's *Dict.* The word is frequently used by Skelton (see, for instance, vol. i. 209, where he introduces it with other terms nearly synonymous,—" reprehending " and " rebukynge ").

v. 102. *creaunser*] i. e. tutor: see *Account of Skelton and his Writings.*—Erasmus in his *Paraph. in Epist. Pauli ad Galat.* cap. 4. v. 2,—*Opp.* vii. 956. ed. 1703-6, has these words; " sed metu cohibetur, sed alieno arbitrio ducitur, sub *tutoribus* et actoribus agens," &c.: which are thus rendered in *The Paraphrase of Erasmus vpon the Newe Testament*, vol. ii. fol xiii. ed. 1548-9 ; " but is kept vnder with feare, and ruled as other men wyll, passyng that tyme vnder *creansers* and gouernours," &c. (Fr. *creanser*.)

v. 105. *primordialle*] i. e. original, earliest.

v. 106. *rybawde*] i. e. ribald.

—— *reclame*] i. e. tame,—a metaphor from falconry ; see note, p. 82. v. 1125.

v. 114. *bawdy*] i. e. foul ; see note, p. 101. v. 90.

Page 151. v. 117. *Thow*] i. e. Though.

—— *pyllyd*] i. e. scaldhead.

—— *sade*] i. e. sad,—sober, discreet,—wise (see the preceding line).

v. 120. *Thowth*] i. e. Though.

v. 122. *throw*] i. e. little while, moment.

v. 125. *thé froo*] i. e. from thee.

v. 127. *lewde*] i. e. ignorant.

Page 151. v. 127. *shrow*] i. e. curse.

v. 132. *Prickyd*] i. e. Pointed.

v. 133.   *I wold sum manys bake ink horne*
          Wher thi nose spectacle case]
—*manys*, i. e. man's: *bake*, i. e. back: *Wher*, i. e.
Were. Compare our author's poem against Dundas,
v. 37. vol. i. 215, and Bale's *Kynge Iohan*, p. 35. Cam-
den ed.

v. 135. *wyll*] i. e. well; as before in this poem.

v. 136. *ouyrthwarthe*] i. e. overthwart,—cross, per-
verse, cavillous, captious.

v. 144. *steuyn*] i. e. voice.

v. 145. *follest*] i. e. foulest.

Page 152. v. 146. *lyddyr*] Or *lither*,—is—sluggish,
slothful, idle; but the word is often used in the more
general meaning of wicked, evil, depraved.

v. 146. *lewde*] i. e. ignorant.

v. 147. *well thewde*] i. e. well dispositioned, well
mannered.

v. 148. *Besy*] i. e. Busy.

v. 149. *Syr Wrig wrag*] A term several times used
by Skelton; see note, p. 139. v. 186.

v. 151. *slyght*] i. e. trick, contrivance.

v. 153. *to mykkylle*] i. e. too much.

v. 154. *I xulde but lese*] i. e. I should but lose.

v. 155. *tragydese*] i. e. tragedies. Skelton does not
mean here dramatic pieces: compare his piece *Against
the Scottes*, v. 72. vol. i. 205. So Lydgate's celebrated
poem, *The* TRAGEDIES, *gathered by Iohn Bochas, of
all such Princes as fell from theyr estates*, &c.

v. 157. *my proces for to saue*]—*proces*, i. e. story;
see notes, p. 75. v. 735. p. 79. v. 969. So our author
in his *Why come ye nat to Courte;*

" Than, our *processe for to stable.*"

v. 533. vol. ii. 294.

Page 152. v. 158. *xall*] i. e. shall.

v. 162. *a tyd*] i. e. betime.

v. 164. *Haruy Haftar*] See note, p. 30. v. 138.

v. 166. *xulde*] i. e. should.

v. 170. *hay . . . ray*] Names of dances, the latter less frequently mentioned than the former:

" I can daunce *the raye*, I can both pipe and sing."

Barclay's *First Egloge*, sig. A ii. ed. 1570.

v. 171. *fonde*] i. e. foolish.

v. 173. *lewdenes*] i. e. ignorance, baseness, worthlessness.

Page 153. v. 176. *spynt*] i. e. spent, employed.

v. 180. *I xall thé aquyte*] i. e. I shall requite thee.

AGAINST VENEMOUS TONGUES.

Page 154. *Psalm cxlij.*] *Vulg.* cxix. 3.

Psal. lxvii.] *Vulg.* li. 7.

v. 4. *Hoyning*] " *Hoigner.* To grumble, mutter, murmure ; to repine ; also, to whyne as a child or dog." Cotgrave's *Dict.* " *Hoi,* a word vsed in driuing hogges," says Minsheu ; who proceeds to derive it " a Gr. κοî, quod est imitatio vocis porcellorum." *Guide into Tongues.*

*—— *groynis*] i. e. grunts. See note, p. 127. v. 2.

—— *wrotes*] i. e. roots.

Page 155. v. 2. *made . . . a windmil of an olde mat*] The same expression occurs again in our author's *Magnyfycence,* v. 1040. vol. ii. 49.

v. 4. *commaunde*] i. e. commend.

—— *Cok wat*] See note, p. 31. v. 173.

Page 155. v. 2. *lack*] i. e. fault, blame.

* v. 3. *In your crosse rowe nor Christ crosse you spede*] — *crosse rowe*, i. e. alphabet; so called, it is commonly said, because a cross was prefixed to it, or perhaps because it was written in the form of a cross. See Nares's *Gloss.* in **v.** *Christ-cross.* [*Christ crosse me spede*, seems to have been the beginning of an early school lesson. Such a lesson preserved in MS. Rawl. 1032, commences, " Christe crosse me spede in alle my worke."

Halliwell, Dict.]

" How long agoo lerned ye *Crist crosse me spede ?* "
Lydgate's Prohemy of a mariage, &c.,—
MS. Harl. 372. fol. 50.

In *The Boke of Curtasye* we find ;

" Yff that thou be a ȝong enfaunt,
And thenke tho scoles for to haunt,
This lessoun schulle thy maister the merke,
Cros Crist the spede in alle thi werke."

The sec. Boke, p. 7.
(printed for the Percy Society.)

and see title of a poem cited p. 109. v. 296.

v. 7. *cognisaunce*] i. e. badge.

v. 1. *scole*] i. e. school, teaching.

—— *haute*] i. e. high, lofty.

v. 2. *faute*] i. e. fault.

* Page 156. v. 2. *faitours*] Used here as a general term of reproach,—scoundrels.

* —— *straught*] i. e. distracted.

v. 4. *liddrous*] i. e. evil, wicked.   See note, p. 147. v. 146.

—— *lewde*] i. e. ignorant, vile.

Page 156. v. 3. *vale of bonet of their proude sayle*]
— *vale*, i. e. lower : *bonet* means a small sail attached
to the larger sails.

* v. 4. *ill hayle*] i. e. ill success.   See note, p. 122.
v. 617.

v. 4. *vntayde*] i. e. untied, loose.

—— *renning*] i. e. running.

v. 7. *lewdly alowed*] i. e., perhaps, ignorantly ap-
proved of.

v. 9. *vertibilite*] i. e. variableness.

v. 10. *folabilite*] i. e. folly.

v. 12. *coarte*] i e. coarct, constrain.

v. 13. *hay the gy of thre*] Perhaps an allusion to the
dance called *heydeguies* (a word variously spelt).

Page 157. v. 2. *Pharaotis*] i. e. (I suppose) Pha-
raoh.

v. 1. *vnhappy*] i. e. mischievous.

v. 2. *atame*] i. e. tame.

Page 158. v. 1. *tratlers*] i. e. prattlers, tattlers.

v. 3. *Scalis Malis*] i. e. Cadiz.   " The tounes men
of Caleis, or *Caleis males*, sodainly rong their common
bell," &c.   Hall's *Chronicle* (Hen. viii.). fol. xiii, ed.
1548.   " His fortunatest piece I esteem the taking of
Cadiz Malez."   *A Parallel of the Earl of Essex and
the Duke of Buckingham,*—*Reliquiæ Wottonianæ,* p,
177. ed. 1672.

v. 4. *nut shalis*] i. e. nutshells.

v. 7. *ren*] i. e. run.

—— *lesinges*] i. e. falsehoods.

v. 8. *wrate suche a bil*] i. e. wrote such a letter.

v. 10. *ill apayed*] i. e. ill pleased, ill satisfied.

v. 1. *hight*] i. e. is called.

v. 2. *quight*] i. e. requite.

Page 158. v. 5. *Although he made it neuer so tough*]
The expression, *to make it tough*, i. e. to make difficulties, occurs frequently, and with several shades of
meaning, in our early writers; see R. of Gloucester's
Chronicle, p. 510. ed. Hearne, and the various passages cited in Tyrwhitt's *Gloss.* to Chaucer's *Cant.
Tales* in v. *Tough*. Palsgrave has " I *Make it tough,*
I make it coye, as maydens do, or persons that be
strange if they be asked a questyon." p. 624.

ON TYME.

Page 160. v. 5. *hym lyst*] i. e. pleases him.
v. 6. *couenable*] i. e. fit.
v. 10. *sad*] i. e. serious.
Page 161. v. 17. *trauell*] i. e. travail, labour.
v. 21. *prease*] i. e. press, throng.
v. 23. *lacke*] i. e. blame.
v. 24. *rotys*] i. e. roots.
—— *vere*] i. e. spring.
Quod] i. e. Quoth.

PRAYER TO THE SECONDE PARSON.

Page 163. v. 7. *Agayne*] i. e. Against.
v. 8. *woundis fyue*] A common expression in our
early poetry;

> " Jhesu, for *thi woundes five*, &c.
>
>   Minot's *Poems*, p. 5. ed. Ritson.

See too Dunbar's *Poems*, i. 229. ed. Laing.
v. 10. *blo*] i. e. livid.

WOFFULLY ARAID

Is mentioned by our author as one of his compositions in the *Garlande of Laurell*, v. 1418. vol. ii. 233.

With the opening of this piece compare Hawes's *Conuercyon of Swerers*, where Christ is made to exclaim,

" They newe agayne do hange me on the rode,
   They tere my sydes, and are nothynge dysmayde,
   My woundes they do open, and deuoure my blode :
   I, god and man, moost *wofully arayde*,
   To you complayne, *it maye not be denayde ;*
   Ye nowe to-lugge me, ye tere me at the roote,
   Yet I to you am chefe refuyte and bote."

and a little after,

   " Why arte thou *harde herted*, &c.
                                    Sig. A iii. ed n. d. 4to.

Barclay too has,

" Some sweareth armes, nayles, heart, and body,
   Tearing our Lorde worse then the Jewes him *arayde*."
                          The Ship of Fooles, fol. 33. ed. 1570.

Woffully araid is, I believe, equivalent to—wofully disposed of or treated, in a woful condition. " *Araye*, condicion or case, *poynt*." Palsgrave, p. 194.—(and see note, p. 105. v. 163).

" *Isaac.*   What have I done, fader, what have I
                     saide ?
   Abraham. Truly, no kyns ille to me.
   Isaac.   And thus gyltles shalle be *arayde*."
                          Abraham,—Towneley Mysteries, p. 40.

—" His [Tybert's] body was al to-beten, and blynde

on the one eye. Whan the kynge wyste this, that tybert was thus *arayed*, he was sore angry, &c." *Reynard the Fox*, sig. b 8. ed. 1481. Again in the same romance, when Isegrym the wolf has received a kick on the head from a mare, he says to Reynard, " I am so foule *arayed* and sore hurte, that an herte of stone myght haue pyte of me." Sig. f 4.

> " Who was wyth loue : more *wofully arayed*
> Than were these twayne."
> > > Hawes's *Pastime of Pleasure*, sig. I iiii.
> > > > ed. 1555.

" I am fowle *arayed* with a chyne cowgh. *Laceor pertussi.*" — " He was sore *arayed* with sycknesse. Morbo atrociter *conflictus est.*" Hormanni *Vulgaria*, sigs. H iii. I ii. ed. 1530.

Page 165. v. 4. *naid*] i. e. denied.

v. 8. *encheson*] i. e. cause.

v. 9. *Sith*] i. e. Since.

* v. 12. *fretid*] i. e. fretted, galled.

* v. 13. *threted*] i. e. threatened.

v. 14. *mowid*] i. e. made mouths at, mocked.

Page 166. v. 19. *hart rote*] i. e. heart-root.

v. 20. *panys*] i. e. pains.

—— *vaynys*] i. e. veins.

—— *crake*] i. e. crack.

v. 24. *Entretid thus in most cruell wyse,*
> *Was like a lombe offerd in sacrifice*]

Entretid, i. e. Treated. So in a " litel dite " by Lydgate, appended to his *Testamentum ;*

> " Drawen as a felon *in moost cruel wyse*
>
> . . . .
>
> *Was lik a lamb offryd in sacrifise.*"
> > > *MS. Harl.* 2255. fol. 64.

Page 166. v. 29. *bobbid*] i. e. struck.   So Lydgate in the piece just cited ;

> " Bete and eke *bobbid*."
>
> *Ibid.*

and in the *Coventry Mysteries*, Nichodemus seeing Christ on the cross, says

> " Why haue ȝe *bobbyd* and thus betyn owth
> All his blyssyd blood ? "
>
> *MS. Cott. Vesp.* D viii. fol. 186.

—— *robbid*] i. e. (I suppose) robed.   [Qy. stript ?]
* v. 30. *Onfayned*] Generally means un-glad, displeased, which even in the forced sense of—to my sorrow, is against the intention of the passage : it seems to be used here for—Unfeignedly : and see note, p. 160. v. 81.   [This word will perhaps bear the interpretation—not entreated, unasked.]
—— *deynyd*] i. e. disdained ;

> " Youth *dayneth* counsell, scorning discretion."
>
> Barclay's *Fifth Egloge*, sig. D ii. ed. 1570.

v. 33. *myȝt*] i. e. might.
Page 167. v. 39. *enterly*] i. e. entirely.
v. 43. *ȝytt*] i. e. yet.
v. 45. *race*] i. e. tear, wound.
v. 48. *Butt gyve me thyne hert*]—*hert*, i. e. heart. With this and v. 41 compare Lydgate's " litel dite " already cited ;

> " *Gyff* me thyn *herte*, and be no mor *vnkynde*."
>
> *MS. Harl.* 2255. fol. 66.

v. 49. *wrouȝt*] i. e. wrought, formed.
—— *bowgȝt*] i. e. bought, redeemed.

Page 167. v. 50. *hy3t*] i. e. high.

v. 55. *sawlys*] i. e. soul's.

v. 59. *Hytt*] i. e. It.

—— *nayd*] i. e. denied.

v. 60. *blow*] i. e. livid.

NOW SYNGE WE, &c.

This piece is mentioned by Skelton as his own composition in the *Garlande of Laurell*, v. 1420. vol. ii. 233.

Page 168. v. 1.

> *Now synge we as we were wont,*
> *Vexilla regis prodeunt*]

Compare Lydgate ;

> " Wherefore *I synge as I was wont,*
> *Vexilla regis prodeunt.*"
>
> > *Poem about various birds singing praises*
> > *to God,—MS. Harl.* 2251. fol. 38.

The hymn *Vexilla regis prodeunt,* &c. may be seen in *Hymni Ecclesiæ e Breviario Parisiensi,* 1838, p. 71. I ought to add that the present poem is not a translation of it.

v. 3. *on felde is* [*s*] *playd*] i. e. is displayed on field.

v. 4. *nayd*] i. e. denied.

v. 11. *thees*] i. e. thighs.

v. 13. *pyne*] i. e. pain.

v. 14. *spylt*] i. e. destroyed, put to death.

Page 169. v. 17. *dong*] i. e. dung, struck.

v. 25. *fote*] i. e. foot.

v. 31. *Syth*] i. e. Since.

v. 33. *chere*] i. e. spirit,—or reception.

v. 35. *lykes*] i. e. pleases.

Page 169. v. 40. *eysell*] i. e. vinegar.

Page 170. v. 51. *doone*] i. e. done.

v. 60. *isprode*] i. e. spread.

Page 171. v. 68. *payne*] i. e. labour, strive.

v. 71. *mys*] i. e. miss, fail.

v. 72. *Withouten nay*] i. e. Without contradiction, assuredly.

v. 74. *hardnes*] i. e. cruelty.

LATIN POEM.

Page 172. v. 7. *gentis Agarenæ*] i. e. of the race of Hagar.

WARE THE HAUKE.

This poem was evidently called forth by a real event; but the name of the " hawking parson " has not transpired. According to Barclay, skill in hawking sometimes advanced its possessor to a benefice;

" But if I durst truth plainely vtter and expresse,
  This is the speciall cause of this inconuenience,
  That greatest fooles, and fullest of lewdnes,
  Hauing least wit, and simplest science,
  Are first promoted, and haue greatest reuerence,
  For if one can flatter, and *beare a Hauke on his fist,*
  He shalbe made Parson of Honington or of Clist."
                        The Ship of Fooles, fol. 2. ed. 1570.

I may add, that afterwards, in the same work, when treating of indecorous behaviour at church, Barclay observes;

  " Into the Church then comes another sotte,
    Without deuotion, ietting vp and downe,

Or to be seene, and to showe his garded cote:
Another on his fiste a Sparhauke or Fawcone," &c.
fol. 85.

Page 173. v. 5. *abused*] i. e. vitiated, depraved.

" Be all yonge galandes of these *abused* sorte,
Whiche in yonge age vnto the court resorte ? "
Barclay's *Third Egloge*, sig. C ii. ed. 1570.

v. 8. *daw*] i. e. simpleton, fool.

* v. 10. *funte*] i. e. font.

v. 16. *him fro*] i. e. from him.

Page 174. v. 22. *dysgysed*] i. e. guilty of unbecoming conduct: so again in our author's *Colyn Cloute*;

" They mought be better aduysed
Then to be so *dysgysed*."
v. 581. v. ii. 145.

v. 30. *apostrofacion*] i. e. apostrophe.

v. 34. *wrate*] i. e. wrote.

v. 35. *lewde*] i. e. ignorant, worthless.

v. 42. *Dis*] Of which Skelton was rector; see *Account of his Life and Writings*.

v. 43. *fonde*] i. e. foolish.

—— *fauconer*] i. e. falconer.

* v. 44. *pawtenar*] i. e. a net-bag. " *Pautner* [*Pawtenere, MS. Harl.* 221.] Cassidile." *Prompt. Parv.* ed. 1499. " Will. Brito: *Cassidile* dicitur pera Aucupis in modum reticuli facta, in quo ponit quos in casse, id est, rete, cepit." Du Cange's *Gloss.* in v. " Pera . . . anglice a skryppe or a *pawtner.*" *Ortus Vocab.* fol. ed. W. de Worde, n. d.

Page 175. v. 48. *hogeous*] i. e. hugeous, huge.

v. 49. *auter*] i. e. altar.

v. 50. *craked*] i. e. talked vauntingly.

Page 175. v. 55. *yede*] i. e. went.

v. 56. *pray*] i. e. prey.

v. 60. *tyrid*] A term in falconry : the hawk *tired* on what was thrown to her, when she pulled at and tore it.

v. 62. *mutid*] i. e. dunged.

* —— *a chase*] i. e. a spot. Compare a passage in that curious tract, by Walter Smith, *xii Mery Jests of the wyddow Edyth ;*

> " Her potage & eke her ale were well poudred
> With an holsome influence that surgeons call
> Pouder Sinipari that wil make on cast his gall : "

in consequence of which, she is compelled suddenly to quit the supper-table, and,

> " When that she was vp, she got her foorth apace,
> And er she had walkt xxx fote, she marked *a chase*
> And eftsones another, thrugh the Hal as she yede," &c.
>
> Sig. f iii. ed. 1573.

" A *chase* at tennis is that spot where a ball falls, beyond which the adversary must strike his ball to gain a point or chace. At long tennis, it is the spot where the ball leaves off rolling." Douce's *Illust. of Shakespeare*, i. 485. Compare our author's *Why come ye nat to Courte*, v. 880. vol. ii. 306.

v. 63. *corporas*] i. e. communion-cloth, the fine linen cloth used to cover the *body*, or consecrated elements.

v. 65. *gambawdis*] i. e. gambols, pranks.

v. 66. *wexid*] i. e. waxed.

—— *gery*] " *Gerysshe*, wylde or lyght heeded, *farouche*." Palsgrave, p. 313.

" Howe *gery* fortune, furyous and wode."
> Lydgate's *Fall of Prynces*, B. iii. leaf lxxvii.
> ed. Wayland.

" And as a swalowe *geryshe* of her flyghte,
Twene slowe and swifte, now croked nowe vpright.'
> *Ibid.* B. vi. leaf cxxxiiii.

Tyrwhitt explains "*gery*—changeable." *Gloss.* to Chaucer's *Cant. Tales*. Richardson observes that in the present passage of Skelton " it seems to be *giddy* (sc.) with turning round." *Dict.* in v.

Page 175. v. 69. *the rode loft*] A loft (generally placed just over the passage out of the church into the chancel,) where stood the *rood*,—an image of Christ on the cross, with figures of the Virgin Mary and Saint John on each side of it: compare v. 126 of the present poem ;

> " His hawke then flew vppon
> *The rode with Mary and John.*"

v. 70. *perkyd*] i. e. perched.
v. 71. *fauconer*] i. e. falconer.
—— *prest*] i. e. ready.
v. 72. *dow*] i. e. pigeon.
* v. 73. *And cryed, Stow, stow, stow !*] So Fansy, in our author's *Magnyfycence*, exclaims to his bird, (which, however, appears to have been an owl)

> " *Stowe*, byrde, *stowe*, *stowe !*
> It is best I fede my hawke now."
> > v. 980. vol. ii. 47

Compare Brathwait's *Merlin ;*

> " But *stow*, bird, stow,
> > See now the game's afoote,

> And white-mail'd Nisus,
> He is flying to't."
> > *Odes*, p. 250, appended to *Natures*
> > *Embassie*, 1621.

" Make them come from it to your fist, eyther much or little, with calling and chirping to them, saying : Towe, Towe, or *Stowe, Stowe*, as Falconers vse." Turbervile's *Booke of Falconrie*, &c. p. 182. ed. 1611.

Page 176. v. 76. *lure*] [i. e. " that whereto faulconers call their young hawks, by casting it up in the aire, being made of feathers and leather in such wise that in the motion it looks not unlike a fowl." Latham, quoted by Halliwell, *Dict.*]

v. 78. *endude*] " She [the hawk] *Enduyth* whan her meete in her bowelles falle to dygestyon." *Book of St. Albans*, by Juliana Berners, sig. C iii.

v. 79. *ensaymed*] i. e. purged from her grease. " *Ensayme* of an hawke," says the lady just quoted, " is the greeys." Sig. A v. See too " How you shall enseame a Hawke," &c. in Turbervile's *Booke of Falconrie*, &c. p. 115. ed. 1611.

v. 80. *reclaymed*] i. e. tamed.

v. 81. *fawconer*] i. e. falconer.

—— *vnfayned*] Either, unfeignedly (in the next line but six is " not *fayne* nor forge ") or un-glad, displeased : see note, p. 154. v. 30.

v. 83. *lyst*] i. e. liking, inclination.

v. 85. *loked*] i. e. looked.

—— *the frounce*] Is a distemper in which a whitish foam gathers in wrinkles (frounces) about the hawk's mouth and palate. " The *Frounce* proceedeth of moist and cold humours, which descend from the hawkes head to their palate and the roote of the tongue. And of that cold is engendred in the tongue the *Frownce*," &c. Turbervile's *Booke of Falconrie*, &c. p. 303. ed. 1611.

Page 176. v. 87. *the gorge*] "Is that part of the Hawk which first receiveth the meat, and is called the Craw or Crop in other fowls." Latham's *Faulconry*. (Explan. of Words of Art,) 1658.

v. 89. *clap*] i. e. stroke.

v. 91. *sparred*] i. e. fastened, shut ("boltyd and barryd" being in the next line).

v. 93. *wyth a prety gyn*]—*gyn*, i. e. contrivance.

" And *with a prety* gynne
Gyue her husbande an horne."
The boke of mayd Emlyn, &c.
n. d. sig. A ii.

v. 100. *On Sainct John decollacion*] i. e. On the festival of the beheading of St. John.

Page 176. v. 103. *secundum Sarum*] So in Sir D. Lyndsay's *Complaynt of the Papingo;*

" Suppose the geis and hennis suld cry alarum,
And we sall serve *secundum usum Sarum*."
Works, i. 327. ed. Chal.

The proverbial expression, " It is done *secundum usum Sarum*," is thus explained by Fuller: " It began on this occasion; Many Offices or forms of service were used in severall Churches in England, as the Office of York, Hereford, Bangor, &c. which caused a deal of Confusion in Gods Worship, untill Osmond Bishop of Sarum, about the year of our Lord 1090, made that Ordinall or Office which was generally received all over England, so that Churches thence forward easily understood one another, all speaking the same words in their Liturgy. It is now applyed to those persons which do, and Actions which are formally and solemnly done, in so Regular a way by Authentick Precedents, and Paterns of unquestionable Authority, that no just exception can be taken thereat." *Worthies* (*Wilt-Shire*), p. 146. ed. 1662.

Page 177. v. 104. *Marche harum*] i. e. March hare.

v. 106. *let*] i. e. leave, desist.

v. 107. *fet*] i. e. fetch.

v. 110. *to halow there the fox*] — *halow*, i. e. halloo. " Men blewe the hornes and cryed and *halowed the foxe*." *Reynard the Fox*, sig. h 5. ed. 1481.

v. 112. *Boke*] i. e. Book.

* v. 114. *lectryne*] [i. e. reading-desk.]

" Sum syng at the *lectorne* with long eares lyke an asse."

Bale's *Kynge Johan*, p, 27. Camd. ed.

v. 116. *With, troll, cytrace, and trouy*] So in *Apius and Virginia*, by R. B., 1575 ;

" *With* hey tricke, how *trowle*, trey trip, and trey trace." Sig. B.

v. 117. *hankin bouy*] Compare *Thersytes*, n. d. ;

" And we wyll haue minstrelsy that shall pype *hankyn boby*."

p. 62. Roxb. ed.

and Nash's *Haue with you to Saffron-walden*, 1596 ; " No vulgar respects haue I, what Hoppenny Hoe and his fellow *Hankin Booby* thinke of mee." Sig. K 2 : and Brome's *Joviall Crew*, 1652 ; " he makes us even sick of his sadness, that were wont to see my Ghossips cock to day, mould Cocklebread, daunce clutterdepouch and *Hannykin booby*, binde barrels, or do any thing before him, and he would laugh at us." Act ii. sc. i. sig. D 2.

* P. 177. vv. 120, 121. *gospellers . . . pystillers*] i. e. [priests that chant the gospel and the epistle, respectively, at mass.]

v. 125. *gydynge*] " He controlled my lyuynge and *gydynge . . . . mores.*" Hormanni *Vulgaria*, sig. N vi. ed. 1530.

" Wise women has wayis, and wonderfull *gydingis.*"
>Dunbar's tale of *The Tua Maryit Wemen and the Wedo,—Poems,* i. 77. ed. Laing.

v. 127. *The rode with Mary and John*] See note on v. 69. p. 159.

v. 128. *fon*] i. e. fool.

v. 129. *daw*] i. e. simpleton.

Page 178. v. 137. *hawkis bels*] i. e. the bells attached to the feet of the hawk.

v. 138. *losels*] i. e. good-for-nothing fellows,—the same as *lorels,* which has several times occurred before (see note, p. 60. v. 488, &c.) : " Lorell or *losell* or lurdeyn." *Prompt. Parv.* ed. 1499. " Lorrell or *losell.*" Palsgrave, p. 241.

v. 142. *snappar*] i. e. stumble ; but see note, p. 12. v. 4.

v. 144. *loke*] i. e. look.

v. 146. *bokis*] i. e. books.

v. 149. *mayden Meed*] See the allegorical account of Meed in *Pierce Plowman ;* where we find,

" That is *mede the maid,* quod she, hath noyed me full oft."

>Sig. B iv. ed. 1561.

Page 178. v. 158. *toke*] i. e. took.

v. 159. *this*] Perhaps for *thus:* compare v. 181.

Page 179. v. 164. *Exodi*] i. e. the book of *Exodus.*

"In *Exodi* ben these mencions."

> Lydgate's *Fall of Prynces*, B. i. leaf vii.
> ed. Wayland.

v. 166. *Regum*] i. e. *The Third*, now called *The First*, *Book of Kings*.

v. 178. *the rode*] i. e. cross. See note on v. 69. p. 159.

v. 181. *this*] i. e. thus; see note, p. 2. v. 38.

v. 183. *dowues donge*] i. e. dove's dung.

Page 180. v. 194. *croked*] i. e. crooked.

—— *Cacus*] See extract from *The Recuyel of the Historyes of Troy*, in note, p. 168. v. 23.

v. 196. *Nother*] i. e. Neither.

—— *Olibrius*] Was " the provost " by whose order Saint Margaret, after being put to sundry tortures, was beheaded at Antioch. *Golden Legende*, fol. ccxiiii. sqq. ed. 1483. See also *The Legend of Seynt Mergrete*, printed from the Auchinleck MS., in Turnbull's *Legendæ Catholicæ*. Most readers will recollect Mr. Milman's dramatic poem, *The Martyr of Antioch*.

v. 198.   —— ——*Phalary,*
          Rehersed in Valery]

i. e. Phalaris, recorded in Valerius Maximus, lib. iii. cap. iii. (where it is related that the Agrigentines, at the instigation of Zeno Eleates, stoned the tyrant Phalaris to death. " 'Tis plain," says Bentley, "he mistakes Phalaris for Nearchus." *Diss. upon the Ep. of Phalaris,—Works*, i. 241. ed. Dyce), and lib. ix. cap. ii.

Page 180. v. 200. *Sardanapall*] So our early writers often spell his name ;

> " Last of all was *Sardanapall*."
>> Lydgate's *Fall of Prynces*, Boke ii.
>> leaf L. ed. Wayland.

v. 204. *Egeas*] Is mentioned with various other evil personages in *The Flyting of Dunbar and Kennedy*,

> " Herod thy uthir eme, and grit *Egeass*."
>> Dunbar's *Poems*, ii. 86. ed. Laing.

and in the Second Part of Marlowe's *Tamburlaine ;*

> " The headstrong jades of Thrace Alcides tamed,
> That King Egeus fed with humane flesh."
>> Last sc. of act iv. sig G 3. ed. 1606.

v. 205. *Syr Pherumbras*] See note, p. 124. v. 15.

v. 211. *poll by poll*] i. e. head by head,—one by one.

> " And ye shall here the names *poll by poll*."
>> *Cocke Lorelles bote*, sig. B ii.

Page 181. v. 212. *Arystobell*] i. e. (I suppose) Aristobulus,—who, having succeeded his father Hyrcanus as high-priest and governor of Judea, assumed the title of king,—cast his mother into prison, and starved her to death,—caused his brother Antigonus to be assassinated,—and died after reigning a year. See Prideaux's *Connect.* Part ii. B. vi.

v. 214. *miscreantys*] i. e. infidels. " These thre kynges were the fyrst of *myscreauntes* that byleued on cryst." *The three kynges of Coleyne*, sig. C ii. ed. 1526.

v. 216. *Sowden*] i. e. Soldan, Sultan.

v. 225. *pekysh*] See note, p. 55. v. 409.

v. 228. *crokid*] i. e. crooked.

Page 181. v. 230. *this*] i. e. thus; as before, see v. 181.

—— *ouerthwarted*] i. e. cavilled, wrangled. "To hafte or *ouerthwarte* in a matter, to wrangle." Baret's *Alvearie* in v.

v. 231. *proces*] i. e. subject-matter; see note, p. 75. v. 735, &c.

Page 182. v. 239. *rehers*] i. e. tell, declare.

v. 240. *sentence*] i. e. meaning.

v. 241. *scholys*] i. e. schools.

v. 242. *folys*] i. e. fools.

* v. 244. *Dawcocke*] i. e. simpleton. See note, p. 36. v. 301.

v. 249. *fista*] i. e. fist.

Page 183. v. 250. *you lista*] i. e. you please.

v. 260. *Dialetica*] i. e. Dialectica.

v. 264. *forica*] Is Latin for a public jakes; and compare vv. 62, 183: but I cannot determine the meaning of it here.

v. 270. *Jacke Harys*] Must not be mistaken for the name of the person who called forth this piece; we have been already told that he "shall be nameless," v. 38. So in our author's *Magnyfycence*, Courtly Abusyon terms Cloked Colusyon "cankard *Jacke Hare*." v. 768. vol. ii. 37. There is a poem by Lydgate (at least attributed to him) concerning a personage called *Jak Hare*, of which the first stanza is as follows

" A froward knave plainly to discryve,
  And a sluggard plainly to declare,
  A precious knave that cast hym never to thryve,
  His mowth wele wet, his slevis right thredebare,
  A tourne broche, a boy for wat of ware
  With louryng face noddyng and slombryng,

Of newe cristened called *Jak Hare,*
Whiche of a bolle can pluk out the lyneng."

MS. Harl. 2251. fol. 14.

Since the above note was written, the ballad on Jack Haré has been edited from *MS. Lansd.* 699. fol. 88. by Mr. Halliwell, among Lydgate's *Minor Poems,* p. 52 (printed for the *Percy Society*). "The original of this," says Mr. H. (p. 267), "is an Anglo-Norman poem of the 13th century, in MS. Digb. Oxon. 86. fol. 94, entitled ' De Maimound mal esquier.'"

Page 183. v. 274. *federis*] i. e. feathers.

Page 184. v. 284. *fisty*] i. e. fist.

v. 290. *Apostata*] This form, as an English word, continued in use long after the time of Skelton.

v. 291. *Nestorianus*] "*Nestoriani* quidam heretici qui beatam mariam non dei, sed hominis dicunt genitricem." *Ortus Vocab.* fol. ed. W. de Worde, n. d. : but here *Nestorianus* seems to be put for Nestorius, the founder of the sect.

v. 300. *This*] i. e. Thus; as before, see v. 181.

v. 301. *Dys church ye thus deprauyd*] To *deprave* generally means—to vilify in words (as in our author's *Colyn Cloute,* " *The Churche to depraue,*" v. 515. vol. ii. 143) ; but (and see the poem *Howe the douty Duke of Albany,* &c. v. 191. vol. ii. 327) here *deprauyd* must be equivalent to—defiled.

v. 305. *Concha*] " *Concha* recensetur vulgo inter vasa ac ministeria sacra, cujus varii fuere usus." Du Cange's *Gloss.*

v. 306. *sonalia*] i. e. the bells attached to the hawk's feet.

Page 185. v. 313. *Et relis et ralis,*
Et reliqualis]

Occurs again in our author's *Garlande of Laurell*, **v.** 1216. vol. ii. 223.

> v. 315. *Galis*] i. e. Galicia.
>
> v. 320. *chalys*] i. e. chalice.
>
> v. 324. *Masyd*] i. e. Bewildered, confounded.
>
> v. 325. *styth*] i. e. anvil.
>
> v. 327. *daw*] i. e. simpleton.

EPITAPHE, &c.

Page 187. v. 3. *this*] i. e. these.

v. 4. *queed*] i. e. evil. The word is common in our earliest poetry :

> " That euer schuld haue don him *qued.*"
>
> *Arthour and Merlin*, p. 51. ed. Abbotsf.

A DEUOUTE TRENTALE, &c.

trentale] i. e. properly, a service of thirty masses for the dead, usually celebrated on as many different days.

Page 190. v. 44. *I faith, dikkon thou crue*] See note, p. 39. v. 360.

> v. 46. *knauate*] i. e. knave.
>
> v. 47. *rode*] i. e. rood, cross ; see note, p. 159. v. 69.
>
> v. 53. *fote ball*] i. e. foot-ball.
>
> v. 61. *Wit*[*h*], *hey, howe, rumbelowe*] See note, p. 33. v. 252.

Page 192. v. 23.

> *Crudelisque Cacus*
> *barathro, peto, sit tumulatus*]

To readers of Skelton's days Cacus was known not so much from the 8th book of Virgil's *Æneid*, as from

The Recuyel of the Historyes of Troy, (a translation by Caxton from the French of Raoul le Fevre), where his story is related at considerable length, and with great variation from the classical fable: "In the cyte of Cartagene, a kynge and geant regned. named Cacus whiche was passyng euyll and full of tyrannye, and had slayn by his cursidnes the kynges of Aragon and of Nauerre. their wyues and their children And possessid her seignouryes and also helde in subieccion alle the contrey into ytaly," &c. Book ii. ed. 1471—about the middle of the volume, which is printed without paging or signatures. His death is afterwards thus described: "But hercules ranne after and retayned hym And enbraced hym in his armes so harde that he myght not meue And brought hym agayn And bare hym vnto a depe pytte that was in the caue where he had caste in all ordures and filthe, hercules cam vnto this fowle pytte that the grekes had founden And planted cacus there Inne. his heed dounward from on hye vnto the ordure benethe, Than the ytaliens cam aboute the pitte and caste so many stones vpon hym that he deyde there myserably. Suche was the ende of the poure kynge Cacus. he deyde in an hooll full of ordure and of styngkynge filthe."

v. 28. *best*] i. e. beast.

Page 193. *Apud Trumpinton scriptum per Curatum ejusdem, &c.*] A passage wrongly understood by Skelton's biographers: see *Account of his Life and Writings.*

Page 194.

Diligo rustincum cum portant bis duo quointum,
   Et cantant delos est mihi dulce melos]

The Rev. J. Mitford proposes to read—

Diligo rusticulum cum portat Dis duo quintum,
Et cantat Delos, est mihi dulce melos:

understanding *duo quintum* to mean decimum, a tenth
or tithe, and explaining the whole, I like the peasant
when he brings his tithe to Dis, and sings " Delos,"—
pays it from motives of devotion.

LAMENTATIO URBIS NORVICEN.

In 1507, the city of Norwich was " almost utterly
defaced " by two dreadful fires : the first broke out on
25th April, and lasted for four days; the second began
4th June, and continued for two days and a night.
See Blomefield's *Hist. of Norfolk*, ii. 131, ed. fol.

IN BEDEL, &c.

Page 195.   *Mortuus est asinus,*
              Qui pinxit mulum]

" *Mulum de asino pingere*, Dici potest, quando exem-
plar et res efficta non multum inter se distant; vel
quando ineptiæ ineptiis repræsentantur, vel mendacia
mendaciis astruuntur.   Magna similitudo inter asinum
et mulum est. Tertullianus. [*Adv. Valent.* cap. xix.]."
Erasmi *Adagia*, p. 1663. ed. 1606.

EPITAPHIUM IN HENRICUM SEPTIMUM.

Page 198. Henry the Seventh died April 21st,
1509, in the 24th year of his reign (see Sir H. Nicolas's
Chron. of Hist. pp. 333, 350. sec. ed.), and in the 52d

(according to some authorities, the 53d) year of his age ; and was interred in the splendid chapel which bears his name.

" Here lieth buried in one of the stateliest Monuments of Europe, both for the Chappell, and for the Sepulchre, the body of Henry the seuenth . . . This glorious rich Tombe is compassed about with verses, penned by that Poet Laureat (as he stiles himselfe) and Kings Orator, Iohn Skelton : I will take onely the shortest of his Epitaphs or Eulogiums, and most to the purpose.

> Septimus hic situs est Henricus, gloria Regum
> Cunctorum, ipsius qui tempestate fuerunt,
> Ingenio atque opibus gestarum et nomine rerum,
> Accessere quibus nature dona benigne :
> Frontis honos, facies augusta, heroica forma,
> Junctaque ei suauis coniux, perpulchra, pudica,
> Et fecunda fuit: felices prole parentes,
> Henricum quibus octauum terra Anglia debes."
>   Weever's *Anc. Fun. Mon.*, p. 476. ed. 1631.

But the above lines are not in Marshe's ed. of Skelton's *Workes ;* nor are they assigned to him in *Reges, Reginæ, Nobiles, et alii in Ecclesia Collegiata B. Petri Westmonasterii sepulti*, &c. 1603,—where they occur, sig. D.

—— *ad sinceram contemplationem reverendi in Christo patris ac domini, domini Johannis Islippæ abbatis Westmonasteriensis*] So Skelton again in his *Replycacion*, &c. " ad cujus auspicatissimam *contemplationem*, sub memorabili prelo gloriosæ immortalitatis, præsens pagella felicitatur, &c." vol. i. 230 ; and in his *Garlande of Laurell*,—

" Of my ladys grace *at the contemplacyoun,*
   Owt of Frenshe into Englysshe prose,
Of Mannes Lyfe the Peregrinacioun,
   He dyd translate," &c.

v. 1219. vol. ii. 224.

Compare also Hollinshed; " *At the contemplation* of
this cardinall, the king lent to the emperour a great
summe of monie." *Chron.* (Hen. viii.) vol. iii. 839. ed.
1587. Concerning the Abbot Islip see *Account of
Skelton and his Writings.*

Page 199. v. 19. *sua*] Used for *ejus.*

—— *Leo candidior Rubeum necat ense Leonem*]
Leo candidior, i. e. the Earl of Surrey, whose badge
was a White Lion : *Rubeum Leonem,* i. e. King James
the Fourth, slain at Flodden, who bore the royal arms
of Scotland, a Red Lion. See note on the poem
Against the Scottes, p. 179. v. 135.

TETRASTICHON VERITATIS.

Page 201. v. 1. *cuprum*] i. e. *cupreum.* " The
Tomb itself [principally of black marble], with the
metal statues which lie upon it, and the beautiful casts
in *alto-relievo* [of copper gilt], which ornament the
sides, were executed by the celebrated Italian artist
Pietro Torrigiano . . for the sum of 1500*l.* Its sur-
rounding Screen, or ' Closure ' [of gilt brass and cop-
per], which is altogether in a different style of work-
manship, though almost equally curious, was, most
probably, both designed and wrought by English
artizans." Neale's *Account of Henry the Seventh's
Chapel,* pp. 54, 59.

AGAINST THE SCOTTES.

The battle of Flodden, one of the most disastrous events in Scottish history, has been rendered so familiar to readers of our own day by the poem of *Marmion*, that a particular account of it here is unnecessary. It took place on September 9th, 1513. The English army was commanded by the Earl of Surrey (created Duke of Norfolk the February following); the Scottish by their rash and gallant monarch James the Fourth, who perished in the field amid heaps of his slaughtered nobles and gentlemen.

Page 202. v. 2. *tratlynge*] i. e. prattling, idle talk.

v. 5. *Lo, these fonde sottes, &c.*]—*fonde*, i. e. foolish. This passage resembles a rhyme made in reproach of the Scots in the reign of Edward the First:

> " These scaterand Scottes
> Holde we for sottes," &c.
> > Fabyan's *Chron.* vol. ii. fol. 140.
> > ed. 1559.

v. 11. *Branxton more*] i. e. Brankston Moor.

v. 12. *stowre*] Means generally—hardy, stout; here perhaps it is equivalent to—obstinate: but in Palsgrave we find " *Stowre* of conversation, *estourdy*," p. 326.

Page 203. v. 22. *closed in led*] The body of James, disfigured with wounds, was found the day after the battle; it was carried to Berwick, and ultimately interred in the priory of Shene: see Weever's *Anc. Fun. Mon.*, p. 394. ed. 1631. After the dissolution of that house, according to Stow's account, the body, enclosed in lead, was thrown into one of the lumber-rooms; and the head, which some workmen hewed off " for their foolish pleasure," was brought to London and buried in St. Michael's Church, Wood Street: *Survey*, B. iii. 81. ed. 1720.

Page 203. v. 26. *byllys*] i. e. bills,—a sort of beaked pikes,—battle-axes.

v. 30. *Folys and sottys*] i. e. Fools and sots.

v. 32. *crake*] i. e. vaunt.

v. 33. *To face, to brace*] So Borde in his *Boke of knowlege* introduces a Scotchman saying,

" I wyll boost my selfe, I wyll *crake and face*."

Sig. G 2. reprint.

Compare our author's *Magnyfycence*;

" *Cl. Col.*

By God, I tell you, I wyll not be *out facyd*.

By the masse, I warrant thé, I wyll not be *bracyd*."

v. 2247. vol. ii. 106.

and his *Garlande of Laurell*;

" Some *facers*, some *bracers*, some make great crackis."

v. 189. vol. ii. 178.

In Hormanni *Vulgaria* we find, " He *faceth* the matter, and maketh great crakes. *Tragice loquitur*, et ampullosa verba proiicit." Sig. P. iiii. ed. 1530. " He is not aferde to *face or brace* with any man of worshyp. Nullius viri magnitudinem *allatrare* dubitat." Sig. O ii. And in Palsgrave, p. 542, " I *face*, as one dothe that brauleth or falleth out with a nother to make hym a frayde, *Je contrefays des mines* . . . I dare nat passe by his dore, he *faceth and braceth* me so: . . . *il contrefayt tellement des mines*." ' I *Brace* or *face*, *Je braggue.* He *braced* and made *a bracyng* here afore the dore as thoughe he wolde haue kylled . . . . *Il braggoyt,*" &c. p. 462.

Page 203. v. 36. *ouerthwart*] i. e. cross, perverse, wrangling.

v. 41. *quayre*] i. e. quire,—pamphlet, book.

Page 204. v. 51. *sumner*] i. e. summoner (it generally meant what we now call apparitor).

v. 52. *greyth*] i. e. agreeth, suiteth.

v. 53. *Our kynge of Englande for to syght*]—*syght,* i. e. cite. While Henry viii. was encamped before Terouenne, James iv. sent his chief herald to him, with a letter (which may be found in Hall's *Chron.* (*Hen. viii.*), fol. xxix. ed. 1548), reckoning up the various injuries and insults he had received from Henry, and containing what amounted to a declaration of war, unless the English monarch should desist from hostilities against the French king.

v. 57. *kynge Koppynge*] Compare the *Coliphizacio,* where Cayphas exclaims—

" Therfor I shalle the name that ever shalle rew the,
  Kyng Copyn in oure game," &c.
                    Towneley Mysteries, p. 194,—

the Glossary informing us that " A coppin is a certain quantity of worsted yarn wound on a spindle, and the spindle then extracted,"—which may be true, though it does not explain the passage. Some game must be alluded to.

v. 59. *Hob Lobbyn of Lowdean*] So again our author in *Speke, Parrot;*
" *Hop Lobyn of Lowdeon* wald haue e byt of bred."
                    v. 74. vol. ii. 249.

Perhaps there is an allusion to some song or ballad : *Lowdean* is, I apprehend, Lothian.

* Page 204. v. 60. *what good ye can*] [i. e. what manners you know.]

v. 61. *Locrian*] i. e. Loch Ryan—a large bay in Wigtonshire, which, by approximating to the bay of Luce, forms the peninsula called the Rinns of Galloway. It is mentioned by Barbour ;

> " And at *Lochriane* in Galloway
> He schippyt, with all his menye."
>> *The Bruce*, B. xi. v. 36. ed. Jam.

In the poem *Howe the douty Duke of Albany*, &c. Skelton speaks of the Scots

> " Of *Locryan*,
> And the ragged ray
> Of *Galaway*."
>> v. 21. vol. ii. 322.

and in his verses against Dundas, he calls him

> " Dundas of *Galaway*."
>> v. 29. vol. i. 215.

See too v. 109 of the present poem. Our author uses Scottish names at random.

v. 62. *sence*] i. e. cense.

v. 63. *Saint Ionis towne*] i. e. Perth. Compare Langtoft's *Chronicle*, p. 333, ed. Hearne ; Minot's *Poems*, p. 6. ed. Ritson ; and Barbour's *Bruce*, B. ii. v. 53. ed. Jam. It is said that the Picts, after their conversion to Christianity, or the Scots, after their king had succeeded to the Pictish throne, consecrated the church and bridge of Perth to St. John the Baptist ; and that hence in process of time many persons gave to the town the name of St. Johnston : see Jamieson's note on the passage last referred to.

Page 204. v. 72. *tragedy*] See note p. 147. v. 155.

Page 205. v. 79. *enbybe*] i. e. wet.

v. 83. *Irysh keteringes*]—*Irysh*, i. e. Highlanders and Islesmen :

> " Than gert he all the *Irschery*
> That war in till his cumpany,
> *Off Arghile, and the Ilis alsua*," &c.
>> Barbour's *Bruce*, B. xiii. v. 233. ed. Jam.

—*keteringes* (see Jamieson's *Et. Dict. of Scot. Lang.* in v. *Cateranes*), i. e. marauders who carried off cattle, corn, &c.

v. 86. *armony*] i. e. harmony.

v. 89. *me adres*] i. e. apply myself.

v. 90. *proces*] i. e. story.

v. 91. *Jocky my jo*] Perhaps a fragment of some song or ballad. In Scotch, *Jocky* is the diminutive of *Jock*, the abbreviation of *John* : *jo* is sweetheart, dear, (*joy*).

v. 92. *summond*] See note on v. 53, page 175.

v. 97. *to*] i. e. too.

v. 98. *harrold*] i. e. herald. See note on v. 53.

v. 100. *pye*] i. e. magpie.

Page 206. v. 101. *Syr skyrgalyard*] So again our author in his *Speke, Parrot ;*

> " With, *skyregalyard*, prowde palyard, vaunteperler,
> ye prate."   v. 427. vol. ii. 269.

and in his poem *Howe the douty Duke of Albany*, &c. ;

> " Suche a *skyrgaliarde*."
>> v. 168. vol. ii. 327.

" William Johnstone of Wamphray, called the *Galliard*, was a noted freebooter. . . . His *nom de guerre* seems to have been derived from the dance called *The Galliard.* The word is still used in Scotland to express an active, gay, dissipated character." Scott's *Minst. of the Scott. Bord.* i. 305. ed. 1810. To *skir* (under which Richardson in his *Dict.* cites Skelton's term " a skyrgaliarde ") is to scour, to move rapidly.

Page 206. v. 101. *skyt*] i. e. hasty, precipitate.

v. 103. *layd*] " I *Laye* for me, or alledge to make my mater good." Palsgrave, p. 602.

v. 104. *not worth a fly*] A common expression in our early poetry ;

> " The goos saide then all this *nys worth a flie*."
> > Chaucer's *Ass. of Foules,—Workes,*
> > > fol. 235. ed. 1602.

v. 106. *brother*] James married Margaret sister of Henry the Eighth.

v. 109. *Gup*] See note, p. 20. v. 17.

—— *Syr Scot of Galawey*] See note on v. 61. p. 176.

v. 110. *fall*] i. e. fallen.

v. 111. *Male vryd*] i. e. ill-fortuned (Fr. *malheur*).

v. 117. *Scipione*] i. e. Scipio.

v. 119. *Thoughe ye vntruly your father haue slayne*] James iii. was slain by a ruffian whose name is not certainly known, under circumstances of great atrocity, in 1488, in a miller's cottage, immediately after his flight from the battle of Sauchie-burn, where his son (then in his 17th year) had appeared in arms against him. The mind of James iv. was haunted by remorse for his father's death ; and he wore in penance an iron girdle, the weight of which he every year increased.

Page 206. v. 121. *Dunde, Dunbar*] Scottish names used at random: so again in our author's verses against Dundas, " *Dunde, Dunbar*," v. 60. vol. i. 216 ; and in his poem *Howe the douty Duke of Albany*, &c. " *Dunbar, Dunde*," v. 24. vol. ii. 322.

v. 122. *Pardy*] i. e. *par dieu*, verily.

v. 124. *shent*] i. e. destroyed, brought to disgrace or punishment.

v. 128. *checkmate*] See note, p. 17. v. 29.

v. 129. *the castell of Norram*] In taking the Castle of Norham, James wasted some days, previous to the battle of Flodden, while he ought to have employed his forces in more important enterprises.

v. 130. *to sone*] i. e. too soon.

Page 207. v. 132. *bylles*] i. e. bills, axes. See note on v. 26. p. 174.

v. 133. *Agaynst you gaue so sharpe a shower*] *Shower* is often applied by our old writers to the storm, assault, encounter of battle :

" The *sharpe shoures* and the cruel rage
    Abyde fully of this mortall werre."
                    Lydgate's *Warres of Troy*, B. iv.
                        sig. Y iiii. ed. 1555.

" He was slawe yn *sharpe showre*."
                    Kyng Roberd of Cysylle,—*MS. Harl.*
                        1701. fol. 94.

and see our author's poem *Howe the douty Duke of Albany*, &c. v. 240. vol. ii. 329.

v. 135.
    The Whyte Lyon, there rampaunt of moode,
    He ragyd and rent out your hart bloode ;
    He the Whyte, and ye the Red]

The White Lion was the badge of the Earl of Surrey, derived from his ancestors the Mowbrays. His arms were Gules, on a bend between six cross croslets, fitchy, argent: after the battle of Flodden, the king granted to him " an honourable augmentation of his arms, to bear *on the bend thereof: in an escutcheon Or, a demi Lion rampant, pierced through the mouth with an arrow, within a double tressure flory and counter-flory Gules;* which tressure is the same as surrounds the royal arms of Scotland." Collins's *Peerage,* i. 77. ed. Brydges.

" If Scotlands Coat no marke of Fame can lend,
  That Lyon plac'd in our bright siluer-bend,
  Which as a Trophy beautifies our shield,
  Since Scottish bloud discoloured Floden-Field;
  When the proud Cheuiot our braue Ensigne bare,
  As a rich Jewell in a Ladies haire,
  And did faire Bramstons neighbouring vallies choke
  With clouds of Canons fire-disgorged smoke."
                    *Epistle from H. Howard Earle of Surrey to
                    Geraldine,*—Drayton's *Poems,* p. 86 [88],
                    ed. 8vo. n. d.

" George Buchanan reporteth that the Earle of Surrey gaue for his badge a Siluer Lion, which from Antiquitie belonged to that name, tearing in pieces a Lion prostrate Gules; and withall, that this which hee termes insolence, was punished in Him and his Posteritie," &c.   Drayton's note on the preceding passage.

—— *the Red*] The royal arms of Scotland.

Page 207. v. 139. *quyt*] i. e. requited.

v. 141. *swete Sainct George, our ladies knyght*] " Our Lady's knight " is the common designation of St. George: so in a song written about the same time as

the present poem, *Cott. MS. Domit.* A. xviii. fol. 248 ;
in *Sir Beues of Hamtoun*, p. 102. Maitl. ed. &c. &c.

Page 207. v. 144. *His grace beyng out of the way*]
i. e. Henry the Eighth being in France : see note on
v. 53. p. 175.

v. 148. *ye lost your sworde*] The sword and dagger,
worn by James at the battle of Flodden, are preserved
in the college of Heralds.   An engraving of them is
prefixed to Weber's ed. of the poem, *Flodden Field*.

v. 149. *buskyd*] i. e. hied.

——— *Huntley bankys*]   So again in our author's
verses against Dundas ;

> " That prates and prankes
>   On *Huntley bankes*."
>
> v. 57. vol. i. 216.

and in his *Why come ye nat to Courte ;*

> " They [the Scottes] play their olde pranckes
>   After *Huntley bankes*."
>
> v. 263. vol. ii. 285.

and in his poem *Howe the douty Duke of Albany*, &c. ;

> " Of the Scottes ranke
>   Of *Huntley banke*."
>
> v. 18. vol. ii. 321.

Here again Skelton uses a Scottish name at random.
The *Huntlybank*, where, according to the charming
old poem, Thomas the Rhymer met the Queen of
Faery, is situated on one of the Eldoun hills.

v. 153.
Of the kyng of Nauerne ye might take heed,
Vngraciously how he doth speed :

> *In double delynge so he did dreme,*
> *That he is kynge without a reme;*
> *And, for example ye would none take, &c.*]

—*reme*, i. e. realm. In a letter despatched from the
camp before Terouenne, in answer to the epistle of
the Scottish king (see note on v. 53. p. 175), Henry
says; "And yf *the example of the kyng of Nauarre*
beynge excluded from his royalme for assistence gyuen
to the Frenche kyng cannot restrayne you from this
vnnaturall dealynge, we suppose ye shall haue lyke
assistence of the sayde Frenche kynge as the kyng of
Nauarre hath nowe: *Who is a kynge withoute a
realme*, &c." Hall's *Chron.* (*Henry viii.*) fol. xxxi. ed.
1548. James, however, never received this letter: he
was slain before the herald who bore it could procure
a passage from Flanders.

Page 207. v. 158. *brake*] See note, p. 111. v. 324.

Page 208. v. 161. *Your beard so brym as bore at
bay*]—*brym*, i. e. fierce,—rugged, bristly. James
wore "his Beerde somethynge longe." Lelandi *Col-
lect.* iv. 285. ed. 1770.

v. 162. *Your Seuen Systers, that gun so gay*] Lind-
say of Pitscottie informs us that when James was
making preparations for his fatal expedition against
England, "he had sewin great cannones out of the
castle of Edinburgh, quhilkis was called the *Sewin
Sisteris*, castin be Robert Borthik; and thrie maister
gunneris, furnisched with pouder and leid to thame at
thair pleasure." *Cron. of Scotl.* i. 266. ed. 1814.
These canons were named *Sisters* because they were
all of the same great size and fine fabric. Concerning
Borthwick, master of the artillery to James, the fol-
lowing mention is made by Lesley: "Rex amplo sti-

pendio Robertum Borthuik, insignem tormenti fabricandi artificem donauit, vt tormenta bellica maiora in arce Edinburgensi aliquamdiu conflaret: quorum permulta hodie in Scotia reperiuntur, hoc versu incisa:

" Machina sum Scoto Borthuik fabricata Roberto."

De or. mor. et reb. gest. Scot. p. 353. ed. 1578.

Page 208. v. 169. *The Popes curse gaue you that clap*]—*clap*, i. e. stroke. James died under a recent sentence of excommunication for infringing the pacification with England.

v. 170. *Of the out yles the roughe foted Scottes*] i. e. the rough-footed Scots of the Hebrides : the epithet *rough-footed* was given to them, because they wore, during the frost, a rude sort of shoe, made of undressed deer-skin, with the hairy side outwards ; see MS. quoted in Pinkerton's *Hist. of Scotland*, ii. 397.

v. 171. *the bottes*] i. e. the worms.

v. 172. *dronken dranes*]—*dranes*, i. e. drones. The Editor of Skelton's *Workes*, 1736, printed " *dronken Danes* ; " and Weber (*Flodden Field*, p. 276) proposes the same alteration ; but though the Danes (as the readers of our early dramatists know) were notorious for deep potations, the text is right. Our author has again, in his poem *Howe the douty Duke of Albany*, &c. ;

" We set nat a prane
By suche a *dronken drane*."

v. 163. vol. ii. 326.

" *Drane*. Fucus." *Prompt. Parv.* ed. 1499. And compare *Pierce Plowman's Crede ;*

" And right as *dranes* doth nought but *drinketh* vp **the** huny." Sig. D i. ed. 1561.

Page 208. v. 175. *sumner*] [i. e. summoner, appa-ritor.] See note on v. 51. p. 175.

    v. 177. *to*] i. e. too.

    Quod] i. e. Quoth.

per desertum Sin] " Profectique sunt de Elim, et venit omnis multitudo filiorum Israel in *desertum Sin,* quod est inter Elim et Sinai," &c. *Exod.* xvi. 1. (*Vulgate*).

VNTO DIUERS PEOPLE THAT REMORD THIS RYMYNGE, &c.

Page 209. *remord*] i. e. censure. See note, p. 146. v. 101.

    v. 7. *makynge*] i. e. composing, composition.

    v. 8. *Their males therat shakynge*]—*males,* i. e. bags, wallets; compare our author's *Colyn Cloute ;*

> " I purpose to *shake oute*
> All my *connyng bagge.*"

v. 50. vol. ii. 127.

    v. 14. *brother*] See note, p. 178. v. 106.

    v. 21. *pyketh mood*] i. e. grows angry, picks a quarrel.

    v. 26. *recrayed*] i. e. recreant, false (the idea of *cowardice* is certainly not implied here.)

Page 210. v. 30. *died excommunycate*] See note, p. 183. v. 169.

    * v. 37. *that*] i. e. they that.

—— *ouerthwartes*] i. e. cross, perverse objections, cavils.

    * v. 38. *percase*] i. e. perchance.

CHORUS DE DIS, &c.

Dis] Of which Skelton was rector; see *Account of his Life and Writings.*

Page 211. vv. 17, 18. *Leo Candidus . . . Leo tu Rubeus*] See note, p. 179. v. 135.

CHORUS DE DIS, &c. SUPER TRIUMPHALI VICTORIA CONTRA GALLOS, &c.

These verses (placed immediately after the poems on the Battle of Flodden, in the eds.) relate to an event which happened about the same period. Henry viii. having in person invaded France, in conjunction with the Emperor Maximilian, they proceeded to the siege of Terouenne. An attempt on the part of Louis to relieve the town occasioned the Battle of the Spurs, August 16, 1513, in which the Duke of Longueville, Clermont, &c. were made prisoners. Terouenne surrendered to Henry on the 22d of that month, and its defences were razed to the ground on the 27th. In these dates I follow Lingard.

Page 212. v. 13. *Gloria Cappadocis, divæ milesque Mariæ*] i. e. St. George, whom our author has before termed " our Ladies knyght," see note, p. 180. v. 141. During this war, the Emperor, to flatter Henry's vanity, wore his badge of the red rose, assumed the cross of St. George, and accepted a hundred crowns daily as the soldier of the English king.

VILITISSIMUS SCOTUS DUNDAS, &c

" Georgius Dundas, Græce Latineque doctissimus habitus, Equitum Hierosolymitanorum intra Regnum Scotiæ præfectus, sed prius Aberdoniæ Professor. Scripsit diligenter, et laboriose. *Historiam Equitum Hierosolymitanorum*, lib. ii. Claruit anno MDXX." Dempsteri *Hist. Eccles. Gentis Scotorum*, &c. 1627. p. 234. This George Dundas was, I apprehend, the person who excited the wrath of Skelton.

Page 213. v. 1.
> *Anglicus a tergo*
> *caudam gerit*, &c.]

These three hexameters are, it would seem, the composition of Dundas.

" After this saynt austyn entryd in to dorsetshyre, and came in to a towne where as were wycked peple & refused his doctryne and prechyng vtterly & droof hym out of the towne castyng on hym the tayles of thornback or like fisshes, wherfore he besought almyghty god to shewe his jugement on them, and god sente to them a shameful token, for the chyldren that were borne after in that place had tayles as it is sayd, tyl they had repented them. It is sayd comynly that thys fyl at strode in kente, but blessyd be god at this day is no suche deformyte." *The lyf of saynt Austyn,* — *Golden Legende*, fol. clxxiiii. ed. 1483. See too *Nova Legenda Anglie* (by Capgrave), 1516. fol. xxx.

" *Anglos quosdam caudatos esse.*

Svspicabar quod de Anglorum caudis traditur, nugatorium esse, nec hoc meminissem loco, nisi ipsi An-

glicarum rerum conditores id serio traderent : nasci
videlicet homines, instar brutorum animalium caudatos
apud Strodum Angliæ vicum, ad ripam fluuii Meduciæ,
qui Roffensem, siue Rocestrensem agrum alluit. Nar-
rantque eius vici incolas, iumento quod D. Thomas
Canthuariensis episcopus insideret, per ludibrium cau-
dam amputasse, ob idque diuina vltione adnatas incolis
eius loci caudas : vt in hos fatidici regis carmen tor-
queri possit : Percussit eos (inquit) in posteriora
eorum, opprobrium sempiternum dedit illis. De
huiusmodi caudis quidam in hunc modum lusit :

Fertur equo Thomæ caudam obtruncasse Britannos,
   Hinc Anglos caudas constat habere breueis."
       *Anglicæ Descriptionis compendium, Per Guliel-
          mum Paradinum Cuyselliensem*, 1545. p. 69.

On the proverbial expression *Kentish Long-Tailes*,
Fuller has the following remarks. " Let me premise,
that those are much mistaken who first found this Pro-
verb on a Miracle of Austin the Monk . . . . . I say
they are much mistaken, for the Scæne of this Lying
Wonder was not laied in any Part of Kent, but pre-
tended many miles off, nigh Cerne in Dorsetshire.
To come closer to the sence of this Proverb, I conceive
it first of outlandish extraction, and cast by forraigners
as a note of disgrace on all the English, though it
chanceth to stick only on the Kentish at this Day.
For when there happened in Palestine a difference
betwixt Robert brother of Saint Lewis King of France
and our William Longspee Earle of Salisbury, heare
how the French-man insulted over our nation :

Matthew Paris. Anno Dom. 1250. pag. 790.

O timidorum caudatorum formidolositas ! quam beatus, quam mundus præsens foret exercitus, si a caudis purgaretur et caudatis.	O the cowardliness of these fearful Long-tails ! How happie, how cleane would this our armie be, were it but purged from tails and Long-tailes.

That the English were nicked by this speech appears by the reply of the Earle of Salisbury following still the metaphor; The son of my father shall presse thither to day, whither you shall not dare to approach his horse taile: Some will have the English so called from wearing a pouch or poake, (a bag to carry their baggage in) behind their backs, whilest probably the proud Monsieurs had their Lacquies for that purpose. In proof whereof they produce ancient pictures of the English Drapery and Armory, wherein such conveyances doe appear. If so, it was neither sin nor shame for the common sort of people to carry their own necessaries, and it matters not much whether the pocket be made on either side, or wholly behinde. If any demand how this nick-name (cut off from the rest of England) continues still entaild on Kent? The best conjecture is, because that county lieth nearest to France, and the French are beheld as the first founders of this aspersion. But if any will have the Kentish so called from drawing and dragging boughs of trees behind them, which afterwards they advanced above their heads and so partly cozened partly threatned King William the Conqueror to continue their ancient customes, I say, if any will impute it to this original, I will not oppose." *Worthies* (*Kent*, p. 63), ed. 1662. The preceding passage of Fuller, somewhat abridged, is copied by Ray into his *Proverbs*, p. 245. ed. 1768. For fanciful stories concerning the origin of Kentish long-tails, see also *Cornv-copiœ, Pasquils Night-cap*, 1612, (attributed to S. Rowlands), p. 42. sqq.; and the commencement of *Robin Good-fellow, His mad Prankes and Merry Jests*, 1628, (a tract which originally appeared at an earlier date).

Page 214. v. 1. *Gup*] See note, p. 20. v. 17.

v. 23. *Agayn*] i. e. Against.

Page 215. v. 26. *dur*] i. e. door.

v. 28. *Go shake thy dog, hey*] In our author's *Magnyfycence*, v. 306. vol. ii. 17, is,—

" *Go, shake the dogge, hay,* syth ye wyll nedys."

and had the expression occurred only in these two passages of Skelton, I should have felt confident that in the present one " thy " was a misprint for " the," and that both were to be explained—" Go shake thee, dog," &c.; but again, in his poem *Howe the douty Duke of Albany*, &c. v. 159, vol. ii. 326, we find,

" Twyt, Scot, *shake thy dogge, hay!* "

v. 34. *hose*] i. e. breeches.

v. 37. *A spectacle case, &c.*] See note, p. 147. v. 133.

v. 40. *A tolman to blot*] A friend queries " tal man ? " but *tolman* is, I believe, pen-man : compare our author's third poem *Against Garnesche ;*

" Had ye gonne with me to scole,
And occupyed no better your *tole* [i. e. pen]," &c.
v. 117. vol. i. 143.

also the commencement of the present piece,—

" Gup, Scot,
Ye *blot*."

Page 215. v. 41. *rough foted*] See note, p. 183. v. 170.

v. 43. *depraue*] i. e. vilify, defame.

v. 44. *reame*] i. e. realm.

* v. 56. *rankis*] i. e. bluster, &c., from, *rank*, proud, haughty.

v. 58. *Huntley bankes*] See note, p. 181. v. 149.

v. 60. *Dunde, Dunbar*] See note 179. v. 121.

v. 63. *to far*] i. e. too far.

ELEGIA IN COMITISSAM DE DERBY.

This illustrious and excellent lady, born in 1441, was Margaret, the only child of John Beaufort, Duke of Somerset. Her first husband was Edmund, Earl of Richmond, who died in 1456, a little more than a year after their marriage, the sole issue of which was Henry, afterwards King Henry the Seventh. Her second husband was Sir Henry Stafford, second son of Humphrey, the great Duke of Buckingham. Her third husband was Thomas Lord Stanley, afterwards the first Earl of Derby of his name. Having survived him, as also her son King Henry, she died June 29, 1509, in her 69th year, and was buried in the magnificent chapel then lately erected in Westminster Abbey.

Page 217. v. 5. *polyandro*] *Polyandrum* or *polyandrium*, (properly, *multorum commune sepulchrum—πολυάνδριον*)—" Interdum et sæpius apud ævi inferioris scriptores sumitur pro monumento aut sepulcro unius hominis." Du Cange's *Gloss.*—Here it means, of course, the tomb of Henry VII.—Whiting has anglicised the word in a poem appended to his *Albino and Bellama*, 1638 ;

" King Ethelbert's clos'd in his *Poliander*."

Sig. H 7.

Page 217. v. 7. *Titus hanc, &c.*] i. e. Livy, who gives an account of Tanaquil, wife of Tarquinius Priscus: see his *Hist.* i. 34, &c.—" Tanaquilem Sidonius Apollinaris et Ausonius pro egregia uxore." Cassellii *Var.* lib. i. c. xiii. p. 210 (Gruteri *Lampas*, iii.).

Page 218. v. 19. *Abyron*] i. e. Abiram: see *Numbers*, ch. xvi.

v. 25. *periturœ parcere chartœ*] Juvenal, *Sat.* i. 18.

—— *phagolœdoros*] i. e. (φαγολοιδόρους) *convicia et maledicta devorantes*.

WHY WERE YE CALLIOPE, &c.

were, i. e. wear: concerning this dress, worn, it would seem, by Skelton as Laureat, see *Account of his Life and Writings*.

Page 219. v. 16. *somdele sere*] i. e. somewhat dry, withered.

v. 17. *fayne*] i. e. glad, willing.

THE BOKE OF THREE FOOLES.

This piece is a paraphrase of three portions of Brant's *Ship of Fools:* see the Latin version by Locher, *Stultifera Nauis*, ed. 1497,—*Vxorem ducere propter opes*, fol. lx., *De livore et inuidia*, fol. lxi., and *De voluptate corporali*, fol. lviii.: the same sections will be found accompanying Barclay's *Ship of Fooles*, ed. 1570,—fol. 95, fol. 97, and fol. 92.

Page 221. v. 3. *lygnage femynatyfe*] i. e. lineage feminine.

v. 9. *sythe*] i. e. since.

Page 222. l. 7. *iyen*] i. e. eyes.

—— *loke*] i. e. look.

l. 8. *folysh*] i. e. foolish.

l. 9. *Pecunyous*] i. e. Money-loving.

l. 10. *bee*] i. e. by.

l. 11. *wyddred*] i. e. withered.

l. 12. *nobles*] i. e. the gold coins so called.

l. 15. *habandoneth*] i. e. abandoneth.

—— *for to gather togyther the donge* . . . . . *grese*]
In the Latin of Locher ;

" Aruinam multi quærunt sub podice asselli :
     Et cumulant trullas : stercora vana petunt."
                                   fol. lx. ed. 1497.

l. 26. *thoughte*] i. e. care. See note p. 27. v. 27.

l. 29. *debylyte*] i. e. debilitated.

—— *vnpropyce*] i. e. unpropitious.

Page 223. l. 2. *esperaunce*] i. e. hope, expectation.

l. 3. *lygnage*] i. e. lineage.

l. 4. *demoraunce*] i. e. abiding.

l. 6. *leseth*] i. e. loseth.

l. 13. *cure*] i. e. care.

Page 224. l. 4. *conninge*] i. e. knowledge, learning,
attainments.

l. 10. *whereas*] i. e. where.

l. 14. *corrompeth*] i. e. corrupteth,—destroyeth.

l. 22. *defende*] i. e. forbid.

l. 29. *condycions*] i. e. qualities. See note, p. 132.
v. 12.

Page 225. l. 2. *dyssypers*] i. e., I suppose, disperser

l. 3. *brennest*] i. e. inflamest.

l. 4. *sleeth*] i. e. slayeth, (slayest).

l. 6. *traueyleth*] i. e. causeth travail (trouble) to.

l. 15. *reclaymeth*] i. e. proclaimeth.

Page 225. l. 16. *courage*] i. e. heart, mind, disposition.

l. 18, *adnychell*] i. e. annihilate.

l. 24. *flambe*] i. e. flame.

l. 26. *where as*] i. e where.

l. 27. *odyfferaunt*] i. e. odoriferous.

l. 30. *tho*] i. e. those.

Page 226. l. 2. *dissolate*] i. e. dissolute.

* l. 15. *glauca*] Properly *glaucus*.

l. 16. *eyen beholdinge a trauers*] i. e. eyes looking cross, awry.

l. 17. *syntillously*] i. e. so as to emit sparks.

l. 25. *were delybered*] i. e. were advised, were minded.

l. 27. *domage*] i. e. damage, loss.

Page 227. l. 2. *brenneth*] i. e. burneth.

l. 4. *edefyed*] i. e. built.

l. 8. *egally*] i. e. equally, justly.

l. 13. *Cayme*] i. e. Cain (a misprint probably).

l. 14. *semblablye*] i. e. likewise.

l. 17. *Thesius*] Should of course be *Thyestes*, as in Locher's Latin: yet Barclay, in his version of the passage, has,

> " Atreus storye and *Theseus* cruel."
>
> *The Ship of Fooles*, fol. 96. [99], ed. 1570.

l. 23. *rested*] i. e. roasted.

l. 26. *Ethiocles*] So written in Locher's Latin for Eteocles ; and so Lydgate,—

> " But make youre myrroure of *Ethyocles*."
>
> *Storye of Thebes, Pars Prima*,
> sig. C v. ed. 4to. n. d.

Page 228. l. 5. *collacion*] Equivalent here, I believe, to comparison.

Page 228. l. 11. *cautellous*] i. e. crafty, wily.

l. 21. *pill*] i. e. strip.

l. 23. *cheseth*] i. e. chooseth.

* Page 229. l. 10. *thoughte*] i. e. sadness. See note, p. 27. v. 27.

l. 22. *sith*] i. e. since.

l. 23. *asprely*] i. e. roughly, severely.

—— *enforce*] i. e. exert.

A REPLYCACION, &c.

Concerning the " yong scolers " against whom this piece was composed, I can give no information.

Page 230. l. 11. *contemplationem*] See note, p. 170, title of Epitaph.

* l. 4. *remordyng*] i. e. rebuking. See note, p. 146. v. 101.

* l. 5, *recrayed*] i. e. recreant. See note, p. 184. v. 26.

Page 232. l. 1. *enbolned*] i. e. swollen, puffed up.

l. 3. *pipplyng*] i. e. piping: compare our author's *Garlande of Laurell*, v. 676. vol. ii. p. 200.

l. 5. *lusty*] i. e. pleasant, desirable.

l. 9. *sped*] i. e. versed.

l. 10. *connyng*] i. e. knowledge, learning.

v. 8. —— *in the Uyntre*
At the Thre Cranes]

Here the tavern with the sign of the Three Cranes is meant: the *three cranes* were originally three strong cranes of timber, placed on the Vintry-wharf, for lifting from the ships the vessels of foreign wine which were landed there.

Page 233. v. 2. *enflamed*] i. e. burned.

Page 233. l. 1 (of prose). *Over*] i. e. besides.

—— *processe*] i. e. treatise.

l. 6. *tetrycall*] i. e. sour, sullen, gloomy.

l. 7. *friscaioly*] So in the *Interlude of the iiii Elementes*, n. d. ;

> " Synge *fryska Joly* with hey troly loly."
>
> Sig. B ii.

* l. 8. *moche better bayned than brayned*] i. e. better boned than brained.

* l. 10. *burblyng*] i. e. bubbling. " I *Burbyll*, a spring up, as water dothe out of a spring." Palsgrave, p. 472.

Page 234. l. 1. *perihermeniall principles*] i. e. principles of interpretation.

l. 3. *leudly*] i. e. ignorantly—or perhaps, wickedly.

l. 9. *surcudant*] i. e. presumptuous, arrogant.

l. 10. *popholy*] Occurs again several times in our author's writings, and with the more correct spelling,— *popeholy*. In *Pierce Plowman* we find,

> " And now so singuler by him selfe, nor so *pope holy*."
>
> Sig. T ii. ed 1561.

In Chaucer's *Romount of the Rose* is the following description ;

> " Another thing was doen their [there] write,
> That seemed like an ipocrite,
> And it was cleped *pope holy*,
> That ilke is she that priuily
> Ne spared neuer a wicked deed
> When men of her taken none heed,
> And maketh her outward precious,
> With pale visage and piteous,
> And seemeth a simple creature," &c.
>
> *Workes*, fol. 111. ed. 1602.

The original French of the preceding passage is,—

> " Une autre imaige estoit escripte,
> Qui sembloit bien estre ypocrite,
> *Papelardie* est appellée," &c.
> > *Le Rom. de la Rose,* vol. i. 15. ed. 1735,

Roquefort (*Gloss. de la Langue Romaine*) cites these lines under "*Papelardie,* papelardise : Hypocrisie, tromperie, subtilité, mauvaise foi." See too Du Cange's *Gloss.* in vv. *Papelardia, Papelardus.* Compare also Lydgate ;

> " And for *popholy* and uyce loke wel aboute."
> > *The prohemy of a mariage,* &c.,—
> > *MS. Harl.* 372. fol. 51.

and Barclay ;

> " Ouer sad or proude, disceitfull and *pope holy.*"
> > *The Ship of Fooles,* fol. 57. ed. 1570.

and the *Interlude of the iiii Elementes,* n. d.

> " For rather than I wolde vse suche foly
> To pray, to study, or be *pope holy,*
> I had as lyf be ded." Sig. B ii.

Page 234. l. 19. *orgulyous*] i. e. proud, insolent.

v. 22. *vnbrent*] i. e. unburnt.

Page 235. v. 23. *content*] As the marginal note has *Convenio,* is it not a misprint for " convent ? "

v. 24. *leudly*] i. e. badly, wickedly.

v. 26. *disable*] i. e. disqualify, degrade, disparage : " *disablinge* hymself in wordes, though his entent was otherwise."

> > Hall's *Chron.* (*Hen. viii.*) fol. lvii. ed. 1548.

v. 37. *ianglyng*] i. e. babbling, chattering,—noisy.

v. 38. *clawes*] i. e. clause.

Page 235. v. 39. *poppyng dawes*] Compare our author's *Why come ye nat to Courte;*

> "*Poppynge* folysshe *dawes.*"
>
> v. 261. vol. ii. 285.

and v. 121 of the present piece ;

> "And porisshly *forthe popped*
> Your sysmaticate sawes."

"*Popping*, blabbing, like a popinjay or parrot." *Gloss.* to *Exmoor Scolding: dawes,* i. e. simpletons.

v. 45. *recrayed*] i. e. recreant. See note, p. 184. v. 26.

v. 48. *baudrie*] i. e. foul language : see note, p. 101. v. 90.

v. 50. *to*] i. e. too.

Page 236. v. 54. *confettred*] i. e. confederated.

v. 61. *attamed*] i. e. tamed.

v. 65. *sorte*] i. e. set, company.

v. 66. *fayne*] i. e. glad.

v. 75. *Te he, &c.*] Expressions of laughter ;

> "*Te he,* quod she, and clapt the window to."
>
> Chaucer's *Milleres Tale,* v. 3738. ed. Tyr.

v. 76. *mo*] i. e. more.

* v. 77. *wo*] i. e. sad.

Page 237. v. 87. *reny*] i. e. renounce, abjure.

v. 89. *brende*] i. e. burnt.

v. 92. *discured*] i. e. discovered.

v. 95.   *Ye are vnhappely vred.*
>   *In your dialecticall, &c.*]

The old (and unique) copy is without punctuation in this passage ; but that the first line closes the sense, and that Skelton did not mean that these heretics were *unhappely ured in their dialectical,* &c. would appear from a comparison of other passages:

> " Agaynst these heretykes,
> Nowe of late abiured,
> Most *vnhappely vred:*
> For be ye wele assured,"
>
> v. 403 of the present piece.

" But men nowe a dayes so *vnhappely be vryd,*
That nothynge than welth may worse be enduryd."

Magnyfycence, v. 6. vol. ii. 3.

> " O Scottes pariured,
> *Vnhaply vred,*
> Ye may be assured," &c.
>
> *Howe the douty Duke of Albany,* &c.
v. 125. vol. ii. 325.

In our author's *Colyn Cloute* we find,

> " Wherfore he hath good *vre,*" &c.
>
> v. 1003. vol. ii. 160.

in the note on which line I have cited various examples of *vre* in the sense of—hap, luck ; and in his poem *Against the Scottes,*

> " *Male vryd* was your fals entent,"
>
> v. 111. vol. i. 206.

which surely means—Ill-fortuned, &c. (Fr. *malheur*). Is *vnhappely vred* to be considered as nearly synonymous with *male vryd,* or is it to be explained,—unhappily (evilly) *used,* practised, habituated ?

Page 237. v. 98.

> *If ye to remembrance call*
> *Howe syllogisari*
> *Non est ex particulari,*

Neque negativis,
Recte concludere si vis]

" *Nullus syllogismus categoricus communis, vel ex solis particularibus, vel ex solis negativis constare potest.* Hanc [regulam] expresse tradit Aristoteles libro primo Prior. capite 24. numero primo. Hinc metrum hoc natum :

> Ex *particulari* non est syllogizari,
> Neque *negativis,* recte concludere si vis."
>> Crakanthorp's *Logicæ Libri Quinque,*
>> 1622. p. 279.

Page 237. v. 107. *Your hertes than were hosed*] i. e. Your hearts were in your hose (breeches) : so again our author in his *Why come ye nat to Courte ;*

> " Their *hertes be in thyr* hose."
>> v. 286. vol. ii. 286.

See too Ray's *Proverbs,* (Scottish), p. 292. ed. 1768.

Page 238. v. 113. *quosshons*] i. e. cushions.

v. 115. *Harpocrates*] The God of Silence.

v. 120. *folysshly*] i. e. foolishly.

—— *fopped*] A singular example of the word as a verb.

v. 121. *porisshly*] In our author's *Garlande of Laurell* is " *porisshly* pynk iyde," v. 626. vol. ii. 197 (and Palsgrave has " *Porisshly,* as one loketh that can nat se well") ; see note on the passage : but I cannot determine the meaning of the word here.

v. 124. *dawes*] i. e. simpletons.

v. 126. *elenkes*] i. e. elenchs (*elenchus*—in logic).

v. 132. *prouoke and tyse*] i. e. incite and entice.

Page 239. v. 143. *exhibycion*] i. e. allowance of money.

Page 239. v. 144. *skoles*] i. e. schools.

v. 145. *foles*] i. e. fools.

v. 147. *founde*] i. e. maintained.

v. 156. *brute*] i. e. saying, proverb.

v. 165. *skyes*] i. e. clouds.

v. 168. *dawns*] i. e. dance.

v. 169. *ray*] A dance: see note, p. 148. v. 170.

v. 171. *lay*] i. e. law.

* v. 172. *shayle*] i. e. walk crookedly. See note, p. 18. v. 19.

Page 240. v. 175. *babyls*] i. e. baubles.

v. 196. *face*] i. e. face out.

y. 199. *to*] i. e. too.

Page 241. v. 204. *lollardy*] i. e. heretical. "*Lollar*, heretique." Palsgrave, p. 240.

v. 206. *predycacion*] i. e. declaration,—or preaching.

v. 207. *knowlege*] i. e. acknowledge.

v. 212. *muse*] Is properly the opening in a fence or thicket, through which a hare, or other beast of sport, is accustomed to pass: see Nares's *Gloss.* in v. and Moor's *Suff. Words*, in v. *Mewse.*

v. 215.   *With blowyng out your hornes,*

.   .   .   .   .   .

With chatyng and rechatyng]
Whatever Skelton may have meant by "chatyng,"— (perhaps he uses it for *chatting*,— in the next line we have "pratyng"),— *rechatyng* is properly a hunting-term, and signifies sounding the *rechate* or *recheat* (Fr.), a certain set of notes blown with the horn to recall the dogs.

v. 219. *pystels*] i. e. epistles.

v. 220. *bremely*] i. e. fiercely, roughly.

Page 242. v. 234. *lydder*] i. e. bad.

v. 247. *popeholy*] See note on prose of this piece, l. 10. p. 195.

v. 260. *echone*] i. e. each one.

Page 243. v. 264. *iangle*] i. e. babble, chatter.

v. 267. *the people of lay fee*] i. e. the laity ; as again in our author's *Colyn Cloute ;*

> " *The lay fee people* rayles."
>
> > v. 403. (where MS. omits " fee ")
> >
> > vol. ii. 138.

fee, i. e. possessions ; see Tyrwhitt's *Gloss.* to Chaucer's *Cant. Tales*, Jamieson's *Et. Dict. of Scot. Lang.*, and Todd's *Johnson's Dict.* in v.

v. 274. *snapper*] i. e. stumble ; but see note, p. 12. v. 4.

v. 280. *mo*] i. e. more.

v. 281. *latria*] " Le culte que nous déférons à Dieu seul, nous l'appellons *Latrie* [λατρεία]." *Perroniana*, p. 312. ed. 1740.

v. 285.

> *But, I trowe, your selfe ye ouersé*
> *What longeth to Christes humanyte.*
> *If ye haue reed de hyperdulia,*
> *Than ye knowe what betokeneth dulia*]

—*ouersé* i. e. overlook : *longeth*, i. e. belongeth. " L'adoration de *Superdulie* est celle qui se défère à la Vierge, et elle est plus eminente pour la grace qu'elle a reçu de Dieu, plus particulière que les autres Saints, pour avoir porté le Fils de Dieu en ses entrailles." *Perroniana*, p. 71. " Aux Saints nous déférons l'honneur qu'on appelle *Dulie*." Id. p. 312. ed. 1740. " *Dulia* [δουλεία] enim adoratio est, quæ etiam creaturæ exhibetur, quæ duas species habet, unam quæ hominibus indifferenter, alteram quæ soli humanitati Christi exhibetur." Gaufridus Abbas in Epist. ad Albinum Cardinalem,—cited by Du Cange, *Gloss.* in v.

Page 244. v. 293. *mased*] i. e. bewildered, confounded.

v. 295. *brent*] i. e. burned.

v. 296. *busynesse*] i. e. trouble.

v. 297. *vyse*] i. e. advise.

v. 298. *scoles*] i. e. schools.

Page 245. v. 303. *replycable*] i. e. such as can be replied to.

* Page 246. v. 323. *remorded*] i. e. carped at, objected to: see note, p. 146. v. 101.

v. 225. *his pystell ad Paulinum*] i. e. his Epistle *ad Paulinum presbyterum de omnibus divinæ historiæ libris,* prefixed to the Vulgate: the passage quoted by Skelton is also to be found in Hieronymi *Opera,* I. 1011. ed. 1609.

—— *Serenus*] The Scholium on this name in Hieronymi *Opera* is; " Aulus Serenus lyricus ipse etiam fuit, et, ut Terentianus est auctor, eleganti ac facili ingenio, et ad jocos amoresque describendos accommodato: Martianus Capella ac Nonius sæpius ejus carmina citant." I. 1017. ed. 1609.—See also an account of Serenus, prefixed to his extant pieces, in Wernsdorf's *Poetæ Latini Minores,* tom. ii.

Page 247. v. 337. *armony*] i. e. harmony.

* —— *processe*] i. e. course, discourse, treatise.

Page 248. v. 359.

> *For if ye sadly loke,*
> *And wesely rede the Boke*

> *Of Good Aduertysement,*
> *With me ye must consent, &c.*]

sadly loke, i. e. seriously look, consider. In the *Garlande of Laurell* Skelton mentions, as one of his own compositions,

Item *Good Aduysement,* that brainles doth blame.

v. 1186. vol. ii. 222.

Qy. does he allude to it here ?

Page 249. v. 395. *avaunce*] i. e. advance.

v. 399. *make*] i. e. compose.

v. 405. *vnhappely vred*] See note on v. 95. p. 197.

NOTES TO VOLUME II.

MAGNYFYCENCE.

That this piece was composed subsequently to the year 1515 seems evident from the mention made in one place [v. 283] of "Kynge Lewes of Fraunce," as an example of liberality [and as dead, v. 285]; and this could only mean Louis XII. who died in that year, as his immediate predecessor of that name [who died in 1483] was the most niggardly of wretches." *MS. note by Ritson in a transcript* of Magnyfycence.

* Page 3. v. 4 *probate*] In our author's *Garlande of Laurell* mention is made of

"Macrobius that did trete
Of Scipions dreme what was the treu *probate*."

v. 367. vol. ii. 186.

where *probate* is proof, meaning, or, perhaps, interpretation: but in what sense Skelton uses the word here I cannot determine [Qy. trial, touchstone?], the greater part of this speech being beyond my comprehension.

Page 3. v. 5. *fole*] i. e. fool.

v. 6. *vnhappely be vryd*] i. e. ill conditioned, &c. p. 197. v. 95.

* v. 9. *The amense therof is far to call agayne*] i. e. apparently, the amends, cure, is far to seek.

v. 10. *by*] i. e. buy, acquire.

Page 4. v. 16. *sad*] i. e. grave, serious, sober.

v. 17. *lure*] i. e. See note, p. 81, v. 1100.

* v. 20. *ouer all*] i. e. all over, everywhere.

v. 22. *wonnys*] i. e. dwells.

—— *and a man wolde wyt*] i. e. if a man could know.

v. 24. *Mary*] i. e. By the Virgin Mary.

v. 33. *Ye, to knackynge ernyst what and it preve*]— i. e. Yea, what if it prove mocking earnest : compare the preceding line, and see Jamieson's *Et. Dict. of Scott. Lang.* in v. *Knack.*

Page 5. v. 35, *in the mew*] i. e. in confinement,— properly, the place in which hawks were kept, or in which fowls were fattened : see note on *Why come ye nat to Courte*, v. 219.

* v. 36. *a cue*] i. e. half a farthing. " *Cu*, halfe a farthynge, or q., *Calcus.*"

Prompt. Parvul. ed. Way. p. 106.

Q. should seem to stand for quadrans, a farthing ; but Minshew, who finished his first edition in Oxford, says it was only half that sum, and thus particularly explains it : " Because they set down in the battling or butterie bookes in Oxford and Cambridge, the letter q. for halfe a farthing, and in Oxford, when they make that cue or q. a farthing, they say, *cap my q.*, and make it a farthing thus $\frac{a}{q}$." Nares's Glossary.

It seems possible that *cue* or q. may have been an abreviation of " *calcus,* quarta pars oboli." Way's note in v.

Page 5. v. 37. *to*] i. e. too.

v. 39. *condyssende*] " I *Condescende,* I agre to a mater." Palsgrave, p. 493.

v. 44. *countenaunce*] i. e. continence, restraint.

v. 45. *let*] i. e. hinder, restrain.

v. 47. *corage*] i. e. inclination, desires.

v. 56. *parcell*] i. e. part, portion.

v. 57. *Ye*] i. e. Yea.

Page 6. v. 60.

> *Somwhat I coulde enferre,*
> *Your consayte to debarre*]

i. e. I could bring in somewhat to hinder, contravene, your conception of the subject. So again in our author's *Garlande of Laurell;*

> " Madame, your apposelle is wele *inferrid,*
> And at your auauntage quikly it is
> Towchid, and hard for to be *debarrid."*
>
> v. 141. vol. ii. 176.

v. 65. *fet*] i. e., fetch.

v. 72. *the surpluse of my sawe*] i. e. the remainder of my saying.

v. 74. *where as*] i. e. where.

v. 80. *ryn*] i. e. run.

Page 7. v. 86. *wonder*] I may observe that the Roxburgh reprint, without authority, and against the sense, has " no *wonder."*

v. 89. *ken*] i. e. instruct.

v. 90. *wonders*] i. e. wondrous.

v. 92. *to*] i. e. too.

Page 7. v. 94. *other*] i. e. either.

v. 95.   *To you I arecte it, and cast*
                    Therof the reformacyon]
So Skelton again;

   " Syth vnto me formest this processe is *erectyd.*"
                              v. 2507 of the present drama.

   " *Arrectinge* vnto your wyse examinacion
   How all that I do is vnder refformation."
                    Garlande of Laurell, v. 410. vol. ii. 188.
He has also,

   " *Arectyng* my syght towarde the zodyake."
                              Id. v. 1. ii. 170.

   " My supplycacyon to you I *arrect.*"
                              Id. v. 55. p. ii. 173.

Arect in our early writers frequently signifies—impute,
a meaning foreign to the present passages : in the two
last cited, there can be no doubt that it is used in the
sense of—raise : in the others it seems to mean—offer,
refer.

   v. 103. *Come of, therfore, let se*] Compare Chaucer;

   " _____ *let see, come off*, and say."
                    Court of Loue—Workes, fol. 331. ed. 1602.
and *Reynard the Fox;* " Why tarye ye thus longe,
come of." Sig. b 7. ed. 1481 : and *Morte d'Arthur;*
" *Come of* thenne sayd they alle, and do hit." Book
xx. cap. iiii. vol. ii. 394. ed. Southey.

   v. 106. *reason and skyll*] An expression which
Skelton has elsewhere ; but the words are nearly
synonymous. " *Skyll.* Racio." *Prompt. Parv.* ed. 1499.

   Page 8. v. 113. *chere*] i. e. spirit,—or reception.

   v. 114. *intere*] i. e. entire.

   v. 115. *Oracius to recorde*] i. e. Horace to witness.

Page 8. v. 117. *to*] i. e. too.

v. 126. *Measure is treasure*] Lydgate mentions this as " an olde prouerbe : " see his verses on Moderation, *MS. Harl.* 2251. fol. 29, and his poem beginning " Men wryte of oold how *mesour is tresour.*" *Id.* 2255. fol. 143.

—— *this*] i. e. thus ; see note, p. 2. v. 38.

v. 131. *Ye*] i. e. Yea.

Page 9. v. 133. *kynde*] i. e. nature.

v. 134. *renne*] i. e. run.

v. 137. *a rest*] i. e. a wrest—by which the strings of harps and other musical instruments were drawn up.

v. 138. *All trebyllys and tenours be rulyd by a meyne*] " Intercentus. a *meane* of a songe." *Ortus Vocab.* fol. ed. W. de Worde, n. d.   In the notes on Shakespeare, in Todd's *Johnson's Dict.* &c., *mean* is wrongly explained—tenor : what the *mean* was, depended entirely on the nature of the composition.

v. 139. *beste*] i. e. beast.

v. 149. *skyll*] i. e. reason : see note on v. 106.

v. 150. *sad*] i. e. grave, serious, sober.

* v. 151. *It is no maystery*] i. e. what you say requires no masterly skill.

> " So me helpe God ! queth Beues tho,
> *Hit were no meistri* me to slo,
> For this is the ferthe dai agon
> Mete ne drinke ne bot I non."
>> *Sir Beues of Hamtoun,* p. 68. Maitl. ed.

" That is *lytel maystry* sayd syre launcelot to slee myn hors." *Morte d'Arthur,* B. xix. c. iiii. vol. ii. 369. ed. Southey.

v. 153. *herdely*] i. e. firmly.

Page 10. v. 166. *hyght*] i. e. am called.

Page 11. v. 175. *Conuenyent*] i. e. Fit, suitable.

—— *ryall*] i. e. royal.

v. 178. *syttynge*] i. e. proper, becoming,—a word very common in our early poetry (altered unnecessarily to "fyttinge" in the Roxburgh reprint of this piece).

v. 182. *his large*] i. e. his range.

v. 184. *hooly*] i. e. wholly.

v. 189. *sawe*] i. e. sow.

v. 190. *nother to*] i. e. neither too.

—— *lawe*] i. e. low: so again in v. 2541, "nowe hy, nowe *lawe* degre."

v. 193. *consayte*] i. e. conception.

Page 12. v. 202. *losyll so lyther*] i. e. scoundrel so wicked.

v. 209. *plenarly*] i. e. fully, entirely.

* v. 213. *Had I wyste*] [i. e. of a mistake which you may have cause to repent.] See note, p. 3. v. 40.

v. 216. *to fer*] i. e. too far.

v. 219. *defaute*] i. e. default, want.

Page 13. v. 226. *mone*] i. e. moon.

v. 230. *lyghtly*] " *Lightly* or sone [i. e. soon]. Leuiter." *Prompt. Parv.* ed. 1499 : or, easily.

v. 231. *to moche*] i. e. too much.

v. 233. *scole*] i. e. school.

v. 234. *a poppynye fole*]—*fole*, i. e. fool. " He •is a *popte fole* or a starke fole for the nones. Homo fatuitate monstrabilis." Hormanni *Vulgaria*, sig. P iii. ed. 1530. And see note, p. 197. v. 39.

v. 239. *delyaunce*] i. e. dalliance, delay.

Page 14. v. 249. *endure*] i. e. remain, dwell.

v. 256. *Here is none forsyth whether you flete or*

synke]—*forsyth*, i. e. regardeth, careth : *flete*, i. e. float, swim. So Chaucer ;

> " Him *recketh neuer whether she flete or sinke*."
> > *Annel. and Ar.,—Workes*, fol. 244. ed. 1602.

Page 14. v. 257. *lokyd*] i. e. looked.

v. 259. *hafter*] See note, p. 30. v. 138.

v. 260. *iangelynge Jacke of the vale*] i. e., chattering, &c.; see note, p. 26. v. 6.

Page 15. v. 266. *Mary*] i. e. by the Virgin Mary.

v. 267. *largesse*] i. e. bounty, liberality.

v. 269. *worshyp*] i. e. honour, dignity.

v. 272. *hyght*] i. e. am called.

v. 274. *Ye*] i. e. Yea.

v. 280. *hardely*] i. e. firmly.

—— *auaunce*] i. e. advance.

v. 283. *reporte me*] i. e. refer.

—— *Kynge Lewes*] i. e. King Louis the Twelfth : see note on title, p. 204.

Page 16. v. 285. *syth*] i. e. since.

v. 290. *Jacke shall haue Gyl*] So Heywood ;

> " Come chat at home, all is well, *Jack shall haue Gill*."
> > *Dialogue*, sig. F 3.—*Workes*, ed. 1598.

* v. 291. *carles*] i. e. careless.

v. 295. *broder*] i. e. brother.

v. 296. *I set not by*] i. e. I value not.

—— *Dauncaster cuttys*] i. e. Doncaster horses.— *Cut* was a term for a common horse, from its having the tail cut short.

v. 297. *bolte*] i. e. arrow (for a description of it, see Nares's *Gloss*. in v.).

—— *shote*] i. e. shoot.

v. 298. *hyght*] i. e. be called.

Page 16. v. 300. *this checke if ye voyde canne*] " *Checke*, a mery taunt." Palsgrave, p. 204.

v. 301. *to longe to scole*] i. e. too long to school.

v. 302. *gose*] i. e. goose.

Page 17. v. 303. *pole*] i. e. pool, water.

v. 304. *fole*] i. e. fool.

v. 306. *Go, shake the dogge, hay*] See note, p. 189. v. 28.

v. 310. *to play with me checke mate*] In allusion to the king being put in *check* at the game of chess.

v. 311. *your noble estate*] Equivalent to—your noble lordship.

v. 312. *recorde*] i. e. testimony.

v. 314. *Sad*] i. e. Grave, serious, sober.

v. 318. *hele*] i. e. health.

v. 319. *commaunde*] i. e. commend.

Page 18. v. 321. *ony*] i. e. any.

v. 322. *sone*] i. e. soon.

v. 323. *kepe*] i. e. heed, care, attention.

v. 327. *Whylest*] i. e. Until.

v. 333. *mynde*] i. e. fancy.

v. 336. *beholde*] i. e. beholden.

Page 19. v. 341. *By lakyn*] i. e. by our Lady ; *lakyn* is the contraction of *ladykyn*, little lady.

v. 346. *Pountesse*] i. e. Pontoise.

v. 347. *taken me*] i. e. committed, consigned to me.

v. 355. *Ye*] i. e. Yea.

v. 357. *They bare me in hande that I was a spye*] i. e. They accused me, laid to my charge, that, &c.

" This false knight, that hath this treson wrought,
   Bereth hire in hond that she hath don this thing."
      Chaucer's *Man of Lawes Tale*, v. 5039. ed. Tyr.

" What crime or yuell mayest thou *beare me in hande
of: Quel crime ou mal me peulx tu mettre sus*." Pals-
grave, p. 450. " Many be *borne an hande* of a faute,
and punysshed therfore, that were neuer gylty. Pleri-
que facinoris *insimulantur*," &c. Hormanni *Vulgaria*,
sig. m ii. ed. 1530. This expression occurs with a dif-
ferent shade of meaning in our author's *Why come ye
nat to Courte*,—

> " *He bereth the kyng on hand,*
> That he must pyll his lande," &c.

v. 449. vol. ii. 291.

* Page 19. v. 362.
*And wolde haue made me Freer Tucke,
To preche out of the pylery hole*]

[An allusion to the punishment called *collistrigium*, a
kind of pillory in which the head (or the head and
hands) was confined in holes, so that the prisoner
would bear a ludicrous resemblance to a preacher
bending over his pulpit.]

v. 364. *antetyme*] i. e. text. So in the absurd story
of Skelton's preaching, *Merie Tales*, (reprinted in
Appendix to *Account of his Life and Writings*), " I
say, as I said before in my *antethem, vos estis*." *Tale
vii.*

Page 20. v. 366. *moche warke*] i. e. much work,
trouble.

v. 369. *made largesse as I hyght*] i. e. made donation
of money according to my name (Fancy's assumed
name being Largesse, see v. 272).

v. 375. *grete estates*] i. e. persons of great estate or
rank.

v. 384. *ye*] i. e. yea.

Page 20. v. 385. *mesure is a mery mene*] Heywood in his *Epigrammes vpon Prouerbs* has ten on " Measure is a mery meane." Sig. N iiii., — *Workes*, ed. 1598.

v. 388. *ryall*] i. e. royal.

v. 391. *oder*] i. e. other.

Page 21. v. 405. *blunderyng*] i. e. disturbance. " I *Blonder, Je perturbe.*" Palsgrave, p. 458.

v. 406. *betake*] i. e. commit, consign.

v. 411. *to put the stone*] i. e. to throw the stone above hand, from the uplifted hand, for trial of strength.

Page 22. v. 413. *gyse*] i. e. guise, fashion, manner.

v. 417. *I set not by*] i. e. I value not.

v. 423. *lurdayne*] i. e. lumpish, lazy fellow, clown,— worthless person in general.

v. 425. *tappyster*] i. e. woman presiding over the tap in a public house.

v. 429. *can*] i. e. know.

—— *praty*] i. e. pretty.

v. 430. *occupy*] i. e. use.

—— *kayes*] i. e. keys.

*v. 433. *at all assayes*] i. e. in all sorts of trials or enterprises. Occurs again in v. 2303. " *At all assayes, En tous poynts,* or *a tous poynts.*" Palsgrave, p. 831. " He is a frende *at all assayes. Omnium horarum* amicus est." Hormanni *Vulgaria,* sig. Y iiii. ed. 1530.

v. 435. *mekyll*] i. e. much.

v. 444. *sleyght*] i. e. trick, artful contrivance.

Page 23. v. 446. *fayty bone geyte*] Perhaps corrupted French — *fait a bon get* or *geste.*

v. 449. *consayte*] i. e. conceit, conception.

v. 453. *noppe is rughe*] i. e. nap is rough.

Page 23. v. 455. *chafer*] i. e. merchandise.

v. 458. *The courtly gyse of the newe iet*] A somewhat pleonastic expression, — the courtly guise of the new fashion. " *Gette,* a custome, *guise nouuelle.*" Palsgrave, p. 224.

" Yit a poynte *of the new gett* to telle wille I not
   blyn."

> *Juditium,* — *Towneley Mysteries,* p 312.

v. 460. *ferre fet*] i. e. far fetched.

v. 461. *ymet*] i. e. met.

v. 462. *Margery Mylke Ducke*] See note, p. 116. **v.** 418.

—— *mermoset*] A kind of ape or monkey.

v. 465. *fresshe*] i. e. smart.

v. 469. *praty*] i. e. pretty.

v. 470. *iet*] i. e. strut.

* **v.** 472. *pope holy*] i. e. hypocritical; see note, p. 195. l. 10.

Page 24. v. 473. *sadnesse*] i. e. gravity, seriousness, soberness, discreetness.

v. 477. *occupy*] i. e. use.

v. 478. *worshyp*] i. e. honour, dignity.

* **v.** 485. *knokylbonyarde*] i. e. a rude clown. Compare Palsgrave's *Acolastus,* 1540 : " Do I raygne here on this facion, being a swynherde amongest swyne of Boeatia. i. amongest a meyny of iacke holde my staues, or *knockyldeboynyardes,* beinge but of late a kynge," &c. Sig. Y iiii.; and Heywood's *Dialogue,* &c.,—

" He is a *knuckilbonyard* very meete
   To match a minion neither fayre nor sweete."

> Sig. D 4., — *Workes,* ed. 1598.

v. 486. *to*] i. e. too.

Page 24. v. 488. *warke*] i. e. work, business, matter.

v. 489. *yarke*] i. e. strike, lash.

v. 490. *custrell*] " *Coustillier:* An Esquire of the body; an Armour-bearer unto a Knight; the servant of a man at Armes; also, a groom of a stable, a horse-keeper." Cotgrave's *Dict.*

v. 492. *this*] i. e. thus; see note, p. 2. v. 38 (and so in the next line.)

——*freers*] i. e. friars.

* v. 498. *Monkys*] i. e. monks.

Page 25. l. 2. *famine*] " *Famen,* sermo, verbum." Du Cange's *Gloss.*

* v. 500. *Conueyaunce*] i. e. Thievery, Cheatery.

v. 506. *By God, I haue bene about a praty pronge*] — *praty*, i. e. pretty: in the present line at least, *pronge* seems to mean — prank (Dutch *pronk*), whatever be its signification in the following passage of our author's *Colyn Cloute;*

> " And howe at *a pronge*
> We tourne ryght into wronge."
>
> v. 1196. vol. ii. 166.

v. 510. *pagent*] i. e. part; see note, p. 6. v. 85.

v. 512. *by lakyn*] See note on v. 341. p. 211.

v. 513. *heyre parent*] i. e. heir apparent.

v. 514. *rome*] i. e. room, place.

v. 516. *to*] i. e. too.

Page 26. v. 518. *Cockys harte*] i. e. God's heart (*Cock,* a corruption of *God*).

v. 521. *thee*] i. e. thrive.

v. 529. *large*] A play on the meanings of the word,— big, and liberal.

Page 26. v. 533. *cofer kay*] i. e. coffer-key.

v. 535. *auowe*] i. e. vow; see note, p. 32. v. **199.**

Page 27. v. 539. *alowde*] i. e. approved.

v. 554. *in same*] i. e. in the same place (a pleon-asm, — since "*togyder*" precedes).

v. 561. *Can*] i. e. Know.

v. 562. *spedde*] i. e. versed.

Page 28. v. 564. *iapes*] i. e. jests, jokes.

v. 568. *ouerwharte*] i. e. overthwart — cross, per-verse, wrangling.

v. 569. *beshrowe*] i. e. curse.

v. 571. *iangle*] i. e. babble, chatter.

v. 573. *Ye*] i. e. Yea.

v. 575. *my botes and my spores*] i. e. my boots and my spurs.

v. 578. *Cockes woundes*] i. e. God's wounds; see note on v. 518.

v. 585. *iurde hayte*] Words (French perhaps) which I do not understand.

Page 29. v. 591. *quod*] i. e. quoth.

v. 592. *a leysshe of ratches to renne an hare*] i. e. a leash of — three — hounds to run a hare.

v. 597. *prece*] i. e. press.

v. 609. *to*] i. e. too.

Page 30. v. 628. *do togyder*] i. e. put it together.

v. 633. *wonne*] i. e. dwell.

v. 635. *a captyuyte*] Is rather, I suspect, a misprint for, than used in the sense of — *in:* compare v. 2543.

Page 31. v. 639. *the playnesse*] i. e. the plain fact.

v. 644. *thee*] i. e. thrive.

Page 32. v. 658. *a pystell of a postyke*] — *pystell*, i. e. epistle, letter; but I do not understand the expres-sion. Cotgrave has " *Postiquer;* to play the vagrant

Impostor," &c.; *Postiqueries*, cousening sleights," &c.
Postiquer, a wandering impostor," &c.

Page 32. v. 659 *fonnysshe*] i. e. foolish.

v. 666 *freke*] i. e. fellow; see notes, p. 32. v. 187.
p. 124. v. 15.

v. 667. *peke*] "I *Peke* or prie." Palsgrave, p. 655.

v. 672. *rome*] i. e. room, place.

Page 33. v. 681. *Ye*] i. e. Yea.

v. 685. *By the armes of Calys*] See note, p. 42.
v. 398.

v. 687. *slyght*] i. e. trick, artful contrivance.

v. 688. *fonde consayte*] i. e. foolish conceit, — fantasies.

* Page 33. v. 690. *sadnesse*] i. e. seriousness, discretion.   See note on v. 473. p. 214.

v. 692. *Cockys body*] i. e. God's body : see note on
v. 518. p. 215.

v. 695. *whylyst*] i. e. until.

v. 698. *quyte*] i. e. acquit.

—— *praty*] i. e. pretty.

Page 34. v. 707. *haftynge*] i. e. cunning.   See note,
p. 30. v. 138.

v. 713. *geste*] i. e. guest.

v. 719. *hynder*] " *Hyndringe* or harmynge.   Dampnificacio." *Prompt. Parv.* ed. 1499.   "I *Hynder*, I
hurte, *Je porte dommage.*" Palsgrave, p. 585.

" Lest the reporte in *hinderyng* of his name," &c.

Lydgate's *Warres of Troy*, B. iii.
sig. Q ii. ed. 1555.

v. 720. *hode*] i. e. hood.

v. 722. *fole*] i. e. fool.

Page 35. v. 730. *lacke*] i. e. blame.

v. 732. *sped*] i. e. versed.

Page 35. v. 733. *lytherly*] i. e. wickedly.

v. 734. *Paynte*] i. e. feign. See note, p. 121. v. 583.

v. 737. *fauell*] See note, p. 30. v. 134.

—— *tyned*] i. e. pointed, pronged.

v. 745. *shrewdenes*] i. e. wickedness, evil.

Page 36. v. 746. *grete estates*] i. e. persons of great estate, or rank.

v. 748. *flery*] i. e. fleer.

—— *pretence*] i. e. intent.

v. 751. *bronde*] i. e. brand.

v. 752. *mase*] i. e. bewilder, confound

—— *fonde*] i. e. foolish.

v. 754. *bale*] i. e. sorrow, trouble.

v. 755. *Huffa, huffa*] See note, p. 129. v. 16.

v. 756. *a*] i. e. he.

v. 757. *Rutty bully*] See note, p. 14. v. 29.

—— *ioly rutterkyn, heyda*] Occurs in a song preserved in the Fairfax MS. which once belonged to Ralph Thoresby, and is now among the Additional MSS. in the British Museum (5465, fol. 114):

> " Hoyda, *joly rutterkyn, hoyda,*
> Lyke a rutterkyn, hoyda!
>
> Rutterkyn is com vnto oure towne,
> In a cloke, withoute cote or gowne,
> Save a raggid hode to kouer his crowne,
> Like a rutter, hoyda!
>
> Rutterkyn can speke no englissh,
> His tonge rennyth all on buttyrd fyssh,
> Besmerde with grece abowte his disshe,
> Like a rutter, hoyda!
>
> Rutterkyn shall bryng you all good luk,
> A stoup of bere vp at a pluk,

Till his brayne be as wise as a duk,
    Like a rutter, hoyda !

When rutterkyn from borde will ryse,
He will piss a galon pott full at twise,
And the ouerplus vndir the table, of the newe gyse,
    Like a rutter, hoyda ! "

Sir John Hawkins printed the above song (with the music) and tells us that it " is supposed to be a satire on those drunken Flemings who came into England with the princess Anne of Cleve, upon her marriage with king Hen. viii." *Hist. of Music*, iii. 2. But if it be the very song quoted in our text, it must allude to "rutterkyns" of a considerably earlier period; and, as the Fairfax MS. contains two other pieces which are certainly known to be from Skelton's pen, there is a probability that this also was composed by him.

    Court. Ab. in his next speech but one says, " am not I a ioly *rutter?* " and (v. 846)

      " My robe russheth
      So *ruttyngly.*"

Rutter, which properly means—a rider, a trooper (Germ. *reiter, reuter*), came to be employed, like its diminutive *rutterkin*, as a cant term, and with various significations, (see Hormanni *Vulgaria*, sig. q iii. ed. 1530; Drant's *Horace His Arte of Poetrie, pistles, &c.* sig. D ii. ed. 1567). When *Court. Ab.* asks " am not I a ioly *rutter?* " he evidently uses the word in the sense of—dashing fellow, gallant, alluding to his dress, on which he afterwards enlarges in a soliloquy. In v. 805 *Cr. Con.* terms him " this ioly *ietter.*" Compare the following passage of Medwall's *Interlude of Nature,* n. d. ;

> " And whan he is in suche aray,
>   There goth *a rutter*, men wyll say,
>   *a rutter, huf a galand.*" Sig. d ii.

Page 36. v. 759. *Decke your hofte, &c.*]—hofte, i. e.
head. If I rightly understand the passage, *Court. Ab.*
desires *Cl. Col.* to put on his hat, or cap : see note
below the text.

v. 760. *Say vous, &c.*] i. e. *Savez vous*, &c. : the
last three words of the line seem to be the beginning
of some French song.

v. 761. *Wyda*] i. e. *Oui da !*

Page 37. v. 763. *rome*] i. e. room, place.

—— *stonde vtter*] i. e. stand out, back.

v. 765. *a betell, or a batowe, or a buskyn lacyd*] In
Ortus Vocab. fol. ed. W. de Worde, n. d., besides
" Feritorium. anglice a battynge staffe a batyll dur or
a betyll," we find " Porticulus. anglice a lytell hand-
staff or a *betyll*." For " batowe " I have proposed in
a note below the text " *batone* " (baton), a conjecture
which is somewhat supported by the preceding word ;
but it seems more probable that the right reading is
" *botowe*," i. e. boot, for the work above cited has
" Ocree . . . anglice botis or *botwes* [ed. 1514—*bo-
towes*]," and *Prompt. Parv.* ed. 1499 gives " *Botewe.*
Coturnus."

v. 768. *Jacke Hare*] See note, p. 166. v. 270.

—— *loke thou be not rusty*] i. e. look that thou be
not cankered, uncivil.

v. 769. *nother*] i. e. neither.

v. 770. *lusty*] i. e. gayly dressed. See note, p. 131,
heading of poem.

v. 773. *Mary*] i. e. By the Virgin Mary.

* Page 37. v. 775. *swap*] i. e. are odd ones : or, qy. *swapping* great ones ?

—— *fotys*] i. e. foots, footest.

v. 776. *Ye*] i. e. Yea.

—— *gere*] i. e. apparel.

Page 38. v. 780. *mo*] i. e. more.

* v. 782. *ale in cornys*] i. e. with the dregs : see note, p. 114. v. 378.

v. 784. *auysed*] i. e. purposed on consideration.

v. 786. *rome*] i. e. room, place, office.

Page 39. v. 789. *Cockys harte*] i. e. God's heart : see note on v. 518.

v. 790. *for the armys of the dyce*] Some cant exclamation.

v. 793. *fayne*] i. e. glad.

v. 795. *rynne*] i. e. run.

v. 796. *cayser*] i. e. Cæsar, or, as it is generally explained, emperor : in the *Coventry Mysteries*, however, a distinction is made between these terms ;

" Bothe kynge and *caysere* and grett empere."
                    MS. Cott. Vesp. D viii. fol. 113.

v. 798. *quod*] i. e. quoth.

v. 799. *tende*] i. e. attend.

Page 40. v. 805. *ietter*] i. e. strutter,—gallant.

v. 806. *supplye*] i. e. supplicate.

v. 810. *I ne tell can*] i. e. I cannot tell.

v. 818. *gyse*] i. e. guise, fashion.

v. 819. *we wyll be aduysed twyse*] i. e. we will consider of it twice.

v. 821. *crake*] i. e. speak vauntingly.

Page 41. v. 827. *bende*] i e. band.

v. 830. *tawle*] i. e. brave, bold.

Page 41. v. 832. *defaute*] i. e. default, defect.

v. 833. *hawte*] i. e. haughty.

v. 834. *pose*] i. e. rheum in the head.

v. 839. *loketh*] i. e. looketh.

v. 843. *gere*] i. e. apparel.

Page 42. v. 844. *My heyre bussheth*]—*heyre*, i. e. hair. So Barclay, alluding to the " newe fassions and disguised garmentes" of the time;

> " To Ship, galants, come nere, I say agayne,
> With your set *bushes* curling as men of Inde."
> *The Ship of Fooles*, fol. 8. ed. 1570.

v. 847. *ruttyngly*] i. e. dashingly, gallantly : see note on v. 757. p. 218.

v. 850. *To daunce delyght*] So afterwards, Magny-fycence, exulting in his prosperity, says, " I dawnce all in delyte," v. 1510.

v. 852. *poynte deuyse*] i. e. perfectly exact: see Gifford's note on B. Jonson's *Works*, iv. 169.

v. 855. *gyse*] i. e. guise, fashion.

v. 857. *route*] i. e. crowd, assembly.

v. 859. *My sleue is wyde*] So Barclay describes the young gallants of the time with " Their *sleues* blasing like to a Cranes winges." *The Ship of Fooles*, fol. 8. ed. 1570. Wide sleeves are also mentioned in the following curious passage of Medwall's *Interlude of Nature*, n. d. (written before the year 1500); the speaker is Pride :

> " Behold the bonet vppon my hed,
> a staryng colour of scarlet red ;
> I promyse you a fyne threde,
> and a soft wull.
> It cost me a noble at one pyche,
> The scald capper sware sythyche

That yt cost hym euen as myche,
But there Pryde had a pull.
I loue yt well to haue syde here
Halfe a wote byneth myne ere ;
For euer more I stande in fere
That myne nek shold take cold.
I knyt yt vp all the nyght,
and the day tyme kemb yt down ryght,
And then yt cryspeth and shyneth as bryght
as any pyrled gold.
My doublet ys on laced byfore
A stomacher of saten and no more.
Rayn yt, snow yt, neuer so sore,
Me thynketh I am to hote.
Than haue I suche a short gown,
Wyth *wyde sleues* that hang a down,
They wold make some lad in thys town
a doublet and a cote.
Som men wold thynk that this were pryde,
But yt ys not so; ho, ho, abyde,
I haue a dagger by my syde,
yet ther of spake not I.
I bought thys dagger at the marte,
A sharp poynt and a tarte,
He that had yt in hys hart
Were as good to dye.
Than haue I a sworde or twayn ;
To bere theym my selfe yt were a payne ;
They ar so heuy that I am fayne
to puruey suche a lad ;
Though I say yt, a praty boy,
It ys halfe my lyues ioy ;
He maketh me laugh wyth many a toy,
The vrchyn ys so mad."   Sig. c ii.

Page 42. v. 861. *hose*] i. e. breeches.

v. 866. *hyght*] i. e. am called.

v. 871. *thee*] i. e. thrive.

v. 872. *fon*] i. e. fool.

Page 43. v. 878. *pore*] i. e. poor.

v. 881. *to to*] So in v. 2121 ;

" To flatterynge, to smatterynge, *to to* out of harre."

Compare *M. Harry Whobals mon to M. Camel,* &c. (folio broadside among the " flytings " of Churchyard and Camell;)

" My master Harry Whoball, sur, is *to to* shamefull
   wrothe.

  .   .   .   .

  .   .   .   for drinke is *to to* nappye."

Ray gives " *Too too* will in two. *Chesh.*" *Proverbs,* p. 163. ed. 1768.

v. 884. *crake*] i. e. vaunt.

v. 885. *I befoule his pate*] i. e. I befool, &c. (not *befoul,*) as it would seem from v. 1057, " I *befole* thy face;" and v. 1829, " I *befole* thy brayne pan."

v. 886. *fonne iet*] i. e. foolish fashion : (see note on v. 458.)

v. 887. *From out of Fraunce*] So Barclay ;

" Reduce courtiers clerely vnto your remembraunce,
 From whence *this disguising* was brought wherin
   ye go,
As I remember *it was brought out of France.*"

     The Ship of Fooles, fol. 9. ed. 1570.

Borde, in his *Boke of knowledge,* introduces a Frenchman saying,

" I am ful of new inuencions,
 And dayly I do make new toyes and fashions :

Al necions of me example do take,
Whan any garment they go about to make."

Sig. T. reprint.

Page 43. v. 889. *purueaunce*] i. e. provision.
Page 44. v. 907. *carlys*] i. e. churl's.
v. 909. *wonne*] i. e. dwell.
v. 915. *slyue*] i. e. sleeve.
v. 918. *preue*] i. e. prove.
v. 919. *A Tyborne checke*] i. e. a rope.
—— *craynge, Stow, stow*] — *craynge*, i. e. crying.
See note, p. 159. v. 73.

* v. 921. *out of harre*] i. e. out of hinge, out of
order: see Jamieson's *Et. Dict. of Scot. Lang.* and
Suppl. in v. *Har.*

" There nas no dore that he nolde heve of *harre*."

Cant. Tales. v. 552. ed. Wright.

The expression occurs again in v. 2121; and is found
in the *Towneley Myst.* and G. Douglas's Virgil's *Æn.*
v. 923. *warre*] i. e. worse.
Page 45. v. 932. *farly*] i. e. strange.
v. 933. *lokys*] i. e. looks.
v. 934. *an hawke of the towre*] So again our author
in the *Garlande of Laurell ;*

" Ientill as fawcoun
Or *hawke of the towre.*"

v. 1006. vol. ii. 214.

i. e., says Warton, " in the king's mews in the Tower,"
Hist. of E. P. ii. 355. ed. 4to : and the following lines
occur in a poem called *Armony of Byrdes*, n. d. (attri-
buted without authority to Skelton), reprinted entire
in *Typograph. Antiq.* iv. 380. ed. Dibdin ;

" The Haukes dyd syng,
    Their belles dyd ryng,
        Thei said *they came frō the tower.*
    We hold with the kyng
    And wyll for him syng
        To God, day, nyght, and hower."

p. 383.

But I apprehend that by a *hawke of the towre* Skelton
means — a hawk that towers aloft, takes a station high
in the air, and thence swoops upon her prey. Juliana
Berners mentions certain hawks which " ben *hawkes
of the toure.*" *Book of St. Albans,* sig. c. v.: and
Turbervile says; " Shee [the hobby] is of the number
of those Hawkes that are hie flying and *towre Hawks.*"
Booke of Falconrie, p. 53. ed. 1611.

Page 45. v. 935. *the malarde*] i. e. the wild-drake.

v. 936. *becked*] i. e. beaked.

v. 938. *Mary*] i. e. By the Virgin Mary.

v. 940. *Ye*] i. e. Yea.

v. 947. *spere*] i. e. spire, shoot, — stripling. So in
our author's third poem *Against Garnesche,* " But a
slendyr *spere.*" v. 41. vol. i. 140.

Page 46. v. 953. *mo*] i. e. more.

v. 954. *in the dyuyls date*] See note, p. 41. v. 375.

v. 956. *he playeth the state*] i. e. he playeth the per-
son of consequence.

v. 957. *pyke out of the gate*] " I *Pycke* me forth out
of a place, or I *pycke* me hence, *Je me tyre auant.*"
Palsgrave, p. 656.

v. 962. *out of consayte*] i. e. out of good opinion,
favour.

v. 964. *a praty slyght*] i. e. a pretty trick, con-
trivance.

Page 46. v. 973. *poynted after my consayte*] i. e. appointed, equipped according to my fancy.

v. 974. *thou iettes it of hyght*] i. e. thou struttest it in high style.

v. 975. *let vs be wyse*] Equivalent to — let us understand.

v. 977. *come of, it were done*] The expression " come of" has occurred before ; see note on v. 103. p. 207. Compare *Mary Magdalene ;*

" *Cum of,* ꝫe harlotts *that yt wer don.*"
An. Mysteries from the Digby MSS.
p. 97. ed. Abbotsf.

Magnus Herodes ;

" Hens now go youre way that ye *were* thore."
Towneley Mysteries, p. 147.

Still's *Gammer Gurtons Nedle ;*

" Sir knaue, make hast diccon *were* here."
Sig. E 3. ed. 1575.

See too our author's *Garlande of Laurell,* v. 243. vol. ii. 181.

Page 47. v. 979. *sone*] i. e. soon.

v. 980. *Stowe*] See note, p. 159. v. 73.

v. 982. *There is many euyll faueryd, and thou be foule*] i. e. There is many a one ill-looking, if thou be ugly : see note, p. 57. v. 442.

v. 985. *I wys*] i. e. truly, certainly (*i-wis*, adv.).

v. 987. *Jesse*] i. e. Jesus.

v. 992. *bent*] i. e. arched ; see note, p. 79. v. 1016.

v. 993. *glent*] i. e. glancing, bright.

v. 1000. *Barbyd lyke a nonne*] — *nonne,* i. e. nun. " The feders vnder the becke [of a hawk] ben callyd the *Barbe feders.*" *Book of Saint Albans,* sig. a 5.

Barbe is explained by Tyrwhitt to mean a hood or muffler, which covered the lower part of the face and the shoulders; *Gloss.* to Chaucer's *Cant. Tales:* and he refers to Du Cange in v. *Barbuta.* According to Strutt, it was a piece of white plaited linen, and belonged properly to mourning : in an edict concerning " The order and manner **of** apparell for greate estates of weomen in tyme of mourninge," made by the mother of Henry vii. in the 8th year of his reign, we find " Everye one not beinge vnder the degree of a Baronesse to weare a *barbe* aboue [Strutt prints by mistake — "about"] the chinne. And all other : as knightes wyfes, to weare yt vnder theire throtes, and other gentleweomen beneath the throte goyll." *MS. Harl.* 1354. fol. 12. See *Dress and Habits*, pp. 323, 325, 326, 368, and plate cxxxv.

Page 47. v. 1002. *donne*] i. e. dun.

v. 1003. *Well faueryd bonne*] So in our author's *Elynour Rummyng*, v. 227, " my prety *bonny;* " see note, p. 107.

Page 48. v. 1005. *rowte*] i. e. crowd, assembly.

v. 1008. *prese*] i. e. press, throng.

v. 1009. *a hole mese*] i. e. a whole mess, set.

v. 1011. *I rede, we sease*] i. e. I advise that we cease.

v. 1012. *farly . . . lokys*] i. e. strangely . . . looks.

v. 1013. *becke . . . crokys*] i. e. beak . . . crooks.

v. 1014. *tenter hokys*] i. e. tenter-hooks.

v. 1015. *wokys*] i. e. weeks.

v. 1018. *The deuyll spede whyt*] So again in our author's *Why come ye nat to Courte;*

> " For as for wytte,
> *The deuyll spede whitte !* "
>
> v. 1013. vol. ii. 310.

Page 48. v. 1020. *to*] i. e. too (as in the next two lines).

v. 1023. *solempne*] i. e. solemn.

v. 1027. *a pere*] i. e. a pear, — used frequently by our early writers for a thing of no value. " Vayne glory of the world, the whiche is not worth *a pere.*" *Morte d'Arthur*, B. xv. cap. vi. vol. ii. 254. ed. Southey.

v. 1028. *lese*] i. e. lose.

v. 1030. *And I may tende*] i. e. If I may attend.

v. 1032. *halfe*] i. e. side.

Page 49. v. 1035. *Fansy seruyce*] i. e. Fancy-service.

v. 1038. *theke*] i. e. thatch.

v. 1040. *Make a wyndmyll of a mat*] Compare v. 2 of our author's third set of verses *Against venemous Tongues*, vol. i. 155.

v. 1041. *and I wyst*] i. e. if I knew.

v. 1049. *blunder*] See note on v. 405. p. 213.

—— *blother*] i. e. gabble; as in our author's *Colyn Cloute*, v. 66. vol. ii. 127.

v. 1054. *this*] i. e. thus.

v. 1055. *euerychone*] i. e. every one.

Page 50. v. 1057. *fonnysshe*] i. e. foolish.

—— *I befole thy face*] See note on v. 885. p. 224.

v. 1058. *a foles case*] i. e. a fool's habit.

v. 1059. *glede*] i. e. kite. Nares, *Gloss.* in v., observes that in the common version of the Bible, *Deut.* xiv. 13, the *glede* and *kite* are erroneously mentioned together as two distinct birds.

v. 1061. *thy lyppes hange in thyne eye*] So in *Thenterlude of Youth*, n. d.;

"Faine of him I wolde haue a sight,
But my *lyppes hange in my lyght.*"

Sig. A iiii.

See too Heywood's *Dialogue*, &c. sig. F 4, — *Workes,* ed. 1598.

Page 50. v. 1066. *pylde*] i. e. bald —mangy : see note, p. 133. v. 68.

v. 1068. *Ye*] i. e. Yea.

v. 1069. *Mackemurre*] A proper name, though not printed as such in the old copy :

"The great Onele, and *Makmurre* also,
And al the lordes and kynges of Ireland."
                    Hardyng's *Chronicle*, fol. cxlix. ed. 1543.

v. 1070. *budge furre*] "*Budge* or Lambes furre." Minsheu's *Guide into Tongues.* In an order respecting the scholastic habit in the University of Cambridge, dated 1414, (quoted by Todd from Farmer's papers, in a note on Milton's *Comus*, v. 707,) mention is made of "*furruris buggeis* aut *agninis.*"

v. 1073. *thou wylte coughe me a dawe*] — *dawe*, i. e. simpleton. So in the fourth line after this, "ye shall *coughe me a fole:*" and in Lilly's *Mother Bombie*, 1594; "I know hee will cough for anger that I yeeld not, but he shall *cough mee a foole* for his labour." Sig. B 2.

v. 1074. *Mary*] i. e. By the Virgin Mary.

v. 1079. *can*] i. e. know.

Page 51. v. 1081. *broder*] i. e. brother.

v. 1082. *so hye fro me doth sprynge*] i. e. doth (dost) grow so much taller than I.

v. 1088. *gere*] i. e. apparel.

v. 1089. *folysshe*] i. e. foolish.

v. 1093. *flete*] i. e. float, flow, abound.

v. 1095. *by*] i. e. buy.

v. 1096. *Cockys harte*] i. e. God's heart.

v. 1103. *syke*] i. e. such.

Page 52. v. 1104. *a fole the tone*] i. e. a fool the one.

Page 52. v. 1107. *warke*] i. e. work, business.

v. 1108. *donnyshe*] i. e. dunnish.

v. 1109. *a fonde gest*] i. e. a foolish guest.

v. 1111. *so folysshe and so fonde*] i. e. so foolish and so silly (one of Skelton's pleonasms.)

v. 1118. *beshrowe*] i. e. curse.

v. 1119. *do*] i. e. done.

v. 1120. *Here is nothynge but the bockyll of a sho*] Compare *The Bowge of Courte*, v. 397. vol. i. 54.

* v. 1126. *a botchment*] i. e. to boot. "*Botchement. Additamentum.*" *Prompt. Parv.* ed. 1499.

Page 53. v. 1127. *forfende*] i. e. prohibit, forbid.

v. 1128. *For Goddes cope*] So we find as an oath, "By gods blew *hood.*" *Tom Tyler and his Wife*, p. 5. ed. 1661.

v. 1131. *be tyme*] i. e. by time.

v. 1134. *praty*] i. e. pretty.

v. 1136. *Aungey*] Does it mean Angers, or Anjou?

v. 1142. *gate*] i. e. got.

v. 1143. *puddynges*] See note, p. 117. v. 443.

—— *wortes*] Is here, I suppose, equivalent to — cabbages.

v. 1147. *marmosete*] A kind of ape, or monkey.

Page 54. v. 1148. *iapes*] i. e. jests, jokes.

v. 1150. *pultre*] i. e. poultry, fowl.

—— *catell*] i. e. beast.

v. 1154. *rode*] i. e. rood, cross: see note, p. 159. v. 69.

v. 1157. *nyfyls*] A word sufficiently explained by the context, and of frequent occurrence. So in *A Mery Play between Johan the Husbande, Tyb his Wyfe, and Syr Jhan the Preest*, 1533, attributed to Heywood;

" By God, I wolde ye had harde the tryfyls,
  The toys, the mokkes, the fables, and the *nyfyls*,
  That I made thy husbande to beleve and thynke."

p. 21. reprint.

Page 54. v. 1158. *canest*] i. e. knowest.

v. 1159. *mased*] i. e bewildered, confounded.

v. 1165. *It forseth not*] i. e. It matters not.

Page 55. v. 1172. *Ye*] i. e. Yea.

v. 1175. *a farle freke*] i. e. a strange fellow: see notes, p. 18. v. 29 ; p. 32. v. 168.

* v. 1176. *play well at the hoddypeke*]—*hoddypeke* is a common term of contempt or reproach (as in our author's *Why come ye nat to Courte*, v. 326. vol. ii. 287), and is generally equivalent to—fool. The original meaning of the word is altogether uncertain. Steevens (note on *Gammer Gurtons Nedle* (explains it—hodmandod (shell-snail) ; and Nares (*Gloss.* in v.) is inclined to agree with him. [Qy. compounded of *hoddy*, i. e. doddy, stupid, and *peke*, fool?] In a passage of Dunbar's *Dance of the Sevin Deidly Synnis* (*Poems*, i. 51. ed. Laing), " *hud-pykis* " has been explained (on account of the context)—misers. In Cotgrave's *Dict.* is " Noddy peke."

v. 1182. *ne reckys*] i. e. recks not.

v. 1185. *mo folys*] i. e. more fools.

Page 56. v. 1189. *kesteryll*] A sort of base-bred hawk.

v. 1190. *I wys*] i. e. truly, certainly (*i-wis*, adv.).

—— *doteryll*] See note, p. 55. v. 409.

* v. 1191. *In a cote thou can play well the dyser*] i. e. a low jester, tale-teller, mimic. Ang. Sax. *dýsig*, foolish, dizzy, &c. "*Dysowre*, that cannot be sadde (i. e. serious). Bomolochus." *Prompt. Parvul.* Way. " *Dissar*, a scoffer, *saigefol.*" Palsgrave, p. 214. " He can play the *desarde* with a contrefet face properly. *Morionem* scite representat." Hormanni *Vulgaria*, sig. bb iiii. ed. 1530. " One that were skylled in the crafte of *dysours* or skoffyng fellowes." Palsgrave's *Acolastus*, 1540. sig. H ii.

Page 56. v. 1195. *gatte*] i. e. got.

v. 1200. *fon*] fool.

* v. 1201. *Syr Johnn*] A contemptuous name for a priest ; here, for a simpleton in general.

* v. 1205. *do mastryes*] i. e. cunning tricks or sleights. See note on v. 151. p. 208.

v. 1206. *cocke wat*] See note, p. 31. v. 173.

Page 57. v. 1211. *rode*] i. e. rood, cross : see note, p. 159. v. 69.

—— *semblaunt*] i. e. semblance.

v. 1215. *lyste*] i. e. liest.

v. 1216. *moght* . . . . *lyste*] i. e. moth . . . . list.

v. 1220. *Johnn a Bonam*] One of the persons who figure in the old metrical tale, *The Hunttyng of the Hare*, is called " Jac of Bonam :" see Weber's *Met. Rom.* iii. 279.

v. 1223. *Shyt*] i. e. Shut.

—— *dawe*] i. e. simpleton.

Page 58. v. 1230. *cayser*] See note on v. 796. p. 221.

v. 1232. *scoles*] i. e. schools,—teaching.

v. 1234. *Ye*] i. e. Yea.

v. 1241. *renneth*] i. e. runneth.

* v. 1242. *thefte and bryboury*]—*bryboury*, i. e. pilfering. " I *Bribe*, I pull, I pyll, *Je bribe, (Romant) Je derobbe.* Palsgrave, p. 465. " *Bribors*, Cometh of the French Bribeur, i. e. Mendicus. It seemeth in a legal

Signification one that pilfereth other Mens Goods, as Cloaths out of a Window, or the like. *Anno* 28 *Ed. 2 Stat.* 1. *cap. unico.*" Cowel's *Law Dictionary, or The Interpreter*, &c. *augmented and improved*, &c. ed. 1727. So again our author;

> " Thefte also and pety *brybery.*"
>
> > v. 1370 of the present drama.

> " Some haue a name for thefte and *brybery.*"
>
> > *Garlande of Laurell*, v. 183. vol. ii. 178.

So too in *The Hye Way to the Spyttell Hous*, by Copland, n. d.;

> " *Brybe*, and conuey, fro mayster and maystres."
>
> > Utterson's *Early Pop. Poet.* ii. 37.

and in *Gentylnes and Nobylyte*, n. d. (attributed without reason to Heywood) ;

> " For *brybe* and stele euery thyng they wyll,
> If they may secretly come theruntyll."
>
> > Sig. B iii.

> " Divide me like a *brib'd* buck, each a haunch."
>
> > Merry W. of W. v. 5. (Cited by Halliwell.)

Other passages might be cited from various poets. And see Tyrwhitt's *Gloss.* to Chaucer's *Cant. Tales*, and Richardson's *Dict.*

Page 58. v. 1244. *a nysot*] In *Prompt. Parv.* ed. 1499 is " *Anysot* or a folt. Stolidus. Baburrus. Insons." But in the present passage *nysot* seems, from the context, to be equivalent to—lazy jade : and in the work just cited we find " *Nyce.* Iners."—" *Nycehede* or *nycete.* Inercia."

v. 1246. *warke*] i. e. work.

Page 58. v. 1247. *lyther*] i. e. wicked, evil.

v. 1249. *Bytwene the tappet and the wall*]—*tappet*, i. e. tapestry.   This line has occurred before, in our author's fourth poem *Against Garnesche*, v. 75. vol. i. 149.

Page 59. v. 1252. *ony*] i. e. any.

v. 1254. *sorte*] i. e. set, company,—people.

v. 1257. *ferre*] i. e. far.

v. 1258. *dawys*] i. e. simpletons.

v. 1261.

> *He frownyth fyersly, brymly browde,*
> *The knaue wolde make it koy, and he cowde*]

—*fyersly* and *brymly* are nearly synonymous : *make it koy* means here—affect (not merely reserve, but) haughtiness;—and so in our author's *Bowge of Courte*,—

" He bote the lyppe, he loked passynge *coye*."

v. 288. vol. i. 50.

v. 1265. *besy*] i. e. busy.

v. 1270. *quod*] i. e. quoth.

v. 1275. *lese moche*] i. e. lose much.

Page 60. v. 1278. *mo*] i. e. more.

v. 1280. *scolys*] i. e. schools.

v. 1281. *folys*] i. e. fools.

v. 1282. *lyther*] i. e. wicked,—rascals (as in the next line but one—" these *lythers*.").

v. 1283. *Symkyn Tytyuell*] See note on *Colyn Cloute*, v. 418.

v. 1284. *lere*] i. e. learn.

v. 1289. *mykyll*] i. e. much.

v. 1291. *dell*] i. e. part.

v. 1293. *shroudly*] i. e. shrewdly.

v. 1297. *fonde*] i. e. foolish.

v. 1299. *auowe*] i. e. vow: see note, p. 32. v. 199.

Page 60. v. 1301. *kynde*] i. e. nature.

Page 61. v. 1303. *rutters*] i. e. gallants.   See note on v. 757. p. 218.

v. 1309. *Ye*] i. e. Yea.

v. 1312. *howe*] i. e. ho! stop!

> " Ye shall haue ay quhill you cry *ho*."
>
> *Philotvs*, sig. B. ed. 1612.

> " Greit God defend I suld be one of tho
> Quhilk of thair feid and malice neuer *ho*."
>
> G. Douglas's *Palice of Honour*,
> p. 30. Bann. ed.

v. 1314. *scrat*] i. e. scratch.

v. 1315. *So how*] i. e. So ho.

v. 1317. *gadde*] Does it mean—gadding ?

v. 1318. *brayne seke*] i. e. brain-sick.

v. 1319. *to shyre shakynge nought*] i. e. to sheer nothing. So in our author's *Elynour Rummyng*, (v. 466. vol. i. 125.), that lady pronounces a couple of stunted goslings to be " *shyre shakyng nought*," i. e. sheer worthless.

v. 1323. *perde*] i. e. *par dieu*, verily.

* —— *ryde or go*] i. e. ride or walk.   See note, p. 51. v. 186.

Page 62. v. 1324. *slyght*] i. e. contrivance.

v. 1325. *hyght*] i. e. be called.

v. 1327. *wonne*] i. e. dwell.

v. 1334. *Ye*] i. e. Yea.

v. 1338. *Cockes armes*] i. e. God's arms : see note on v. 518. p. 215.

v. 1339. *whylest*] i. e. till.

v. 1341. *slee*] i. e. slay.

v. 1342. *away the mare*] See note, p. 102. v. 110.

Page 63. v. 1345. *a rome* . . *in euery route*] i. e. a place in every crowd, assembly.

v. 1347. *face and brace*] See note, p. 174. v. 33.

v. 1348. *fotyth*] i. e. footeth.

v. 1353. *poyntmentys*] i. e. appointments.

v. 1356. *mykyll praty*] i. e. much pretty.

* v. 1358. *an hoby can make larkys to dare*]—*to dare*, i. e. to lurk, lie hid. So in the poem *Howe the douty Duke of Albany*, &c. ;

> " Therin, lyke a royle,
>   Sir Dunkan, ye *dared*."   v. 270.

> " . . . . . let his grace go forward,
>   And *dare* us with his cap, like *larks*."
>   Henry VIII. Act. III. Sc. 2.

To *dare larks* was an expression applied to the catching of larks by terrifying them; and there were several modes of *daring* them. When the *hobby* (a small hawk, see note, p. 64. v. 567) was employed for that purpose, the larks lay still in terror till a net was thrown over them.—On the word *dare*, see *Notes & Queries*, vol. vii. p. 542.

v. 1360. *almesse*] i. e. alms.

v. 1363. *howe*] i. e. ho.

v. 1365. *loke*] i. e. look.

v. 1368. *hardely*] i. e. assuredly.

Page 64. v. 1370. *pety brybery*] See note on v. 1242.

* v. 1372. *inwyt*] i. e. crafty : A. Sax. *inwit*.

v. 1373. *be*] i. e. by.

v. 1376. *trew*] i. e. honest.

v. 1378. *checke*] i. e. taunt: see note on v. 300. p. 211

* v. 1379. *weltyth*] i. e. defeats, ruins. " *Welt*, to upset." Halliwell. *Dict.* "*Welten*, overturn." Jamieson, *Scot. Dict.*

Page 64. v. 1382. *sadnesse*] i. e. gravity, seriousness, soberness, discreetness.

v. 1389. *sorte*] i. e. set, company.

* v. 1390. *hokes vnhappy*] i. e. knavish chaps.—*hokes*, i. e. hooks, a word frequently applied to persons as a term of reproach. " *Vnhappy* of maners, *mauluays*." Palsgrave, p. 328. So in *Jacke Jugelar*, n. d. ;

" Loo, yender cumithe that *vnhappye hooke*."
p. 26. Roxb. ed.

and in Heywood's *Dialogue*, &c.;

" Since thou art crosse sailde, auale, *vnhappie hooke*."
Sig. E,—*Workes*, ed. 1598.

Page 65. v. 1395. *dawe*] i. e. simpleton.

v. 1396. *occupyed*] i. e. used, employed.

v. 1397. *reason and skyll*] See note on v. 106. p. 207.

v. 1405. *largesse*] i. e. liberality.

* Page 66. v. 1411. *Had I wyst*] i. e. repenting too late. See note, p. 3. v. 40.

v. 1416. *Ye*] i. e. Yea.

v. 1421. *Ye haue eten sauce*] Compare our author's *Bowge of Courte*, v. 72. vol. i. p. 40.

v. 1422. *to*] i. e. too.

* —— *bere a brayne*] i. e. look out, take heed.

v. 1425. *worshyp*] i. e. honour, dignity.

Page 67. v. 1436. *repryuable*] i. e. reprovable.

v. 1441. *menys of to moche*] i. e. means of too much.

v. 1442. *What, can ye agree thus and appose ?*]— *and appose*, i. e. and yet keep questioning, disputing: see note on *Colyn Cloute*, v. 267.

v. 1443. *faute*] i. e. fault.

Page 67. v. 1444. *Ye*] i. e. Yea.

—— *Jacke a thrommys bybyll*] See note, p. 140. v. 204.

—— *glose*] i. e. gloss.

* v. 1445. *Sore*] i. e. Smartly.

v. 1446. *loke you vnder kay*] i. e. lock you under key.

* Page 68. v. 1456. *Take it in worthe*] i. e. Be satisfied with it.   See note, p. 16. v. 68.

v. 1458. *largesse*] i. e. liberality.

—— *kynde*] i. e. nature.

v. 1467. *stonde*] i. e. stand.

Page 69. v. 1473. *fonde*] i. e. foolish.

v. 1474. *loke that ye occupye*] i. e. look that ye use.

v. 1475. *For nowe, syrs, 1 am lyke as a prynce sholde be, &c.*] This speech of Magnyfycence is very much in the style of Herod in the old miracle-plays : see, for instance, the *Coventry Mysteries, MS. Cott. Vesp. D.* viii. fol. 92. sqq.

v. 1477. *abandune*] i. e. subject.

> " For *abandonit* will, he noght be to berne that is
>   borne."
>
> > *Golagros and Gawane*, p. 142,—
> > *Syr Gawayne*, &c.
>
> " Till all to yow *abandownyt* be."
> > Barbour's *Bruce*, B. iii. v. 883. ed. **Jam.**

v. 1481. *mene*] See note on v. 138. p. 208.

* v. 1482. *over all*] i. e. everywhere.

Page 70. v. 1491. *syar*] i. e. sire, lord.

v. 1493. *ryall trone*] i. e. royal throne.

v. 1496. *spyll*] i. e. destroy.

v. 1502. *loke*] i. e. look.

v. 1504. *dynt*] i. e. blow.

Page 70. v. 1505. *the cane*] Does it mean—the khan ?

v. 1507. *I set not by*] i. e. I value not, regard not.

—— *prane*] i. e. prawn.

v. 1508. *Ne*] i. e. Nor.

—— *rehersse*] i. e. mention.

Page 71. v. 1513. *cache*] i. e. couch.

v. 1515. *mell*] i. e. meddle.

v. 1518. *to lowte man be sene*] i. e. (if the text be right ; see footnote *ad l.*) must be seen to bow, pay obeisance.

v. 1520. *brymme*] i. e. fierce, rugged, bristly.

v. 1521. *Basyan the bolde, for all his brybaunce*] *Basyan* is, I suppose, Antoninus Bassianus Caracalla (he is called " *Basian* " in Robert of Gloucester's *Chron.* p. 76. sqq.) ; *brybaunce* would seem to mean—plundering (properly, pilfering) ; see note on v. 1242.

v. 1522. *Alerycus*] i. e. Alaric.

—— *the Gothyaunce*] i. e. the Goths.

—— *swerd*] i. e. sword.

* 1523. *on molde*] i. e. on the earth.

v. 1524. *maysyd*] i. e. bewildered, confounded— stupid.

v. 1525. *fole*] i. e. fool.

v. 1526. *Galba, whom his galantys garde for a gaspe*] i. e. (I suppose) Galba, whom his gallants (soldiers) made to gasp :—they assassinated him :—see *gar* in v. 1532.

v. 1527. *nother set by*] i. e. neither valued, regarded.

v. 1528. *Vaspasyan, that bare in his nose a waspe*] This passage is explained by the following lines of a poem never printed, entitled *The Sege of Jerusalem :*

"His fader Vaspasiane ferly bytydde ;
  A byke of waspes bredde in his nose,

Hyved vp in his hedde he hadde hem of thoght,
And Vaspasiane is called by cause of his waspes."
MS. Cott. Calig. A. ii. fol. 109.

Page 71. v. 1529. *agayne*] i. e. against.

v. 1531. *crake*] i. e. vaunt, talk bigly.

v. 1532. *I shall frounce them on the foretop*] To
frounce is — to wrinkle, ruffle up, &c. In our author's
Phyllyp Sparowe, v. 1340. vol. i. 107, Charon is de-
scribed as having a "*frownsid* fore top;" and in his
Colyn Cloute, v. 533. vol. ii. 143, "fore top" means
simply — head, pate.

—— *gar*] i. e. make, cause.

Page 72. v. 1538. *auaunce*] i. e. advance.

v. 1539. *take it in degre*] Seems equivalent here
to — "take it in gre" (which occurs in v. 2005), i. e.
take it kindly : see note, p. 16. v. 68.

v. 1544. *ferre*] i. e. far.

v. 1547. *supprysed*] i. e. overpowered, smitten.

v. 1549. *Pullyshyd*] i. e. Polished.

—— *ornacy*] i. e. ornate diction.

v. 1551. *electe vtteraunce*] i. e. choice expression.

v. 1554. *feffyd and seasyd*] i. e. enfeoffed and seised,
— law-terms.

Page 73. v. 1556. *Mary*] i. e. By the Virgin Mary.

v. 1557. *comon*] i. e. communing, discourse.

v. 1558. *Poynt deuyse*] See note on v. 852. p. 222.

v. 1561. *pore*] i. e. poor.

v. 1564. *semynge*] i. e. beseeming, fitting.

v. 1568. *maystresse*] i. e. mistress.

v. 1569. *That quyckly is enuyued with rudyes of the
rose*] i. e. That is lively envived with hues, or com-
plexion, of the rose. This somewhat pleonastic ex-

pression is found again in our author's *Garlande of Laurell;*

> " *Enuyuid* picturis well touchid and *quikly.*"
>
> v. 1161. vol. ii. 220.

Page 73. v. 1570. *Inpurtured*] i. e. Portrayed, pic-, tured, — adorned.

v. 1571. *The streynes of her vaynes*] i. e. The strains, runnings of her veins.

> " Rills rising out of euery banck,
>   In wilde meanders *strayne.*"
>
> Drayton's *Muses Elizium*, p. 2. ed. 1630.

——— *as asure inde blewe*] See note, p. 23. v. 17.

v. 1573. *loke*] i. e. look.

—— *leyre*] i. e. complexion, skin.

v. 1576. *lusty*] i. e. pleasant, desirable.

Page 74. v. 1578. *to brace and to basse*] i. e. to embrace and to kiss.

v. 1579. *by hym that hell dyd harowe*] i. e. by our Saviour: see note, p. 85. v. 1291.

v. 1580. *a Phylyp sparowe*] See note, p. 47. v. 7.

v. 1581. *whylest my hede dyd warke*] i. e. until my head did work, ache. " *Hedwerke*, sekenesse. Cephalia." *Prompt. Parv.* ed. 1499. " *Wark*, to ache." Hunter's *Hallam. Gloss.* " But I may not stonde, *myn hede werches soo.*" *Morte d' Arthur*, B. xxi. c. v. vol. ii. 440. ed. Southey.

v. 1582. *hobby for suche a lusty larke*] See note on v. 1358. p. 237. The same metaphorical use of this expression occurs in our author's *Colyn Cloute*, v. 194. vol. ii. 131.

v. 1584. *my flesshe wolde be wroken*] —*wroken*, i. e. wreaked, satiated.

" Whyles thou art yonge   .   .   .   .   .   .
   Wreke the with wiueryng, if thou wilt be excused."
          Pierce Plowman, sig. M iii. ed. 1561.

Page 74. v. 1585. *consayte*] i. e. conceit, fancy.

v. 1586. *weryed I wolde be on*] i. e. I would worry, eagerly devour: compare our author's *Phyllyp Sparowe,* v. 29. vol. i. 62.

v. 1587. *Cockes armes*] i. è. God's arms : see note on v. 518. p. 215.

v. 1588. *ony*] i. e. any.

v. 1589. *Ye*] i. e. Yea.

v. 1590. *to be sped*] i. e. to be made successful.

v. 1592. *make suche one to the call*] A metaphor from falconry.

* v. 1598. *over all*] i. e. everywhere. See v. 1482.

Page 75. v. 1600. *a sawte*] i. e. an assault.

v. 1601. *prece*] i. e. press.

v. 1603. *sone*] i. e. soon.

v. 1604. *intreted*] i. e. prevailed on by solicitation.

v. 1606. *broken*] Seems to mean here — tame, assuage. [?]

v. 1610. *consayte*] i. e. conceit, conception.

v. 1615. *it shall not gretely skyll*] i. e. it shall not make much difference, it shall not much signify.

Page 76. v. 1620. *face it*] i. e. bluster. See note, p. 174. v. 33.

v. 1621. *Frete*] i. e. Gnaw, fret.

v. 1626. *lust and lykynge*] See note, p. 19, v. 23.

v. 1633. *your gorge*] i. e. what you have swallowed, the contents of your stomach.

* v. 1636. *wambleth*] i. e. turns. " Nauseo . . . to *wamble.*"   *Ortus Vocab.* fol. ed. W. de Worde, n. d.

v. 1638. *wonder*] i. e. wondrous.

Page 77. v. 1640. *harte seke*] i. e. heart-sick.

—— *me lyst*] i. e. it pleases me.

v. 1641. *coryed*] i. e. curried, drubbed.

—— *blyst*] i. e. wounded, — thumped.

"Your lasy bones I pretende so to *blisse*,
That you shall haue small luste to prate any more."
The Triall of Treasure, 1567. sig. A. iiii.

v. 1642. *loute*] i. e. bow, pay obeisance.

v. 1652. *at the contemplacyon*] See note, p. 171, heading of Epitaph.

v. 1653. *pore*] i. e. poor.

v. 1657. *sone*] i. e. soon.

Page 78. v. 1664. *rowne*] i. e. whisper; see note, p. 45, v. 513.

v. 1671. *dyssayued*] i. e. deceived.

v. 1673. *wete*] i. e. know.

v. 1677. *I wyll haue hym rehayted and dyspysed*] Our early poets frequently use *rehete* in the sense of— revive, cheer; a meaning foreign to the present passage. In the *Towneley Mysteries*, we find " *rehett* " and " *rehete*," pp. 143, 198, which the *Gloss.* explains " to threaten;" qy. if rightly? In some copies of Chaucer's *Troilus and Creseide*, B. iii. 350, is " reheting;" of which, says Tyrwhitt (*Gloss.* to *Cant. Tales*), " I can make no sense." In G. Douglas's Virgil's *Æneidos*, B. xiii. p. 467. l. 53. ed. Rudd., and in the *Flyting of Dunbar and Kennedy*, Dunbar's *Poems*, ii. 74, 80. ed. Laing, is " rehatoure," which has been referred to the French *rehair*: and perhaps *rehayted* in our text is — re-hated (Skelton afterwards in this piece, v. 2458, has the uncommon word *inhateth*).

v. 1679. *rest*] i. e. remain.

Page 79. v. 1682. *supplyed*] i. e. supplicated.

Page 79. v. 1687. *But for all that he is lyke to haue a glent*] *Glent* is frequently found in the sense of — glance ; but its meaning here, as would seem from the context, is—slip, fall : and in our author's *Garlande of Laurell* we find,

" Go softly, she sayd, the stones be full *glint* [i. e, slippery]."   v. 572. vol. ii. 195.

v. 1688.   *Ye*] i. e. Yea.

v. 1692. *What force ye*] i. e. What care ye.

v. 1695. *loke*] i. e. look.

* v. 1698. *haftynge*] i. e. cunning.   See note, p. 30. v. 138.

Page 80. v. 1702. *woke*] i. e. week.

v. 1703. *sone*] i. e. soon.

v. 1709. *comonynge*] i. e. communing, conversing.

v. 1711. *sad*] i. e. grave, serious, sober, discreet.

v. 1713. *doute*] i. e. fear.

v. 1715. *ony*] i. e. any.

v. 1718. *be lykelyhod*] i. e. by likelihood, — as it appeared.

v. 1719. *to fode*] i. e. to feed with words, — deceive. So in our author's *Bowge of Courte ;*

" Than Fauell gan *wyth fayre speche me to fede.*"   v. 147. vol. i. 43.

Page 81. v. 1723. *reserued*] i. e. retained.

v. 1725. *set a gnat By*] i. e. value at a gnat, care a gnat for.

v. 1738. *suche maystryes gan make*] — *suche maystryes,* i. e. such disturbances from the consequence which you assumed ; and see note on v. 151. p. 208.

Page 82. v. 1745. *lurden*] See note on v. 423, p. 213.

* v. 1748. *haynyarde*] A term of reproach which I

do not understand : but in our author's *Bowge of Courte*, v. 327, vol. i. 51, *hayne* seems to mean — hind, slave, peasant. [Probably from Ang. Sax. *hean*, poor, mean, despicable. " *Hanniel*, a bad fellow." Halliwell. *Dict.*]

Page 82. v. 1749. *cast*] i. e. throw up.

v. 1751. *bolle*] i. e. bowl.

—— *Goddes brede*] i. e. God's bread.

v. 1754. *praty*] i. e. pretty.

v. 1758. *Cockes armes*] i. e. God's arms ; see note on v. 518. p. 215.

Page 83. v. 1759. *Ye*] i. e. Yea.

v. 1766. *ony*] i. e. any.

v. 1772. *Where as*] i. e. Where.

v. 1775. *No force*] i. e. No matter.

v. 1776. *pollynge*] i. e. plundering.

v. 1778. *parde*] i. e. *par dieu*, verily.

—— *largesse*] i. e. liberality.

v. 1779. *vergesse*] i. e. verjuice.

Page 84. v. 1782. *gyse*] i. e. guise, fashion.

v. 1786. *taken*] i. e. committed, consigned.

v. 1802. *lowte*] i. e. bow, pay obeisance.

Page 85. v. 1813. *syth*] i. e. since.

v. 1817. *acquyte*] i. e. requite.

v. 1820. *solace*] i. e. pleasure.

v. 1821. *dyntes*] i. e. blows.

v. 1822. *Well were*] i. e. In good condition were.

Page 86. v. 1824. *halse*] } Both words signify —
v. 1825. *clepe*] } embrace ; with this distinction, that the former means properly — to throw the arms round the neck.

v. 1829. *I befole thy brayne pan*] i. e. I befool thy skull, head : see note, p. 22, v. 31.

* Page 86. v. 1830. *By our lakyn*] i. e. our lady. See note on v. 341. p. 211.

v. 1831. *My hawke is rammysshe*] " *Ramage* is when a Hawk is wilde, coy, or disdainfull to the man, and contrary to be reclamed." Latham's *Faulconry* (*Explan. of Words of Art*), 1658.

v. 1833. *warne*] i. e. prevent.

v. 1835. *ronner*] i. e. runner.

—— *fole*] i. e. fool.

v. 1836. *iarfawcon*] See note, p. 63. v. 557.

v. 1838. *ydder*] i. e. udder.

v. 1840. *slydder*] i. e. slippery.

v. 1841. *for God auowe*] So presently, v. 1851, " I make God *auowe:*" see note, p. 32. v. 199.

—— *chydder*] i. e. shiver.

v. 1842. *Thy wordes hange togyder as fethers in the wynde*] An expression which occurs again in our author's *Speke, Parrot*, v. 295. vol. ii. 261. So too in a comedy (before quoted), *The longer thou liuest, the more foole thou art*, &c. *Newly compiled by W. Wager*, n. d. ;

> " A song much like thauthour of the same,
>   *It hangeth together like fethers in the winde.*"
>   Sig. D ii.

Page 87. v. 1844. *carle*] i. e. churl.

v. 1848. *a losell lede a lurden*] i. e. one good-for-nothing fellow lead another : see note, p. 163. v. 138, and note on v. 423 of the present poem, p. 213.

v. 1849. *sowter*] i. e. shoemaker, cobbler.

v. 1850. *Cockes harte*] i. e. God's heart : see note on v. 518. p. 215.

v. 1854. *I shall gyue you a gaude of a goslynge that I gaue*] *Gaud* is found in the sense of—jest, trick, toy, &c. : but the line (perhaps corrupted) is beyond my comprehension.

Page 87. v. 1856. *reue*] i. e. steward, bailiff.

v. 1858. *syke*] i. e. such.

v. 1859. *Sadylgose*] i. e. Saddle-goose.

—— *Dawcocke*] See note, p. 36. v. 301.

Page 88. v. 1860. *garre*] i. e. make, cause.

v. 1862. *bytter*] i. e. bittern.

* v. 186**3**. *frame*] i. e. succeed, go well.

v. 1864. *to grame*] i. e. to be angry, — or perhaps to grieve ; the word being found in both senses.

v. 1865. *snyte*] i. e. snipe.

v. 1868. *loke*] i. e. look.

v. 1871. *Ye*] i. e. Yea.

—— *iapes*] i. e. jests, jokes.

v. 1876. *sone*] i. e. soon.

Page 89. v. 1882. *mo*] i. e. more.

v. 1886. *payntyd*] See note, p. 121. v. 583.

v. 1887. *demenour*] i. e. director : see note, p. 62. v. 553.

v. 1891. *largesse*] i. e. liberality.

v. 1892. *fondnesse*] i. e. folly.

Page 90. v. 1896. *rode*] i. e. rood, cross : see note, p. 159. v. 69.

v. 1898. *broder*] i. e. brother.

v. 1899. *lokys*] i. e. looks.

v. 1900. *clokys*] i. e. claws — clutches ; see Jamieson's *Et. Dict. of Scot. Lang.* in v. *Cleuck.*

v. 1903. *quyte*] i. e. requite.

v. 1904. *velyarde*] i. e. old man, dotard.

—— *dynt*] i. e. blow.

v. 1906. *losell*] i. e. good-for-nothing fellow. See note, p. 163. v. 138.

Page 90. v. 1908. *hyght*] i. e. am called.

v. 1910. *rughly*] i. e. roughly.

v. 1912. *lust*] i. e. pleasure, liking.

v. 1913. *lurden*] i. e. worthless fellow. See note on v. 423. p. 213.

Page 91. v. 1915. *set by hym a flye*] i. e. value him at a fly, care a fly for him.

v. 1916. *brace*] i. e. swagger. See note, p. 174. v. 33.

v. 1917. *loke*] i. e. look.

v. 1918. *to*] i. e. too.

v. 1928. *carbuckyls*] i. e. carbuncles.

v. 1930. *lyppers*] i. e. lepers.

v. 1932. *Some with the marmoll to halte I them make*] — *marmoll*, i. e. old sore, ulcer, gangrene. " *Marmoll*, a sore, *lovp.*" Palsgrave, p. 243. Skelton recollected Chaucer ;

> " But gret harm was it, as it thoughte me,
>   That *on his shinne a mormal* hadde he."
>   *Prol. to Cant. Tales*, v. 387.

on which passage see Tyrwhitt's note.

v. 1934. *brennynge*] i. e. burning.

v. 1936. *walter*] i. e. tumble, roll. " I *Walter*, I tumble, *Je me voystre.*" Palsgrave, p. 771.

Page 92. v. 1939. *sle*] i. e. slay.

v. 1945. *Lydderyns*] i. e. *Lydder*, wicked, persons : so in our author's *Garlande of Laurell*, " Some *lidderons*, some losels*," &c. v. 188. vol. ii. 178.

—— *set by*] i. e. value, regard.

v. 1958. *franesy*] i. e. frensy.

v. 1960. *worshyp*] i. e. honour, dignity.

v. 1961. *fole*] i. e. fool.

v. 1962. *loke*] i. e. look.

Page 93. v. 1966. *sadly*] i. e. gravely, seriously, soberly, discreetly.

v. 1967. *preposytour*] i. e. a scholar appointed by the master to overlook the rest. "I am *preposyter* of my boke. Duco classem." Hormanni *Vulgaria*, sig. R viii. ed. 1530.

v. 1968. *theyr wanton vagys*] — *vagys*, i. e. vagaries, strayings. Richardson in his *Dict.* gives an example of this substantive (*vagues*) from Holinshed.

v. 1977. *mo*] i. e. more.

v. 1979. *Howe*] i. e. Ho.

v. 1980. *lore*] i. e. teaching.

v. 1984. *vnlykynge*] i. e. in poor condition of body. " The strength and lustinesse, or *well lykyng* of my body." Palsgrave's *Acolastus*, 1540. sig. U iiii. " I am withered," says Falstaff, "like an old apple-John. Well, I'll repent, and that suddenly, while I am in some *liking*." Shakespeare's *Henry IV*. Part i. act iii. sc. 3.

Page 94. v. 1989. *enuy*] i. e. ill-will, grudge.

*v. 1993. *fe*] i. e. possessions.

v. 1995. *thought*] i. e. sorrow; see note, p. 23. v. 10.

v. 2004. *syth*] i. e. since.

—— *no nother*] A not unfrequent form in our early writers, — i. e. none other.

v. 2005. *take it in gre*] i. e. take it kindly : see note, p. 16. v. 68.

v. 2006. *a noble estate*] i. e. a person of noble estate or rank.

Page 95. v. 2014. *Ye*] i. e. Yea.

v. 2026. *loke*] i. e. look.

v. 2034. *cawdels*] According to the custom of great persons. So in the ballad of *Glasgerion ;*

" He harped in the kinges chambere,
     Where cuppe and *caudle* stoode."
       Percy's *Rel. of A. E P.*, iii. 43. ed. 1794.

Page 95. v. 2035. *mamockes*] " *Mammocks*, leavings, wasted fragments." Forby's *Vocab. of East Anglia.*

Page 96. v. 2037. *fayne*] i. e. glad.

v. 2038. *pomped*] In our text at least is equivalent to — pampered.

" The *pomped* clerkes with foles [fodes] delicous
     Erth often fedeth," &c.

Hawes's *Pastime of Pleasure*, sig. B b iiii. ed. 1555.

v. 2040. *to be drawe*] i. e. to be drawn over, covered.

v. 2042. *shertes of Raynes*] i. e. shirts made of the delicate species of linen manufactured at Rennes in Brittany.

v. 2044. *happed*] i. e. covered.

v. 2054. *sykernesse*] i. e. security, sureness.

Page 97. v. 2061. *plete*] i. e. plead.

* v. 2064. *lyther*] i. e. lazy, heavy.

v. 2066. *leuer*] i. e. more willingly.

v. 2070. *they rynne to in manus tuas quecke*] — *rynne*, i. e. run, — they quickly come to be hanged, when they say *In manus tuas, Domine, commendo spiritum meum.*

—— *mote*] i. e. may.

v. 2073. *too*] i. e. toe.

v. 2077. *rydlesse*] In v. 2445 is "*redlesse*," which properly means — devoid of counsel: but Skelton seems to use both forms in the sense of — unavailing, [helpless.]

Page 98. v. 2080. *bloo*] i. e. livid: see note, p. 25. v. 3.

v. 2093. *I garde her gaspe, I garde her gle*] — *garde,*

i. e. made, caused: *gle*, i. e., perhaps, squint; see Jamieson's *Et. Dict. of Scot. Lang.* in v. *Gley.*

Page 98. v. 2094. *daunce on the le*] A fragment, it would seem, of some song: *le*, i. e. lea.

v. 2095. *bassed*] i. e. kissed.

v. 2096. *the bote of all my bale*] i. e. the remedy or help of all my evil or sorrow.

> " God send every good man *bote of his bale*."
>
> Chaucer's *Chanones Yemannes Tale,*
>
> v. 16949. ed. Tyr.

v. 2097. *farre fet*] i. e. far-fetched.

v. 2098. *louesome*] i. e. lovely one.

v. 2098. *let*] i. e. leave, desist.

v. 2100. *patlet*] — or *partlet*, — i. e. a sort of ruff, or rather neckkerchief: see Strutt's *Dress and Habits*, &c. ii. 368.

Page 99. v. 2104. *lust and lykynge*] See note, p. 19. v. 23.

v. 2106. *me lyst*] i. e. pleases me.

v. 2113. *hardely*] i. e. assuredly.

v. 2114. *to moche*] i. e. too much.

v. 2115. *not worth an hawe*] A common expression in our early poetry;

> " Your wo appease which is *not worth an haw*."
>
> Lydgate's *Warres of Troy*, B. ii.
>
> sig. I iiii. ed. 1555.

v. 2116. *to free of the dawe*] Equivalent, I suppose, to — too much fooling: see note, p. 36. v. 301.

* v. 2117. *sad*] i. e. serious.

* v. 2121. *to to out of harre*] too much out of hinge, out of order.   See notes on v. 881. p. 224, and v. 921. p. 225.

Page 99. v. 2123. *iettynge*] i. e. strutting : see note, p. 15. v. 43.

——— *iapes*] i. e. jests, jokes.

v. 2124. *mowynge*] i. e. making mouths, grimacing.

——— *iackenapes*] i. e. monkey.

Page 100. v. 2132. *brothell*] Was formerly applied as a term of reproach to the worthless of either sex :

> " Of this daye gladde was many a *brothell*
> That myght haue an ore with Cocke Lorell."
>> *Cocke Lorelles bote*, n. d. sig. C ii.

v. 2135. *Cockes armes*] i. e. God's arms : see note on v. 518. p. 215.

v. 2138. *lurden*] i. e. good-for-nothing, wretched fellow : see note on v. 423. p. 213.

v. 2141. *largesse*] i. e. liberality.

v. 2143. *conuenyent*] i. e. fit, suitable.

v. 2148. *poddynge prycke*] i. e. skewer that fastens the pudding-bag.

v. 2150. *pot sharde*] i. e. potsherd.

v. 2151. *the spence of a noble*] i. e. the expense or spending of a noble, — the gold coin so called.

Page 101. v. 2152. *c. s̄.*] i. e. a hundred shillings.

v. 2155. *occupyed*] Though our author, according to his occasionally pleonastic style, has in the next line but one " *occupyed* and vsyd," the words are synonymous : see note, p. 3. v. 52.

v. 2156. *Ye*] i. e. Yea.

v. 2159. *retchlesse*] i. e. reckless.

v. 2162. *rynne*] i. e. run.

* v. 2164. *skyll*] i. e. matter : see note on v. 1615 of the present poem.

v. 2165. *spyll*] i. e. destroy.

Page 101. v. 2166. *some fall prechynge at the Toure Hyll*] So in *Thenterlude of Youth*, n. d. ;

> " By our Lady he dyd promote the
> To make the *preche* at the galowe tre."

Sig. B i.

v. 2168. *nother they set by*] i. e. neither they value, regard.

v. 2171. *lusty to loke on*] i. e. pleasant to look on.

Page 102. v. 2172. *nonnes*] i. e. nuns.

v. 2173. *Freers*] i. e. Friars.

—— *fayne*] i. e. glad, joyful.

* v. 2175. *ouer all*] i. e. everywhere.

* v. 2177. *rechate*] i. e. sound a recheat, recall : see note, p. 200. v. 215.

v. 2186. *brast*] i. e. burst.

v. 2187. *spewe and cast*] One of Skelton's pleonasms.

v. 2188. *gotted . . to thy share*] —*gotted*, i. e. gotten.

Page 103. v. 2193. *ye*] i. e. yea.

v. 2194. *to wed*] i. e. for a pawn, pledge.

v. 2195. *a daggeswane*] i. e. a rough sort of coverlet. " *Dagswayne.* Lodex." *Prompt. Parv.* ed. 1499. " My bedde is couered with a *daggeswayne* and a quylte . . . *gausape* . . ." — " Some *daggeswaynes* haue longe thrummes & iagges on bothe sydes : some but on one." Hormanni *Vulgaria*, sig. g iii. ed. 1530.

—— *ony*] i. e. any.

v. 2196. *metely well*] " *Metely : Moyennement, Assez . . . Passablement.*" Palsgrave, p. 839. " He is *metely* lerned. *Mediocriter* doctus est." Hormanni *Vulgaria*, sig. R viii. ed. 1530.

v. 2197. *dele*] i. e. part, bit.

Page 103. v. 2198. *in the deuyls date*] See note, p. 41. v. 375.

v. 2201. *the messe*] i. e. the Mass.

Page 104. v. 2204. *hose*] i. e. breeches.

v. 2207. *skelpe*] i. e. slap, strike : see Jamieson's *Et. Dict. of Scot. Lang.*

v. 2208. *loke*] i. e. look.

v. 2209. *Cockes bones*] i. e. God's bones : see note on v. 518. p. 215.

*—— *blysse*] i. e. wound, bruise, &c. : see note on v. 1641.

v. 2210. *dynge the deuyll*] — *dynge*, i. e. strike, knock. So again in our author's poem *Howe the douty Duke of Albany*, &c. ;

"And *the deuill downe dynge.*"

v. 210. vol. ii. 328.

Compare *The Droichis Part of the Play*, attributed to Dunbar ;

" That *dang the devill*, and gart him yowle."

Dunbar's *Poems*, ii. 38. ed. Laing.

—— *holde*] i. e. holden, held.

v. 2211. *rede*] i. e. advise.

v. 2214. *wrynge thy be in a brake*] Some cant expression : *brake*, see note, p. 111. v. 324, and note on *Why come ye nat to Courte*, v. 980.

v. 2215. *dawe*] i. e. simpleton.

v. 2216. *fawchyn*] i. e. cut.

v. 2217. *cauell*] " *Kevil, Kephyl*, A horse, contemptuously applied to a person, ' thou girt *kevil.'* " *The Dialect of Craven*, &c. Compare Lydgate's verses, entitled in the Catalogue, *Advices for people to keep a guard over their tongues* ;

"I saugh a *kevell* corpulent of stature,
  Lyk a materas redlyd was his coote," &c.

                              MS. Harl. 2255. fol. 132.

* Page 104. v. 2218. *iauell*] " *Iauell.* Ioppus." *Prompt. Parv.* ed. 1499. Of this common term of contempt (which Skelton uses in other passages) the meaning and etymology are uncertain. Todd (Johnson's *Dict.* in v.) explains it " A wandering or dirty fellow ; " shews that it is sometimes written *jabel;* and would derive it from the verb, *javel, jable,* or *jarble,* to bemire, to bedew. Nares (*Gloss.* in v.) refers it to the French *javelle,* which sometimes means " a faggot of brushwood or other worthless materials." The compiler of the *Gloss.* to *The Towneley Mysteries* (under *Hawvelle*) considers it equivalent to — jabberer. [It has not been suggested that this word may be only a shortened form of *javellone, jevellone,* jailer. The Lieutenant of the Tower, advising Sir Thos. More to put on worse clothes at his execution, gave this reason," because he that is to have them is but a *Javel.*" Halliwell's *Dict.*]

Page 105. v. 2223. *iche*] i. e. I.

v. 2229. *all one*] i. e. all agreed.

v. 2233. *rode*] i. e. rood, cross: see note, p. 159. v. 69.

v. 2235. *By our lakyn*] i. e. by our Lady. See note on v. 341. p. 211.

Page 106. v. 2242. *acomberyd*] i. e. encumbered, troubled.

v. 2243. *Goddys fote*] i. e. God's foot.

* v. 2244. *facyd*] i. e. outbraved, hectored. See note, p. 174, v. 33.

v. 2246. *condycyons*] i. e. qualities, dispositions. See note, p. 132. v. 12.

* Page 106. v. 2248. *bracyd*] i. e. bullied.   See note, p. 174. v. 33.

v. 2249. *defaute*] i. e. default, defect.

v. 2250. *to haute*] i. e. too haughty.

v. 2252. *pratyer*] i. e. prettier.

* Page 107. v. 2258. *gardeuyaunce*] In a note on Dunbar's *Freir of Tungland*, Lord Hailes observes that *gardyvians* is "literally *garde de viande*, or cupboard; but there it implies his cabinet;" and Mr. D. Laing adds, "rather, a portable cabinet." Dunbar's *Poems*, ii. 243. Skelton appears to use the word in the sense of—trunk. ["' *Scriniolum ;* a kasket or forsar, a *gardiviance.*' Elyot. 1559." Halliwell's *Dict.*]

v. 2259. *bowget*] i. e. budget.

v. 2260. *male*] i. e. bag, wallet.

v. 2262. *Your trymynge and tramynge by me must be tangyd*] The reader will hardly expect that I should attempt any precise explanation of this line.

v. 2264. *When we with Magnyfycence goodys made cheuysaunce*]—*cheuysaunce*, i. e. booty : see note, p. 30. v. 100.   Compare Gower ;

"Right as a thefe *maketh his cheuesance*,
And robbeth mens gooddes aboute," &c.
Conf. Am. B. v. fol. cxvi. ed. 1554.

v. 2265. *wengaunce*] i. e. vengeance.

v. 2266. *banne and wary*] "I *warrye*, I *banne* or curse. *Je mauldis.*" Palsgrave, p. 772.   Barclay is even more pleonastic than Skelton ;

"And your vnkindness *weray, ban and curse.*"
The Ship of Fooles, fol. 22. ed. 1570.

v. 2268. *Cockys bonys*] i. e. God's bones; see note on v. 518. p. 215.

v. 2270. *Ye*] i. e. Yea.

Page 108. v. 2275. *gaure*] i. e. stare : see Tyrwhitt's *Gloss.* to Chaucer's *Cant. Tales.* Yet Palsgrave has " I *Gaure*, I krye, *Je hue.* Howe he *gaureth* after his hauke : *Cōment il heue apres son oyseau.*" p. 561.

v. 2276. *yll hayle*] See note, p. 122. v. 617.

v. 2283. *the gowte and the gyn*] If *gyn* means (as the context seems to prove) some bodily ailment, I know not what it is.

v. 2287. *murre*] i. e. severe cold with hoarseness.

—— *pose*] i. e. rheum in the head.

v. 2288. *requiem æternam groweth forth of his nose*] Heywood has a similar expression ;

" Hunger droppeth *euen out of both their noses.*"
    Dialogue, &c. sig. D 4. — *Workes,* ed. 1598.

And Cotgrave ; " *Chishe-face* . . . one *out of whose nose* hunger drops." *Dict.*

v. 2291. *the halfe strete*] On the Bank-side, South-wark, — where the stews were : it is mentioned in the following curious passage of *Cocke Lorelles bote*, n. d. (where the " wynde fro wynchester" alludes to the temporary suppression of the Southwark stews at the intercession of the Bishop of Winchester) ;

" Syr this pardon is newe founde
By syde London brydge, in a holy grounde
Late called the stewes banke.
Ye knowe well all that there was
Some relygyous women in that place,
To whome men offred many a franke,
And bycause they were so kynde and lyberall,
A merueylous auenture there is be fall.
Yf ye lyst to here how,
There came suche a wynde fro wynchester,
That blewe these women ouer the ryuer,

In wherye, as I wyll you tell,
Some at saynt Kateryns stroke a grounde,
And many in holborne were founde.
Some at saynt Gyles, I trowe,
Also in aue maria aly, and at westmenster,
And some in shordyche drewe theder,
With grete lamentacyon ;
And by cause they haue lost that fayre place,
They wyll bylde at colman hedge in space
Another noble mansyon,
Fayrer and euer *the halfe strete* was.
For euery house newe paued is with gras,
Shall be full of fayre floures ;
The walles shall be of hauthorne, I wote well,
And hanged wᵗ whyte motly yᵗ swete doth smell ;
Grene shall be the coloures,
And as for this olde place, these wenches holy
They wyll not haue it called the stewys for foly,
But maketh it strabery banke."   Sig. B iv.

Page 109. v. 2293. *motton*] Long after Skelton's time, as the readers of our early dramatists will recollect, *mutton* was a favorite cant term for a prostitute.

v. 2294. *Ye . . . to*] i. e. Yea . . . too.

v. 2295. *queysy mete*] " *Quaisy* as meate or drinke is, *dangereux*." Palsgrave, p. 321. Compare *Jyl of Braintfords Testament*, n. d. ;

" I pray you fil you not to much of the *mutton ;*
I promise you that it is very *queisy*."   Sig. A.

v. 2297. *In fay*] i. e. In faith.

v. 2302. *froty*] Is frequently, as here, used by our early writers for — *forty*.

v. 2303. *at all assayes*] See note on v. 433, p. 213.

Page 110. v. 2311. *sleeth*] i. e. slayeth.

v. 2315. *bronde*] i. e. brand.

v. 2316. *stonde*] i. e. stand.

v. 2319. *lewdly*] i. e. vilely, basely (but here it seems to be used as an adjective).

v. 2320. *to*] i. e. too.

v. 2322. *fer*] i. e. far.

v. 2324. *loke*] i. e. look.

v. 2330. *agayne*] i. e. against.

Page 111. v. 2332. *wyte*] i. e. blame.

v. 2333. *rede*] i. e. counsel.

v. 2335. *Ye*] i. e. Yea.

—— *ryd thy selfe*] i. e. set free thyself, — despatch thyself.

v. 2340. *honge*] i. e. hang.

v. 2342. *tonge*] i. e. thong.

v. 2343. *throte bole*] i. e. throat-bowl, — protuberance of the throat. " Throte gole or *throte bole, neu de la gorge, gosier.*" Palsgrave, p. 281. In *Ortus Vocab.* fol. ed. W. de Worde, n. d. is " Epiglotum, *a throte bolle.*"—" It is not impossible," says Warton, alluding to this passage, " that Despare [Myschefe] offering the knife and the halter, might give a distant hint to Spenser." *Hist. of E. P.* (Em. and Ad. to p. 363 of vol. ii.) ed. 4to. See *The Faerie Queene*, i. ix. 50.

Page 112. v. 2352. *Out, harowe*] — *harowe* (variously spelt) is common in our early poetry as an exclamation of alarm or sudden distress, or an outcry for help. " Interiectyons of outkrye : *Haro*, as Haro, alarme, *trahy, trahy.*" Palsgrave, p. 888. On the origin of the word see Du Cange's *Gloss.* in vv. *Haro, Haroep ;* Tyrwhitt's note on v. 3286 of Chaucer's *Cant. Tales ;* Jamieson's

Et. Dict. of Scot. Lang. in v. *Harro ;* and Roquefort's *Gloss. to La Lang. Rom.* in v. *Harau.*

Page 112. v. 2352. *hyll*] i. e. hell.

v. 2353. *combred*] i. e. encumbered, troubled.

v. 2354. *sloo*] i. e. slay.

—— *nature and kynde*] A pleonastic expression.

v. 2357. *sautes*] i. e. assaults.

v. 2361. *soner*] i. e. sooner.

v. 2362. *luge*] i. e. (I suppose) lodge, abode.

* v. 2365. *wanhope*] i. e. want of hope,—despair. In some of our early writers, however, we find a distinction made between *wanhope* and *despair.*

Page 113. v. 2370. *dysease*] i. e. uneasiness, pain.

v. 2373. *ony*] i. e. any.

v. 2375. *ne*] i. e. nor.

v. 2383. *lectuary*] i. e. electuary.

v. 2387. *gommes goostly*] i. e. gums ghostly, spiritual.

—— *herte*] i. e. heart.

v. 2388. *To thanke God of his sonde*]—*his sonde,* i. e. his sending,—his providential dispensation.

Page 114. v. 2392. *fote*] i. e. foot.

v. 2394. *mode*] i. e. mood.

v. 2398. *dyscryue*] Signifies—describe; but in the present passage it would seem to mean—discover, search, try.

v. 2406. *Ye*] i. e. Yea.

v. 2411. *sone*] i. e. soon.

Page 116. v. 2430. *apayed*] i. e. satisfied, pleased.

v. 2433. *abylyment*] i. e. habiliment.

v. 2434. *aduysement*] i. e. consideration, heed.

v. 2435. *confyrmable*] i. e. conformable.

Page 116. v. 2444. *to*] i. e. too.

v. 2445. *redlesse*] See note on v. 2077.

Page 117. v. 2449. *to accompte you the contynewe of my consayte*] i. e. to tell you the continuation, the rest, of my conceit, conception.

v. 2455. *sad*] i. e. serious, discreet. See note on v. 1711.

v. 2457. *that is no nay*] i. e. that is not to be denied.

v. 2458. *inhateth*] Skelton's fondness for compound words has been already noticed (see note, p. 28. v. 31); and here most probably *inhateth* was not intended to convey a stronger meaning than—hateth.

—— *rennynge*] i. e. runnning.

v. 2460. *ne can*] i. e. can not.

v. 2465. *largesse*] i. e. liberality.

Page 118. v. 2467. *thorowly ingrosed*] i. e. (as the context would seem to shew) fully written out.

v. 2468. *Pountes*] i. e. Pontoise.

v. 2469. *hyght*] i. e. is called.

v. 2479. *ouerthrow*] i. e. overthrown.

* Page 119. v. 2485. *hafters*] i. e. cheats, sharpers. See note, p. 30. v. 138.

—— *forfende*] i. e. forbid, prohibit.

v. 2493. *sentence*] i. e. meaning.

v. 2494. *corage*] i. e. heart, affection.

—— *flyt*] i. e. remove.

Page 120. v. 2499. *worshyp*] i. e. honour, dignity.

v. 2500. *sadnesse*] i. e. seriousness, discretion. See note on v. 1382. p. 238.

v. 2503. *I wyll refrayne you ferther, or we flyt*] i. e. I will question you farther before we remove (*refrayne* being here, it would seem, according to Skelton's use of such compounds, equivalent to the simple, and not uncommon word,—*frayne*).

Page 120. v. 2506. *processe*] i. e. relation, discourse : see notes, p. 75. v. 735.

v. 2507. *Syth*] i. e. Since.

* —— *erectyd*] i. e. directed, referred. Seē note on v. 95. p. 207.

v. 2508. *aforse me*] i. e. exert myself, do my endeavour.

* v. 2511. *corage*] i. e. heart, disposition.

v. 2510. *warkys*] i. e. works.

v. 2513. *largesse*] i. e. liberality.

—— *to*] i. e. too.

v. 2517. *the nygarde nor the chyncherde*] Synonymous terms. " *Chynche* or *chynchare*. Preparcus." *Prompt. Parv.* ed. 1499.

Page 121. v. 2518. *negarship*] i. e. niggardship.

* v. 2522. *fumously adresse you with magnanymyte*] i. e. hotly, vigorously provide, furnish yourself with, &c. [Qy. famously ?]

v. 2525. *affyaunce*] i. e. trust.

v. 2534. *this processe*] i. e. this drama of *Magnyfycence:* (so presently, " this interlude " v. 2548, " this treatyse " v. 2562, " this mater " v. 2576 :) see note on v. 2506, above.

v. 2539. *seke[r]nesse*] i. e. security, sureness.

v. 2541. *lawe*] i. e. low ; as in v. 190.

Page 122. v. 2544. *leue*] i. e. willing.

v. 2550. *auaunsyd*] i. e. advanced.

v. 2557. *lacke*] i. e. fault, blame.

v. 2563. *comberyd*] i. e. encumbered, troubled.

Page 123. v. 2573. *maysterfest*] i. e. master-fast.

* v. 2577. *Precely purposyd*] i. e. Briefly discoursed.

v. 2583. *the terestre rechery*] If " *rechery* " be the

right reading, I know not what it means. Qy. " trech-
ery ? " as before, v. 2046,

> " Fye on *this worlde, full of trechery.*"

—— *flode*] i. e. flood.

v. 2585. *Ensordyd*] Could only, I presume, mean—
defiled : but qy., as the context seems to require,
" Ensorbyd," i. e. sucked in, swallowed ?

—— *wawys*] i. e. waves.

—— *wode*] i. e. mad, raging.

v. 2586. *brast*] i. e. burst,—break.

v. 2588. *hym*] Must be an error of the press for
" hymselfe ; " compare v. 2581.

v. 2590. *syttynge*] i. e. proper, becoming.

v. 2591. *ryalte*] i. e. royalty.

v. 2593, *indeuer*] i. e. endure, continue, dwell.

COLYN CLOUTE.

This powerful and original poem must have been
circulated in MS., probably for a considerable time,
before it was given to the press ; for from a passage
towards the conclusion, v. 1239, we learn that those
against whom its satire was directed would not " suffer
it to be printed." In *Colyn Cloute*, Skelton appears to
have commenced his attacks on Wolsey.

" I could never conceive, Mr. Warton, to what Dray-
ton alludes, in the preface to his Eclogues, where he
says, that ' the Colin Clout of SCOGAN, under Henry
the Seventh, is pretty.' He is speaking of pastoral
poetry ; and adds that ' Barklays ship of fools hath

twenty wiser in it.' You somewhere say [*Hist. of E. P.* iii. 76, note, ed. 4to], 'he must mean SKELTON; but what PASTORAL did HE write?'" Ritson's *Obs. on Warton's Hist. of E. P.*, p. 20 (note); see too his *Bibl. Poet.*, p. 99. I believe that Drayton did mean Skelton. *Colyn Cloute* is surely as much a *pastoral* as Barclay's *Ship of Fooles*,—as much perhaps as even Barclay's *Egloges.*

Page 125. *Quis consurget mecum, &c.*] *Vulg. Psal.* xciii. 16, where "Quis consurget *mihi*," &c.

—— *Nemo, Domine*] *Id. Joan.* viii. 11.

v. 1.   *What can it auayle*
                To dryue forth a snayle]

So in *Gentylnes and Nobylyte*, n. d. (attributed without grounds to Heywood);

        "In effect it shall no more *auayle*
        Than with a whyp *to dryfe a snayle*."
                                Sig. C ii.

v. 9. *bokes*] i. e. books.

Page 126. v. 20. *He pryeth and he peketh*] See note, p. 217. v. 667. So Gascoigne;

        "That other *pries and peekes* in euerie place."
        The Steele Glasse, fol. 301,—*Workes*, ed. 1587.

v. 28. *fole*] i. e. fool.

v. 29. *scole*] i. e. school.

v. 30. *a thre foted stole*] i. e. a three-footed stool.

v. 36. *The deuyll, they say, is dede*] Heywood has six Epigrams on this proverbial expression,—*Workes*, sig. N 2. ed. 1598. Ray gives, "Heigh ho, *the Devil is dead.*" *Proverbs*, p. 55. ed. 1768.

Page 127. v. 51. *connyng bagge*] i. e. bag, store, of knowledge or learning.

v. 52. *hagge*] See note, p. 21. v. 19.

v. 53. *though my ryme be ragged*] So Sir D. Lyndsay; "my rural *raggit* vers." *Prol. to Monarchie,—Works*, ii. 330. ed. Chalmers; and Spenser, "My *ragged rimes.*" *F. Queene*, i. xii. 23.

v. 56. *moughte eaten*] i. e. moth-eaten.

v. 66. *blother*] i. e. gabble.

v. 67. *The tone agayng*] i. e. The one against.

v. 68. *shoder*] i. e. shudder.

v. 69. *hoder moder*] i. e. hugger-mugger.

v. 70. *faute*] i. e. fault.

v. 71. *ben so haut*] i. e. be so haughty.

v. 72. *loke*] i. e. look.

Page 128. v. 77. *sely*] i. e. silly, simple, harmless.

v. 79. *wull*] i. e. wool.

v. 80. *Vnethes*] i. e. Scarcely.

v. 82. *connynge*] i. e. knowledge, learning.

v. 83. *A glommynge*] i. e. A glumming, a looking gloomy, sour.

—— *a mummynge*] Compare our author elsewhere;

> "Men of suche maters make but a *mummynge*."
> *Garlande of Laurell*, v. 200. vol. ii. 179.

> "Thhere was amonge them no worde then but *mum*."
> *Id.* v. 1118. p. 218.

> "But play scylens and glum,
> Can say nothynge but *mum*."
> v. 906 of the present poem.

v. 84. *iape*] i. e. jest, joke.

v. 86. *hole*] i. e. whole.

Page 128. v. 89. *the forked cap*] i. e. the mitre.

" No wise man is desirous to obtayne
The forked cappe without he worthy be."

Barclay's *Ship of Fooles*, fol. 236. ed. 1570.

v. 90. *to lewd*] i. e. too wicked, vile.

v. 91. *all beshrewd*] i. e. altogether cursed.

v. 99. *For other mennes skyll*]—*skyll*, i. e. reason : the line seems to mean—Notwithstanding other men's reasons.

Page 129. v. 107. *solfa so alamyre*]—*alamire* is the lowest note but one in Guido Aretine's scale of music : Gayton, in his *Notes upon Don Quixote*, 1654, says (metaphorically) that Maritornes "plaid her part so wel, that she run through all the keyes from *A-la-mi-re* to double Gammut," &c. p. 83.

v. 108. *premenyre*] i. e. præmunire.

v. 115. *heedes*] i. e. heads.

v. 119. *warke*] i. e. work.

Page 130. v. 137.

A great parte is for slouth,
But the greattest parte
Is for they haue but small arte
And ryght sklender connyng
Within theyr heedes wonnyng]

—*sklender connyng*, i. e. slender knowledge, learning : *wonnyng*, i. e dwelling. The meaning of the passage is—a great part of this is owing to their laziness, but it is chiefly to be attributed to their ignorance, &c.

v. 151. *werkes*] i. e. works.

v. 152. *Ure*] i. e. Urias.

v. 154. *werryn*] i. e. hinder, ward off.

v. 159. *heery*] i. e. hairy.

v. 160. *Set nought by*] i. e. Value not.

Page 130. v. 160. *ne*] i. e. nor.

v. 162. *mell*] i. e. meddle.

v. 163.   *loth to hang the bell*
          Aboute the cattes necke]

So Heywood ;

" And I will *hang the bell about the cats necke :*
For I will first breake and ieoperd the first checke."
          Dialogue, &c. sig. D 3,—*Workes*, ed. 1598.

See *Pierce Plowman*, where one of the rats proposes
that a bell should be hung about the cat's neck. Sig.
A iii. ed. 1561 ; and Ray's *Proverbs*, p. 85. ed. 1768.

Page 131. v. 166. *to play deuz decke*] An allusion,
I suppose, to some game.

v. 167. *for the becke*] i. e. to obey the nod of com-
mand.

v. 169. *Moche herted*] i. e. Much hearted.

v. 178. *combred*] i. e. encumbered.

v. 181. *Sho the mockysshe mare*] So in our author's
Why come ye nat to Courte ;
          " And *Mocke* hath lost her shoo."
                    v. 83. vol. ii. 279.

v. 182. *Wynche and keke*] i. e. wince and kick.

v. 183. *not worth a leke*] An expression not uncom-
mon in our early poetry :
          " No fallow *wourth ane leik*."
                    G. Douglas's *King Hart*—Pinkerton's *An.*
                    Scot. Poems from Maitl. MSS. i. 42.
          " Such loue I preise not *at a leke*."
                    Chaucer's *Rom. of the Rose*, fol. 130,—
                    Workes, ed. 1602.

v. 190.   *Amende whan ye may,*
          For, usque ad montem Sare,
          Men say ye can not appare]

—*appare*, i. e. impair. The meaning of this passage,
—in which (as I have already noted *ad loc.*) it seems
probable from a comparison of the MS. and the print-
ed copies, that Skelton used the forms " Seire " and
" appeire,"—is—Amend when ye may, for it is said
by every body, even as far as Mount Seir, that ye
cannot be worse than ye are. The Latin words are a
quotation from the Vulgate : " Et circuit de Baala
contra occidentem, *usque ad montem Seir.*" *Josue,*
xv. 10.

Page 131. v. 194. *hauke on hobby larkes*] See notes,
p. 237. v. 1358. p. 242. v. 1582.

v. 195. *warkes*] i. e. works.

Page 132. v. 198. *The gray gose for to sho*] Hoc-
cleve uses this proverbial expression ;

" Ye medle of al thyng, ye moot *shoo the goos.*"
Poems, p. 13. ed. 1796.

and Heywood has the following Epigram ;

" *Of common medlers.*
" He that medleth with all thing, may *shoe the gosling.*
If all such medlers were set to goose shoing,
No goose need go barefoote betweene this and
    Greece,
For so we should haue as many goose shoers as
    geese."
Sig. P 2,—*Workes*, ed. 1598.

See also Davies's *Scourge of Follie* (*Prouerbs*), n. d.
p. 175.

v. 209. *pranes*] i. e. prawns.

v. 211. *werynge*] i. e. wearing.

v. 213. *ne peason*] i. e. nor peas.

v. 214. *loke to be let lose*] i. e. look to be let loose.

Page 132. v. 215. *gose*] i. e. goose.

v. 216.   *Your gorge not endewed*
Without a capon, &c.]

Equivalent to—You not digesting any thing except,
&c.: see notes, p. 160. v. 78, and p. 161. v. 87.

v. 218. *a stewed cocke*] Compare the following pas-
sage in the *Interlude of the iiii Elementes*, n. d. ;

"*Tauerner*.   Though all capons be gone, what than ?
yet I can get you *a stewed hen*
That is redy dyght.
Humanyte. yf she be fat yt wyll do well.
Tauerner.   Fat or lene I cannot tell,
But as for this, I wot well
She lay at the stewes all nyght."

Sig. **B. vi.**

v. 219.   *To knowe whate ys a clocke*
Vnder her surfled [MS. *surfuld*] *smocke*]

Compare Heywood's *Dialogue*, &c. ;

" Howbeit suddenly she minded on a day,
To pick the chest locke, wherein this bagge lay :

. . . .

But streight as she had forthwith opened the locke,
And look't in the bagge, *what it was a clocke*," &c.
Sig. K 3,—*Workes*, ed. 1598.

In our author's *Garlande of Laurell* we find,

" With burris rowth and bottons *surffillyng* [MS. *sur-*
fullinge]."   v. 803. vol. ii. 206.

which is cited (*Dict.* in v. *Surfel*) by Richardson, who,
after quoting from Gifford that " To *surphule* or *surfel*
the cheeks, is to wash them with mercurial or sulphur
water," &c., adds that Gifford's " explanation does not

extend to the passage from Skelton." The fact seems
to be that Skelton uses *surfle* for *purfle*, i. e. border,
embroider : and I may notice that Brathwait, on the
other hand, seems to employ *purfle* for *surfle ;*
" With painting, *purfling*, and a face of Art."
                    A Strappado for the Diuell, 1615, p. 150.
    Page 132. v. 222.
            And howe whan ye gyue orders
            In your prouinciall borders,
            As at Sitientes, &c.]
Sitientes is the first word of the Introit of the Mass for
Passion Sunday (" *Sitientes, venite ad aquas, dicit Do-*
minus," *&c., Isaiah* lv. 1). For this note I am indebt-
ed to W. Dyce, Esq., who further observes that *Siti-*
entes Saturday was of old, and is now abroad, the
Saturday before Passion Sunday.

    Page 133. v. 233. *renne they in euery stede*] i. e. run
they in every place.

    v. 234. *nolles*] i. e. heads.

    v. 239. *Pystle*] i. e. Epistle.

    v. 243. *prymes and houres*] i. e. the devotions so
named.

    v. 248. *vagabundus*] i. e. vagabonds.

    v. 251. *ale stake*] i. e. stake set up before an ale-
house by way of sign.

    v. 252. *welcome hake and make*] An expression
which I have not elsewhere met with. Ray gives
among *North Country words*, " To *hake*, To sneak, or
loiter : " in Hunter's *Hallam. Gloss.* is " A *haking* fel-
low, an idle loiterer ; " and in a song cited by Mr. J.
P. Collier (*Hist. of Engl. Dram. Poet.*, ii. 472) from a
MS. drama called *Misogonus* by T. Richards, we
find,—

" With Bes and Nell we love to dwell,
In kissinge and in *hakinge*."

—*make* is common in the sense of—mate, companion.

Page 134. v. 262. *stylla*] i. e. still.

v. 263. *wylla*] i. e. will.

v. 264. *pekes*] See note, p. 55. v. 409.

v. 266. *faute*] i. e. fault.

v. 267. *apposed*] i. e. questioned, examined. " He was *apposed*, or examyned of his byleue. De religione *appellatus est*." Hormanni *Vulgaria*, sig. D ii. ed. 1530.

v. 269. *connyng*] i. e. knowledge, learning.

v. 284. *Tom a thrum*] See note, p. 140. v. 204.

Page 135. v. 293.

> *There shall no clergy appose*
> *A myter nor a crose,*
> *But a full purse*]—*clergy*, i. e. erudition.

" Androgeus by kyng Mynos was sent,
For he should profite in *cleargy*,
To Athens."

Lydgate's Fall of Prynces, B. i. leaf xii.
ed. Wayland.

—*appose* seems to be used in a different sense from that in which we have just had it (v. 267), and to be equivalent to—procure : *crose*, i. e. crosier.

Page 136. v. 299. *a hermoniake*] A term I am unable to explain.

v. 303. *Ouer*] i. e. Besides.

—— *the foresayd laye*] i. e. the above-mentioned laity.

v. 305. *anker*] i. e. anchorite.

v. 310.   *To ryde vpon a mule*
           With golde all betrapped]

Perhaps, as Warton thinks (note on *Hist. of E. P.*, ii. 347. ed. 4to), an allusion to Wolsey : afterwards in this poem, the Cardinal appears to be pointed at more plainly.

Page 136. v. 312. *purple and paule*] An expression which frequently occurs, more particularly in ballad-poetry (considered by Percy and others as equivalent to—purple robe) : *paule*, i. e. pall, rich or fine cloth.

v. 316. *Raynes*] See note, p. 251. v. 2042.

Page 137. v. 317. *morowes mylke*] i. e. morning's milk.

v. 318. *tabertes*] Tabards,—jackets or coats, without sleeves, close before and behind, and open at the sides, are still worn by heralds : but those mentioned in the text were longer,—a sort of riding-cloaks. " *Tabard*, a garment, *manteau*." Palsgrave, p. 278. And see Du Cange's *Gloss.* in v. *Tabartum ;* Roquefort's *Gloss.* in v. *Tabar ;* and Strutt's *Dress and Habits*, &c, ii. 301.

v. 319. *Theyr styrops of myxt gold begared*]—*begared*, or *begarded*, means—faced, bordered,—adorned. The line, I suspect, (see various readings *ad l.*) ought to stand,—

" Theyr styrops *with* gold begared."

v. 321. *moyles*] i. e. mules.

v. 323. *What care they though Gil sweate,*
Or Jacke of the Noke]

So afterwards, v. 857, the same terms are used to signify the labouring poor of both sexes. *Jacke of the Noke*, i. e. (I suppose) Jack of the Nook: see " *Nocata terræ* " in Cowel's *Law Dictionary*, &c. ed. 1727.

v. 325. *pore*] i. e. poor.

Page 137. v. 331. *farly*] i. e. strange.

v. 332. *iangle*] i. e. babble, chatter.

v. 335. *all to-mangle*] See note, p. 22. v. 32.

v. 337. *ascrye*] i. e. call out against: see notes, p. 78. v. 903. p. 88. v. 1358.

v. 341. *Ware*] i. e. Were. (MS. "Was:" see note *ad loc.*)

v. 342. *Poules*] i. e. Paul's.

v. 346. *trones*] i. e. thrones.

v. 347. *Lyke prynces aquilonis*] i. e. Like so many Lucifers.

v. 352. *For prestes and for lones*]—*prestes*, i. e. sums in advance. "*Prest* and *loan*," Sir H. Nicolas observes to me, "seem to have been used in nearly, if not precisely, the same sense in the 16th century. Perhaps, strictly, *prest* meant a compulsory advance. In fiscal records it has much the meaning of *charge* or *imprest.*"

v. 356. *tonge tayde*] i. e. tongue-tied.

v. 360. *shrewd*] i. e. evil.

v. 362. *poollynge*] i. e. polling, plundering.

* v. 365. *Ye make monkes to haue the culerage, &c.*] A passage which I do not understand: but *culerage* perhaps has here the meaning which it conveys as the name of an herb, " Arse-smart. *Cul-rage.*" Cotgrave's *Dict.* [Qy. *cullage*, the tribute called *culagium?*]

v. 373. *ouerthwarted*] Has been explained before (p. 166. v. 230)—cavilled, wrangled: but here it seems to mean—crossly, perversely opposed or controlled.

v. 376. *fayne*] i. e. glad.

Page 138. v. 379. *corum*] i. e. quorum.

v. 388. *apostataas*] See note, p. 167. v. 290.

Page 138. v. 391. *sely nonnes*] i. e. silly, simple, harmless nuns.

v. 392. *ronnes*] i. e. runs.

v. 396. *quere*] i. e. quire.

v. 397. *heuy chere*] " *Heavy chear*, Tristitia, Mœstitia." Coles's *Dict.*

v. 399. *fucke sayles*] So in a copy of verses attributed to Dunbar ;

" The dust upskaillis, mony fillok with *fuk saillis.*"
Poems, ii. 27. ed. Laing.

and in another by Sir R. Maitland ;

" Of fynest camroche thair *fuk saillis.*"
Anc. Scot. Poems from Maitland MSS.,
ii. 326. ed. Pink.

Focksegel, a foresail, German. In the Expenses of Sir John Howard, first Duke of Norfolk, we find, " Item, the same day my mastyr paid to the said Clayson, for a *fuk* maste for the said kervelle, iijs. iiijd." *Manners and Household Expenses of England*, &c., p. 206. ed. Roxb.

v. 401. *shales*] i. e. goest wry. See note, p. 18. v. 19.

v. 403. *The lay fee people*] i. e. the laity : see note, p. 201. v. 267.

v. 404. *fawte*] i. e. fault.

Page 139. v. 409. *Boke and chalys*] i. e. Book and chalice.

v. 410. *leedes*] i. e. leads.

v. 417. *melles*] i. e. meddles.

v. 418. *tytyuelles*] This word occurs not unfrequently, and with some variety of spelling, in our early writers. So Lydgate ;

" *Tytyuylles* tyrauntes with tormentoures."
Le Assemble de dyeus, sig. c i. n. d. 4to.

and Heywood ;

" There is no moe such *titifyls* in Englandes ground,
To hold with the hare, and run with the hound."
Dialogue, &c. sig. C,—Workes, ed. 1598.

Some have considered the word as derived from the Latin, *titivilitium,* a thing of no worth. Jamieson " suspects that it is a personal designation," *Et. Dict. of Scot. Lang.* in v. *Tutivillaris.* In *Juditium, Towneley Mysteries,* p. 310, *Tutivillus* is a fiend ; and in the Moral Play of *Mankind* he represents the sin of the flesh, *Hist. of Eng. Dram. Poet.,* ii. 297, by Mr. J. P. Collier, who says (ii. 223) that " the name afterwards came to mean any person with evil propensities," and refers to the comedy of *Rauf Royster Doyster,* Skelton's Works, and the Enterlude of *Thersytes :* when he objected to the derivation of the word from *titivilitium* and proposed " the more simple etymology, *totus* and *vilis,*" he was probably not aware that some writers (wrongly) " *totivillitium* volunt, quasi *totum vile :* " see Gronovius's note on the *Casina* of Plautus, ii. 5, 39. ed. Var.

Page 139. v. 421. *Of an abbay ye make a graunge*] A proverbial expression.

" Our changes are soch that *an abbeye turneth to a graunge.*"
Bale's Kynge Iohan, p. 23. Camd. ed.

" To bring *an Abbey to a Grange.*" Ray's *Proverbs,* p. 174. ed. 1768.

v. 424. *beade rolles*] i. e. prayers,—properly, lists of those to be prayed for.

Page 139. v. 429.

> *But where theyr soules dwell,*
> *Therwith I wyll not mell*]

—*mell*, i. e. meddle. So Dunbar;

" Now *with thair sawle we will nocht mell.*"

Poems, ii. 52. ed. Laing.

v. 434. *reporte me*] i. e. refer.

Page 140. v. 440. *the lay fee*] i. e. the laity; see note, p. 201. v. 267.

v. 447. *splendore*
Fulgurantis hastœ]

From the Vulgate. " Ibunt in *splendore fulgurantis hastœ* tuæ." *Habac.* iii. 11. " Et micantis gladii, et *fulgurantis hastœ.*" *Nahum*, iii. 3.

v. 456. *eysell*] i. e. vinegar.

v. 458. *ypocras*] Was a favourite medicated drink, composed of wine (usually red), with spices and sugar. It is generally supposed to have been so named from Hippocrates (often contracted, as in our author's *Garlande of Laurell*, v. 1426. vol. ii. 233., to " Ipocras "); perhaps because it was strained,—the woollen bag used by apothecaries to strain syrups and decoctions for clarification being termed *Hippocrates's sleeve.*

v. 459. *Let the cat wynke*] See note, p. 110. v. 305.

v. 460. *Iche wot*] Seems to mean here—Each knows (not, I know).

v. 467. *theologys*] i. e. theologians.

Page 141. v. 468. *astrologys*] i. e. astrologers.

v. 474. *pretendynge*] Equivalent to—portending.

" What misfortune, aduersitie, or blame,
  Can all the planets to man or childe *pretende,*
  If God most glorious by his might vs defende? "

Barclay's Ship of Fooles, fol. 129. ed. 1570.

Here Skelton seems to allude to Wolsey ; and from these lines (called in the Lansdown MS., see note *ad loc.*, " The profecy of Skelton ") perhaps originated the story of our poet having prophesied the downfall of the Cardinal.

Page 141. v. 476. *trone*] i. e. throne.

v. 479. *euerychone*] i. e. every one.

Page 142. v. 489. *bruted*] i. e. reported, talked of.

v. 492. *wrest vp*] i. e. screw up : see note, p. 208. v. 137.

v. 493. *twynkyng*] i. e. tinking, tinkling.

v. 498. *the lay fee*] i. e. the laity : see note, p. 201. v. 267.

Page 143. v. 504. *to*] i. e. too.

v. 515. *depraue*] i. e. vilify, defame.

v. 523. *resydeuacyon*] i. e. recidivation, backsliding.

* v. 525. *aquarde*] i. e. awkward.

v. 528. *ipostacis*] i. e. hypostasis.

v. 533. *fore top*] i. e. (as the context shews) simply,—head, pate.

Page 144. v. 542.

> And some haue a smacke
> Of Luthers sacke]

Concerning the wine called *sack* (about which so much has been written) see Henderson's *Hist. of Anc. and Mod. Wines*, p. 298.

v. 544. *brennyng*] i. e. burning.

v. 545. *warke*] i. e. work.

v. 549. *carpe*] i. e. talk, prate.

v. 551. *Called Wicleuista*] From Wicliffe.

v. 553. *Hussyans*] i. e. followers of Huss.

Page 144. v. 554. *Arryans*] i. e. followers of Arius.

v. 555. *Pollegians*] i. e. Pelagians.

v. 559. *to mykel*] i. e. too much.

Page 145. v. 564. *tryalytes*] i. e. three benefices united.

v. 565. *tot quottes*] So Barclay ;

" Then yf this lorde haue in him fauour, he hath hope
To haue another benefyce of greater dignitie,
And so maketh a false suggestion to the pope
For a *tot quot*, or else a pluralitie."
                    Ship of Fooles, fol. 60. ed. 1570.

v. 572. *persons and vycaryes*] i. e. parsons and vicars.

v. 576. *loselles*] i. e. good-for-nothing fellows. See note, p. 163. v. 138.

v. 577. *lewdely*] i. e. wickedly, vilely.

v. 578. *sely*] i. e. silly, simple, harmless.

v. 581. *mought*] i. e. might.

* v. 582. *dysgysed*] i. e. ill-behaved. See note, p. 157. v. 22.

Page 146. v. 597. *lokes*] i. e. looks.

v. 598. *bokes*] i. e. books.

v. 600. *wroken*] i. e. wreaked.

* v. 602. *iauell*] i. e. a low, base fellow. See note, p. 256. v. 2218.

* v. 604. *face*] i. e. bluster. See note, p. 174. v. 33.

—— *crake*] i. e. vaunt, talk bigly.

* v. 606. *kayser*] i. e. emperor. See note, p. 221. v. 796.

v. 607. *layser*] i. e. leisure.

Page 147. v. 619. *connyng*] i. e. knowledge, learning.

—— *auaunce*] i. e. advance.

Page 147. v. 624. *dykes*] i. e. ditches.

" Where the blinde leadeth the blinde, both fall in the
    dyke."

Heywood's *Dialogue*, &c.—*Workes*, ed. 1598, sig. G 2.

v. 625. *Set nothyng by*] i. e. Value not, regard not.

v. 637. *ye, shall*] i. e. yea, I shall.

Page 148. v. 648. *shule*] i. e. shovel.

* v. 654. *mamockes*] i. e. fragments, leavings. See
note, p. 251. v. 2035.

v. 663. *kynde*] i. e. nature.

v. 664. *Many one ye haue vntwynde*] The reading
of the MS., which at least gives a sense to the line ;
vntwynde, i. e. destroyed ; see note, p. 53. v. 284.

v. 668. *fote*] i. e. foot.

v. 672. *in the deuyll way*] A common expression in
our early writers.

" Our Hoste answerd ; Tell on *a devil way.*"
        Chaucer's *Milleres Prol.*, v. 3136. ed. Tyr.

" In the *twenty deuyll way, Au nom du grant diable.*"
Palsgrave, p. 838.   " What reason is that, *in the twenty
deuell waye,* that he shulde bere suche a rule ? Quæ-
nam (*malum*) ratio est," &c.   Hormanni *Vulgaria,* sig.
dd iii. ed. 1530.

v. 673. *ouer*] i. e. besides.

Page 149. v. 675. *hear*] i. e. hair.

v. 679. *tonsors*] i. e. *tonsures.*

v. 688. *the male dothe wrye*] See note, p. 74. v. 700.

v. 692. *Ye bysshops of estates*]—*of estates,* i. e. of
great estate, rank, dignity.

v. 698. *awtentyke*] i. e. authentic.

v. 704. *intoxicate*] i. e. poison (Lat. *intoxico*).

Page 150. v. 705. *conquinate*] i. e. coinquinate,—
pollute, defile, defame.

Page 150. v. 710. *The Churchis hygh estates*] i. e. the dignitaries of the Church.

v. 728. *marke*] i. e. marks,—the coins so called.

v. 730. *werke*] i. e. work.

v 734. *sawe*] i. e. saying,—branch of learning.

Page 151. v. 737. *pore*] i. e. poor.

v. 739. *frere*] i. e. friar.

v. 747.   *of the order*
                          Vpon Grenewyche border,
                          Called Obseruaunce]

The statement that Edward the Third founded a religious house at Greenwich in 1376 appears to rest on no authority. A grant of Edward the Fourth to certain Minorites or Observant Friars of the order of St. Francis of a piece of ground which adjoined the palace at Greenwich, and on which they had begun to build several small mansions, was confirmed in 1486 by a charter of Henry the Seventh, who founded there a convent of friars of that order, to consist of a warden and twelve brethren at the least; and who is said to have afterwards rebuilt their convent from the foundation. The friars of Greenwich were much favoured by Katherine, Queen of Henry the Eighth; and when, during the question of her divorce, they had openly espoused her cause, the king was so greatly enraged that he suppressed the whole order throughout England. The convent at Greenwich was dissolved in 1534. Queen Mary reinstated them in their possessions, and new-founded and repaired their monastery. Queen Elizabeth suppressed them, &c. See Lysons's *Environs of London*, iv. 464. ed. 1796.

v. 754. *Babuell besyde Bery*] When by an order of Pope Urban the Fourth, the Grey Friars were removed out of the town and jurisdiction of Bury St. Edmund, in 1263, " they retired to a place just without the bounds, beyond the north gate, called Babwell, now the Toll-gate, which the abbat and convent generously gave them to build on ; and here they continued till the dissolution." Tanner's *Not. Mon.* p. 527. ed. 1744.

Page 151. v. 755. *To postell vpon a kyry*] i. e. to comment upon a Kyrie eleison : (a *postil* is a short gloss, or note).

v. 757. *coted*] i. e. quoted.

Page 152. v. 779. *blother*] i. e. gabble.

v. 780.   *make a Walshmans hose*
           Of the texte and of the glose]

So again our author in his *Garlande of Laurell ;*

" And after conueyauns as the world goos,
    It is no foly to vse *the Walshemannys hose.*"
                              v. 1238. vol. ii. 225.

Compare *The Legend of the Bischop of St. Androis ;*

" Of omnigatherene now his glose,
    He *maid it lyk a Wealchman hose.*"
                    Scot. Poems of the Sixteenth Century,
                              (by Dalzell), p. 332.

" WELCHMAN'S HOSE. Equivalent, I imagine, to the breeches of a Highlander, or the dress of a naked Pict ; upon the presumption that Welchmen had no hose." Nares's *Gloss.* in v. Unfortunately, however, for this ingenious conjecture, the expression is found varied to " *shipman's hose,*"—which certainly cannot be considered as a non-entity. " Hereunto they adde also a Similitude not very agreeable, how the Scriptures be like to a Nose of Waxe, or *a Shipmans Hose :*

how thei may be fashioned, and plied al manner of waies, and serue al mennes turnes." Jewel's *Defence of the Apologie*, &c. p. 465. ed. 1567. " And not made as *a shippe mans hose* to serue for euery legge." Wilson's *Arte of Rhetorike*, p. 102. ed. 1580. Surely *Welshman's hose* (as well as shipman's) became proverbial from their pliability, power of being stretched, &c.

Page 152. v. 784. *broke*] i. e. brook.

Page 153. v. 800. *the brode gatus*] Means, perhaps, Broadgates Hall, Oxford, on the site of which Pembroke College was erected.

v. 801. *Daupatus*] i. e. Simple-pate : see note, p. 36. v. 301.

v. 803. *Dronken as a mouse*] So Chaucer ;

" We faren as he that *dronke is as a mous*."
        The Knightes Tale, v. 1263. ed. Tyr.

* v. 803. *his pyllyon and his cap*]—*pyllyon*, from Lat. *pileus*. " Hic pilleus est ornamentum capitis sacerdotis vel graduati, Anglice a hure or a *pyllyon*." Halliwell, *Dict.* Compare Barclay ;

" Mercury shall geue thee giftes manyfolde,
    His *pillion*, scepter, his winges, and his harpe."
        Fourth Egloge, sig. C iiii. ed. 1570.

v. 811. *As wyse as Waltoms calfe*] So Heywood ;

" And thinke me *as wise as Waltams calfe*, to talke," &c.
        Dialogue, &c. sig. F 3,—*Workes*, ed. 1598.

Ray gives, " *As wise as Waltham's calf*, that ran nine miles to suck a bull." *Proverbs*, p. 220. ed. 1768.

v. 812. *a Goddes halfe*] i. e. for God's sake. See note, p. 119. v. 501.

Page 153. v. 817. *scole matter*] i. e. school-matter.

v. 820. *elenkes*] i. e. elenchs (*elenchus*—in logic).

v. 822. *mell*] i. e. meddle.

v. 826. *neuen*] i. e. name.

Page 154. v. 831. *mo*] i. e. more.

v. 836. *Lymyters*] i. e. Friars licensed to beg within certain districts.

v. 840. *Flatterynge, &c.*] Compare Barclay ;

" We geue wooll and *cheese*, our wiues coyne and
    egges,
When *freers flatter* and prayse their proper legges."
            Fifth Egloge, sig. D v. ed. 1570.

v. 843. *lese*] i. e. lose.

v. 846. *bacon flycke*] i. e. flitch of bacon.

v. 849. *couent*] i. e. convent.

v. 852. *theyr tonges fyle*]—*fyle*, i. e. smooth, polish : the expression occurs in earlier and in much later writers.

v. 854.   *To Margery and to Maude,*
        Howe they haue no fraude]

As we find the name "Mawte" in our author's *Elynour Rummyng*, v. 159. vol. i. 115, and as in the second of these lines the MS. has "fawte" (i. e. fault), the right reading is probably,

    " To Margery and to *Mawte*,
      Howe they haue no *fawte*."

v. 856. *prouoke*] i. e. incite.

Page 155. v. 857. *Gyll and Jacke at Noke*] See note on v. 323. p. 273.

v. 861. *In open tyme*] i. e. In the time when no fasts are imposed.

Page 155. v. 864. *an olde sayd sawe*] " *Oulde sayd sawe, prouerbe.*" Palsgrave, p. 250.

v. 866. *Some walke aboute in melottes*] " Circuierunt in melotis." *Vulgate,—Heb.* xi. 37. " *Melotes*," as Mr. Albert Way observes to me, " is explained in the *Catholicon* to be a garment used by the monks during laborious occupation, made of the skin of the badger, and reaching from the neck to the loins," and according to other early dictionaries, it was made of the hair or skin of other animals. So the original Greek word, μηλωτή, which properly means *pellis ovina*, signifies also *pellis quævis*.

v. 867. *heery*] i. e. hairy.

v. 868. *ne*] i. e. nor.

v. 869. *in remotes*] i. e. in retired places.

v. 874.

> *And by Dudum, theyr Clementine,*
> *Agaynst curates they repyne ;*
> *And say propreli they ar sacerdotes,*
> *To shryue, assoyle, and reles*
> *Dame Margeries soule out of hell*]

—*shruye, assoyle,* i. e. confess, absolve.—" On a de Clément V une compilation nouvelle, tant des décrets du concile général de Vienne, que de ses épîtres ou constitutions. C'est ce qu'on appelle les *Clémentines.*" *L'Art de vérifier les Dates, &c. (depuis la naissance de Notre-seigneur*), iii. 382. ed. 1818. Skelton alludes here to *Clement.* lib. iii. tit. vii. cap. ii. which begins, " *Dvdum* à Bonifacio Papa octauo prædecessore nostro," &c., and contains the following passages. " Ab olim siquidem inter Prælatos & Rectores, seu Sacerdotes ac Clericos parochialium Ecclesiarum per diuersas Mundi prouincias constitutos ex vna parte, & Prædi-

catorum & Minorum ordinum fratres ex altera (pacis
æmulo, satore zizaniæ procurante), grauis & periculosa
discordia extitit, suscitata·super prædicationib. fidelium
populis faciendis, eorum confessionibus audiendis, pœni-
tentiis iniungendis eisdem, & tumulandis defunctorum
corporibus, qui apud fratrum ipsorum Ecclesias siue
loca noscuntur eligere sepulturam. . . . . . .
Statuimus etiam & ordinamus auctoritate prædicta, vt
in singulis ciuitatibus & diœcesibus, in quibus loca
fratrum ipsorum consistere dignoscuntur, vel in ciuita-
tibus & diœcesibus locis ipsis vicinis, in quibus loca
huiusmodi non habentur, Magistri, Priores prouinciales
Prædicatorum, aut eorum Vicarij & Generales, et Pro-
uinciales Ministri & custodes Minorum & ordinum præ-
dictorum ad præsentiam Prælatorum eorundem locorum
se conferant per se, vel per fratres, quos ad hoc idoneos
fore putauerint, humiliter petituri, vt fratres, qui ad
hoc electi fuerint, in eorum ciuitatibus & diœcesibus
confessiones subditorum suorum confiteri sibi volentium
audire liberè valeant, & huiusmodi confitentibus (prout
secundùm Deum expedire cognouerint) pœnitentias
imponere salutares, atque eisdem absolutionis bene-
ficium impendere de licentia, gratia, & beneplacito
eorundem: Ac deinde præfati Magistri, Priores, Pro-
uinciales, & Ministri ordinum prædictorum eligere
studeant personas sufficientes, idoneas, vita probatas,
discretas, modestas, atque peritas, ad tam salubre min-
isterium et officium exequendum: quas sic ab ipsis
electas repræsentent, vel faciant præsentari Prælatis,
vt de eorum licentia, gratia, & beneplacito in ciuitatib.
& diœcesibus eorundem huiusmodi personæ sic electæ
confessiones confiteri sibi volentium audiant, imponant
pœnitentias salutares, & beneficium absolutionis (in

posterum) impendant, prout superiùs est expressum : extra ciuitates & diœceses, in quibus fuerint deputatæ, per quas eas volumus & non per prouincias deputari, confessiones nullatenus audituræ. Numerus autem personarum assumendarum ad huiusmodi officium exercendum esse debet, prout vniuersitas cleri & populi, ac multitudo vel paucitas exigit eorundem. Et si iidem Prælati petitam licentiam confessionum huiusmodi audiendarum concesserint : illam præfati Magistri, Ministri, & alij cum gratiarum recipiant actione, dictæque personæ sic electæ' commissum sibi officium exequantur. Quòd si fortè iam dicti Prælati quenquam ex dictis fratribus præsentatis eisdem ad huiusmodi officium nollent habere, vel non ducerent admittendum : eo amoto, vel subtracto loco ipsius similiter eisdem præsentandus Prælatis possit, & debeat alius surrogari. Si verò iidem Prælati præfatis fratribus ad confessiones (vt præmittitur) audiendas electis, huiusmodi exhibere licentiam recusârint, nos ex nunc ipsis, vt confessiones sibi confiteri volentium liberè licitèque audire valeant, & eisdem pœnitentias imponere salutares, atque eisdem beneficium absolutionis impertiri, gratiosè concedimus de plenitudine Apostolicæ potestatis. Per huiusmodi autem concessionem nequaquam intendimus personis, seu fratribus ipsis ad id taliter deputatis, potestatem in hoc impendere ampliorem quàm in eo curatis vel parochialibus Sacerdotib. est à iure concessa : nisi forsan eis Ecclesiarum Prælati vberiorem in hac parte gratiam specialiter ducerent faciendam." Pp. 184–190. (*Decret.* tom. iii. ed. 1600.)

Page 155. v. 879.

> *But when the freare fell in the well,*
> *He coud not syng himselfe therout*
> *But by the helpe of Christyan Clout]*

The name " *Cristian Clowte* " has occurred before in
our author's *Manerly Margery Mylk and Ale,* vol. i. 35.
The story alluded to in this passage appears to be
nearly the same as that which is related in a compara-
tively modern ballad, entitled,

" *The Fryer Well-fitted :*

or,

A Pretty Jest that once befel,

How a Maid put a Fryer to cool in the Well.

To a merry new Tune.

Licens'd and Enter'd according to Order."

The Friar wishes to seduce the Maid;

" But she denyed his Desire,
  And told him, that she feared Hell-fire;
            fa, la, &c.
  Tush, (quoth the Fryer) thou needst not doubt,
            fa, la, &c.
  If thou wert in Hell, I could sing thee out;
            fa, la, &c.

The Maid then tells him that he " shall have his re-
quest," but only on condition that he brings her " an
angel of money." While he is absent, " She hung a
Cloth before the Well;" and, when he has returned,
and given her the angel,—

  " Oh stay, (quoth she) some Respite make,
    My Father comes, he will me take;
            fa, la, &c.
    Alas, (qouth the Fryer) where shall I run,
            fa, la, &c.
    To hide me till that he be gone ?
            fa, la, &c.
    Behind the Cloth run thou (quoth she),
    And there my Father cannot thee see;
            fa, la, &c.

Behind the Cloth the Fryer crept,
  fa, la, &c.
And into the Well on sudden he leapt,
  fa, la, &c.
Alas, (quoth he) I am in the Well ;
No matter, (quoth she) if thou wert in Hell ;
  fa, la, &c.
Thou say'st thou could'st sing me out of Hell,
  fa, la, &c.
Now prithee sing thyself out of the Well,
  fa, la, &c."

The Maid at last helps him out, and bids him be gone ;
but when he asks her to give him back the angel,—
 " Good Sir, (said she) there's no such matter,
 I'll make you pay for fouling my Water ;
  fa, la, &c.
 The Fryer went along the Street,
  fa, la, &c.
 Drapping wet, like a new-wash'd Sheep,
  fa, la, &c.
 Both Old and Young commended the Maid,
 That such a witty Prank had plaid ;
  fa, la, la, la, la,
  fa, la, la, lang-tree down-dily."
     Ballads, Brit. Mus. 643. m.

Page 155. v. 882.
  Another Clementyne also,
  How frere Fabian, with other mo,
  Exivit de Paradiso]

—*mo,* i. e. more. Some corruption, if not considera-
ble mutilation of the text, may be suspected here.
There seems to be an allusion to *Clement.* lib. v.
tit. xi. cap. i., which begins, " *Exiui de paradiso,* dixi,

rigabo hortum plantationum, ait ille cœlestis agricola,"
&c. P. 313. (*Decret.* tom. iii. ed. 1600).

Page 156. v. 892. *abiections*] i. e. objections.

v. 901. *hertes*] i. e. hearts.

v. 903. *coueytous*] i. e. covetise, covetousness.

v. 906. *play scylens and glum, &c.*] See note on v. 83. p. 266.

v. 911. *leuer*] i. e. more willingly, rather.

Page 157. v. 914. *Worsshepfully*] i. e. According to their honour, or dignity.

* v. 915. *bate*] i. e. debate, contention.

v. 922. *payntes*] i. e. feigns. See note, p. 121. v. 583.

v. 924. *them lyke*] i. e. please them.

v. 931. *crosse*] i. e. coin. See note, p. 40, v. 363.

v. 932. *predyall landes*] i. e. farm-lands.

Page 158. v. 943. *palles*] See note on v. 312. p. 273.

v. 944. *Arras*] i. e. tapestry : see note, p. 145. v. 78.

v. 947. *lusty*] i. e. pleasant, desirable,—beautiful.

v. 950. *shote*] i. e. shoot.

v. 951. *tyrly tyrlowe*] This passage was strangely misunderstood by the late Mr. Douce, who thought that " *tyrly tyrlowe* " alluded to the note of the crow, that bird being mentioned in the preceding line ! *Illust. of Shakespeare*, i. 353. The expression has occurred before, in our author's *Elynour Rummyng*, v. 292. vol. i. 49 : here it is equivalent to the modern *fa, la, la*, which is often used with a sly or wanton allusion,—as, for instance, at the end of each stanza of Pope's court-ballad, *The Challenge*.

v. 953. *a lege de moy*] See note, p. 121. v. 587.

v. 956. *With suche storyes bydene*]—*bydene*, that is, " by the dozen," says Warton, erroneously, quoting this passage, *Hist. of E. P.*, ii. 343. ed. 4to (note). The word occurs frequently in our early poetry, with different significations: here it may be explained—together—(with *a collection of* such stories); so in *The Worlde and the Chylde*, 1522;

" Now cryst   .   .   .   .

.   .   .   .

Saue all this company that is gathered here *bydene*."

Sig. C iiii.

Page 158. v. 957. *Their chambres well besene*]—*well besene*, i. e. of a good appearance,—well-furnished, or adorned.

v. 962. *Nowe all the worlde stares, &c.*] " This is still," as Warton observes (*Hist. of E. P.*, ii. 343. ed. 4to, note), " a description of tapestry."

v. 963. *chares*] i. e. chariots.

v. 964. *olyphantes*] i. e. elephants.

v. 965. *garlantes*] i. e. garlands.

Page 159. v. 974. *estate*] i. e. high rank, dignity.

v. 975. *courage*] i. e. heart, affections.

v. 977.   *Theyr chambres thus to dresse*
            With suche parfetnesse]
—*parfetnesse*, i. e. perfectness. " We should observe," says Warton, after citing the passage, " that the satire is here pointed at the subject of these tapestries. The graver ecclesiastics, who did not follow the levities of the world, were contented with religious subjects, or such as were merely historical." *Hist. of E. P.*, ii. 344. ed. 4to.

v. 983. *remorde*] i. e. find fault with. See note, p. 146. v. 101.

v. 987. *mellyng*] i. e. meddling.

v. 990. *besy*] i. e. busy.

v. 991. *For one man to rule a kyng*] An allusion, I

apprehend, to Wolsey's influence over Henry the Eighth: so again our author speaking of Wolsey, in the Latin lines at the end of *Why Come ye nat to Courte*, " Qui regnum *regemque regit*." Vol. ii. 320. I may observe too, in further confirmation of the reading " *kyng* " instead of " gyng " [Kele's ed.], that we have had, in an earlier passage of the present poem,

> " *To rule* bothe *kynge* and kayser."   v. 606.

Page 159. v. 996. *flyt*] i. e. remove.

v. 998. *quysshon*] i. e. cushion.

v. 1000. *Cum regibus amicare*] " *Amico*, to be frend." *Medulla Gramatice*, MS. (now in the possession of Mr. Rodd.)

v. 1002. *pravare*] In *Ortus Vocab.* fol. ed. W. de Worde, n. d., is " *Prauo* . . prauum facere. *or to shrewe*," and " Tirannus. *shrewe* or tyrande." The meaning therefore of *pravare* in our text may be—to play the tyrant.

Page 160. v. 1003. *vre*] " *Evr,* happe or lucke, with his compoundes *bonevr* and *malevr*," &c. Palsgrave, p. 166.

> " My goddesse bright, my fortune, and my *vre*."
> > Chaucer's *Court of Loue*, fol. 330,—
> > > *Workes*, ed. 1602.

> " The grace and *ewer* and hap of olde fortune."
> > Lydgate's *Warres of Troy*, B. iv.
> > > sig. Z v. ed. 1555.

> " But wayte his death & his fatall *eure*."
> > *Id.* sig. A a i,

> " And fortune which hath the such *vre* y sent."
> > *Poems by C. Duke of Orleans*,—
> > > *MS. Harl.* 682. fol. 24.

Page 160. v. 1014. *played so checkemate*] In allu-
sion to the king's being put in *check* at the game of
chess.

v. 1017. *mell*] i. e. meddle.

v. 1019. *kayser*] i. e. emperor.   See note, p. 221.
v. 796.

v. 1020. *at the playsure of one, &c.*] Meaning, surely,
Wolsey.

v. 1025. *not so hardy on his hede*] An elliptical ex-
pression; compare v. 1154.   In the *Morte d'Arthur*
when Bors is on the point of slaying King Arthur,
" *Not soo hardy*, sayd syr launcelot, *vpon payn of thy
hede*, &c." B. xx. c. xiii. vol. ii. 411. ed. Southey.

v. 1026. *To loke on God in forme of brede*] — *loke*,
i. e. look : *brede*, i. e. bread..   A not unfrequent expres-
sion in our early writers.

> " Whan I sacred our lordes body,
> Chryste Jesu *in fourme of brede.*"
>> *The Lyfe of saint Gregoryes mother*,
>> n. d. sig. A v.

See too Ritson's *An. Pop. Poetry*, p. 84 ; and Harts-
horne's *An. Met. Tales*, p. 134.

v. 1030. *sacryng*] " *Sacryng* of the masse, *sacre-
ment.*" Palsgrave, p. 264.   And see Todd's *Johnson's
Dict.* in v.

Page 161. v. 1041. *preas*] i. e. press.

v. 1047. *ne*] i. e. nor.

v. 1050. *warke*] i. e. work, business.

v. 1051. *this*] Perhaps for—thus ; see note, p. **2.**
v. 38.

v. 1054. *vncouthes*] i. e. strange matters.

v. 1855. *ken*] i. e. know.

Page 162. v. 1070. *premenire*] i. e. præmunire.

v. 1074. *fotyng*] i. e. footing.

v. 1075. *motyng*] i. e. mooting. " Certamen . . . anglice flytynge chydynge or *motynge*." *Ortus Vocab.* fol. ed. W. de Worde, n. d.

v. 1076. *totyng*] i. e. prying, peeping.

v. 1084. *hole route*] i. e. whole crowd, set.

Page 163. v. 1098. *escrye*] i. e. call out against : see notes, p. 78. v. 903. p. 88. v. 1358.

v. 1106. *hynderyng*] i. e. harming. See note, p. 217. v. 719.

—— *dysauaylyng*] "*Disauayle* one, I hynder his auauntage, *Ie luy porte domaige*." Palsgrave, p. 517.

v. 1116. *to be gramed*] i. e. to be angered : *gramed* is doubtless the right reading here, though the eds. have " greued " and the MS. " grevyd "—(*grame* has already occurred in *Magnyfycence*, v. 1864).

Page 164. v. 1134. *depraue*] i. e. vilify, defame.

Page 165. v. 1154. *Not so hardy on theyr pates*] See note on v. 1025, preceding page.

v. 1155. *losell*] i. e. good-for-nothing. See note, p. 163. v. 138.

v. 1156. *wesaunt*] i. e. weasand.

v. 1157. *syr Guy of Gaunt*] See note. p. 133. v. 70.

v. 1158. *lewde*] i. e. wicked, vile.

v. 1159. *doctour Deuyas*] See note, p. 16. v. 55.

v. 1162. *dawcocke*] i. e. simpleton : see note, p. 36. v. 301.

—— *mell*] i. e. meddle.

v. 1164. *Allygate*] i. e. Allege.

v. 1170. *lurdeyne*] i. e. worthless fellow. See note, p. 213. v. 423.

Page 165. v. 1171. *Lytell Ease*] "*Little Ease* (prison), mala mansio, arcæ robustæ." Cole's *Dict.*— " LITTLE-EASE. A familiar term for a pillory, or stocks; or an engine uniting both purposes, the bilboes." Nares's *Gloss.*

v. 1178. *rechelesse*] i. e. reckless.

Page 166. v. 1184. *Poules Crosse*] i. e. Paul's Cross.

v. 1186. *Saynt Mary Spyttell*] In Bishopsgate Ward: see Stow's *Survey*, B. ii. 97. ed. 1720.

v. 1187. *set not by vs a whystell*] i. e. value us not at a whistle, care not a whistle for us. Compare Lydgate;

" For he *set not by* his wrethe *a whistel*."
The prohemy of a mariage, &c.,—
MS. Harl. 372. fol. 45.

v. 1188. *the Austen fryers*] In Broad-street Ward: see Stow's *Survey*, B. ii. 114. ed. 1720.

v. 1190. *Saynt Thomas of Akers*] Concerning the Hospital intituled of S. Thomas of Acon or Acars [Acre in the Holy Land], near to the great Conduit in Cheape," see Stow's *Survey*, B. iii. 37. ed. 1720, and Maitland's *Hist. of London*, ii. 886. ed. 1756.

v. 1191. *carpe vs*] Is explained by the various reading of the MS.,—" clacke of us."

—— *crakers*] i. e., as the context shews, (not— vaunters, but) noisy talkers.

v. 1193. *reason or skyll*] See note, p. 207. v. 106.

v. 1196. *at a pronge*] See note, p. 215. v. 506.

v. 1199. *fonge*] i. e. take, get.

v. 1201. *the ryght of a rambes horne*] An expression which our author has again in *Speke, Parrot*, v. 498.

vol. ii. 274. So in a metrical fragment, temp. Edward ii. ;

> " As *ryt as ramis orn.*"
>
>> *Reliquiæ Antiquæ* (by Wright and
>> Halliwell), ii. 19.

And Lydgate has a copy of verses, the burden of which is,—

> " Conveyede by lyne *ryght as a rammes horne.*"
>
>> *MS. Harl.* 172. fol. 71.

See too Ray's *Proverbs*, p. 225. ed. 1768.

Page 166. v. 1206. *yawde*] i. e. hewed, cut down. " To *Yaw*, to hew." *Gloss.* appended to *A Dialogue in the Devonshire Dialect*, 1837.

v. 1208. *Isaias*] According to a Jewish tradition, Isaiah was cut in two with a wooden saw by order of King Manasseh.

Page 167. v. 1216. *agayne*] i. e. against.

v. 1223. *cough, rough, or sneuyll*]—*rough*, i. e., perhaps, *rout*, snore, snort. I may just observe that Palsgrave not only gives " *rowte* " in that sense, but also " I *Rowte*, I belche as one dothe that voydeth wynde out of his stomacke, *Je roucte*," (p. 695.) and that Coles has " To *rout*, Crepo, pedo." *Dict.*

v. 1224. *Renne*] i. e. Run.

v. 1227. *set not a nut shell*] i. e. value not at a nutshell, care not a nut-shell for.

v. 1229. *gyse*] i. e. guise, fashion.

v. 1232. *sayd sayne*] A sort of pleonastic expression,—equivalent to—called commonly or proverbially : see note on v. 864. p. 28.

v. 1235. *domis day*] i. e. doomsday.

v. 1239. *boke*] i. e. book.

Page 167. v. 1240. *By hoke ne by croke*] i. e. By hook nor by crook.

Page 168. v. 1244. *nolles*] i. e. heads.

v. 1245. *noddy polles*] i. e. silly heads.

v. 1246. *sely*] i. e. *silly*.

v. 1248. *great estates*] i. e. persons of great estate, or rank.

v. 1255. *wawes wod*] i. e. waves mad, raging.

v. 1257. *Shote*] i. e. Shoot, cast.

v. 1258. *farre*] i. e. farther:

> "I wyl no *farr* mell."
>> *Gentylnes and Nobylyte*, n. d. (attributed
>> without grounds to Heywood) sig C ii.

Page 169. v. 1262. *the porte salu*] i. e. the safe port. Skelton has the term again in his *Garlande of Laurell*, v. 541. vol. ii. 194. Compare Hoccleve;

> "whether our taill
> Shall soone make us with our shippes saill
> To *port salu*." *Poems*, p. 61. ed. 1796,—

where the editor observes, "*Port salut* was a kind of proverbial expression, and so used in the translation of *Cicero de senectute* printed by Caxton."

A RYGHT DELECTABLE TRATYSE VPON A GOODLY GARLANDE OR CHAPELET OF LAURELL ... STUDYOUSLY DYUYSED AT SHERYFHOTTON CASTELL, IN THE FORESTE OF GALTRES, &c.

Sheriff-Hutton Castle " is situated in the Wapentake of Bulmer, and is distant ten miles north-east from York . . . The slender accounts of it that have reached our times, ascribe its origin to Bertram de

Bulmer, an English Baron, who is recorded by Camden
to have built it in the reign of King Stephen, A. D.
1140 . . . From the Bulmers it descended by mar-
riage to the noble family of the Nevilles, and continued
in their possession upwards of 300 years, through a
regular series of reigns, until seized by Edward IV.
in 1471, who soon after gave the Castle and Manor to
his brother the Duke of Gloucester, afterwards Rich-
ard III. In 1485, in consequence of the death of
Richard at the Battle of Bosworth Field, it became
the property of King Henry VII., and continued in
the hands of the Crown, until James the First granted
it to his son, Prince Charles, about 1616. The Castle
and Manor were subsequently granted (also by King
James, according to Camden, and the original grant
confirmed by Prince Charles after he ascended the
throne) to the family of the Ingrams, about 1624–5,
and are now in possession of their lineal descendant,
the present Marchioness of Hertford." *Some Account
of Sheriff-Hutton Castle*, &c. pp. 3–5, York, 1824.

Leland (who says, erroneously it would seem, that
Sheriff-Hutton Castle "was buildid by Rafe Nevill of
Raby the fyrst Erl of Westmerland of the Nevilles,")
gives the following description of it. "There is a
Base Court with Houses of Office afore the Entering
of the Castelle. The Castelle self in the Front is not
dichid, but it stondith *in loco utcunque vdito*. I markid
yn the fore Front of the first Area of the Castelle self
3. great and high Toures, of the which the Gate House
was the Midle. In the secunde Area ther be a 5. or
6. Toures, and the stately Staire up to the Haul is
very Magnificent, and so in the Haul it self, and al the
residew of the House : in so much that I saw no House

in the North so like a Princely Logginges. I lernid
ther that the Stone that the Castel was buildid with
was fetchid from a Quarre at Terington a 2. Miles of.
There is a Park by the Castel. This Castel was wel
maintainid, by reason that the late Duke of Northfolk
lay ther x. Yers, and sins the Duk of Richemond.
From Shirhuten to York vij. Miles, and in the Forest
of Galtres, wherof 4. Miles or more was low Medowes
and Morisch Ground ful of Carres, the Residew by
better Ground but not very high." *Itin.* i. 67. ed.
1770.

"Report asserts, that during the civil wars in the
time of Charles the First, it [the Castle] was dis-
mantled, and the greater part of its walls taken down,
by order of the Parliament. But this is certainly not
the fact, as will be seen by reference to the ' Royal
Survey' made in 1624 . . . From this Survey it will
appear evident, that the Castle was dismantled and
almost in total ruin in the time of James I.,—how long
it had been so, previous to the Survey alluded to, is
now difficult to say. From the present appearance
of the ruins, it is plain that the Castle was purposely
demolished and taken down by workmen, (probably
under an order from the Crown, in whatever reign it
might happen,) and not destroyed by violence of war.
However, since this devastation by human hands, the
yet more powerful and corroding hand of Time has
still further contributed to its destruction. . . . . The
Castle stands upon a rising bank or eminence in front
of the village, and its ruins may be seen on every side
at a great distance." *Some Account*, &c. (already
cited), pp. 5, 6. The vast forest of Galtres formerly
extended nearly all round Sheriff-Hutton.

When Skelton wrote the present poem, Sheriff-Hutton Castle was in possession of the.Duke of Norfolk, to whom it had been granted by the crown for life : see note on v. 769.

Page 170. v. 1. *Arectyng*] i. e. Raising.

v. 6. *plenarly*] i. e. fully—at full.

Page 171. v. 9. *somer flower*] i. e. summer-flower.

v. 10. *halfe*] i. e. side, part.

v. 15. *dumpe*] "I Dumpe, I fall in a *dumpe* or musyng vpon thynges." Palsgrave, p. 530.

v. 16. *Encraumpysshed*] i. e. encramped. Skelton's fondness for compounds of this kind has been already noticed. The simple word occurs in other writers :

"*Crampisheth* her limmes crokedly."

Chaucer's *Annel. and Ar.,—Workes,*
fol. 244. ed. 1602.

"As marbyll colde her lymmes *craumpishing.*"

Lydgate's *Warres of Troy,* B. iv. sig. X v. ed. 1555.

—— *conceyte*] i. e. conceit, conception.

v. 20. *boystors*] i. e. boisterous.

v. 22. *Thus stode I in the frytthy forest of Galtres,*
Ensowkid with sylt of the myry mose]
—*stode,* i. e. stood : *frytthy,* i. e. woody : *ensowkid,* i. e. ensoaked : *sylt,* i. e. mud : *mose,* i. e. moss. The forest of Galtres (which, as already noticed, extended nearly all round Sheriff-Hutton) was, when Camden wrote, "in some places shaded with trees, *in others swampy.*" *Britannia* (by Gough), iii. 20.

v. 24. *hartis belluyng*] In the *Book of Saint Albans,* Juliana Berners, treating " Of the cryenge of thyse bestys," says,

"*An harte belowyth* and a bucke groynyth.I fynde."

Sig. d ii.

Page 171. v. 24. *embosyd*] " When he [the hart] is foamy at the mouth, we say that he is *embost.*" Turbervile's *Noble Art of Venerie*, p. 244. ed. 1611.

v. 26. *the hynde calfe*] " Ceruula. a *hynde calfe.*" *Ortus Vocab.* fol. ed. W. de Worde, n. d.   In the *Book of Saint Albans* we are told ;

" And for to speke of the harte yf ye woll it lere :
Ye shall hym a *Calfe* call at the fyrste yere."
Sig. C vi.

v. 27. *forster*] i. e. forester.

—— *bate*] Does it mean—set on, or train ?

v. 28. *torne*] i. e. turn.

Page 172. v. 32. *superflue*] i. e. superfluous.

" Ye blabbering fooles *superflue* of language."
Barclay's *Ship of Fooles*, fol. 38. ed. 1570.

v. 35. *wele*] i. e. well.

v. 38. *disgysede*] i. e. decked out in an unusual manner.

" Of his straunge aray merueyled I sore

 .   .   .   .

Me thought he was gayly *dysgysed* at that fest."
Lydgate's *Assemble de dyeus*,
sig. b ii. n. d. 4to.

v. 39. *fresshe*] " *Fresshe*, gorgyouse, gay." Palsgrave, p. 313—which I ought to have cited earlier for the meaning of this word.

v. 40. *Enhachyde with perle, &c.*] i. e. Inlaid, adorned with pearl, &c.   Our author in his *Phyllyp Sparowe* tells us that a lady had a wart (or as he also calls it, a scar) " *enhached* on her fayre skyn," v. 1078. vol. i. 98. Gifford observes that " literally, to *hatch* is to inlay [originally, I believe, to cut, engrave, mark with lines] ;

metaphorically, it is to adorn, to beautify, with silver, gold, &c." Note on Shirley's *Works*, ii. 301. " The ladies apparell was after the fashion of Inde, with kerchifes of pleasance, *hatched* with fine gold." Holinshed's *Chron.* (Hen. viii.) vol. iii. 849. ed. 1587. " *Hatching*, is to Silver or gild the Hilt and Pomell of a Sword or Hanger." R. Holme's *Ac. of Armory.* 1688. B. iii. p. 91.

Page 172. v. 41. *The grounde engrosyd and bet with bourne golde*]—*grounde*, i. e. (not floor, but) groundwork; as in Lydgate's verses entitled *For the better abyde* ;

" I see a rybaun ryche and newe

. . . .

The *grownde* was alle of brente golde bryght."
MS. Cott. Calig. A ii. fol. 65.

engrosyd, i. e. thickened, enriched : *bet* has here the same meaning as in *Le Bone Florence of Rome* ;

" Hur clothys wyth bestes and byrdes wer *bete*."
Met. Rom. iii. 9. ed. Ritson,

who somewhat copiously explains it " beaten, plaited, inlay'd, embroider'd :" *bourne*, i. e. burnished.

v. 44. *abylyment*] i. e. habiliment.

v. 45. *estates*] i. e. persons of estate or rank.

v. 49. *supplyed*] i. e. supplicated.

v. 50. *pusant*] i. e. puissant, powerful, mighty.

v. 52. *of very congruence*] i. e. of very fitness.

" Such ought of duetie and *very congruence*," &c.
Barclay's *Ship of Fooles*, fol. 188. ed. 1570

Page 173. v. 54. *astate*] i. e. estate, rank, dignity.

—— *most lenen*] i. e. must lean, bend, bow.

v. 55. *arrect*] i. e. raise.

Page 173. v. 58. *ryall*] i. e. royal.

v. 65. *wele*] i. e. well.

v. 66. *embesy*] i. e. embusy.

—— *holl corage*] i. e. whole heart.

v. 68. *were*] i. e. wear.

v. 69. *wonder slake*] i. e. wonderfully slack.

v. 70. *lake*] i. e. lack, fault.

v. 71. *ne were*] i. e. were it not.

v. 72. *bokis . . sone . . rase*] i. e. books . . soon . erase.

v. 73. *sith*] i. e. since.

v. 74. *Elyconis*] i. e. Helicon's.

v. 75. *endeuour hymselfe*] i. e. exert himself (compare v. 936).

v. 77. *sittynge*] i. e. proper, becoming.

Page 174. v. 79 *to*] i. e. too.

v. 80. *comprised*] Compare our author in *Lenuoy* to Wolsey ;

> " And hym moost lowly pray,
>   In his mynde to *comprise*
>   Those wordes," &c.   vol. ii. 329.

v. 81. *rin*] i. e. run.

v. 83. *pullishe*] i. e. polish.

v. 86. *remorde*] i. e. rebuke. See note, p. 146. v. 101.

v. 94. *mo . . . enduce*] i. e. more . . . bring in, adduce.

v. 95. *parde for to kyll*] i. e. *par dieu*, verily, for to be killed.

v. 96. *enuectyfys*] i. e. invectives.

Page 175. v. 101. *the grey*] i. e. the badger. Juliana Berners says ;

> " That beest a bausyn hyght: a brok or a *graye*:
>   Thyse thre names he hath the soth for to saye."
>   *The Book of St. Albans*, sig. D **vi.**

Page 175. v. 102. *gose* ... *oliphaunt*] i. e. goose ... elephant.

v. 103. *ageyne*] i. e. against.

v. 110. *confecture*] i. e. composition.

v. 111. *diffuse is to expounde*] i. e. is difficult to expound : see note, p. 76. v. 768.

v. 112. *make* . . . *fawt*] i. e. compose . . . fault.

v. 114. *motyue*] i. e. motion. So in the next line but one is " promotyue," i. e. promotion : and so Lydgate has " ymaginatyfe " for—imagination. *Fall of Prynces*, B. v. leaf cxvii. ed. Wayland.

v. 115. *auaunce*] i. e. advance.

v. 116. *rowme*] i. e. room, place.

v. 121. *gyse*] i. e. guise, fashion.

v. 122. *iche man doth hym dres*] i. e. each man doth address, apply, himself.

v. 124. *bokis*] i. e. books.

Page 176. v. 127. *loke*] i. e. look.

v. 129. *mo*] i. e. more.

v. 133. *Ageyne*] i. e. Against.

v. 136. *wele*] i. e. well.

v. 137. *rasid*] i. e. erased.

v. 140. *Sith*] i. e. Since.

—— *defaut*] i. e. default, want.

—— *konnyng*] i. e. (not so much — knowledge, learning, as) skill, ability.

v. 141. *apposelle*] i. e. question.

" And to pouert she put this *opposayle*."
Lydgate's *Fall of Prynces*, B. iii. leaf lxvi.
ed. Wayland.

" Made vnto her this vncouth *apposayle* :
Why wepe ye so," &c.
Id. B. v. leaf. cxxviii.

Page 176. v. 141. *wele inferrid*] i. e. well brought in.

v. 142.   *quikly it is*

           Towchid]

i. e. it is lively, subtly expressed: compare v. 592 and v. 1161, where the words are applied to visible objects.

—— *debarrid*] See note, p. 206. v. 60 ; and compare *Gentylnes and Nobylyte* (attributed without grounds to Heywood) n. d. ;

   " That reason is so grete no man can *debarr*."

                                    Sig. C iii.

v. 149. *sittyng*] i. e. proper, becoming.

Page 177. v. 152. *corage*] i. e. encourage.

v. 153. *fresshely*] i. e. elegantly : see note on v. 39. p. 301.

v. 155. *bruitid*] i. e. reported, spoken of.

v. 156. *outray*] i. e. vanquish. See note, p. 49, v. 87, where this passage is examined.

v. 162. *Ierome, in his preamble Frater Ambrosius, &c.*] The Epistle of Jerome to Paulinus, prefixed to the Vulgate, begins, " *Frater Ambrosius* tua mihi munuscula perferens," &c., and contains this passage : " Unde et Æschines, cum Rhodi exularet, et legeretur illa Demosthenis oratio, quam adversus eum habuerat, mirantibus cunctis atque laudantibus, suspirans ait, Quid, si ipsam audissetis bestiam sua verba resonantem ? " It may be found also in *Hieronymi Opp. I.* 1005. ed. 1609.

v. 172. *most*] i. e. must.

Page 178. v. 180. *wele . . . avaunce*] i. e. well . . . advance.

v. 183. *brybery*] i. e. pilfering. See note, p. 233. v. 1242.

Page 178. v. 186. *cokwoldes*] i. e. cuckolds.

v. 187. *wetewoldis*] i. e. wittols, tame cuckolds.

" *Wetewoldis* that suffre synne in her syghtes."
Lydgate's Assemble de dyeus,
sig. c i. n. d. 4to.

v. 188. *lidderons*] So before, *lydderyns;* see note, p. 249. v. 1945 : but here, it would seem, the word is used in the more confined sense of—sluggish, slothful, idle fellows.

—— *losels*] i. e. good-for-nothings. See note, p. 163. v. 138.

—— *noughty packis*] i. e. worthless, loose persons, (properly, it would seem, cheaters ; see Richardson's *Dict.* in v. *Pack.*)—If Skelton had been required to distinguish exactly between the meanings of these terms of reproach, he would perhaps have been nearly as much at a loss as his editor.

v. 189. *Some facers, some bracers, some make great crackis*] See note, p. 174. v. 33.

v. 192. *courte rowlis*] i. e. court-rolls.—Warton cites this and the next two verses as " nervous and manly lines." *Hist. of E. P.* ii. 354. ed. 4to.

v. 196. *rinne*] i. e. run.

Page 179. v. 198. *cunnyng*] i. e. knowledge, learning.

v. 200. *a mummynge*] See note, p. 266. v. 83.

v. 201. *sadnesse*] i. e. discretion. See note, p. 238. v. 1382.

v. 203. *faute*] i. e. fault.

v. 204. *to*] i. e. too.

v. 205. *can . . . scole*] i. e. knows . . . school.

v. 207. *fole*] i. e. fool.

v. 208. *stole*] i. e. stool.

Page 179. v. 209. *Iacke a thrummis bybille*] See note, p. 140. v. 204.

v. 211. *agayne*] i. e. against.

v. 212. *dwte*] i. e. duty.

Page 180. v. 218. *to*] i. e. too.

v. 223. *lay*] i. e. allege. See note, p. 178. v. 103.

—— *werkis*] i. e. works.

v. 227. *most*] i. e. must.

v. 232. *condiscendid*] i. e. agreed. See note, p. 206. v. 39.

v. 233. *clarionar*] Is used here for—trumpeter : but the words properly are not synonymous;

> " Of *trumpeters* and eke of *clarioneres*."
>
> Lydgate's *Warres of Troy*, B. i. sig. C v.
> ed. 1555.

and Skelton himself has afterwards in the present poem, "*trumpettis* and *clariouns*." v. 1507.

v. 235. *Eolus, your trumpet*] i. e. Æolus, your trumpeter.

> " A *trumpet* stode and proudly gan to blowe,
> Which slayne was and fro the tre doun throw."
>
> Lydgate's *Fall of Prynces*, B. v. leaf cxxx.
> ed. Wayland.

So Chaucer makes Æolus trumpeter to Fame : see *House of Fame*, B. iii.

v. 236. *mercyall*] i. e. martial.

v. 239. *prease*] i. e. press, throng.

v. 240. *hole rowte*] i. e. whole crowd, assembly.

Page 181. v. 243. *were founde out*] See note, p 227. v. 977.

v. 244. *hardely*] i. e. assuredly.

v. 245. *eyne*] i. e. eyes.

v. 248. *presid . . . to*] i. e. pressed . . . too.

* Page 181. v. 250. *Some whispred, some rownyd*]
—to *rown* is to speak low. See note, p. 45. v. 513.

* v. 252. *nexte*] i. e. nearest.

v. 255. *quod*] i. e. quoth.

v. 258. *plumpe*] i. e. cluster, mass. " Stode stille as
hit had ben a *plompe* of wood." *Morte d'Arthur*, B. i.
cap. xvi. vol. i. 27. ed. Southey. Dryden has the
word; and the first writer perhaps after his time who
used it was Sir W. Scott.

v. 260. *timorous*] i. e. terrible.

Page 182. v. 264. *rowte*] i. e. crowd, assembly.

v. 265. *girnid*] i. e. grinned.

v. 266. *peuysshe*] i. e. silly, foolish.

—— *masyd*] i. e. bewildered, confounded.

v. 267. *whyste*] i. e. still.

—— *the nonys*] i. e. the occasion.

v. 268. *iche . . . stode*] i. e. each . . . stood.

v. 269. *wonderly*] i. e. wonderfully.

v. 270. *A murmur of mynstrels*] So in many of our
early English dramas " a noise of musicians " is used
for a company or band of musicians.

v. 272. *Traciane*] i. e. Thracian.

—— *herped meledyously*] i. e. harped melodiously.

v. 274. *armony*] i. e. harmony.

v. 275. *gree*] i. e. agree.

v. 278. *gle*] i. e. music.

v. 279. *auaunce*] i. e. advance.

v. 282. *Sterte . . . fote*] i. e. Started . . . foot.

v. 285. ——————— *lake
Of*]
i. e. lack of,—less than.

Page 183. v. 288. *cronell*] i. e. coronal, garland.

Page 183. v. 289. *heris encrisped*] i. e. hairs formed
into curls, curling.

   v. 290. *Daphnes*] i. e. Daphne.   So our early poets
wrote the name ;

> " A maiden whilom there was one
> Which *Daphnes* hight."
>
> > Gower's *Conf. Am.* B. iii. fol. lvi.
> > ed. 1554.

" Her name was *Daphnys* which was deuoyed of loue."

> *The Castell of pleasure*, (by Nevil, son of
> Lord Latimer), sig. A iii. 1518.

So afterwards in the present poem we find *Cidippes*
for Cydippe, v. 885 ; and see note, p. 49. v. 70.

   —— *the darte of lede*] From Ovid, *Met.* i. 471.

   v. 291. *ne wolde*] i. e. would not.

   v. 292. *herte*] i. e. heart.

   v. 295. *Meddelyd with murnynge*] i. e. Mingled with
mourning.

   v. 296. *O thoughtfull herte*] See note, p. 23. v. 10.

   v. 298. *loke*] i. e. look.

   v. 300.   *the tre as he did take*
Betwene his armes, he felt her body quake]
From Ovid, *Met.* i. 553.

   v. 302. *he assurded into this exclamacyon*]—*assurded*,
i. e. broke forth—a word which I have not elsewhere
met with, but evidently formed from the not uncom-
mon verb *sourd*, to rise. " Ther withinne *sourdeth*
and spryngeth a fontayne or welle."   Caxton's *Mir-
rour of the world*, 1480, sig. e v.: in that work, a few
lines after, occurs " *resourdeth*."

   v. 306. *adyment*] i. e. adamant.

   v. 307. *ouerthwhart*] i. e. cross, perverse, adverse.

   v. 310. *Sith*] i. e. Since.

Page 184. v. 314. *gresse*] i. e. grass. This stanza is also imitated from Ovid, *Met*. i. 521.

* v. 315. *axes*] i. e. access, feverish pain. See note, p. 22. v. 9.

* v. 317. *raist*] i. e. arrayest :—*to array* is to put into a condition or plight : see note on title of poem, p. 152.

v. 318. *But sith I haue lost, &c.*] Again from Ovid, *Met*. i. 557.

* v. 323. *by and by*] i. e. straightway.

v. 324. *poetis laureat, &c.*] It must be remembered that formerly a *poet laureat* meant a person who had taken a degree in grammar, including rhetoric and versification : and that the word *poet* was applied to a writer of prose as well as of verse ; " *Poet*, a connyng man." Palsgrave, p. 256.

> " And *poetes* to preoven hit. Porfirie and Plato
> Aristotle. Ovidius," &c.
> > *Peirs Plouhman*, p. 210. ed. Whit.

> " Nor sugred deties [ditties] of Tullius Cicero."
> > Lydgate's *Lyfe and passion of seint Albon*,
> > sig. B ii. ed. 1534.

v. 328. *Esiodus, the iconomicar*] i. e. Hesiod, the writer on husbandry (the eds. by a misprint have "icononucar,"—which Warton says he " cannot decypher." *Hist. of E. P.*, ii. 352 (note), ed. 4to. Among *MSS. Dig. Bod.* 147. is " Carmen Domini Walteri de Henleye quod vocatur *Yconomia* sive Housbundria : " compare Cicero ; " quam copiose ab eo [Xenophonte] agricultura laudatur in eo libro, qui est de tuenda re familiari, qui *Œconomicus* inscribitur." *Cato Major*, c. 17.

v. 329. *fresshe*] i. e. elegant : see note, p. 301. v. 39

Page 185. v. 335. *engrosyd*] i. e. plumped up, swollen.

—— *flotis*] i. e. flowings,—drops : Faukes's ed. "droppes;" ("*Flotyce.* Spuma." *Prompt. Parv.* ed. 1499, is a distinct word.)

v. 338. *Percius presed forth with problemes diffuse*] —*presed*, i. e. pressed : *diffuse*, i. e. difficult to be understood : see note, p. 76. v. 768.

v. 340. *satirray*] Is this word to be explained—satirist, or satirical ?

v. 344. *auaunce*] i. e. advance.

v. 345. *mengith*] i. e. mingleth.

v. 347. *wrate . . . mercyall*] i. e. wrote . . . martial.

v. 352. *Orace also with his new poetry*] "That is, Horace's *Art of Poetry.* Vinesauf wrote *De Nova Poetria.* Horace's *Art* is frequently mentioned under this title." Warton's *Hist. of E. P.*, ii. 353 (note), ed. 4to.

Page 186. v. 359. *Boyce*] i. e. Boethius.

—— *recounfortyd*] i. e. recomforted,—comforted.

v. 360.

Maxymyane, with his madde ditiis,
How dotynge age wolde iape with yonge foly]

—*iape*, i. e. jest, joke. The *Elegiarum Liber* of Maximianus, which has been often printed as the production of Cornelius Gallus, may be found, with all that can be told concerning its author, in Wernsdorf's *Poetæ Latini Minores, tomi sexti pars prior.* In these six elegies, Maximianus deplores the evils of old age, relates the pursuits and loves of his youth, &c. &c. Perhaps the line " *How dotynge age wolde iape with yonge foly* " (in which case *iape* would have the same meaning here as in our author's *Manerly Margery Mylk and Ale,* v. 20. vol. i. 36.) is a particular allusion to Elegy v., where Maximianus informs us, that, having been sent on an embassy, at an advanced period of life, he became enamoured of a " Graia puella," &c., the adventure being described in the grossest terms.

Page 186. v. 365. *Johnn Bochas with his volumys grete*] In Skelton's time, the *De Genealogia Deorum,* the *De Casibus Virorum et Fœminarum Illustrium,* and other now-forgotten works of Boccaccio, were highly esteemed,—more, perhaps, than the *Decamerone.*

v. 366. *full craftely that wrate*] i. e. that wrote full skillfully.

v. 368. *probate*] i. e. proof, meaning, or, perhaps, interpretation.   See note, p. 204. v. 4.

v. 372. *Poggeus . . . with many a mad tale*] When this poem was written, the *Facetiæ* of Poggio enjoyed the highest popularity.   In *The Palice of Honour,* Gawen Douglas, enumerating the illustrious writers at the Court of the Muses, says,

" Thair was Plautus, *Poggius,* and Persius."
      · p. 27. ed. Ban. 1827.

v. 374. *a frere of Fraunce men call sir Gagwyne, &c.*]—*frere,* i e. friar: concerning Gaguin, see *Account of Skelton and his Writings.*

v. 376. *bote is of all bale*] i. e. remedy of all evil. See note, p. 252. v. 2096.

v. 380. *Valerius Maximus by name*] i. e. Valerius who has the name Maximus (to distinguish him from Valerius Flaccus).

v. 381. *Vincencius in Speculo, that wrote noble warkis*]—*warkis,* i. e. works.   The *Speculum Majus* of Vincentius Bellovacensis (*naturale, morale, doc-*

trinale, et historiale), a vast treatise in ten volumes folio, usually bound in four, was first printed in 1473. See the *Biog. Univ.*, and Hallam's *Introd. to the Lit. of Europe*, i. 160.

Page 187. v. 382. *Pisandros*] " Our author," says Warton, "got the name of Pisander, a Greek poet, from Macrobius, who cites a few of his verses." *Hist. of E. P.*, ii. 353 (note), ed. 4to. A mistake: Macrobius (*Sat.* v. 2.) mentions, but does not cite, Pisander.

v. 383. *blissed Bachus, that mastris oft doth frame*]— *mastris*, i. e. disturbances, strifes : see note, p. 245. v. 1738.

v. 386. *sadly . . . auysid*] i. e. seriously, earnestly . . . considered, observed.

v. 389. *fresshely be ennewed*] i. e. be elegantly polished. See notes, p. 76. v. 775. p. 301. v. 39.

v. 390.   *The monke of Bury . . .*
    Dane Johnn Lydgate]

— *Dane*, equivalent to *Dominus*. So at the commencement of his *Lyfe of our Lady*, printed by Caxton, folio, n. d.; " This book was compyled by *dan John lydgate, monke of Burye*," &c. He belonged to the Benedictine abbey of Bury in Suffolk.

v. 391. *theis Englysshe poetis thre*] " That only these three English poets [Gower, Chaucer, Lydgate] are here mentioned, may be considered as a proof that only these three were yet thought to deserve the name." Warton's *Hist. of E. P.*, ii. 354. ed. 4to. So the Scottish poets of Skelton's time invariably selected these three as most worthy of praise : see Laing's note on Dunbar's *Poems*, ii. 355.

v. 393. *Togeder in armes, as brethern, enbrasid*] So Lydgate ;

" *Embraced in armes* as they had be knet
Togyder with a gyrdell."
Le Assemble de dyeus, sig. d iii. n. d.

Page 187. v. 395. *tabers*] i. e. tabards : see the earlier portion of note, p. 273. v. 318.

v. 397. *Thei wantid nothynge but the laurell*] Meaning,—that they were not poets laureate : see note on v. 324. p. 310.

v. 398. *godely*] i. e. goodly.

v. 402. *enplement*] i. e. employment, place.

Page 188. v. 405. *The brutid Britons of Brutus Albion*]—*brutid*, i. e. famed. So Lydgate ;

" Reioyse ye folkes that borne be in Bretayne,
Called otherwise *Brutus Albion.*"
Fall of Prynces, B. viii. fol. viii. ed. Wayland.

* v. 410. *Arrectinge vnto your wyse examinacion*] i. e. referring, subjecting. See note, p. 207, v. 95.

v. 414. *besy*] i. e. busy.

v. 417. *hooll*] i. e. whole.

v. 420. *poynted*] i. e. appointed.

v. 421. *pullisshyd*] i. e. polished.

v. 425. *mowte*] i. e. might.

Page 189. v. 428. *preuentid*] i. e. anticipated.

v. 429. *meritory*] i. e. deserved, due.

v. 431. *regraciatory*] i. e. return of thanks.

v. 432. *poynt*] i. e. appoint.

v. 433. *holl*] i. e. whole.

v. 434. *Auaunced*] i. e. Advanced.

v. 439. *warkes*] i. e. works.

v. 444. *I made it straunge*] i. e. I made it a matter of nicety, scruple.

v. 445. *presed*] i. e. pressed.

Page 190. v. 455. *prese*] i. e. press, throng.

* Page 190. v. 455. *lesse and more*] i. e. the smaller and the greater.

v. 460. *Engolerid*] i. e. Engalleried.

v. 466. *turkis and grossolitis*] i. e. turquoises and chrysolites.

v. 467. *birrall enbosid*] i. e. beryl embossed.

v. 469.   *Enlosenged with many goodly platis*
             Of golde]

i. e. Having many goodly plates of gold shaped like lozenges (quadrilateral figures of equal sides, but unequal angles).

—— *entachid with many a precyous stone*]—*entachid* may be used in the sense of—tacked on; but qy. is the right reading " *enhachid?* " as in v. 40 of the present poem, " *Enhachyde* with perle," &c., (and v. 1078 of *Phyllyp Sparowe*,) see note, p. 301.

v. 472. *whalis bone*] In our early poetry " white as whales bone " is a common simile; and there is reason to believe that some of our ancient writers supposed the ivory then in use (which was made from the teeth of the horse-whale, morse, or walrus) to be part of the bones of a whale. Skelton, however, makes a distinction between " whalis bone " and the real ivory (see v. 468). The latter was still scarce in the reign of Henry the Eighth; but, before that period, Caxton had told his readers that " the tooth of an olyfaunt is yuorye." *Mirrour of the world*, 1480. sig. f i.

Page 191. v. 474. *The carpettis within and tappettis of pall*]—*tappettis of pall*, i. e. coverings of rich or fine stuff (perhaps table-covers) : that *tappettis* does not here mean tapestry, is proved by the next line; and compare v. 787,

" With that the *tappettis* and carpettis were layd,

Whereon theis ladys softly myght rest,
The saumpler to sow on," &c.

In an unpublished book of King's Payments, in the
Chapter-House, we find, under the first year of
Henry 8;

" Item to Corneles Vanderstrete opon his ⎫
waraunt for xv *Tappettes made for Wyndowes* ⎬ ix s."
at the towre ⎭

Page 191. v. 475. *clothes of arace*] See note, p. 145.
v. 78.

v. 476. *Enuawtyd . . . vawte*] i. e. Envaulted . . .
vault.

v. 477. *pretory*] Lat. prætorium.

v. 478. *enbulyoned*] i. e. studded ; see note on **v.**
1165.

—— *indy blew*] i. e. azure. See note, p. 23. v. 17.

* v. 480. *Iacinctis and smaragdis out of the florthe
they grew*]—*Iacinctis*, i. e. Jacinths : *smaragdis*, i. e.
emeralds (but see note, p. 24. v. 20) : *Planché*, the
florthe of any thyng that is borded." Palsgrave, p. 49
" *Florthe* of a house, *astre*." *Id.* p. 221.—" Gyst that
gothe ouer the *florthe soliue, giste*." *Id.* p. 225. " I
Plaster a wall or *florthe* with plaster . . . I wyl plaster
the *florthe* of my chambre to make a gernyer there,
*Je plastreray latre de ma châbre pour en faire vng
grenier.*" *Id.* p. 660.

v. 483. *most rychely besene*] i. e. of a most rich ap-
pearance,—most richly arrayed : see notes, p. 35. v.
283. p. 291. v. 957.

v. 484. *cloth of astate*] i. e. cloth of estate,—canopy.

v. 487. *ryally*] i. e. royally.

v. 489. *enuyrowne*] i. e. in compass, about.

Page 191. v. 490. *stode*] i. e. stood.

v. 492. *presid*] i. e. pressed.

v. 493. *Poyle . . . Trace*] i. e. Apulia . . . Thrace.

Page 192. v. 499. *metely wele*] See note, p. 254. v. 2196.

v. 502. *a kyby hele*] i. e. chapped. See note, p. 119. v. 493.

v. 503. *salfecundight*] i. e. safe-conduct.

v. 504. *lokyd . . . a fals quarter*]—*lokyd*, i. e. looked: "The *false quarters* is a soreness on the inside of the hoofs, which are commonly called quarters, which is as much as to say, crased unsound quarters, which comes from evil Shooing and paring the Hoof." R. Holme's *Ac. of Armroy*, 1688. B. ii. p. 152.

v. 505. *I pray you, a lytyll tyne stande back*] So Heywood;

"For when prouender prickt them *a little tine*," &c.
                Dialogue, &c. sig. D,—*Workes*, ed. 1598.

v. 514. *the ballyuis of the v portis*] i. e. the bailiffs of the Cinque Ports.

Page 193. v. 519. *besines*] i. e. business.

v. 520. *most*] i. e. must.

v. 521. *maystres*] i. e. mistress.

v. 523. *sufferayne*] i. e. sovereign.

v. 525. *And we shall se you ageyne or it be pryme*] I have my doubts about what hour is here meant by *pryme*. Concerning that word see Du Cange's *Gloss.* in *Prima* and *Horæ Canonicæ*, Tyrwhitt's *Gloss.* to Chaucer's *Cant. Tales*, Sibbald's *Gloss.* to *Chron. of Scot. Poetry*, and Sir F. Madden's *Gloss.* to *Syr Gawayne*, &c.

v. 531. *kest . . . loke*] i. e. cast . . . look.

v. 537. *supprysed*] i. e. overpowered, smitten.

Page 194. v. 541. *the port salu*] See note, p. 297. v. 1262.

v. 547. *hertely as herte*] i. e. heartily as heart.

v. 550. *aquyte*] i. e. discharge, pay.

v. 554. *moche*] i. e. much.

v. 555. *Affyaunsynge her myne hole assuraunce*] i. e. Pledging her my whole, &c.

v. 559. *stonde*] i. e. stand.

Page 195. v. 566. *iangelers*] i. e. babblers, chatterers.

v. 570. *moche costious*] i. e. much costly.

v. 572. *the stones be full glint*]—*glint* must mean here—slippery : see note, p. 245. v. 1687

v. 574. *yatis*] i. e. gates.

v. 581. *seryously*] i. e. seriatim.

v. 585. *carectis*] i. e. characters.

v. 586. *where as I stode*] i. e. where I stood.

Page 196. v. 590. *a lybbard*] i. e. a leopard.—" There is," says Warton, who quotes the stanza, " some boldness and animation in the figure and attitude of this ferocious animal." *Hist. of E. P.*, ii. 252. ed. 4to.

v. 592. *As quikly towchyd*] i. e. touched, executed, as much to the life.

v. 595. *forme foote*] i. e. fore-foot.

—— *shoke*] i. e. shook.

v. 597.

Unguibus ire parat loca singula livida curvis
Quam modo per Phœbes nummos raptura Celœno."

The whole of this " Cacosyntheton ex industria " is beyond my comprehension. Here Skelton has an eye to Juvenal ;

" Nec per conventus nec cuncta per oppida *curvis*
Unguibus ire parat nummos raptura Celœno."

Sat. viii. 129.

Page 196. v. 601. *Spreto spineto cedat saliunca ro-*
seto] Here he was thinking of Virgil;

> " Lenta salix quantum pallenti *cedit* olivæ,
> Puniceis humilis quantum *saliunca rosetis*."
>
> *Ecl.* v. 16.

v. 602. *loked*] i. e. looked.

v. 605. *to*] i. e. too.

v. 606. *astate*] i. e. estate, condition.

v. 607. *haskardis*] " *Haskerdes* went in the queste :
not honeste men. *Proletarii & capite censi:* non clas-
sici rem transegerunt." Hormanni *Vulgaria*, sig. n iiii.
ed. 1530.

> " Wyne was not made for euery *haskerde*."
>
> Copland's *Hye Way to the Spyttell Hous,*
> *Early Pop. Poetry*, ii. 33. ed. Utterson.

who in the Gloss. queries if *haskerde* mean " dirty fel-
low ? from the Scotch *hasky*." [Rough, rude fellows.
See Halliwell's *Dict.* where " hastarddis," (p. 8. v. 24.)
is referred to this word.]

—— *rebawdis*] i. e. ribalds.

v. 608. *Dysers, carders*] Dicers, card-players.

—— *gambawdis*] i. e. gambols.

Page 197. v. 609. *Furdrers of loue*] i. e. Furtherers
of love—pimps, pandars.

v. 610. *blow at the cole*] A friend suggests that there
is an allusion here to alchemists; but I believe he is
mistaken. It is a proverbial expression. So our
author again;

> " We may *blowe at the cole*."
>
> *Why come ye nat to Courte*, **v. 81.**
> vol. ii. 29.

The proverb given by Davies of Hereford ;

" *Let them that bee colde, blow at the cole.*
So may a man do, and yet play the foole.*"
Scourge of Folly,—Prouerbes, p. 171.
and by Ray, *Proverbs*, p. 90. ed. 1768, seems to have
a quite different meaning.

Page 197. v. 611. *kownnage*] i. e. coinage—coining.

v. 612. *Pope holy ypocrytis*] i. e. Pope-holy hypo-
crites: see note, p. 195. l. 10 (prose).

—— *as they were golde and hole*]—*hole*, i. e. whole.
Heywood also has this expression ;
" In words *gold and hole*, as men by wit could wish,
She will [lie] as fast as a dog will lick a dish."
Dialogue, &c.—*Workes*, sig. H 2, ed. 1598.

v. 613. *Powle hatchettis*] See note, p. 20. v. 28.

—— *ale pole*] i. e. pole, or stake, set up before an
ale-house by way of sign.

v. 614. *brybery*] i. e. pilfering. See note, p. 233.
v. 1242.

* v. 615. *condycyons*] i. e. qualities, dispositions,
habits. See note, p. 132. v. 12.

v. 616. *folys*] i. e. fools.

v. 618. *dysdanous dawcokkis*] i. e. disdainful simple-
tons, empty fellows: see note, p. 36. v. 301.

v. 619. *fawne thé*] i. e. fawn on thee.

—— *kurris of kynde*] i. e. curs by nature.

v. 620. *shrewdly*] i. e. evilly.

v. 625. *broisid*] i. e. bruised, broke.

v. 626. *peuysshe*] i. e. foolish, silly.

—— *porisshly pynk iyde*] " *Porisshly*, as one loketh
y[t] can nat se well, *Louchement.*" Palsgrave, p. 840.
pynk iyde, i. e. pink-eyed; " Some haue myghty eyes,
and some be *pynkeyed . . . peti.*" Hormanni *Vulgaria*,
sig. G vi. ed. 1530 ; and see Nares's *Gloss.* in v.

Page 197. v. 627. *aspyid*] i. e. espied, marked.

v. 620. *a gun stone*] After the introduction of iron shot (instead of balls of stone) for heavy artillery, the term *gunstone* was retained in the sense of—bullet: " *Gonne stone, plombee, boulet, bovle de fonte.*" Palsgrave, p. 226.

—— *all to-iaggid*] See note p. 22. v. 32.

* Page 198. v. 630. *daggid*] i. e. jagged, or foliated.

v. 631. *byrnston*] i. e. brimstone.

v. 632. *Masid*] i. e. Bewildered, confounded.

—— *a scut*] " *Scut* or hare. Lepus." *Prompt. Parv.* ed. 1499.

—— *a deuyl way*] See note, p. 280. v. 672.

v. 637. *peuisshenes*] i. e. foolishness, silliness : compare v. 626.

v. 639. *foisty bawdias*] See note, p. 144. v. 76.

v. 641. *Dasing after dotrellis, lyke drunkardis that dribbis*]—*Dasyng*, i. e. gazing with a stupefied look : *dotrellis;* see note, p. 55. v. 409 : *dribbis*, i. e. drip, drivel, slaver.

v. 642. *titiuyllis*] See note, p. 275. v. 418.

—— *taumpinnis*] i. e. tampions,—wooden stoppers, put into the mouths of cannon to keep out rain or sea-water. In *The foure P. P.* by Heywood, the Poticary tells a facetious story about " a thampyon." Sig D i. ed. n. d. (Fr. *tampon*).

v. 643. *I hyght you*] i. e. I assure you.

v. 649. *auenturis*] i. e. adventure.

* Page 199. v. 652. *herber*] i. e. arbour.

v. 653. *brere*] i. e. briar.

v. 654. *With alys ensandid about in compas*] " i. e. it was surrounded with sand-walks." Warton's *Hist. of E. P.*, ii. 350 (note), ed. 4to. So the garden, in which Chaucer describes Cressid walking, was " *sonded* all the waies." *Troilus and Creseide*, B. ii. fol. 152,— *Workes*, ed. 1602 : and compare Lydgate ;

> " Alle the *aleis* were made playne with *sond*."
>
> > *The Chorle and the Bird,—MS. Harl.*
> > > 116. fol. 147.

Page 199. v. 655. *with singular solas*] i. e. in a particularly pleasant manner.

v. 656. *rosers*] i. e. rose-bushes.

v. 658. *coundight*] i. e. conduit.

—— *coryously*] i. e. curiously.

v. 662. *ensilured again the son beames*] i. e. ensilvered against the sunbeams.

v. 664. *reuolde*] i. e. revolved, turned.

* 669. *bet vp a fyre*] i. e. made a fire, (properly, mended).

v. 671. *flagraunt flower*]—*flagraunt*, i. e. fragrant. Compare v. 978.   So Hawes ;

> " Strowed with *floures flagraunte* of ayre."
>
> > *The Pastime of pleasure*, sig. A a iiii.
> > > ed. 1555.

v. 673. *baratows broisiours*] i. e. contentious bruisers, —unless (as the context seems rather to shew) *broisiours* means—bruisures, bruises.

Page 200. v. 674. *passid all bawmys*] i. e. surpassed all balms.

v. 676. *piplyng*] i. e. piping ; as in our author's *Replycacion*, &c. vol. i. 232. l. 3. (prose).

v. 680. *the nyne Muses, Pierides by name*] So Chaucer ;

> " *Muses, that men clepe Pierides.*"
>
> > *The Man of Lawes Prol.* v. 4512 (but
> > > see Tyrwhitt's note).

Page 200. v. 681. *Testalis*] i. e. Thestylis. So Bar-
clay;

" Neera, Malkin, or lustie *Testalis.*"
Second Egloge, sig. B ii. ed. 1570,

v. 682. *enbybid*] i. e. made wet, soaked.

v. 683. *moche solacyous*] i. e. much pleasant, mirth-
ful.

v. 686. *fotid*] i. e. footed.

v. 687. *twynklyng vpon his harpe stringis*]—*twynk-
lyng*, i. e. tinkling. So, at a much later period, Dek-
ker; " Thou (most cleare throated singing man,) with
thy Harpe, (to the *twinckling* of which inferior Spirits
skipt like Goates ouer the Welsh mountaines)," &c.
A Knights Coniuring, 1607. sig. D 2.

v. 688. *And Iopas, &c.*] Here, and in the next two
stanzas, Skelton has an eye to Virgil;

" Cithara crinitus Iopas
Personat aurata, docuit quæ maxumus Atlas.
Hic canit errantem lunam, solisque labores ;
Unde hominum genus, et pecudes ; unde imber, et
        ignes ;
Arcturum, pluviasque Hyadas, geminosque Triones ;
Quid tantum Oceano properent se tinguere soles
Hiberni, vel quæ tardis mora noctibus obstet."
Æn. i. 740.

—— *auaunce*] i. e. advance.

v. 694. *spere*] i. e. sphere.

Page 201. v. 697. *prechid*] i. e. discoursed, told.

—— *chere*] i. e. countenance, look.

v. 699. *aspy*] i. e. espy.

v. 705. *counteryng*] See note, p. 11.

v. 712. *conuenable*] i. e. fitting.

Page 201. v. 718. *wcle were hym*] i. e. he were in good condition.

Page 202. v. 720. *maystres*] i. e. mistress.

v. 725. *losyd ful sone*] i. e. loosed full soon.

v. 731. *That I ne force what though it be discurid*] i. e. That I do not care although it be discovered, shewn.

v. 733. *ladyn of liddyrnes with lumpis*]—*liddyrnes*, i. e. sluggishness, slothfulness (the construction is—ladyn with lumpis of liddyrness).

v. 734. *dasid*] i. e. stupefied.

—— *dumpis*] i. e. musings. See note on v. 15. p. 300: but here the word implies greater dulness of mind.

v. 735. *coniect*] i. e. conjecture.

v. 736. *Gog*] A corruption of the sacred name.

v. 737. *be*] i. e. by.

Page 203. v. 741. *fonde*] i. e. foolish.

v. 742. *Tressis agasonis species prior, altera Davi*] " Hic Dama est non *tressis agaso.*" Persius, *Sat.* v. 76. *Davus* is a slave's name in Plautus, Terence, &c.

v. 748. *tacita sudant præcordia culpa*] From Juvenal, *Sat.* i. 167.

v. 751. *Labra movens tacitus*] " *Labra* moves *tacitus.*" Persius, *Sat.* v. 184.

—— *rumpantur ut ilia Codro*] From Virgil, *Ecl.* vii. 26.

v. 754. *and ye wist*] i. e. if ye knew.

Page 204. v. 758. *hole reame*] i. e. whole realm.

v. 763. *leue warke whylis it is wele*] i. e. leave work while it is well.

* v. 764. *towchis*] i. e. tricks. " *Touche*, a crafty dede, *tour.*" Palsgrave, p. 282.

Page 204. v. 764. *to*] i. e. too.

v. 768. *astate*] i. e. estate, state.

v. 769. *Countes of Surrey*] Was Elizabeth Stafford, eldest daughter of Edward Duke of Buckingham, and second wife of Thomas Howard, Earl of Surrey, who afterwards (on the death of his father in 1524) became the third Duke of Norfolk. She had previously been attached and engaged to the Earl of Westmoreland with the consent of both families ; but her father, having broken off the intended match, compelled her to accept the hand of Lord Thomas Howard in 1513. She was twenty years younger than her husband. After many domestic quarrels, they separated about 1533. Of their five children, one was Henry Howard, the illustrious poet. She died in 1558. See *Memorials of the Howard Family*, &c. by H. Howard, 1834, folio.

The Countess of Surrey appears to have been fond of literature ; and, as she calls Skelton her "clerk," we may suppose that she particularly patronised him. The probability is, that the present poem was really composed at Sheriff-Hutton Castle, which (as already noticed, p. 300) had been granted by the king to the Duke of Norfolk for life, and that the Countess was residing there on a visit to her father-in-law.

The *Garlande of Laurell* was written, I apprehend, about 1520, or perhaps a little later : in v. 1192 Skelton mentions his *Magnyfycence*, which was certainly produced after 1515,—see note on title of that piece, p. 204.

v. 771. *beue*] i. e. bevy.

v. 774. *warke*] i. e. work.

Page 205. v. 775. *asayde*] i. e. tried, proved.

Page 205. v. 776. *cronell*] i. e. coronal, garland.

* v. 786. *of there lewdnesse*] i. e. out of their vile-ness.

v. 787. *tappettis and carpettis*] See note on v. 474. p. 315.

v. 790. *To weue in the stoule*] So Chaucer;

" And *weauen in stole* the radevore."

Leg. of Philomene, fol. 195.—*Workes*, ed. 1602.

and Hall; " On their heades bonets of Damaske syluer flatte *wouen in the stole*, and therupon wrought with gold," &c. *Chron. (Hen. viii.)* fol. vii. ed. 1548.—Mr. Albert Way observes to me that in *Prompt. Parv. MS. Harl.* 221, is " Lyncent, werkynge instrument for sylke women. Liniarium," while the ed. of 1499 has " Lyncet, a werkynge *stole;*" and he supposes the *stole* (i. e. stool) to have been a kind of frame, much like what is still used for worsted work, but, instead of being arranged like a cheval glass, that it was made like a stool,—the top being merely a frame or stretcher for the work.

—— *preste*] i. e. ready.

v. 791. *With slaiis, with tauellis, with hedellis well drest*]—*slaiis*, i. e. sleys, weavers' reeds: *tauellis*, see note, p. 15. v. 34 : " *Heddles, Hedeles, Hiddles.* The small cords through which the warp is passed in a loom, after going through the reed." *Et. Dict. of Scot. Lang.* by Jamieson, who cites from G. Douglas's *Æneid ;*

" With subtell slayis, and hir *hedeles* slee,
Riche lenze wobbis naitly weiffit sche." *

B. vii. p. 204. 45. ed. Rudd.

v. 794. *to enbrowder put them in prese*] i. e. put

themselves in press (applied themselves earnestly) to embroider.

Page 205. v. 795. *glowtonn*] Does it mean — ball, clue ? or, as Mr. Albert Way suggests, — a sort of needle, a stiletto as it is now called,—something by which the silk was to be inwrought ?

v. 796. *pirlyng*] " I *Pyrle* wyer of golde or syluer, I wynde it vpon a whele as sylke women do." Palsgrave, p. 658.

Page 206. v. 798. *tewly sylk*] Richardson in his *Dict.* under the verb *Tew* places *tewly*, as derived from it, and cites the present passage. But *tewly* seems to have nothing to do with that verb. " *Tuly* colowre. Puniceus vel punicus." *Prompt. Parv. MS. Harl.* 221. In *MS. Sloane*, 73. fol. 214, are directions "for to make bokerham, *tuly*, or *tuly* thred," where it appears that this colour was " a manere of reed colour as it were of croppe mader," that is, probably, of the tops or sprouts of the madder, which would give a red less intense or full : the dye was " safflour " (saffron ?) and " asches of wyn [whin] ballis ybrent; " and a little red vinegar was to be used to bring the colour up to a fuller red.—For this information I am indebted to Mr. Albert Way.

v. 799. *botowme*] " I can make no *bottoms* of this threde . . . *glomera*." Hormanni *Vulgaria*, sig. t i. ed. 1530.

v. 801. *warkis*] i. e. works.

v. 803. *With burris rowth and bottons surffillyng*]— *burris rowth*, i. e. burrs rough : *bottons*, i. e. buds : *surffillyng*, see note, p. 270. v. 219.

v. 805. *enbesid*] i. e. embusied.

v. 815. *captacyons of beneuolence*] Todd gives

" *Captation* (old Fr. *captation*, ruse, artifice). The practice of catching favour or applause ; courtship ; flattery." *Johnson's Dict.* Richardson, after noticing the use of the verb *captive* " with a subaudition of gentle, attractive, persuasive means or qualities," adds that in the present passage of Skelton *captation* is used with that subaudition. *Dict.* in v.

Page 206. v. 816. *pullysshid*] i. e. polished.

> v. 817. *Sith ye must nedis afforce it by pretence*
> *Of your professyoun vnto vmanyte*]

i. e. Since you must needs attempt, undertake, it by your claim to the profession of humanity,—*humaniores literæ*, polite literature.

v. 819. *proces*] i. e. discourse ; see notes, p. 75. v. 735. p. 195 (first note on prose), p. 263. v. 2506, &c

v. 820. *iche*] i. e. each.

v. 821. *sentence . . . couenable*] i. e. meaning . . fitting.

Page 207. v. 822. *Auaunsynge*] i. e. Advancing.

v. 824. *arrectyng*] i. e. raising.

v. 825. *ken*] i. e. instruct (pleonastically coupled with " informe," as in v. 1428).

v. 828. *dredfull*] i. e. full of dread, timorous.

v. 830. *bestad*] i. e. bested, circumstanced.

v. 833. *gabyll rope*] i. e. cable-rope. "A *Gable*, Ru dens." Coles's *Dict.*

v. 835. *beseke*] i. e. beseech.

—— *Countes of Surrey*] See note on v. 769. p. 325.

v. 838. *reconusaunce*] i. e. acknowledgment.

v. 841. *astate*] i. e. estate, state.

v. 842. *honour and worshyp*] Terms nearly synonymous : *worshyp*, i. e. dignity.

Page 207. v. 842. *formar*] i. e. first, highest: see Todd's *Johnson's Dict.* in v.   *Former.*

v. 843. *Argyua*] i. e. Argia.

v. 844. *Polimites*] i. e. Polynices;

> "his fellaw dan *Polimites*,
> Of which the brother dan Ethiocles," &c.
>> Chaucer's *Troilus and Creseide*, B. v. fol. 180,—
>> *Workes*, ed. 1602.

> "Lete *Polymyte* reioyse his herytage."
>> Lydgate's *Storye of Thebes, Pars tert.*
>> sig. i v. ed. 4to. n. d.

Page 208. v. 847. *counterwayng*] i. e. counter-weighing.

v. 850. *Pamphila*] "Telas araneorum modo texunt ad vestem luxumque fœminarum, quæ bombycina appellatur. Prima eas redordiri, rursusque texere invenit in Ceo mulier *Pamphila*, Latoi filia, non fraudanda gloria excogitatæ rationis ut denudet fœminas vestis." Plinii *Nat. Hist.* lib. xi. 26.

—— *quene of the Grekis londe*]—*londe*, i. e. land: qy. does any writer except Skelton call her a queen?

v. 852. *Thamer also wrought with her goodly honde*
  Many diuisis passynge curyously]

It is plain that Skelton, while writing these complimentary stanzas, consulted Boccaccio *De Claris Mulieribus:* there this lady is called *Thamyris* (see, in that work, "De *Thamyri* Pictrice," cap. liiii. ed. 1539). Her name is properly *Timarete;* she was daughter to Mycon the painter; vide Plinii *Nat. Hist.: honde,* i. e. hand: *diuisis,* i. e. devices.

v. 857. *toke*] i. e. took.

Page 208. v. 860. *corage* . . . *perfight*] i. e heart, affection . . . perfect.

—— *lady Elisabeth Howarde*] Was the third daughter of the second Duke of Norfolk by his second wife, Agnes Tylney, daughter of Sir Hugh Tylney, and sister and heir to Sir Philip Tylney of Boston, Lincolnshire, knight (I follow Howard's *Memorials of the Howard Family*, &c.; Collins says " daughter of Hugh Tilney "). Lady Elizabeth married Henry Ratcliff, Earl of Sussex.

v. 865. *Aryna*] i. e. perhaps—Irene. In the work of Boccaccio just referred to is a portion " De *Hyrene* C[r]atini filia," cap. lvii. ; and Pliny notices her together with the above-mentioned Timarete.

v. 866. *konnyng*] i. e. knowledge.

v. 867. *wele*] i. e. well.

Page 209. v. 868. *enbewtid*] i. e. beautified.

v. 871. *Creisseid*] See Chaucer's *Troilus and Creseide*.

—— *Polexene*] i. e. Polyxena, the daughter of Priam.

v. 872. *enuyue*] i. e. envive, enliven, excite.

—— *lady Mirriell Howarde*] Could not have been Muriel, daughter of the second Duke of Norfolk ; for she, after having been twice married, died in 1512, anterior to the composition of the present poem. Qy. was the Muriel here celebrated the Duke's grandchild, —one of those children of the Earl and Countess of Surrey, whose names, as they died early, have not been recorded ? .Though Skelton compares her to Cidippe, and terms her " madame," he begins by calling her " mi *litell* lady."

v. 880. *curteyse*] i. e. courteous.

Page 209. v. 881. *Whome fortune and fate playnly haue discust*]—*discust*, i. e. determined.   So again our author in *Why come ye nat to Courte ;*

" Allmyghty God, I trust,
    Hath for him *dyscust*," &c.   v. 747. vol. ii. 301.

and Barclay ;

" But if thou iudge amisse, then shall Eacus
    (As Poetes saith) hell thy iust rewarde *discusse.*"
                    The Ship of Fooles, fol. 4. ed. 1570.

and Drayton ;

" In vaine was valour, and in vaine was feare,
    In vaine to fight, in vaine it was to yeeld,
    In vaine to fly ; for destiny *discust*,
    By their owne hands or others' dye they must."
                    The Miseries of Queene Margarite,
                        p. 115. ed. 1627.

v. 882. *plesure, delyght, and lust*] One of Skelton's pleonastic expressions.

v. 885.   *Cidippes, the mayd,*
    That of Aconcyus whan she founde the byll, &c.]

—*Cidippes*, i. e. Cydippe ; see note on v. 290. p. 309 : *the byll ;* i. e. the writing,—the verses which Acontius had written on the apple.

v. 888. *fyll*] i. e. fell.

Page 210. *lady Anne Dakers of the Sowth*] The wife of Thomas Lord Dacre, was daughter of Sir Humphrey Bourchier, son of John Lord Berners and of Elizabeth Tylney, who (see note on v. 399) afterwards became the first wife of the second Duke of Norfolk.

v. 893. *his crafte were to seke*] i. e. his skill were at a loss.

v. 897. *Princes*] i. e. Princess.

Page 210. v. 898. *conyng*] i. e. knowledge.

v. 899. *Paregall*] i. e. Equal (thoroughly equal).

v. 901. *surmountynge*) i. e. surpassing.

v. 902. *sad*] i. e. grave, discreet.   See note, p. 245. v. 1711.

v. 903. *lusty lokis*] i. e. pleasant looks.

—— *mastres Margery Wentworthe*] Perhaps the second daughter of Sir Richard Wentworth, afterwards married to Christopher Glemham of Glemham in Suffolk.

v. 906. *margerain ientyll*] "Marierome is called . . . in English, Sweet Marierome, Fine Marierome, and *Marierome gentle ;* of the best sort Marjerane." Gerard's *Herball*, p. 664. ed. 1633.

v. 907. *goodlyhede*] i. e. goodness.

v. 908. *Enbrowdred*] i. e. Embroidered.

v. 912. *praty*] i. e. pretty.

Page 211. —— *mastres Margaret Tylney*] A sister-in-law, most probably, of the second Duke of Norfolk. His first wife was Elizabeth, daughter and heir of Sir Frederick Tylney of Ashwell-Thorpe, Norfolk, knight, and widow of Sir Humphrey Bourchier, son of John Lord Berners : his second wife was Agnes, daughter of Sir Hugh Tylney, and sister and heir to Sir Philip Tylney of Boston, Lincolnshire, knight ; see second note, p. 330.

v. 928. *besy cure*] i. e. busy care.

v. 933.   *As Machareus*
                 Fayre Canace]

Their tale is told in the *Conf. Am.* by Gower ; he expresses no horror at their incestuous passion, but remarks on the cruelty of their father, who

" for he was to loue strange,
    He wolde not his herte change
    To be benigne and fauourable
    To loue, but vnmerciable ! "
                  B. iii. fol. xlviii. ed. 1554.

(and see the lines cited in note on v. 1048. p. 335).
Lydgate (*Fall of Prynces*, B. i. leaf xxxv. ed. Wayland) relates the story with a somewhat better moral feeling.

Page 211. v. 935. *iwus*] Or *i-wis* (adv.),—i. e. truly, certainly.

v. 941. *Wele*] i. e. Well.

* v. 942. *Intentyfe*] i. e. Attentive.

Page 212. v. 948. *Perle orient*] In allusion to her Christian name just mentioned, " Margarite."

v. 949. *Lede sterre*] i. e. Load-star.

v. 950. *Moche*] i. e. Much.

—— *maystres Iane Blenner-Haiset*] Perhaps a daughter of Sir Thomas Blennerhasset, who was executor (in conjunction with the Duchess) to the second Duke of Norfolk : see Sir H. Nicolas's *Test. Vet.* ii. 604.

v. 955. *smale lust*] i. e. small liking.

v. 958. *prese*] i. e. press, band.

v. 962. *ententifly*] See above, note on v. 942.

v. 963. *stellyfye*] " I *Stellifye*, I sette vp amongest the starres." Palsgrave, p. 734.

v. 965. *ne swarue*] i. e. swerve not.

v. 968. *Sith*] i. e. Since.

v. 972. *Laodomi*] i. e. Laodamia.

Page 213. v. 975. *godely*] i. e. goodly.

v. 977. *Reflaring rosabell*] i. e. odorous fair-rose : see note, p. 62. v. 524.

Page 213. v. 978. *flagrant*] i. e. fragrant. See note on v. 671. p. 322.

v. 979. *The ruddy rosary*]—*rosary* must mean here —rose-bush, not rose-bed.

v. 982. *nepte*] " Cats mint or *nept* is a kind of cala-mint," &c. *The Countrie Farme*, p. 320. ed. 1600.

v. 983. *ieloffer*] See note, p. 80. v. 1052.

v. 984. *propre*] i. e. pretty.

* v. 985. *Enuwyd*] i. e. freshly put on or painted. See note, p. 76. v. 775.

Page 214. v. 1006. *Ientill as fawcoun*] The *Falcon gentle*, says Turbervile, is so called " for her *gentle* and courteous condition and fashions." *The Booke of Falconrie*, &c. p. 26. ed. 1611.

v. 1007. *hawke of the towre*] See note, p. 225. v. 934.

v. 1025. *fayre Isaphill*] The Hypsipyle of the an-cients.

" *Isiphile*,

. . . .

She that dyd *in fayrnesse so excell.*"
Lydgate's Fall of Prynces, B. i. leaf xviii.
ed. Wayland.

She figures in the *Storye of Thebes* by the same inde-fatigable versifier, who there says,

" But to knowe the auentures all
Of this lady, *Isyphyle the fayre*,"
(Pars tert. sig. h iiii. n. d. 4to.)
we must have recourse to Boccaccio *De Claris Muli-eribus* (see that work, cap. xv. ed. 1539).

v. 1027. *pomaunder*] Was a composition of per-fumes, wrought into the shape of a ball, or other form, and worn in the pocket, or about the neck (Fr. *pomme d'ambre*). In the following entry from an unpublished

Boke of Kyngs Paymentis from i to ix of Henry viii, preserved in the Chapter-House, Westminster, *pomaunder* means a case for holding the composition ;

"Item to the frenche quenes seruaunt, ⎫ xx.s." (9th
  that brought *a pomaunder of gold* to ⎬ year
  the princes, in Re[ward] ⎭ of reign.

Page 215. v. 1030. *Wele*] i. e. Well.

v. 1048. *Pasiphe*] Lest the reader should be surprised at finding Skelton compare Mistress Statham to Pasiphae, I cite the following lines from Feylde's *Contrauersye bytwene a Louer and a Iaye* (printed by W. de Worde), n. d., in which she and Taurus are mentioned as examples of true love ;

> " Phedra and Theseus,
>   Progne and Thereus,
>   *Pasyphe and Taurus,*
>   Who lyketh to proue,
>   Canace and Machareus,
>   Galathea and Pamphylus,
>   Was neuer more dolorous,
>   *And all for true loue."* Sig. B iiii.

I may add too a passage from Caxton's *Boke of Eneydos,* &c. (translated from the French), 1490 ; " The wyffe of kynge Mynos of Crete was named Pasyfa that was a grete lady and a fayr aboue alle other ladyes of the royame . . . . . . The quene Pasyfa *was wyth chylde by kynge Mynos,* and whan her tyme was comen she was delyuered of a creature that was halfe a man and halfe a bulle." Sig. h 6.

Page 216. v. 1062. *aquyte*] i. e. requite.

v. 1068. *gyse*] i. e. guise, fashion.

Page 216. v. 1076.

> *Galathea, the made well besene, &c.*

. . . .

By Maro]

—*the made well besene*, i. e. the maid of good appearance, fair to see : the expression applied, as here, to personal appearance, independent of dress, is, I apprehend, very unusual; see notes, p. 35. v. 283. p. 291. v. 957. p. 316. v. 483 : *By Maro;* vide *Ecl.* i. and iii.

v. 1082. *leyser*] i. e. leisure.

Page 217. v. 1094. *ich*] i. e. each.

v. 1103. *where as*] i. e. where.

Page 218. v. 1109. *Wele was hym*] i. e. He was in good condition.

v. 1114. *astate*] i. e. estate,—meaning here—state, raised chair or throne with a canopy : compare v. 484.

v. 1117. *loked . . . a glum*] i. e. looked . . . a gloomy, sour look.

v. 1118. *Thhere was amonge them no worde then but mum*] See note, p. 266. v. 83.

v. 1121. *sith*] i. e. since.

v. 1124. *pretence*] i. e. pretension, claim.

v. 1128. *princes of astate*] i. e. princess of estate rank, dignity.

* Page 219. v. 1132. *condiscendyng*] i. e. agreeing, conformable with. See note, p. 206. v. 39.

v. 1135. *enduce*] i. e. bring in, adduce.

v. 1136. *lay*] i. e. allege, or make good. See note, p. 178. v. 103.

v. 1139. *bokis*] i. e. books.

v. 1144. *presid*] i. e. pressed.

v. 1150. *ony*] i. e. any.

Page 220. v. 1154. *wote wele*] i. e. know well.

v. 1156. *losende*] i. e. loosened, loosed.

* v. 1158. *byse*] Hearne in his Gloss. to *Langtoft's Chron.* has " *bis*, grey, black," [the original signification of the word: see Ducange, *Bisa*, and, *Gloss. Franc., Bis.*] with an eye, no doubt, to the line at p. 230.

  " In a marble *bis* of him is mad story."

and Sir F. Madden explains the word " white or grey " in his Gloss. to *Syr Gawayne*, &c., referring to the line " Of golde, azure, and *byse* " in *Syre Gawene and The Carle of Carelyle*, p. 204. But we also find " *Byce*, a colour, *azur*." Palsgrave, p. 198. " Scryueners wryte with blacke, red, purple, grene, *blewe or byce*, and suche other." Hormanni *Vulgaria*, sig. Q i. ed. 1530. " *Bize*, Blew, Byze, a delicate Blew." Holme's *Acad. of Arm.*, 1688. B. iii. p. 145.

v. 1158. *gressoppes*] i. e. grasshoppers: see note, p. 51. v. 137.

v. 1159. *fresshe*] i. e. gay, gorgeous: see note on v. 39. p. 301.

v. 1160. *Enflorid*] i. e. Enflowered (embellished, for it applies partly to the " snaylis ").

v. 1161. *Enuyuid picturis well towchid and quikly*] —*Enuyuid*, i. e. envived: *quikly*, livelily, to the life; a somewhat pleonastic line, as before, see note, p. 241. v. 1569.

v. 1163. *garnysshyd*] ⎫ " I hadde leuer haue my
    . . . .   ⎬ boke sowed in a forel [*in*
v. 1165. *bullyons* ⎭ *cuculli involucro*] than
bounde in bourdes, and couered and clasped, and *garnyshed with bolyons* [*vmbilicis*]." Hormanni *Vulgaria*, sig. Q iiii. ed. 1530: *bullyons*, i. e. bosses, studs.

Page 220. v. 1165. *worth a thousande pounde*] An expression found in other early poets ;

> " And euery bosse of bridle and paitrell
> That they had, was *worth*, as I would wene,
> *A thousand pound.*"

Chaucer's *Floure and Leafe,—Workes*,
fol. 345. ed. 1602.

v. 1166. *balassis*] Tyrwhitt (Gloss. to *Chaucer's Cant. Tales*) explains *Bales* to be " a sort of bastard Ruby." Du Cange (*Gloss.*) has " *Balascus*, Carbunculus, cujus rubor et fulgor dilutiores sunt . . . . . a Balascia Indiæ regione . . . dicti ejusmodi lapides pretiosi." Marco Polo tells us, " In this country [*Balashan* or *Badakhshan*] are found the precious stones called *balass* rubies, of fine quality and great value." *Travels*, p. 129, translated by Marsden, who in his learned note on the passage (p. 132) observes that in the Latin version it is said expressly that these stones have their name from the country. See too Sir F. Madden's note on *Privy Purse Expenses of the Princess Mary*, p. 209.

v. 1167. *aurum musicum*] i. e. *aurum musaicum* or *musivum*,—mosaic gold.

Page 221. v. 1172. *Boke of Honorous Astate*] i. e. Book of Honourable Estate. Like many other of the pieces which Skelton proceeds to enumerate, it is not known to exist. When any of his still extant writings are mentioned in this catalogue, I shall refer to the places where they may be found in the present volumes.

v. 1176. *to lerne you to dye when ye wyll*] A version probably of the same piece which was translated and published by Caxton under the title of *A lityll treatise shorte and abredged spekynge of the arte and crafte to knowe well to dye*, 1490, folio. Caxton translated it from the French: the original Latin was a work of great celebrity.

Page 221. v. 1178. *Rosiar*] i. e. Rose-bush.

—— *Prince Arturis Creacyoun*] Arthur, the eldest son of King Henry the Seventh, was created Prince of Wales and Earl of Chester, 1st Oct. 1489: see Sandford's *Geneal. Hist.* p. 475. ed. 1707.

Page 222. v. 1183. *Bowche of Courte*] In vol. i. 37.

v. 1185. *Of Tullis Familiars the translacyoun*] Is noticed with praise in Caxton's Preface to *The Boke of Eneydos*, &c. 1490 ; see the passage cited in *Account of Skelton and his Writings*.

v. 1187. *The Recule ageinst Gaguyne of the Frenshe nacyoun*]—*Recule*, Fr. *recueil*, is properly—a collection of several writings: it occurs again in v. 1390; and in *Speke, Parrot*, v. 232. vol. ii. 257. Concerning Gaguin, see *Account of Skelton and his Writings*.

v. 1188.

the Popingay, that hath in commendacyoun
Ladyes and gentylwomen suche as deseruyd,
And suche as be counterfettis they be reseruyd]

—*Popingay*, i. e. Parrot: " *Reserued*, excepte, *sauf*." Palsgrave, p. 322.—No part of *Speke, Parrot* (in vol. ii. 245), answers to this description: but " *the Popingay* " is certainly only another name for *Speke, Parrot* (see v. 280. vol. ii. 260) ; and Skelton must allude here to some portion, now lost, of that composition.

v. 1192. *Magnyfycence*] In vol. ii. 3.

v. 1193. *new get*] i. e. new fashion. See note, p. 214. v. 458.

v. 1196. *wele*] i. e. well.

Page 223. v. 1198. *Of manerly maistres Margery Mylke and Ale, &c.*] In vol. i. 35. is one of the " many maters of myrthe " which Skelton here says that he " wrote to her."

v. 1202. *Lor*] A corruption of Lord.

v. 1206. *This fustiane maistres and this giggisse gase*] —*maistres,* i. e. mistress : *giggisse,* i. e. giggish,— which Forby gives, with the sense of—trifling, silly, flighty (*Vocab. of East Anglia*) ; but here perhaps the word implies something of wantonness : *gase,* i. e. goose.

* v. 1207. *wrenchis*] i. e. tricks.

v. 1209. *shuld not crase*] i. e. that it should not break.

v. 1210. *It may wele ryme, but shroudly it doth accorde*]—*wele,* i. e. well: *shroudly,* i. e. shrewdly, badly. A copy of verses on Inconsistency by Lydgate has for its burden,

" *It may wele ryme, but it accordith nought.*"

MS. Harl. 2251. fol. 26.

v. 1211. *pyke . . . potshorde*] i. e. pick . . . potsherd.

Page 224. v. 1219.

Of my ladys grace at the contemplacyoun,
Owt of Frenshe into Englysshe prose,
Of Mannes Lyfe the Peregrynacioun,
He did translate, enterprete, and disclose]

—*at the contemplacyoun ;* see note on heading of Epitaph, p. 171 : *my ladys grace* means perhaps the mother of Henry the Seventh, the Countess of Derby; see note on title of Elegy, p. 190. Warton says that this piece was " from the French, perhaps, of Guillaume [de Guilleville] prior of Chalis. But it should be observed that Pynson printed *Peregrinatio humani generis*, 1508, 4to." *Hist. of E. P.*, ii. 337 (note), ed. 4to. *The Pylgremage of the Soule translatid oute of Frensshe in to Englysshe with somwhat of addicions, the yere of our lord* M.CCCC & *thyrten, and endeth in the Vigyle of seynt Bartholomew Emprynted at Westmestre by William Caxton, And fynysshed the sixth day of Juyn, the yere of our lord,* M.CCCC.LXXXIII *And the first yere of the regne of kynge Edward the fyfthe.* fol., was taken from the French of Guillaume de Guilleville (see *Biog. Univ.* xix. 169); but, though Skelton was in all probability an author as early as 1483, there is no reason for supposing that the volume just described had received any revision from him. *Peregrinatio Humani Generis*, printed by Pynson in 4to., 1508, is, according to Herbert (*Typ. Ant.* ii. 430. ed. Dibdin), "in ballad verse, or stanzas of seven lines;" it cannot therefore be the piece mentioned here by Skelton, which he expressly tells us was in "*prose.*"

Page 224. v. 1226. *creauncer*] i. e. tutor. See note, p. 146. v. 102.

v. 1229. *Speculum Principis*] A piece by Skelton entitled *Methodos Skeltonidis Laureati*, sc. *Præcepta quædam moralia Henrico principi, postea Hen. viii. missa. Dat. apud Eltham.* A. D. MDI. was once among the MSS. in the Library of Lincoln Cathedral, but is now marked as missing in the Catalogue of that collection, and has been sought for in vain. Whether it was the same work as that mentioned in the present passage, I am unable to determine.

—— *honde*] i. e. hand.

v. 1231. *astate*] i. e. estate, state.

Page 224. v. 1233. *the Tunnynge of Elinour Rummyng*] In vol. i. 109.

v. 1234. *Colyn Clowt*] In vol. ii. 125.

—— *Iohnn Iue, with Ioforth Iack*] In 1511, a woman being indicted for heresy, " her husband deposed, that in the end of the reign of King Edward the Fourth, one *John Ive* had persuaded her into these opinions, in which she had persisted ever since." Burnet's *Hist. of the Reform*, i. 51. ed. 1816. The words " with *Ioforth, Iack*," were perhaps a portion of Skelton's poem concerning this John Ive : *ioforth* is an exclamation used in driving horses ;

> " Harrer, Morelle, *iofurthe*, hyte."
>
> *Mactacio Abel*,—*Towneley Mysteries*, p. 9.

Page 225. v. 1235. *make . . konnyng*] i. e. compose . . . knowledge, skill, ability.

v. 1236. *parde*] i. e. *par dieu*, verily.

v. 1238. *conueyauns*] See the long speech of Crafty Conueyaunce in our author's *Magnyfycence*, v. 1343 sqq. vol. ii. 62.

v. 1239. *the Walshemannys hoos*] See note, p. 282. v. 780.

v. 1240. *vmblis*] i. e. parts of the inwards of a deer. " *Noumbles* of a dere or beest, *entrailles*." Palsgrave, p. 248. And see Sir F. Madden's note, *Syr Gawayne*, &c. p. 322.

—————— *the botell of wyne,*
To fayre maistres Anne that shuld haue be sent]

Such a present seems to have been not uncommon ;

" Beddes, brochys, and *botelles of wyen he to the lady sent*."

> Lydgate's *Ballad of A Prioress and her three Wooers*,—*MS. Harl.* 78. fol. 74.

The "maistres Anne" here mentioned is doubtless the lady to whom the lines in vol. i. 25 are addressed.

Page 225. v. 1246. *longyth*] i. e. belongeth.

v. 1247. *Of one Adame all a knaue* .

. . . . . .

He wrate an Epitaph, &c.] In vol. i. 191.

v. 1250. *agerdows*] i. e. eager, keen, severe.

v. 1254. *Phillip Sparow*] In vol. i. 61.

Page 226. v. 1257. *Yet sum there be therewith that take greuaunce*] See notes, p. 84 sqq., where will be found illustrations of the portion of *Phyllyp Sparowe* which is inserted in the present poem.

Page 230. v. 1376. *The Gruntyng and the groynninge of the gronnyng swyne*] See note, p. 127. v. 2.

v. 1377. *the Murnyng of the mapely rote*]—*mapely rote*, i. e. maple-root. — In Ravenscroft's *Pammelia*, 1609, part of a nonsensical song (No. 31) is as follows;

> " My Ladies gone to Canterbury,
> S. Thomas be her boote.
> Shee met with Kate of Malmsbury,
> *Why weepst thou maple roote ?* "

a recollection perhaps of Skelton's lost ballad.

v. 1378. *pine*] i. e. pain, grief.

v. 1379. *a cote*] i. e. a coot (water-fowl.)

v. 1380. *birdbolt*] i. e. a blunt arrow used to kill birds ; see Nares's *Gloss.* in v. and in v. *Bolt.*

—— *hart rote*] i. e. heart-root.

v. 1381. *Moyses hornis*] So Lydgate ;

> " *Moyses*
> With *golden hornes* liche phebus beames bright."
> *Process. of Corpus Christi,—MS. Harl.*
> 2251. fol. 251.

" Cumque descenderet Moyses de monte Sinai . . .
ignorabat quod *cornuta* esset facies sua ex consortio
sermonis Domini." Vulgate,—*Exod.* xxxiv. 29.

Page 230. v. 1382. *merely, medelyd*] i. e. merrily,
mingled.

v. 1383. *Of paiauntis that were played in Ioyows
Garde*] Bale, in his enumeration of Skelton's writ-
ings, alluding to this line (as is evident from his
arrangement of the pieces), gives " *Theatrales ludos.*"
Script. Illust. Bryt. p. 652. ed. 1557: and Mr. J. P.
Collier states that " one of Skelton's earlier works had
been a series of pageants, ' played in Joyous Garde,'
or Arthur's Castle." *Hist. of Eng. Dram Poet.* ii. 142.
But, assuredly, in the present line, *paiauntis*, i. e.
pageants, means nothing of a dramatic nature. The
expression to " play a pageant" has occurred several
times already in our author's poems; " I haue *played*
my *pageyond*" (my part on the stage of life), see note,
p. 6. v. 85 ; " Suche pollyng *paiaunttis* ye *pley*" (such
thievish pranks), see note p. 140. v. 190: and though
it may be doubted whether the *paiauntis that were
played* IN *Ioyows Garde*,—i. e. in the Castle of Sir
Launcelot, according to the romances—are to be un-
derstood as connected with feats of arms, I cite the
following passage in further illustration of the expres-
sion ; " The fyrste that was redy to Juste was sir
Palomydes and sir Kaynus le straunge a knyghte of
the table round. And soo they two encountred to
gyders, but sire Palomydes smote sir Kaynus soo hard
that he smote hym quyte ouer his hors croupe, and
forth with alle sir Palomydes smote doune another
knyght and brake thenne his spere & pulled oute his
swerd and did wonderly wel. And thenne the noyse
beganne gretely vpon sir palomydes. loo said Kynge

Arthur yonder palomydes begynneth *to play his pagent.*
So god me help said Arthur he is a passynge good
knyght. And ryght as they stood talkyng thus, in
came sir Tristram as thonder, and he encountred with
syre Kay the Seneschall, and there he smote hym
doune quyte from his hors, and with that same spere
sir Tristram smote doune thre knyghtes moo, and
thenne he pulled oute his swerd and dyd merueyl-
lously. Thenne the noyse and crye chaunged from
syr Palomydes and torned to sir Tristram and alle the
peple cryed O Tristram, O Tristram. And thenne
was sir Palomydes clene forgeten. How now said
Launcelot vnto Arthur, yonder rydeth a knyght *that
playeth his pagents."* *Morte d' Arthur*, B. x. cap. lxxix.
vol. ii. 140. ed. Southey.

Page 230. v. 1384. *wrate*] i. e. wrote.

—— *muse*] See note, p. 200. v. 212.

v. 1385. *do*] i. e. doe.

v. 1386. *parker . . . with all*] i. e. park-keeper . . .
withal.

v. 1387. *Castell Aungell*] " And the pope fled unto
Castle Angell." Cavendish's *Life of Wolsey*, p. 143.
ed. 1827.

* —— *fenestrall*] " Before the general introduction
of glazed windows, their place was supplied by framed
blinds of cloth or canvas, termed *fenestralls.* . . . .
Horman says that " paper or lyn clothe straked acrosse
with losyngys make *fenestrals* in stede of glasen wyn-
dowes." Harrison, who wrote his description of Eng-
land about 1579, . . . states that glass had become so
cheap and plentiful, being imported from Burgundy,
Normandy, and Flanders, as well as made in England,
of good quality, that every one who chose might have

abundance." Way's *Prompt. Parv.* i. 155. *Fenestrall* appears to be used here for a glazed window: see v. 1388.

Page 231. v. 1389. *eyn dasild and dasid*]—*eyn*, i. e. eyes: *dasid*, i. e. dulled.

v. 1390. *The Repete of the recule of Rosamundis bowre*]—*Repete*, i. e. Repetition, Recital: *recule;* see note on v. 1187. p. 339.

v. 1392. *proprc*] i. e. pretty.

—— *ieloffer flowre*] See note, p. 80. v. 1052.

v. 1393. *to recheles*] i. e. too reckless.

v. 1396. *Mok there loste her sho*] A proverbial expression, which occurs again in our author's *Why come ye nat to Courte*, v. 83. vol. ii. 279. In his *Colyn Cloute* we find

" Sho the *mockysshe* mare."

v. 181. vol. ii. 131.

v. 1397. *barbican*] " A *Barbican*, antemurale, promurale, tormentorum bellicorum sedes, locus." Coles's *Dict.* " It was generally," says Nares (referring to King on Anc. Castles, *Archael.*), " a small round tower, for the station of an advanced guard, placed just before the outward gate of the castle yard, or ballium." *Gloss.* in v. And see Richardson's *Dict.* in v.

v. 1398. *sawte*] i. e. assault.

v. 1399. *blo*] i. e. livid: see note, p. 25. v. 3.

v. 1400. *Of Exione, her lambis, &c.*] See note *ad loc.* If the reader understands the line, it is more than I do.

Page 232. v. 1407. *forster*] i. e. forester.

v. 1409. *to yerne and to quest*] Coles renders both these hunting-terms by the same word, " *nicto* " (i. e. open, give tongue). *Dict.* Turbervile, enumerating

" the sundry noyses of houndes," tells us that " when they are earnest eyther in the chace or in the earth, we say *They yearne.*" *Noble Art of Venerie,* &c. p. 242. ed. 1611. " *Quest,* united cry of the hounds." Sir F. Madden's Gloss. to *Syr Gawayne,* &c.

Page 232. v. 1410. *With litell besynes standith moche rest*]

> " *Great rest standeth in little businesse.*"
>
> *Good Counsaile,*—Chaucer's *Workes,*
> fol. 319, ed. 1602.

v. 1411. *make*] i. e. mate, wife.

v. 1412. *ble*] i. e. colour, complexion.

v. 1413. *wele*] i. e. well.

v. 1416. *Some*] i. e. Soham.

Page 233. v. 1418. *Wofully arayd*] In vol. i. 165.

v. 1419. *making*] i. e. composing.

v. 1420. *Vexilla regis*] In vol. i. 168.

v. 1421. *Sacris solemniis*] As the still-extant piece mentioned in the preceding line, and headed *Vexilla regis,* &c., is not a translation of that hymn, so we may with probability conclude that this was not a version of the hymn beginning " *Sacris solemniis* juncta sint gaudia," which may be found in *Hymni Ecclesiæ e Breviario Parisiensi,* 1838. p. 94.

v. 1424. *sadnes*] i. e. seriousness.

v. 1425. *Galiene* ⎱ i. e. Galen, Hippocrates.
v. 1426. *Ipocras* ⎰

> " Old *Hippocras,* Hali, and *Gallien.*"
>
> Chaucer's *Prol. to Cant. Tales,*
> v. 433. ed. Tyr.

> " For *Ipocras* nor yet *Galien.*"
>
> *Poems* by C. Duke of Orleans,—
> *MS. Harl.* 682. fol. 103.

Page 233. v. 1426. *Auycen*] An Arabian physician of the tenth century.

v. 1428. *Albumasar*] See note, p. 61. v. 501.

—— *ken*] i. e. instruct (pleonastically coupled with "enforme," as in v. 825.)

v. 1430. *gose*] i. e. goose.

v. 1432. *ageyne*] i. e. against.

v. 1433. *Dun is in the myre*] A proverbial expression, which occurs in Chaucer's *Manciples Prol.* v. 16954. ed. Tyrwhitt, and is common in writers long after the time of Skelton. Gifford was the first to shew that the allusion is to a Christmas gambol, in which *Dun* (the cart-horse) is supposed to be stuck *in the mire;* see his note on Jonson's *Works,* vii. 283.

Page 234. v. 1434. *rin*] i. e. run.

v. 1435. *spar the stable dur*] i. e. fasten, shut the stable-door.

v. 1437. *sone aspyed*] i. e. soon espied.

v. 1438. *wele wotith*] i. e. well knoweth.

v. 1439. *lucerne*] i. e. lamp. So in the *Lenvoye* to Chaucer's *Cuckow and Nightingale;*

> " Aurore of gladnesse, and day of lustinesse,
> *Lucerne* a night with heauenly influence
> Illumined "   *Workes,* fol. 318, ed. 1602.

v. 1442. *wedder*] i. e. weather.

v. 1443. *cokwolde*] i. e. cuckold.

v. 1445. *vntwynde*] i. e. torn to pieces, destroyed. See note, p. 53. v. 284.

v. 1446. *ieloffer*] See note, p. 80. v. 1052.

v. 1447. *propre*] i. e. pretty.

v. 1450. *all to-fret*] i. e. altogether eaten up, consumed : see note, p. 22. v. 32.

Page 234. v. 1451.

But who may haue a more vngracyous lyfe .
Than a chyldis birde and a knauis wyfe]
This proverbial expression occurs in Lydgate ;
" Vnto purpos this prouerd is full ryfe
  Rade and reported by olde remembraunce ;
A childes birdde and a knavis wyfe
Haue often sieth gret sorowe and myschaunce."
The Chorle and the Bird,—MS. Harl.
116. fol. 151.

v. 1454. *byll*] i. e. writing.

Page 235. v. 1455. *By Mary Gipcy*] In much later writers we find, as an interjection, *marry gep*, *marry gip*, *marry guep*, *marry gup*.

v. 1456. *Quod scripsi, scripsi*] From the Vulgate, *Joan.* xix. 22.

v. 1460. *Secundum Lucam, &c.*] Skelton seems to allude to the Vulgate, *Luc.* i. 13, " *Et uxor tua* Elizabeth," &c.

v. 1461.

the Bonehoms of Ashrige besyde Barkamstede,

. . . .

Where the sank royall is, Crystes blode so rede]
The college of the Bonhommes, completed in 1285, was founded by Edmund, Earl of Cornwall, son and heir of Richard, Earl of Cornwall, who was King of the Romans and brother of Henry the Third, for a rector and twenty brethren or canons, of whom thirteen were to be priests. It was founded expressly in honour of the blood of Jesus, (" *the sank royall* "), which had once formed part of the precious reliques belonging to the German emperors, and which Edmund had brought over from Germany to England.

See Todd's *History of the College of Bonhommes at Ashridge*, 1823. p. 1–3.

The pretended blood of Christ drew to Ashridge many persons of all ranks, greatly to the enrichment of the society. " But," Speed tells us, " when the sunne-shine of the Gospell had pierced thorow such cloudes of darkenesse, it was perceiued apparantly to be onely hony clarified and coloured with Saffron, as was openly shewed at Paules Crosse by the Bishop of Rochester, the twentie foure of Februarie, and yeare of Christ 1538." *A Prospect of The Most Famous Parts of the World*, 1631, (in *Buck*. p. 43).

Page 235. v. 1466. *Fraxinus in clivo, &c.*] " As to the name *Ashridge*," says Kennett, " it is no doubt from a hill set with Ashes ; the old word was *Aescrugge, Rugge*, as after *Ridge*, signifying a hill or steep place, and the Ashen-tree being first *Aesc*, as after *Ashche*, &c." *Parochial Antiquities*, p. 302. ed. 1695.

v. 1470. *The Nacyoun of Folys*] Most probably *The Boke of Three Fooles*, in vol. i. 221.

v. 1471. *Apollo that whirllid vp his chare*] Concerning the piece, of which these were the initial words, a particular notice will be found in *The Account of Skelton and his Writings : chare*, i. e. chariot ; compare the first of the two lines, which in the old eds. and some MSS. of Chaucer stand as the commencement of a third part of *The Squieres Tale ;*

" *Apollo whirleth vp his chare* so hie."

Workes, fol. 25. ed. 1602.

and the opening of *The Floure and the Leafe ;*

" When that *Phebus his chaire* of gold so hie
Had *whirled* vp the sterye sky aloft."

Id. fol. 344.

See also *Poems* by C. Duke of Orleans, *MS. Harl.* 682. fol. 47.

Page 235. v. 1472. *snurre*] i. e. snort.

v. 1475. *mell*] i. e. meddle.

Page 236. v. 1478. *Suppleyng*] i. e. Supplicating.

v. 1483. *rin*] i. e. run.

v. 1487. *take it in gre*] i. e. take it kindly : see note, p. 16. v. 68.

v. 1490. *ragman rollis*] i. e. lists or rolls. The collection of deeds in which the Scottish nobility and gentry were compelled to subscribe allegiance to Edward I. of England in 1296, and which were more particularly recorded in four large rolls of parchment, &c., was known by the name of *Ragman's Roll :* but what has been written on the origin of this expression appears to be so unsatisfactory that I shall merely refer the reader to Cowel's *Law Dictionary*, &c., ed. 1727, in v., Jamieson's *Et. Dict. of Scot. Lang.* in v., Nares's *Gloss.* in v., Gloss. to *The Towneley Myst.* in v., Todd's *Johnson's Dict.* in v. *Rigmarole*, [See also Wright's *Anecdota Literaria*, and his Glossary to *Piers Plouhman*.]

v. 1491. *lenger*] i. e. longer.

v. 1495. *Counforte*] i. e. Comfort.

Page 237. v. 1498.

> *Diodorus Siculus of my translacyoun*
> *Out of fresshe Latine, &c.*]

—*fresshe*, i. e. elegant: see note, p. 301. v. 39. This translation from the Latin of *Poggio* is mentioned with praise in Caxton's Preface to *The Boke of Eneydos*, &c. 1490, and is still preserved in MS. among Parker's Collection, in Corpus Ch. College, Cambridge : see *Account of Skelton and his Writings*, and *Appendix* ii.

Page 237. v. 1505. *dome*] i. e. judgment, thinking.

v. 1507. *the noyse went to Rome*] So Chaucer ;

> " And there came out so great *a noyse*,
> That had it stónde vpon Oyse,
> *Men might haue heard it easely*
> To Rome, I trowe sikerly."
>
> House of Fame, B. iii.— *Workes*,
> fol. 270. ed. 1602.

Page 238. v. 1512. *somdele*] i. e. somewhat.

v. 1514. *sperycall*] i. e. spherical.

v. 1515. *Ianus, with his double chere*]—*chere*, i. e. visage, countenance.

v. 1517. *He turnyd his tirikkis, his voluell ran fast*] What is meant by *tirikkis*, I know not : it occurs again in our author's *Speke, Parrot ;*

> " Some trete of theyr *tirykis*, som of astrology."
>
> v. 139. vol. ii. 252.

For the following note I am indebted to W. H. Black, Esq. " The volvell is an instrument, called *volvella* or *volvellum* in the Latin of the middle age, consisting of graduated and figured circles drawn on the leaf of a book, to the centre of which is attached one movable circle or more, in the form of what is called a geographical clock. There is a very fine one, of the fourteenth century, in the Ashmolean MS. 789. f. 363, and others exist in that collection, which affords likewise, in an Introduction to the Knowledge of the Calendar, (in the MS. 191. iv. art. 2. f. 199,) written in old English of the fifteenth century, a curious description of the volvell, with directions for its use. The passage is entitled ' The Rewle of the Volvelle.'— ' Now folowith here the *volvelle*, that sum men clepen

a *lunarie;* and thus most ghe governe ghou ther ynne.
First take the grettist cercle that is maad in the leef,
for that schewith the 24 houris of the day naturel, that
is of the nyght and day, of the whiche the firste houre
is at noon bitwene 12 and oon.   Thanne above him is
another cercle, that hathe write in hem the 12 monthis
withe here dayes, and 12 signes with here degrees;
and with ynne that, ther is writen a rewle to knowe
whanne the sunne ariseth and the mone bothe ; if ghe
biholde weel these noumbris writen in reed, 8. 7. 6. 5.
4. +. 4. 5. 6. 7. 8.'   The rule proceeds to shew that
there is another row of the same figures in black, and
that the red cross stands in the place of Cancer, the
black at Capricorn : the red figures were used to shew
the rising of the sun and moon, the black for their set-
ting.   Over this is ' another cercle that hath a tunge,'
(tongue, or projecting angle to point with,) the figure
of the sun on it, and 29½ days figured, for the age of
the moon.   Upon this is the least circle, ' which hath
a tunge with the figure of the moon on it, and with
ynne it is an hole, the whiche schewith bi symylitude
howe the moone wexith and wansith.'   It was used
by setting ' the tunge of the moone ' to the moon's age,
and ' the tunge of the sunne ' to the day of the month,
then moving the circle of months and signs to bring
the hour of the day to the last named ' tunge,' where-
by might be found ' in what signe he ' (the *moon,* mas-
culine in Anglo-Saxon) ' sittith and the sunne also,
and in what tyme of the day thei arisen, eny of hem,
either goone downe, and what it is of the watir, whe-
ther it be flood or eb.'   The rule concludes by observ-
ing that the wind sometimes alters the time of the tide
' at Londone brigge.' "

Page 238. v. 1533. *quaire*] i. e. quire,—pamphlet, book.

Page 239. v. 1542. *warkis*] i. e. works.

v. 1552. *brede*] i. e. breadth.

v. 1556. *harnnes*] i. e. armour.

v. 1558. *ageyne*] i. e. against.

v. 1563. *derayne*] i. e. contest.

Page 240. v. 1575. *sad*] i. e. sober, grave.

v. 1581. *Any worde defacid*] i. e. Any disfigured, deformed, unseemly word.

v. 1582. *Lautre Enuoy, &c.*] Concerning this curious Envoy, see *Account of Skelton and his Writings.*

Page 241. v. 1597. *sekernes*] i. e. security, sureness.

v. 1598. *rede*] i. e. conceive, consider.

OWT OF LATYNE INTO ENGLYSSHE.

Page 243. v. 5. *kepe*] i. e. heed, regard, care.

v. 7. *Gone to seke hallows*]—*hallows,* i. e. saints.

> " On pilgremage then must they go,
>   To Wilsdon, Barking, or to some *hallowes.*"
>   *The Schole House of Women,* 1572,—
>   Utterson's *Early Pop. Poetry,* ii. 66.

But " to seek hallows " seems to have been a proverbial expression ;

> " O many woman hath caught be in a trayne,
>   By goyng out such *halowes for to seke.*"
>   Lydgate's *Warres of Troy,* B. ii. sig. I ii.
>   ed. 1555.

Page 244. v. 13. *withholde*] i. e. withheld.

v. 14. *sayne*] i. e. say.

SPEKE, PARROT.

That the extant portion of this very obscure production were written at intervals, is not to be doubted ; and that we do not possess all that Skelton composed under the title of *Speke, Parrot*, is proved by the following passage of the *Garlande of Laurell*, where, enumerating his various works, he mentions

" *the Popingay*, that hath in commendacyoun
Ladyes and gentylwomen suche as deseruyd,
And suche as be counterfettis they be reseruyd."

v. 1188. vol. ii. 222.

a description which, as it answers to no part of the existing poem (or poems), must apply to some portion which has perished, and which, I apprehend, was of an earlier date. " *The Popingay* " is assuredly only another name for *Speke, Parrot;*

" Go, litell quayre, *namyd the Popagay.*"

Speke, Parrot, v. 280.

Page 245. v. 3. *Parrot, a byrd of paradyse*] So Lydgate (in a poem, entitled in the Catalogue, *Advices for people to keep a guard over their tongues*) ;

" *Popyngayes froo paradys* comyn al grene."

MS. Harl. 2255. fol. 133.

" Than spake *the popynge Jay of paradyse.*"

Parlyament of Byrdes, sig. A ii. n. d.

v. 5. *Dyentely*] i. e. Daintily.

Page 246. v. 8. *estate*] i. e. state, rank.

v. 9. *Then Parot must haue an almon*] In Jonson's *Magnetic Lady*, act v. sc. 5, we find,—

" Pol is a fine bird ! O fine lady Pol !

Almond for Parrot, Parrot's a brave bird ; "—

and Gifford, citing the last line (he ought rather to have cited v. 50), observes that Jonson was indebted to Skelton for " most of this jargon." *Works*, vi. 109.

Page 246. v. 11. *couertowre*] i. e. shelter.

v. 12. *toote*] i. e. peep.

v. 17. *becke*] i. e. beak.

v. 18. *My fedders freshe as is the emrawde grene*]—*emrawde*, i. e. emerald. So Ovid in his charming verses on Corinna's parrot;

"Tu poteras virides pennis hebetare smaragdos."

Am. lib. ii. vi. 21.

v. 20. *fete*] i. e. well made, neat.

v. 22. *My proper Parrot, my lytyll prety foole*]—*proper*, i. e. pretty, handsome (elsewhere Skelton uses "proper" and "prety" as synonymes: see note, p. 51. v. 127).

"I pray thee what hath ere the Parret got,
And yet they say he talkes in great mens bowers?

.   .   .   .

A good *foole* call'd with paine perhaps may be."

Sidney's *Arcadia*, lib. ii. p. 229. ed. 1613.

Page 247. v. 26. *mute*] i. e. mew.

v. 30. *Quis expedivit psittaco suum chaire*]—*chaire* XAIPE. From Persius, *Prol.* 8.

v. 31. *Dowse French of Parryse*] *Dowse*, i. e. sweet, soft. Chaucer's Prioress spoke French

"After the scole of Stratford atte bowe,
For *Frenche of Paris* was to hire unknowe."

Prol. to Cant. Tales, v. 125. ed. Tyr.

v. 35. *supple*] i. e. supplicate, pray.

v. 38. *ryall*] i. e. royal. In the marginal note on this line, "Katerina universalis vitii ruina, Græcum est," is an allusion to the Greek καθαρίζω or καθαρός.

v. 39. *pomegarnet*] i. e. pomegranate.

v. 40. *Parrot, saves habler Castiliano*] See note *ad l.*

" Parrot, can you speak Castilian ? " is a question which Spanish boys at the present day frequently address to that bird.

* Page 248. v. 41. *With fidasso de cosso in Turkey and in Trace*]—*fidasso de cosso* [Old editions, *sidasso de cosso*, and *sidasso* de *costo*] is perhaps lingua franca, —some corruption of the Italian *fidarsi di se stesso: Trace*, i. e. Thrace.

v. 42. *Vis consilii expers* . . . ⎫ From Horace, *Carm.*
⎬ iii. iv. 65 (where
v. 43. *Mole ruit sua*] ⎭ " consilf").

—— *dictes*] i. e. sayings.

v. 45. *maystres*] i. e. mistress.

v. 50. *An almon now for Parrot*] I know not if these words occur in any writer anterior to the time of Skelton ; but they afterwards became a sort of proverbial expression.

v. 51. *In Salve festa dies, toto theyr doth best*]— *theyr*, i. e. there. Skelton has two copies of verses, which begin " Salve, festa dies, toto," &c.: see vol i. pp. 211, 212.

v. 54. *Myden agan*] i. e. Μηδὲν ἄγαν.

v. 59. *Besy*] i. e. Busy.

Page 249. v. 63. *To*] i. e. Too.

v. 67. *Iobab was brought vp in the lande of Hus*] " Verisimile est Jobum eumdem esse cum Jobabo, qui quartus est ab Esaü . . . Duces in ista opinione sequimur omnes fere antiquos Patres quos persuasit, ut ita sentirent, additamentum in exemplaribus Græcis, Arabicis et in antiqua Vulgata Latina appositum : ' Job vero habitabat in terra Hus, inter terminos Edom et Arabiæ, et antea vocabatur Jobab,' " &c. *Concordantiæ Bibl. Sacr. Vulg. Ed.* by Dutripon, in v. *Job. ii.*

Page 249. v. 71. *Howst thé, lyuer god van hemrik, ic seg*]—*Howst thé* is (I suppose) Hist thee: what follows is German,—*lieber Gott von Himmelreich, ich sage*— Dear God of heaven's kingdom, I say,—spoken by way of oath.

v. 72. *In Popering grew peres*] From *Popering*, a parish in the Marches of Calais (see Tyrwhitt's note on Chaucer's *Cant. Tales*, v. 13650), the *poprin, poperin*, or *popperin* pear, frequently mentioned in our early dramas, was introduced into this country.

v. 73. *Ouer in a whynny meg*] The initial words of a ballad or song. Laneham (or Langham) in his strange *Letter* concerning the entertainment to Queen Elizabeth at Kenilworth Castle in 1575, mentions it as extant in the collection of Captain Cox, who figured in the shows on that occasion: " What shoold I re-hearz heer what a bunch of Ballets and songs all aun-cient: Az Broom broom on hill, So wo iz me begon, Troly lo, *Over a whinny Meg*," &c. See Collier's *Bridgewater-House Catalogue*, p. 164.

v. 74. *Hop Lobyn of Lowdeon*] See note, p. 175. v. 59.

v. 75. *The iebet of Baldock*] Is mentioned again in our author's *Why come ye nat to Courte*, v. 953. vol. ii. 308. " And in Caldee the chief Cytee is *Baldak*." *Voiage and Travaile of Sir J. Maundevile*, p. 51. ed. 1725.

v. 78. *to*] i. e. too.

v. 80. *erstrych fether*] i. e. ostrich-feather.

v. 81. *Beme*] i. e. Bohemia.

v. 82. *byrsa*] An allusion to Virgil;

" Mercatique solum, facti de nomine *Byrsam*,
    Taurino quantum possent circumdare tergo."

Æn. i. 367.

Perhaps too Skelton recollected a passage in Lydgate's *Fall of Prynces*, B. ii. leaf xlviii. ed. Wayland.

Page 249. v. 84. *Colostrum*] i. e. the biesting,—the first milk after the birth given by a cow (or other milch animal). This form of the word occurs in the title of an epigram by Martial, lib. xiii. 38, and in Servius's commentary on Virgil, *Ecl.* ii. 22.

Page 250. v. 85. *shayle*] i. e. walk crookedly. See note, p. 18. v. 19.

v. 87. *Moryshe myne owne shelfe, the costermonger sayth*] From the next line it would seem that " Moryshe " is meant for the Irish correction of some English word ; but of what word I know not.

v. 88. *Fate, fate, fate, ye Irysh waterlag*] Mr. Crofton Croker obligingly observes to me that he has no doubt of " fate " being intended for the Irish pronunciation of the word *water*.—" There is rysen a fray amonge *the water laggers*.   Coorta est rixa inter *amphorarios*." Hormanni *Vulgaria*, sig. q vi. ed. 1530.

v. 91. *Let syr Wrigrag wrastell with syr Delarag*] See note, p. 139. v. 186. p. 147. v. 149.

v. 93. *Pawbe une aruer*] Either *Paub un arver*, Every one his manner, or *Paub yn ei arver*, Every one in his manner.

v. 95. *mo*] i. e. more.

v. 97. *conseyt*] i. e. conceit.

v. 104. *how*] i. e. ho!

v. 106. *Bas*] i. e. Kiss.

Page 251. v. 109. *pyke . . too*] i. e. pick . . toe.

v. 110. *solas, pleasure, dysporte, and pley*] One of Skelton's pleonasms.

v. 112. *Parot can say, Cæsar, ave, also*] " Ut plurimum docebantur hæ aves salutationis verba . . . interdum etiam plurium vocum versus aut sententias docebantur : ut illi corvi, qui admirationi fuerunt Augusto ex Actiaca victoria revertenti, quorum alter institutus fuerat dicere, *Ave Cæsar*," &c.   Casaubonus *ad Persii Prol.* v. 8.

Page 251. v. 116. *ruly doth loke*] i. e. ruefully doth look.

v. 118. *vndertoke*] i. e. undertook.

v. 119. *of Judicum rede the boke*] i. e. read the Book of Judges.

> " In *Iudicum* the storye ye may rede."
>> Lydgate's *Fall of Prynces*, B. i. leaf xiv.
>>> ed. Wayland.

v. 122.

> *O Esebon, Esebon! to thé is cum agayne*
> *Seon, the regent Amorræorum,*
> *And Og, that fat hog of Basan, doth retayne,*
> *The crafty coistronus Cananæorum*]

—*coistronus* is a Latinised form of *coistroun*, see note on title of poem, p. 11.   Though in an earlier part of *Speke, Parrot*, we find " Cryst. saue Kyng Henry the viii, our royall kyng," &c. v. 36, yet it would almost seem that he is alluded to here under the name of Seon.   Og must mean Wolsey.   This portion of the poem is not found in *MS. Harl.* (see note on v. 59 *ad l.*) ; and there can be no doubt that *Speke, Parrot* is made up of pieces composed at various times.   After Skelton's anger had been kindled against Wolsey, perhaps the monarch came in for a share of his indignation.

v. 126. *asylum, whilom refugium miserorum, &c.*]
—*whilom*, i. e. once, formerly.   So afterwards in this

piece, v. 496, among the evils which Skelton attributes to Wolsey, mention is made of "myche sayntuary brekyng;" i. e. much sanctuary-breaking; and in *Why come ye nat to Courte* he says of the Cardinal that

> " all priuileged places
> He brekes and defaces," &c.
>   v. 1086. vol. ii. 313.

Page 251. v. 130. *trym tram*] See note, p. 101. v. 76.

Page 252. v. 131. *chaffer far fet*] i. e. merchandise far fetched.

v. 133. *Scarpary*] In Tuscany. So afterwards, " Over Scarpary," v. 408; and in *The Flyting of Dunbar and Kennedy*, " Mont Scarpry." Dunbar's *Poems*, ii. 82. ed. Laing.

v. 134. *ich wot*] i. e. I know.

v. 136. *Haly*] See note, p. 61. v. 505.

v. 137. *nolvell* ⎫
                          ⎬ See note, p. 352. v. 1517.
v. 139. *tirykis* ⎭

v. 142. *ren*] i. e. run.

v. 143. *Monon calon agaton*] i. e. Μόνον καλὸν ἀγαθόν.

v. 144. *Quod Parato*] i. e. Quoth Parrot.

v. 149. *in scole matter occupyed*] i. e. used in school-matter.

Page 253. v. 152. *How*] i. e. Ho!

v. 153. *a silogisme in phrisesomorum*] " Sic [indirecte] in prima figura concludunt quinque illi modi, qui ab interpretibus fere omnibus (excepto Zabarella) pro legitimis agnoscuntur, quique hoc versu comprehendi solent, *Celantes, Baralip, Dabilis, Fapesmo,* FRISESOM." Crakanthorp's *Logicæ Libri Quinque*, 1622. p. 275.

v. 165. *Jack Raker*] See note, p. 135. v. 108.

v. 166. *maker*] i. e. composer.

Page 254. v. 170. *Sturbrydge fayre*] The fair kept annually in the neighbourhood of Cambridge, and so named from the rivulet *Stour* and *bridge*.

v. 171. *Tryuyals and quatryuyals*] The *trivials* were the first three sciences taught in the schools, viz. Grammar, Rhetoric, and Logic ; the *quatrivials* were the higher set, viz, Astrology (or Astronomy), Geometry, Arithmetic, and Music. See Du Cange's *Gloss.* in vv. *Trivium, Quadrivium ;* and Hallam's *Introd. to the Lit. of Europe,* i. 4.

v. 171. *appayre*] i. e. impair, are impaired, come to decay.

v. 174. *Albertus de modo significandi*] " Albertus," says Warton, after citing this stanza, " is the author of the *Margarita Poetica*, a collection of *Flores* from the classics and other writers, printed at Nurenberg, 1472, fol." *Hist. of E. P.*, ii. 347 (note), ed. 4to. The work mentioned here by Skelton is stated to have been first printed in 1480. The title of an edition by Wynkyn de Worde, dated 1515, is as follows ; *Modi significādi Alberti sine quibus grammaticæ notitia haberi nullo pacto potest :* there is said to be another edition n. d. by the same printer : see *Typ. Ant.*, ii. 208. ed. Dibdin.

v. 175. *Donatus*] i. e. the work attributed to Ælius Donatus, the Roman grammarian : see the *Bibliog. Dictionary* of Dr. Clarke (iii. 144), who observes : " It has been printed with several titles, such as *Donatus ; Donatus Minor ; Donatus pro puerulis, Donati Ars*, &c., but the work is the same, viz. Elements of the Latin Language for the Use of Children." See too Warton's *Hist. of E. P.*, i. 281 (note), ed. 4to.

—— *scole*] i. e. school.

v. 177. *Inter didascolos*] "*Interdidascolos* is the

name of an old grammar." Warton's *Hist. of E. P.*, ii. 347 (note), ed. 4to. Warton may be right; but I have never met with any grammar that bears such a title.

Page 254. v. 177. *fole*] i. e. fool.

v. 178. *Alexander*] i. e. Alexander de Villa Dei, " author of the *Doctrinale Puerorum*, which for some centuries continued to be the most favourite manual of grammar used in schools, and was first printed at Venice in the year 1473 [at Treviso, in 1472 ; see *Typ. Ant.*, ii. 116. ed. Dibdin]. It is compiled from Priscian, and in Leonine verse. See Henr. Gandav. *Scriptor. Eccles.* cap. lix. This admired system has been loaded with glosses and lucubrations ; but, on the authority of an ecclesiastical synod, it was superseded by the *Commentarii Grammatici* of Despauterius, in 1512. It was printed in England as early as the year 1503 by W. de Worde. [The existence of this ed. has been questioned. The work was printed by Pynson in 1505,·1513, 1516 : see *Typ. Ant.*, ii. 116, 426, 427, ed. Dibdin, and Lowndes's *Bibliog Man.*, i. 27]. Barklay, in the *Ship of Fooles*, mentions Alexander's book, which he calls ' The *olde Doctrinall* with his diffuse and vnperfite breuitie.' fol. 53. b [ed. 1570]." Warton's *Hist. of E. P.*, ii. 347 (note), ed. 4to.

—— *Menanders pole*] See note, p. 57. v. 434 : *pole*, i. e. pool.

v. 179. *Da Cansales*] " He perhaps means *Concilia*, or the canon law." Warton's *Hist. of E. P.*, ii. 347 (note), ed. 4to. ·

v. 180. *Da Racionales*] " He seems to intend *Logic.*" *Id. ibid.*

v. 183. *Pety Caton*] *Cato Parvus* (a sort **of**

supplement to *Cato Magnus*, i. e. *Dionysii Catoni*
Disticha de Moribus) was written by Daniel Churche,
or Ecclesiensis, a domestic in the court of Henry the
Second · see Warton's *Hist. of E. P.*, ii. 170, and
Dibdin's ed. of *Typ. Ant.*, i. 120.

Page 254. v. 187. *scole maters*] i. e. school-matters.

—— *hole sentens*] i. e. whole meaning.

v. 188. *gariopholo*] So, I believe, Skelton wrote,
though the classical form of the word is *garyophyllo*.

v. 189. *pyke*] i. e. pick.

Page 255. v. 190. *synamum styckis*] i. e. cinnamon-
sticks.

v. 191. *perdurable*] i. e. everlasting.

v. 192. *fauorable*] i. e. well-favoured, beautiful.

v. 195. *tote*] i. e. peep.

v. 199. *freshe humanyte*] i. e. elegant literature :
see notes, p. 301. v. 39. p. 328. v. 817.

v. 201. *chekmate*] In allusion to the king's being
put in *check* at the game of chess.

v. 205. *processe*] i. e. discourse.

v. 207. *with all*] i. e. withal.

v. 208. *pauys*] i. e. shield. See note, p. 9. v. 48.

Page 256. v. 209. *flekyd pye*] i. e. spotted, varie-
gated magpie.

v. 210. *pendugum, that men call a carlyng*]—"*pen-
dugum*," says the Rev. J. Mitford, "is penguin ;" and
he supposes that *carlyng* has some connexion with the
term gair-fowl, which is another name for the penguin.

v. 222. *moche . . . popegay ryall*] i. e. much . . .
parrot royal.

v. 226. *amonge*] i. e. together, at the same time.

v. 228. *worldly lust*] i. e. worldly pleasure.

Page 257. v. 232. *recule*] i. e. collection. See note,
p. 339. v. 1187.

Page 257. v. 232. *Itaque consolamini invicem in verbis istis*] From the Vulgate, 1 *Thess.* iv. 17.

v. 239. *when Pamphylus loste hys make*]—make, i. e. mate. As the heading " *Galathea* " precedes this couplet, there is an allusion to a once popular poem concerning the loves of Pamphilus and Galathea,— *Pamphili Mauriliani Pamphilus, sive De Arte Amandi Elegiæ.* It is of considerable length, and though written in barbarous Latin, was by some attributed to Ovid. It may be found in a little volume edited by Goldastus, *Ovidii Nasonis Pelignensis Erotica et Amatoria Opuscula*, &c. 1610.   See too the lines cited in note, p. 335. v. 1048.

v. 240. *propire*] i. e. handsome, pretty.

v. 241. *praty*] i. e. pretty.

Page 258. v. 245. *herte hyt ys*] i. e. heart it is.

v. 262. *Be*] i. e. By.

Page 259. v. 265. *reclaymed*] i. e. tamed, appeased. See note, p. 335. v. 1125.

v. 269. *kus*] i. e. kiss.

v. 270. *mus*] i. e. muzzle, mouth.

—— *Zoe kai psyche*] i. e. Ζωὴ καὶ ψυχή.

Page 260. v. 274. *spuria vitulamina*] From the Vulgate, " *Spuria vitulamina* non dabunt radices altas." *Sap.* iv. 3.

v. 280. *quayre*] i. e. quire,—pamphlet, book.— From this *Lenuoy primere* inclusive to the end of *Speke, Parrot*, with the exception of a few stanzas, the satire is directed wholly against Wolsey. The very obscure allusions to the Cardinal's being employed in some negotiation abroad are to be referred probably to his mission in 1521. That *Speke, Parrot* consists of pieces written at various periods has been already

noticed : and " Pope Julius," v. 425, means, I appre-
hend, (not Julius ii., for *he* died in 1513, but) Clement
vii., Julius de Medici, who was elected Pope in 1523.
With respect to the dates which occur after the present
Lenuoy,—" *Penultimo die Octobris*, 33°," " *In diebus
Novembris*, 34," &c., if " 33° " and " 34 " stand for
1533 and 1534 (when both Skelton and the Cardinal
were dead), they must have been added by the tran-
scriber ; and yet in the volume from which these por-
tions of *Speke, Parrot* are now printed (*MS. Harl.*
2252) we find, only a few pages before, the name
" John Colyn mercer of London," with the date
" 1517." At the end of *Why come ye nat to Courte*
(vol. ii. 320) we find (what is equally puzzling)
" xxxiiii."

Page 260. v. 285. *lyclyhode*] i. e. likelihood.

v. 288. *agayne*] i. e. against.

v. 289. *tonsan*] i. e. *toison*.

v. 291. *Lyacon*] Occurs again in v. 393 : is it—
Lycaon ?

Page 261. v. 294. *folys*] i. e. fools.

——— *knakkes*] " *Knacke* or toye, *friuolle*." Pals-
grave, p. 236.

v. 295. *hang togedyr as fethyrs in the wynde*] See
note, p. 247. v. 1842.

v. 296. *lewdlye ar they lettyrd that your lernyng
lackys*] i. e. badly, meanly, are they lettered that find
fault with your learning.

v. 297. *currys of kynde*] i. e. curs by nature.

v. 298. *lokythe . . . warkys*] i. e. looketh . . . works.

v. 300. *Agayne all remordes*] i. e. Against all blam-
ings, censures, carpings : see note, p. 146. v. 101 : but
as in v. 368, where MS. has " remordes," the sense

absolutely requires "remorders," there is perhaps the same error here.

Page 261. v. 300. *Morda puros mal desires*] This strange gibberish (which occurs twice afterwards) seems to mean,—To bite the pure, is an evil desire.

v. 304. *sadde*] i. e. grave, serious. See note, p. 245. v. 1711.

v. 305. *ower soleyne seigneour Sadoke*]—*soleyne*, i. e. sullen: in applying the name *Sadoke* to Wolsey, Skelton alludes to the high-priest of Scripture, not to the knight of the Round Table.

v. 306. *nostre dame de Crome*] So in *A Mery Play between Johan the Husbande, Tyb his Wyfe, and Syr Jhan the Preest*, 1533, attributed to Heywood;

> " But, by goggis blod, were she come home
> Unto this my house, by *our lady of Crome*,
> I wolde bete her or that I drynke."
>
> p. 1. reprint.

v. 307. *assone*] i. e. as soon.

v. 308. *to exployte the man owte of the mone*] i. e. to achieve the feat of driving the man out of the moon.

v. 309.

With porpose and graundepose he may fede hym fatte,
Thowghe he pampyr not hys paunche with the grete
seall]

—*porpose and graundepose*, i. e. porpoise and grampus. The pun in the second line is sufficiently plain.

Page 262. v. 311. *lokyd*] i. e. looked.

v. 313. *every deall*] i. e. every part.

v. 319. *nodypollys*] i. e. silly-heads.

—— *gramatolys*] i. e. smatterers.

v. 320. *To . . . sentence*] i. e. Too . . . meaning.

Page 263. v. 326. *sadlye*] i. e. gravely. See note, p. 250. v. 1966.

———— *Sydrake*] So Wolsey is termed here in allusion to a romance (characterised by Warton as " rather a romance of Arabian philosophy than of chivalry," *Hist. of E. P.*, i. 143. ed. 4to), which was translated from the French by Hugh of Caumpeden, and printed in 1510, under the title of *The Historie of King Boccus and Sydracke*, &c.

v. 327. *coniecte*} i. e. conjecture.

v. 328. *mellis*] i. e. meddles.

v. 330. *Hyt*] i. e. It.

v. 331. *a cheryston pytte*] An allusion to a game played with cherry-stones ;

> " I can playe at the *chery pytte*,
> And I can wystell you a fytte,
> Syres, in a whylowe ryne."
>
> *The Worlde and the Chylde*,
> 1522. sig. A iii.

v. 332. *sterrys*] i. e. stars.

v. 337. *syn*] i. e. since.

v. 339. *Non sine postica sanna*] " ———— *posticæ* occurrite *sannæ*." Persius, *Sat.* i. 65.

Page 264. v. 354. *quod*] i. e. quoth.

Page 265. v. 356. *propyr*] i. e. pretty, handsome.

v. 358. *supply*] i. e. supplicate.

v. 360. *agayne*] i. e. against.

v. 362. *slaundrys obliqui*] i. e. slanderous obloquy.

v. 365. *jacounce*] i. e. jacinth.

v. 366. *balas*] See note, p. 338. v. 1166.

v. 367. *eyndye sapher*] See note, p. 23. v. 17.

v. 368. *remorde[r]s*] i. e. blamers, censurers : see note, p. 146. v. 101.

Page 266. v. 368. *votorum meorum omnis lapis, lapis pretiosus operimentum tuum*] From the Vulgate, " Omnis lapis pretiosus operimentum tuum." *Ezech.* xxviii. 13.

374. *myche*] i. e. much.

v. 378. *on and hothyr*] i. e. one and other.

v. 380. *recheles*] i. e. reckless.

Page 267. v. 382. *prosses*] Equivalent here to— matter : see p. 195. (first line of prose).

v. 383. *cowardes*] i. e. cowardice.

v. 385. *connyng*] i. e. knowing, learned.

v. 386. *postyll*] i. e. comment upon. See note, p. 282. v. 755.

* v. 389. *plucke the crowe*] i. e. enter into a quarrel.

v. 393. *Lyacon*] See note on v. 291. p. 366.

v. 394. *Racell, rulye*] i. e. Rachel, ruefully ; compare v. 116.

v. 395. *mawmett*] See note, p. 138. v. 170.

—— *quod*] i. e. quoth.

Page 268. v. 407. *For passe a pase apase ys gon to cache a molle*] Qy. is there an allusion here to Secretary Pace ?

v. 408. *Scarpary*] See note on v. 133. p. 361.

—— *sliddyr*] i. e. slippery.

v. 409. *pendugims*] See note on v. 210. p. 364.

v. 412. *Difficille hit ys*] i. e. Difficult it is.

v. 415. *raye*] i. e. array.

v. 416. *Agayne*] i. e. Against.

Page 269. v. 417. *ensembyll*] i. e. together. (Fr.)

v. 418. *The nebbis of a lyon they make to trete and trembyll*]—*nebbis*, i. e. neb, nib, nose : *to trete*, i. e. (I suppose) to become tractable.

Page 269. v. 419. *folys*] i. e. fools.

v. 420. *to play cowche quale*] So in *Thersytes*, n. d. ;
" Howe I haue made the knaues for *to play cowch*
quaile." p. 42. Roxb. ed.
" And thou shalt make him *couche as doth a quaille.*"
The Clerkes Tale, v. 9082. ed. Tyr.

v. 421. *polys*] i. e. pools.

v. 422. *babylles*] i. e. (fools') bawbles.

v. 424. *He facithe owte at a fflusshe*] Compare *The
Bowge of Courte*, v. 315.

" And soo outface hym with a carde of ten."
v. 315. vol. i. 51.
fflusshe, i. e. a hand of cards all of a sort.

v. 425. *cardys*] i. e. cards.

v. 427. *skyregalyard*] See note, p. 177. v. 101.

—— *prowde palyard*] So, afterwards, the Duke of
Albany is termed by Skelton in his tirade against that
nobleman, v. 167. vol. ii. 326. " *Paillard.* A lecher,
wencher, whoremunger, whorehunter; also, a knave,
rascall, varlet, scoundrell, filthy fellow." Cotgrave's
Dict.

—— *vaunteperler*] " *Avant-parleur.* A forespeaker ;
or one that is too forward to speak." Cotgrave's *Dict.*
" Whiche bee the *vauntperlers* and heddes of thair
faction." *Letter of Bedyll to Crumwell,—State Papers*
(1830), i. 424.

v. 428. *woluys hede*] i. e. wolf's head.

—— *bloo*] i. e. livid : see note. p. 25. v. 3.

v. 429. *Hyt ys to fere*] i. e. It is to fear,—be feared.

v. 430. *Peregall*] i. e. Equal (thoroughly equal).

Page 270. v. 431. *regiment*] i. e. rule.

v. 432. *quod ex vi bolte harvi*]—*quod*, i. e. quoth : of
the rest, the reader may make what he can.

Page 270. v. 435. *groynyd at*] i. e. grumbled at.
v. 436.

Grete reysons with resons be now reprobitante,
For reysons ar no resons, but resons currant]

Perhaps this is the earliest instance of a quibble be-
tween *raisins* and *reasons*. The same pun is used by
Shakespeare in *Much ado about Nothing,* act v. sc. 1,
and (though Steevens thinks not) in *Troilus and Cres-
sida,* act ii. sc. 2: compare also Dekker; "*Raisons*
will be much askt for, especially in an action of in-
iury." *The Owles Almanacke,* 1618. p. 36.

v. 438. *Ryn*] i. e. Run.

v. 439. *the date of the Devyll*] See note. p. 41. v.
375.

—— *shrewlye*] i. e. shrewdly, badly.

v. 442. *So many morall maters, &c.*] There is a con-
siderable resemblance between this concluding portion
of *Speke, Parrot,* and a piece attributed to Dunbar,
entitled *A General Satyre;* see his *Poems,* ii. 24. ed.
Laing.

v. 443. *So myche newe makyng*] i. e. So much new
composing.

Page 271. v. 457. *stondythe*] i. e. standeth.

v. 460. *on dawys hedd*] i. e. one daw's head: see
note, p. 36. v. 301.

Page 272. v. 467. *dowȝtfull daunger*] i. e. doubtful
danger,—danger that ought to cause dread.

v. 471. *not worth an hawe*] See note, p. 252. v.
2115.

v. 472. *So myche papers weryng for ryghte a smalle
exesse*] — *exesse,* i. e. excess, offence. "And for a
truthe he [the Cardinal] so punyshed periurye with
open punyshment & *open papers werynge,* that in his

tyme it was lesse vsed." Hall's *Chron.* (Hen. viii.),
fol. lix. ed. 1548.

Page 272. v. 473. *pelory pajauntes*] i. e. pillory-
pageants.

v. 474. *the cooke stole*] i. e. cucking-stool. See note,
p. 131. v. 38.

—— *guy gaw*] i. e. gewgaw, trifle.

v. 478.

So bolde a braggyng bocher . . . . .

. . . .

So mangye a mastyfe curre, the grete grey houndes pere]
Again, in his *Why come ye nat to Courte*, Skelton
alludes to the report that Wolsey was the son of a
butcher, vv. 295. 491. vol. ii. 286. 293. Compare too
Roy's satire against Wolsey, *Rede me, and be nott
wrothe*, &c.;

" *The mastif curre*, bred in Ypswitch towne.

. . . .

Wat. He commeth then of some noble stocke ?
Jeff. His father coulde snatche a bullock,
    A butcher by his occupacion."

Harl. Miscell. ix. 3. 31. ed. Park.

and a poem *Of the Cardnalle Wolse ;*

" To se a churle *a Bochers curre*,
    To rayne & rule in soche honour," &c.

MS. Harl. 2252. fol. 156.

Cavendish says that Wolsey. " was an honest poor
man's son ; " and the will of his father (printed by
Fiddes) shews that he possessed some property : but,
as Mr. Sharon Turner observes, that Wolsey was the
son of a butcher " was reported and believed while he
lived." *Hist. of Reign. of Hen. the Eighth*, i. 167. ed.
8vo.

With the second line of the present passage com-
pare our author's *Why come ye nat to Courte*, where
he wishes that " that mastyfe " Wolsey, may

> . . . " neuer confounde
> The gentyll *greyhownde*."
>
> v. 775. vol. ii. 302.

By the *greyhound* seems to be meant Henry viii., in
allusion to the royal arms.

Page 273. v. 481. *So bygge a bulke of brow auntlers
cabagyd that yere*] " *Cabusser*. To cabbidge ; to grow
to a head," &c.—" The Cabbage of the Deeres head.
Meule de cerf." Cotgrave's *Dict*. " I Kabage a deere,
Je cabaiche . . . I wyll kabage my dere and go with
you : *Je cabacheray*," &c. Palsgrave, p. 596.

v. 485. *banketyng*] i. e. banqueting.

v. 487. *howgye*] i. e. hugy, huge.

v. 488. *apon*] i. e. upon.

—— *suche pyllyng and pollyng*] i. e. such stripping
and plundering (exactions of various kinds).

v. 489. *reson and skylle*] See note, p. 207. v. 106.

Page 274. v. 496. *So myche sayntuary brekyng*] See
note on v. 126. p. 360.

v. 497. *lyerd*] i. e. learned.

v. 498. *ryghte of a rammes horne*] See note, p. 295.
v. 1201.

v. 501. *lokes* . . . *dysdayneslye*] i. e. looks . . . dis-
dainfully.

v. 503. *ffylty gorgon*] i. e. filthy Gorgon.

v. 506. *loselles* . . . *lewde*] i. e. worthless fellows,
scoundrels . . . bad, evil, (or perhaps, lascivious)

v. 507. *myday sprettes*] i. e. mid-day sprites.

v. 508. *puplysshyd*] i. e. published.

v. 509. *all beshrewde*] i. e. altogether cursed.

Page 274. v. 510. *Suche pollaxis and pyllers, suche mvlys trapte with gold*]—*mvlys*, i. e. mules. So Roy in his satire against Wolsey, *Rede me, and be nott wrothe,* &c.;

" *Wat.* Doth he use then on mules to ryde ?
  Jeff. Ye ; and that with so shamfull pryde
            That to tell it is not possible :
      More lyke a god celestiall
      Than eny creature mortall,
            With worldly pompe incredible.
    Before him rydeth two prestes stronge,
    And they beare two crosses ryght longe,
            Gapynge in every mans face :
    After theym folowe two laye-men secular,
    And eache of theym holdynge a pillar
            In their hondes, steade of a mace.
    Then foloweth my lorde on his mule,
    Trapped with golde under her cule,
            In every poynt most curiously ;
    On each syde a pollaxe is borne,
    Which in none wother use are worne,
            Pretendynge some hid mistery.
    Then hath he servauntes fyve or six score,
    Some behynde and some before,
            A marvelous great company :
    Of which are lordes and gentlemen,
    With many gromes and yemen,
            And also knaves amonge.
    Thus dayly he procedeth forthe," &c.
                    Harl. Miscell. ix. 29. ed. Park.

" Then," says Cavendish, " had he two great crosses of silver, whereof one of them was for his Archbishoprick, and the other for his Legacy, borne always before him whither soever he went or rode, by two of the most tallest and comeliest priests that he could get within all this realm." *Life of Wolsey*, 94. ed. 1827. " And as soon as he was entered into his chamber of presence, where there was attending his coming to await upon him to Westminster Hall, as well noblemen and other worthy gentlemen, as noblemen and gentlemen of his own family ; thus passing forth with two great crosses of silver borne before him ; with also two great pillars of silver, and his pursuivant at arms with a great mace of silver gilt : Then his gentlemen ushers cried, and said, ' On, my lords and masters, on before ; make way for my Lord's Grace ! ' Thus passed he down from the chamber through the hall ; and when he came to the hall door, there was attendant for him his mule, trapped all together [altogether] in crimson velvet, and gilt stirrups.   When he was mounted, with his cross bearers, and pillar bearers, also upon great horses trapped with [fine] scarlet : Then marched he forward, with his train and furniture in manner as I have declared, having about him four footmen, with gilt pollaxes in their hands ; and thus he went until he came to Westminster Hall door." *Id.* 106.   See also Cavendish's *Metrical Legend of Wolsey*, p. 533. *ibid.* The pillars implied that the person before whom they were carried was a pillar of the church.   That the Cardinal had a right to the " ensigns and ornaments " which he used, is shewn by Anstis in a letter to Fiddes,—Appendix to Fiddes's *Life of Wolsey.*

WHY COME YE NAT TO COURTE?

This poem appears to have been produced (at intervals perhaps) during 1522 and part of the following year.

Page 274. v. 510. *sadly*] i. e. seriously : *loke*, i. e. look.

Page 276. v. 3. *To*] i. e. Too (as in the next seven lines).

v. 5. *scarce*] i. e. sparing.

v. 6. *large*] i. e. liberal.

v. 8. *haute*] i. e. haughty.

Page 277. v. 23. *appall*] i. e. make pale, make to decay.

v. 33. *rage*] i. e. toy wantonly (see Tyrwhitt's Gloss. to Chaucer's *Cant. Tales*).

v. 34. *basse*] i. e. kiss.

Page 278. v. 37. *corage*] i. e. desire, inclination.

v. 39. *ouerage*] Seems here to be—over-age (excessive age) ; while, again, in our author's poem *Howe the douty duke of Albany*, &c., it appears to be—over-rage (excessive rage) ;

> " It is a rechelesse rage,
> And a lunatyke ouerage." v. 417. vol. ii. 335.

v. 43. *a graunt domage*] Meant for French perhaps.

v. 44. *set by*] i. e. valued, regarded.

v. 46. *rynne*] i. e. run.

v. 50. *boskage*] i. e. thicket, wood.

v. 56. *defaute*] i. e. default, want.

v 58. *theyr hedes mew*] i. e. hide their heads ; see note on v. 219.

v. 62. *to*] i. e. too.

Page 279. v. 63. *In faythe, dycken, thou krew*] See note, p. 39. v. 360.

Page 279. v. 68. *banketynge*] i. e. banqueting.

v. 69. *rechelesse*] i. e. reckless.

v. 70. *gambaudynge*] i. e. gambolling.

v. 74. *The countrynge at Cales*] — *countrynge* does not, I apprehend, mean—encountering, but is a musical term (see note on heading of poem, p. 11) used here metaphorically, as in other parts of Skelton's works. The allusion seems to be to the meeting between Henry the Eighth and Francis in 1520, when (as perhaps few readers need be informed) Henry went over to Calais, proceeded thence to Guisnes, and met Francis in the fields between the latter town and Ardres. If " *Cales* " is to be understood as—Cadiz (see note, p. 150. v. 3.) I know not any occurrence there of sufficient consequence to suit the present passage.

v. 75. *Wrang vs on the males*] See note, p. 74. v. 700.

v. 77. *grouchyng*] i. e. grudging.

v. 79. *talwod*] " Talshide or *Talwood* (Taliatura) is Fire-wood, cleft and cut into Billets of a certain Length . . . This was anciently written *Talghwode.*" Cowel's *Law Dictionary*, &c. ed. 1727.

—— *brent*] i. e. burned.

v. 81. *We may blowe at the cole*] See note, p. 319. v. 610.

v. 83. *Mocke hath lost her sho*] See note, p. 346. v. 1396.

v. 87. *As ryght as a rammes horne*] See note, p. 295. v. 1201.

* v. 90. *all to-torne*] i. e. torn to pieces. See note, p. 22. v. 32.

* v. 92. *Fauell*] i. e. Flattery. See note, p. 30. v. 134.

Page 280. v. 93. *Iauell*] See note, p. 256. v. 2218.

v. 94. *Hauell*] Which occurs again in v. 604, is a term of reproach found less frequently than *javel* in our early writers : whether it be connected with *haveril*,—one who *havers* (see the Gloss. to *The Towneley Myst.* in v. *Hawvelle*), I cannot pretend to determine.

—— *Haruy Hafter*] See note, p. 30. v. 138.

v. 95. *Iack Trauell*] Among payments made in the year 1428 (in the reign of Hen. vi.), *Jack Travel* occurs as the name of a real person ; "Et a Iakke Travaill et ses compaignons, feisans diverses Jeues et Enterludes, dedeins le Feste de Noell, devant nostre dit Sire le Roi," &c. Rymer's *Fœd.* T. iv. p. 133.

v. 97. *pollynge and shauynge*]—*pollynge*, i. e. shearing, clipping,—plundering.

v. 99. *reuynge*] i. e. reaving.

v. 101. *vayleth*] i. e. availeth.

v. 105. *reason and . . . skyll*] See note, p. 207. v. 106.

v. 106. *garlycke pyll*] i. e. peel garlic.

v. 108. *shyll*] i. e. shell.

v. 109. *rost a stone*] So Heywood ;
> "I doe but *roste a stone*
In warming her."
> *Dialogue,* &c. sig. F 2,—*Workes*, ed. 1598.

v. 110. *no man but one*] i. e. Wolsey.

v. 114. *cammocke*] i. e. a crooked beam, or knee of timber. See note, p. 126. v. 30.

v. 115. *This byll well ouer loked*] i. e. This writing being well overlooked, examined.

v. 117. *There went the hare away*] A proverbial expression :
> "*Man.* By my fayth, a lytell season
> I folowed the counsell and dyet of reason.

Gloto. There went the hare away;
  Hys dyet quod a," &c.
      Medwall's *Interlude of Nature*, n. d., sig. g ii.

          " heere's the King, nay stay ;
And heere, I heare [ay, here] : *there goes the Hare
    away."*   *The Spanish Tragedie* (by Kyd),
                    sig. G 3. ed. 1618.

Page 280. v. 118. *the gray*] i. e. the badger : see note, p. 303. v. 101.

  v. 119. *the buck*] Qy. does Skelton, under these names of animals, allude to certain persons ? If he does, " the buck " must mean Edward Duke of Buckingham, who, according to the popular belief, was impeached and brought to the block by Wolsey's means in 1521 : so in an unprinted poem against the Cardinal;

" Wherfor nevyr looke ther mowthes to be stoppyd
  Tyll ther money be restoryd, thow sum hedes be of
      As thowe dyd serue *the Buckke;*   [choppyd,
  For as men sey, by the that was done,
      That sens had this lande no good lucke."
                    MS. Harl. 2252. fol. 158.

  v. 123. *Ge hame*] i. e. Scottice for—Go home.

  * Page 281. v. 125. *tot quot*] See note, p. 279. v. 565. [A general dispensation. Halliwell.]

  v. 127. *lome*] i. e. loom.

  v. 128. *lylse wulse*] i. e. linsey-woolsey,—an evident play on the Cardinal's name.

  v. 130. *cule*] i. e. fundament.

  v. 132. *warse*] i. e. worse.

  v. 136. *Bothombar*] I know not what place is meant here.

* Page 281. v. 139. *gup, leuell suse*]—*gup* has occurred frequently before : see note, p. 17. v. 17. [*leuell suse*, or *level*-sice, (*levez sus ?*) is the same as level-coil (*levez cul?*), a noisy Christmas game, in which one player hunted another from his seat; hence applied to any riot or disturbance. *Level-coil* was also applied to games of skill, when, three persons playing, two at a time, the loser gave up his place and sat out. See Halliwell's *Dict.*]

v. 145. *nat worth a flye*] See note, p. 178. v. 104.

v. 150. *Yet the good Erle of Surray,*
  The Frenche men he doth fray, &c.]

This nobleman (before mentioned, see note, p. 325. v. 769), Thomas Howard (afterwards third Duke of Norfolk), commanded, in 1522, the English force which was sent against France, when Henry the Eighth and the Emperor Charles had united in an attack on that kingdom. In Stow's *Annales*, p. 517. ed. 1615, the marginal note " Earle of Surrey brent Morles in Brytaine. I. Skelton," evidently alludes to the present passage of our poem. Both Turner and Lingard in their *Histories of Engl.* mistake this nobleman for his father.

Page 282. v. 158. *mated*] i. e. confounded I may just observe that Palsgrave, besides " I *Mate* at the chesses, *Jè matte*," gives "I *Mate* or ouercome, *Je amatte.*" p. 633.

v. 163. *vrcheons*] i. e. hedge-hogs.

v. 166. *ouer shote*] i. e. over-shoot.

v. 167. *scutus*] " *Scutum*, Moneta Regum Francorum, ita appellata quod in ea descripta essent Franciæ insignia in scuto." Du Cange's *Gloss.* (Ital. *scudo*, Fr. *écu*).

Page 282. v. 170. *wonders warke*] i. e. work of wonder.

v. 175. *They shote at him with crownes, &c.*] On the immense gifts and annuities which Wolsey received from foreign powers, see Turner's *Hist. of Reign of Hen. the Eighth*, i. 236. ed. 8vo.

v. 178. *his eyen so dased*]—*dased*, i. e. dazzled, or, according to Skelton's distinction—dulled ; for in his *Garlande of Laurell* we find " eyn dasild and *dasid.*" v. 1389. vol. ii. 231.

v. 179. *ne se can*] i. e. can not see.

Page 283. v. 185. *the Chambre of Starres*] i. e. the Star-Chamber.

v. 190. *renayenge*] i. e. contradicting.

v. 194. *Good euyn, good Robyn Hood*] " Good even, good Robin Hood," was, as Ritson observes, a proverbial expression ; "the allusion is to *civility* extorted by *fear.*" *Robin Hood*, i. lxxxvii. Warton mistook the meaning of this line, as is proved by his mode of pointing it: see *Hist. of E. P.*, ii. 346. ed. 4to.

v. 197. *thwartyng ouer thom*] i. e. overthwarting them, perversely controlling them.

v. 202. *With, trompe up, alleluya*] i. e. says Warton, " the pomp in which he celebrates divine service." *Hist. of E. P.*, ii. 346 (note), ed. 4to.   Compare Wager's *Mary Magdalene*, 1567 ;

" Ite Missa est, *with pipe vp, Alleluya.*"

Sig. A iii.

v. 203. *Philargerya*] i. e. Φιλαργυρία, argenti amor, pecuniæ cupiditas.   She was one of the characters in Skelton's lost drama, *The Nigramansir.*

v. 206. *Asmodeus*] The name of the evil spirit in in the Book of *Tobit.*

Page 283. v. 208. *Dalyda*] i. e. Dalilah.

"Unto his lemman *Dalida* he told,
  That in his heres all his strengthe lay."
  Chaucer's *Monkes Tale*, v. 14069. ed. Tyr.

See too Gower's *Conf. Am.*, Lib. viii. fol. clxxxix. ed.
1554, and Lydgate's *Fall of Prynces*, B. i. leaf xxxiii.
ed. Wayland.

v. 208. *mell*] i. e. meddle (in sensu obsc.).

v. 212. *Simonia*] i. e. Simony.

v. 213. *Castrimergia*] "The true reading is CAS-
TRIMARGIA, or *Gulæ concupiscentia*, Gluttony. From
the Greek, Γαστριμαργία, ingluvies, helluatio. Not an
uncommon word in the monkish latinity. Du Cange
cites an old Litany of the tenth century, 'A spiritu
CASTRIMARGIÆ *Libera nos*, domine!' Lat. Gloss. i.
p. 398. Carpentier adds, among other examples, from
the statutes of the Cistercian order, 1375 [1357],
'Item, cum propter detestabile CASTRIMARGIÆ vitium
in labyrinthum vitiorum descendatur, &c.' Suppl.
tom. i. p. 862.' Warton's *Hist. of E. P.*, ii. 346 (note),
ed. 4to.

Page 284. v. 215. *ypocras*] See note, p. 277. v. 458.

v. 217. *In Lent for a repast, &c.*] So Roy in his
satire against Wolsey, *Rede me, and be nott wrothe*, &c.;

"*Wat.* Whatt abstinence useth he to take?
  Jeff. In Lent all fysshe he doth forsake,
      Fedde with partriges and plovers.
  Wat. He leadeth then a Lutheran's lyfe?
  Jeff. O naye, for he hath no wyfe,
      But whoares that be his lovers."
      Harl. Miscel. ix. 32. ed. Park.

v. 219. *partriche mewed*]—*mewed*, i. e. cooped up.

" I kepe *partryches in a mewe* agaynst your comyng."
Hormanni *Vulgaria*, sig. e ii. ed. 1530.

    Page 284. v. 222. *ne*] i. e. nor.

    v. 223. *a postyls lyfe*] i. e. an apostle's life.

    v. 232. *kues*] i. e. half-farthings. See note, p. 205.
v. 36.

    v. 235. *The sygne of the Cardynall Hat*] " These
allowed Stewhouses [in Southwark] had Signs on
their Fronts, towards the Thames, not hanged out,
but painted on the Walls, as a Boar's-Head, the Cross
Keys, the Gun, the Castle, the Crane, *the Cardinal's
Hat*," &c. Stow's *Survey*, B. iv. 7. ed. 1720.

    v. 236. *shyt*] i. e. shut.

    v. 237. *gup*]⎫
    . . . . . ⎬ See note, p. 17. v. 17.
    v. 239. *iast*] ⎭

    v. 240. *Wyll ye bere no coles*] Steevens, in his note
on the opening of Shakespeare's *Romeo and Juliet*,
cites the present line among the examples which he
gives of the expression to *bear* or *carry coals*, i. e. to
bear insults, to submit to degradation. In the royal
residences and great houses the lowest drudges appear
to have been selected to carry coals to the kitchens,
halls, &c.; see note on Jonson's *Works*, ii. 169, by
Gifford, who afterwards (p. 179) observes, " From the
mean nature of this occupation it seems to have been
somewhat hastily concluded, that a man who would
carry coals would submit to any indignity."

    v. 241. *A mayny of marefoles*] i. e. (as appears from
the expressions applied to horses four lines above) a
set of marefoals, fillies.

    Page 285. v. 257. *next*] i. e. nearest.

    v. 261. *Poppynge folysshe dawes*] See note, p. 197.
v. 39.

Page 285. v. 262. *pyll'strawes*]—*pyll*, i. e. peel.

v. 264. *Huntley bankes*] See note, p. 181. v. 149.

v. 269. *Lorde Dakers*] Thomas Lord Dacre (of Gillesland, or of the North) was warden of the West Marches. The accusation here thrown out against him (because, perhaps, he was on the best terms with Wolsey) of "agreeing too well with the Scots" is altogether unfounded. He was for many years the able and active agent of Henry in corrupting by gold and intrigues the nobles of Scotland, and in exciting ceaseless commotions in that kingdom, to the destruction of its tranquillity and good government. He died in 1525. And see notes on vv. 283, 353.

v. 270. *Jacke Rakers*] See note, p. 135. v. 108.

v. 271. *crakers*] i. e. vaunters, big-talkers.

v. 278. *the red hat*] i. e. Wolsey.

v. 280. *lure*] See note, p. 81. v. 1100.

v. 281. *cure*] i. e. care.

v. 283. *Lorde Rose*] i. e. Thomas Manners, Lord Roos. In 14 Henry viii. he was constituted warden of the East Marches towards Scotland; and by letters patent in 17 Henry viii. he was created Earl of Rutland. He died in 1543. See Collins's *Peerage*, i. 465. sqq. ed. Brydges. Hall makes the following mention of him: "In this sommer [xiiii yere of Henry the viii] the lorde Rosse and the lorde Dacres of the North whiche were appointed to kepe the borders against Scotland did so valiantly that they burned the good toune of Kelsy and lxxx. villages and ouerthrew xviii. towers of stone with all their Barnkyns or Bulwerkes." *Chron.* fol. ci. ed. 1548.

v. 285. *a cockly fose*] A term which I do not understand.

Page 286. v. 286. *Their hertcs be in thyr hose*] See note, p. 199. v. 107.

v. 287. *The Erle of Northumberlande, &c.*] i. e. Henry Algernon Percy, fifth Earl of Northumberland. In 14 Henry viii. he was made warden of the whole Marches, a charge which for some reason or other he soon after resigned : *vide* Collins's *Peerage*, ii. 305. ed. Brydges. That he found himself obliged to pay great deference to the Cardinal, is evident from Cavendish's *Life of Wolsey*, where (pp. 120–128. ed. 1827) see the account of his being summoned from the north, &c. when his son Lord Percy, (who was then, according to the custom of the age, a "servitor" in Wolsey's house) had become enamoured of Anne Boleyn. This nobleman, who encouraged literature, and appears to have patronised our poet (see *Account of Skelton*, &c.), died in 1527.

v. 291. *Rynne*] i. e. Run.

v. 292. *mayny of shepe*] i. e. flock of sheep.

v. 293. *loke . . . dur*] i. e. look . . . door.

v. 294. *mastyue cur*]   ⎫ i. e. Wolsey : see note, p.
v. 295. *bochers dogge*] ⎭   372. v. 478.

v. 297. *gnar*] i. e. snarl, growl.

Page 287. v. 308. *astate*] i. e. estate, state, rank, dignity.

v. 312. *foles and dawes*] i. e. fools and simpletons ; see note, p. 36. v. 301.

v. 315. *pletynge*] i. e. pleading.

v. 316. *Commune Place*] i. e. Common Pleas.

* v. 326. *huddypeke*] i. e. fool. See note, p. 232. v. 1176.

v. 327. *Thy lernynge is to lewde*]—*to lewde*, i. e too

bad, too mean. So in our author's *Speke, Parrot,* we find " *lewdlye* ar they *lettyrd.*" v. 296. vol. ii. 261.

Page 287. v. 328. *well thewde*] i. e. well mannered.

Page 288. v. 338. *rowte*] See note, p. 296. v. 1223.

v. 343. *the Scottysh kynge*] i. e. James the Fifth.

v. 347. *whipling*] Perhaps the same as—*pipling.* see note on l. 3 (prose), p. 194.

* v. 352. *calstocke*] i. e. cole, or cabbage stalk.

v. 353. *There goth many a lye*
            Of the Duke of Albany, &c.]

This passage relates to the various rumours which were afloat concerning the Scottish affairs in 1522, during the regency of John Duke of Albany. (The last and disastrous expedition of Albany against England in 1523 had not yet taken place: its failure called forth from Skelton a long and furious invective against the Duke ; see vol. ii. 321.) In 1522, when Albany with an army eighty thousand strong had advanced to Carlisle, Lord Dacre, by a course of able negotiations, prevailed on him to agree to a truce for a month and to disband his forces: see *Hist. of Scot.,* v. 156 sqq. by Tytler,—who defends the conduct of Albany on this occasion from the charge of cowardice and weakness.

v. 358. *The mountenaunce of two houres*] " *Mowntenaunce.* Quantitas. Estimata mensura." *Prompt. Parv.* ed. 1499.

" And largely *the mountenaunce of an houre*
    They gonne on it to reden and to poure.*"
            Chaucer's *Troil. and Cress.,* B. ii. fol. 157.
                    Workes, ed. 1602.

" Racynge and foynynge to *the mountenaunce of an houre.*" *Morte d'Arthur,* B. vii. cap. iiii. vol. i. 191. ed. Southey.

Page 288. v. 359. *sayne*] i. e. say.

Page 289. v. 367. *Burgonyons*] i. e. Burgundians.

v. 373.   *God saue my lorde admyrell!*
        What here ye of Mutrell?]

—*Mutrell* is Montreuil; and the allusion must be to some attack intended or actual on that town, of which I can find no account agreeing with the date of the present poem. To suppose that the reference is to the siege of Montreuil in 1544, would be equivalent to pronouncing that the passage is an interpolation by some writer posterior to the time of Skelton.

v. 375. *mell*] i. e. meddle.

v. 380.   *For drede of the red hat*
        Take peper in the nose]

i. e. For dread that the Cardinal, Wolsey, take offence.

    " Hee *taketh pepper in the nose*, that I complayne
       Vpon his faultes."

                 Heywood's *Dialogue*, &c. sig. G.,—
                      Workes, ed. 1598.

* v. 382. *of gose*] i. e. off goes.

v. 383. *Of by the harde arse*] Compare the *Interlude of the iiii Elementes*, n. d.;

      " Ye but yet I seruyd another wors :
       I smot *of* his legge *by the hard ars*
       As sone as I met hym there."   Sig. E i.

v. 384. *trauarse*] i. e. thwarting contrivance.

v. 386. *makys our syre to glum.*] i. e. makes our lord (Wolsey) have a gloomy or sour look.

* v. 391. *go or ryde*] i. e. walk or ride. See note, p. 51. v. 186.

Page 290. v. 397. *frayne*] i. e. ask, inquire.

v. 401. *Hampton Court*] The palace of Wolsey; which he afterwards, with all its magnificent furniture, presented to the King.

v. 407. *Yorkes Place*] The palace of Wolsey, as Archbishop of York, which he had furnished in the most sumptuous manner : after his disgrace, it became a royal residence under the name of Whitehall.

v. 409.   *To whose magnifycence, &c.*

. . . .

Embassades of all nacyons]

—*Embassades*, i. e. Embassies. " All ambassadors of foreign potentates were always dispatched by his discretion, to whom they had always access for their dispatch. His house was always resorted and furnished with noblemen, gentlemen, and other persons, with going and coming in and out, feasting and banqueting all ambassadors diverse times, and other strangers right nobly." Cavendish's *Life of Wolsey*, p. 112. ed. 1827.

v. 417. *tancrete*] " *Tancrit* : Transcrit, copié." Roquefort's *Gloss. de la Lang. Rom.*

v. 418. *obstract*] i. e. abstract.

Page 291. v. 425. *Whan him lyst*] i. e. When it pleases him.

v. 434. *vndermynde*] i. e. undermine.

v. 435. *sleyghtes*] i. e. artful contrivances.

v. 438. *coarted*] i. e. coarcted, confined.

v. 444. *taken in gre*] i. e. taken kindly, in good part : see note, p. 16. v. 68.

v. 449.   *He bereth the kyny on hand,*
           That he must pyll his lande]

—*bereth on hand*, i. e. leads on to a belief, persuades.

" Lordings, right thus, as ye han understond,
  Bare I stifly min old husbondes *on hond,*
  That thus they saiden in hir dronkennesse."
              Chaucer's *Wif of Bathes Prol.,* 5961.
                                ed. Tyr.

." He is my countre man : as he *bereth me an hande,*—
vti mihi vult persuasum." Hormanni *Vulgaria,* sig. X
viii. ed. 1530. The expression occurs in a somewhat
different sense in our author's *Magnyfycence,* see note,
p. 211. v. 357 : *pyll,* i. e. strip, spoil.

   Page 292. v. 463. *a cœciam*] " *Cœcia,* σκοτοδινία [a
vertigo with loss of sight]." Du Cange's *Gloss.* The
editions give *Acisiam.* Qy. is " *accidiam* " the right
reading (" *Acedia, Accidia* . . . tædium . . tristitia,
molestia, anxietas," &c. (Gr. ἀκηδία) : see *Du Cange)* ?

   v. 476. *a Mamelek*] i. e. a Mameluke. Compare
The Image of Ipocrisy, (a poem in imitation of Skel-
ton, which is appended to the present edition) ;

        " And crafty inquisitors,
         Worse then *Mamalokes.*"   Part Four.

   v. 478. *potshordes*] i. e. potsherds.

   v. 483. *God to recorde*] i. e. God to witness.

   Page 293. v. 485. *reason or skyll*] See note, p. 207.
v. 106.

   v. 486.   *the primordyall*
               Of his wretched originall]
—*primordyall,* i. e. first beginning.

   v. 490. *sank*] i. e. blood.

   v. 491. *bochers*] i. e. butcher's : see note, p. 372.
v. 478.

   v. 495. *rowme*] i. e. room, place, office.

   v. 505. *parde*] i. e. *par dieu,* verily.

Page 293. v. 508. *saw*] i. e. saying,—branch of learning. So in our author's *Colyn Cloute;*
    " Some lernde in other *sawe.*"
                                        v. 734. vol. ii. 150.

v. 511. *quatriuials*] ⎱ See note, p. 362. v. 171. This
v. 515. *triuials*]   ⎰ depreciation of Wolsey's ac-
quirements is very unjust: his learning, there is rea-
son to believe, was far from contemptible.

Page 294. v. 517. *worth a fly*] See note, p. 178. v. 104.

v. 518. *Haly*]   ⎱ See notes, p. 61. vv. 505.
v. 520. *Albumasar*]   ⎰ 501.

v. 522. *mobyll*] i. e. movable.

v. 526. *humanyte*] i. e. *humaniores literæ,* polite lite-
rature.

v. 533. *our processe for to stable*]—*processe.* i. e.
story, account; see notes, p. 75. v. 735. p. 79. v. 969,
&c. and compare our author's Fourth Poem *Against
Garnesche,* " But now my *proces for to saue,*" v. 157.
vol. i. 152.

v. 538. *conceyght*] i. e. conceit,—good opinion, fa-
vour.

v. 540. *exemplyfyenge*] i. e. following the example of.

Page 295. v. 550. *A wretched poore man, &c.*] i. e.
Abdalonimus (or Abdolonimus) whom Alexander
made king of Sidon: see Justin, xi. 10. Cowley
touches on the story at the commencement of *Plant.
Lib. iv.;* and in his English version of that commence-
ment, under the title of *The Country Life,* he has
greatly improved the passage.

v. 557. *occupyed a showell*] i. e. used a shovel: see
note, p. 3. v. 52.

Page 295. v. 566. *renowme*] i. e. renown.

v. 569. *with lewde condicyons cotyd*] i. e. quoted, noted, marked, with evil qualities : see note, p. 132. v. 12.

v. 570. *ben*] i. e. be.

v. 573. *Couetys*] i. e. Covetise, covetousness.

Page 296. v. 575. *wode*] i. e. mad.

v. 576. *mode*] i. e. mood, passion.

v. 577. *swerde*] i. e. sword.

v. 579. *sone*] i. e. soon.

v. 583. *trone*] i. e. throne.

v. 584. *a great astate*] i. e. a person of great estate, or rank.

v. 585. *play checke mate*] In allusion to the king's being put in *check* at the game of chess.

v. 586. *ryall*] i. e. royal.

v. 591. *fynd*] i. e. fiend.

v. 594. *Lyke Mahounde in a play*] In none of the early miracle-plays which have come down to us is Mahound (Mahomet) a character, though he is mentioned and sworn by.

v. 601. *rebads*] i. e. ribalds.

v. 602. *beggers reiagged*] i. e. beggars all-tattered.

v. 603. *recrayed*] i. e. recreant.

Page 297. v. 604. *hauell*] See note on v. 94. p. 378.

v. 605. *Rynne*] i. e. Run.

—— *iauell*] See note, p. 256. v. 2218.

v. 606. *peuysshe pye*] i. e. silly magpie.

v. 607. *losell*] i. e. good-for-nothing fellow, scoundrel.

v. 613. *Iacke breche*] i. e. Jack-ass (·arse).

v. 618. *shrewdly*] i. e. badly.

Page 297. v. 621. *kayser*] i. e. emperor. See note,
p. 221. v. 796.

v. 622.   *My lorde is nat at layser ;*
          Syr, ye must tary a stounde, &c.]

—*layser*, i. e. leisure: *a stounde*, i. e. a time, a while.
Compare *A Character of the insolent behaviour of Car-*
dinal Wolsey, *as given by Thomas Allen, Priest and*
Chaplain to the Earl of Shrewsbury, in a Letter to his
Lordshyp about Apr. 1517, among Kennett's Collec-
tions,—*MS. Lansd.* 978. fol. 213. " Pleseth your
Lordshyp to understande upon Monday was sennight
last past I delivered your Letter with the examinacyon
to my Lord Cardynall at Guilford, whence he com-
manded me to wait on him to the Court. I followed
him and there gave attendance and could have no
Answer. Upon ffriday last he came from thence to
Hampton Court, where he lyeth. The morrow after
I·besought his Grace I might know his plesure ; I
could have no Answer. Upon Mondaye last as he
walked in the parke at Hampton Court, I besought his
Grace I might knowe if he wolde command me anye
servyce. He was not content with me that I spoke to
hym. So that who shall be a Suitour to him may
have no other busynesse but give attendance upon his
plesure. He that shall so doe, it is needfull shuld be a
wyser man then I am. I sawe no remedy, but came
without Answere, except I wolde have done as my
Lord Dacre's Servaunt doth, who came with Letters
for the Kynges servyce five moneths since and yet
hath no Answere. And another Servaunt of the De-
puty of Calais likewyse who came before the other to
Walsyngham, I heard, when he aunswered them, ' If ye
be not contente to tary my leysure, departe when ye

wille.' This is truthe, I had rather your Lordshyp commaunded me to Rome then deliver him Letters, and bring Aunswers to the same. When he walketh in the Parke he will suffer no Servaunt to come nyghe him, but commands them awaye as farre as one might shoote an arrowe."

Page 297. v. 631. *flyt*] i. e. remove.

v. 635. *neuer the nere*]—*nere*, i. e. nearer.

" That they were early vp, and *neuer the neere*."
> Heywood's *Dialogue*, &c. sig. A 3,—
> *Workes*, ed. 1598.

v. 636. *daungerous dowsypere*] " He hath a *daung-erous* loke. Atollit supercilium, adducit, contrahit supercilia."—" I can not away with suche *daungorous* felowes. Ferre non possum horum supercilium, vel superciliosos, arrogantes, fastuosos, vel arrogantiam, aut fastum talium." Hormanni *Vulgaria*, sigs. L i, P iiii. ed. 1530 :—*dowsypere*, i. e. lord, noble (properly, one of the *Douze-Pairs* of France) ;

" Erll, duke, and *douch-spere*."
> *Golagros and Gawane*, p. 182,—*Syr Gawayne*, &c. ed. Madden.

See too Spenser's *F. Queene*, iii. x. 31.

v. 642. *With a poore knyght*] " He [Wolsey] fell in acquaintance with one Sir John Nanphant, a very grave and ancient knight, who had a great room in Calais under King Henry the Seventh. This knight he served, and behaved him so discreetly and justly, that he obtained the special favour of his said master ; insomuch that for his wit, gravity, and just behaviour, he committed all the charge of his office unto his chaplain. And, as I understand, the office was the treasurership of Calais, who was, in consideration of his great age, discharged of his chargeable room, and returned again into England, intending to live more at quiet. And through his instant labour and especial favour his chaplain was promoted to the king's service, and made his chaplain." Cavendish's *Life of Wolsey*, p. 70. ed. 1827. According to Nash, it was Sir *Richard* Nanfan (father of Sir John) who was "captain of Calais, made a knight, and esquire of the body to Henry vii." *Hist. of Worcestershire*, i. 85.

Page 298. v. 646. *mell*] i. e. meddle.

v. 649. *doddypatis*] i. e. thick-heads.

v. 651. *iack napis*] i. e. jackanapes, ape, monkey.

v. 652. *bedleme*] i. e. bedlamite.

v. 653. *reame*] i. e. realm.

v. 661. *loselry*] i. e. wickedness, evil practice.

Page 299. v. 664. *hart rote*] i. e. heart-root.

v. 665. *kote*] i. e. coot, (water-fowl).

v. 668. *he wyll tere it asonder*] So Roy, in his satire against Wolsey, *Rede me, and be nott wrothe*, &c. ;

> " His power he doth so extende,
> That *the Kyngis letters to rende*
> He will not forbeare in his rage."
>
> *Harl. Miscell.*, ix. 69. ed. Park.

v. 670. *hoddypoule*] i. e. dunder-head.

v. 674. *settys nat by it a myte*] i. e. values it not at a mite, cares not a mite for it.

v. 679. *demensy*] i. e. madness.

v. 683. *wele*] i. e. well.

v. 684. *How Frauncis Petrarke, &c.*] " Vidi Aquensem Caroli sedem, & in templo marmoreo verendum barbaris gentibus illius principis sepulchrum, vbi fabellam audiui, non inamœnam cognitu, a quibusdam

templi sacerdotibus, quam scriptam mihi ostenderunt,
& postea apud modernos scriptores accuratius etiam
tractatam legi, quam tibi quoque ut referam incidit
animus: ita tamen, ut rei fides non apud me quæratur,
sed (vt aiunt) penes auctores maneat. Carolum Re-
gem quem Magni nomine [ed Bas. cognomine] æquare
Pompeio & Alexandro audent, mulierculam quandam
perdite & efflictim amasse memorant, eius blanditiis
eneruatum, neglecta fama (cui plurimum inseruire
consueuerat) & posthabitis regni curis, aliarum rerum
omnium & postremo suiipsius oblitum, diu nulla pror-
sus in re nisi illius amplexibus acquieuisse, summa cum
indignatione suorum ac dolore. Tandem cum iam
spei nihil superesset (quoniam aures regias salutaribus
consiliis insanus amor obstruxerat), fœminam ipsam
malorum causam insperata mors abstulit, cuius rei in-
gens primum in regia sed latens gaudium fuit: deinde
dolore tantum priore grauiore, quantum fœdiori morbo
correptum regis animum videbant, cuius nec morte
lenitus furor, sed in ipsum obscœnum cadauer &
exangue translatus est, quod balsamo & aromatibus
conditum, onustum gemmis, & velatum purpura, die-
bus ac noctibus. tam miserabili quam cupido fouebat
amplexu. Dici nequit quam discors & quam male se
compassura conditio est amantis ac regis: nunquam
profecto contraria sine lite iunguntur. Quid est autem
regnum, nisi iusta & gloriosa dominatio? Contra quid
est amor, nisi fœda seruitus & iniusta? Itaque cum
certatim ad amantem (seu rectius ad amentem) Regem,
pro summis regni negotiis legationes gentium, præfec-
tique & prouinciarum præsides conuenirent, is in lec-
tulo suo miser, omnibus exclusis & obseratis foribus,
amato corpusculo cohærebat, amicam suam crebro,

velut spirantem responsuramque compellans, illi curas
laboresque suos narrabat, illi blandum murmur & noc-
turna suspiria, illi semper amoris comites lachrymas
instillabat, horrendum miseriæ solamen, sed quod vnum
ex omnibus Rex alioquin (vt aiunt) sapientissimus
elegisset.   Addunt fabulæ quod ego nec fieri potuisse
nec narrari debere arbitror.   Erat ea tempestate in
aula Coloniensis Antistes vir, vt memorant, sanctitate
& sapientia clarus, necnon comis, et consilii Regii
prima vox, qui domini sui statum miseratus, vbi ani-
maduertit humanis remediis nihil agi, ad Deum versus,
illum assidue precari, in illo spem reponere, ab eo
finem mali poscere multo cum gemitu : quod cum diu
fecisset, nec desiturus videretur, die quodam illustri
miraculo recreatus est : siquidem ex more sacrificanti,
& post deuotissimas preces pectus & aram lachrymis
implenti, de cœlo vox insonuit, Sub extinctæ mulieris
lingua furoris Regii causam latere.   Quo lætior, mox
peracto sacrificio, ad locum vbi corpus erat se prori-
puit, & iure notissimæ familiaritatis regiæ introgressus,
os digito clam scrutatus, gemmam perexiguo annulo
inclusam sub gelida rigentique lingua repertam festina-
bundus auexit.   Nec multo post rediens Carolus, & ex
consuetudine ad optatum mortuæ congressum proper-
ans, repente aridi cadaueris spectaculo concussus,
obriguit, exhorruitque contactum, auferri eam quan-
tocius ac sepeliri iubens.   Inde totus in Antistitem
conuersus, illum amare, illum colere, illum indies arc-
tius amplecti.   Denique nihil nisi ex sententia illius
agere, ab illo nec diebus nec noctibus auelli.   Quod
vbi sensit vir iustus ac prudens, optabilem forte multis
sed onerosam sibi sarcinam abiicere statuit, veritusque
ne si vel ad manus alterius perueniret, vel flammis

NOTES TO VOLUME II.

consumeretur, domino suo aliquid periculi afferret, annulum in vicinæ paludis præaltam voraginem demersit. Aquis forte tum rex cum proceribus suis habitabat, ex eoque tempore cunctis ciuitatibus sedes illa prælata est, in ea nil sibi palude gratius, ibi assidere & illis aquis mira cum voluptate, illius odore velut suauissimo delectari. Postremo illuc regiam suam transtulit, & in medio palustris limi, immenso sumptu, iactis molibus, palatium templumque construxit, vt nihil diuinæ vel humanæ rei eum inde abstraheret. Postremo ibi vitæ suæ reliquum egit, ibique sepultus est : cauto prius vt successores sui primam inde coronam & prima imperii auspicia capescerent, quod hodie quoque seruatur, seruabiturque quam diu Romani frena imperii Theutonica manus aget." Petrarchæ *Fam. Epist.*, lib. i. Ep. iii. p. 10, *et seq.*, ed. 1601.— On this story, which he found in a French author, Mr. Southey has composed a ballad : see his *Minor Poems.*

Page 300. v. 694. *carectes*] i. e. characters, magical inscriptions.

v. 703. *Acon*] i. e. Aix la Chapelle ; " *Acon* in Almayne whyche is a moche fayr cytee, where as kyng charles had made his paleys moche fayr & ryche and a ryght deuoute chapel in thonour of our lady, wherin hymself is buryed." Caxton's *History and Lyf of Charles the Grete*, &c. 1485. sig. b 7.

v. 709. *obsolute*] i. e. absolute, absolved.

v. 710. *practyue*] i. e. practise.

—— *abolete*] i. e. antiquated, abolished.

v. 713.
> But I wyll make further relacion
> Of this isagogicall colation]

—*isagogicall colation* seems to be equivalent here to—

comparison introduced, or discourse introduced for the sake of comparison.

Page 300. v. 715. *How maister Gaguine, &c.*] Concerning Gaguin see the *Account of Skelton's Life*, &c. The passage here alluded to, will be found in *Roberti Gaguini ordinis sanctæ trinitatis ministri generalis de origine et gestis francorum perquamutile compendium*, lib. x. fol. cxiiii. (where the marginal note is " Balluæ cardinalis iniquitas "), ed. 1497. Cardinal Balue (whom the reader will probably recollect as a character in Sir W. Scott's *Quentin Durward*) was confined by order of Louis XI. in an iron cage at the Castle of Loches, in which durance he remained for eleven years. But there is no truth in Skelton's assertion that he " was hedyd, drawen, and quartered," v. 737; for though he appears to have deserved that punishment, he terminated his days prosperously in Italy.

v. 720. *a great astate*] i. e. a person of great estate, or rank.

Page 301. v. 728. *so wele apayed*] i. e. so well satisfied, pleased.

v. 731. *hym lyst*] i. e. pleased him.

v. 732. *cheked at the fyst*] Seems to be equivalent here to—attacked, turned against the hand which fed him. " *Check* is when Crowes, Rooks, Pyes, or other birds comming in the view of the Hawk, she forsaketh her naturall flight to fly at them." Latham's *Faulconry* (*Explan. of Words of Art*), 1658.

v. 733. *agayne*] i. e. against.

v. 748. *dyscust*] i. e. determined. See note, p. 331. v. 881.

Page 302. v. 752. *rote*] i. e. root.

v. 753. *Yet it is a wyly mouse*

That can bylde his dwellinge house
Within the cattes eare]

This proverbial saying occurs in a poem attributed to Lydgate;

" An hardy *mowse that is bold to breede*
In cattis eeris."
            The Order of Foles,—MS. Harl. 2251. fol. 304.

And so Heywood;

" I haue heard tell, it had need to bee
A wylie mouse that should breed in the cats eare."
            Dialogue, &c. sig. G 4,—*Workes,* ed. 1598.

Page 302. v. 766. *sad*] i. e. grave, discreet. See note, p. 245. v. 1711.

v. 768. *heale*] i. e. health.

v. 774.   *that mastyfe . . .*
            Let him neuer confounde
            The gentyll greyhownde]

See note, p. 372. v. 478.

v. 782. *borde*] i. e. jest.

Page 303. v. 783. *stede*] i. e. place.

v. 784. *maister Mewtas*] John Meautis was secretary for the French language to Henry the Seventh and Henry the Eighth. It appears from Rymer's *Fœdera* that he was allowed, in consideration of his services, to import Gascon wine and to dispose of it to the best advantage, T. v. P. iv. p. 78 (anno 1494), T. vi. P. i. p. 146 (anno 1518), ed. Hagæ ; and that he was occasionally employed on business with foreign powers, T. v. P. iv. pp. 110, 113 (anno 1497). Among some, says Ashmole, who became Poor Knights of Windsor " probably out of devotion, rather than cause of poverty," was " John Mewtes Secretary of the French

Tongue (Pat. 18. H. 7. p. 1)." *Order of the Garter*,
p. 161.   Several unimportant entries concerning this
person occur in the unpublished Books of Payments
preserved in the Chapter House, Westminster.

Page 303. v. 795. *a bull vnder lead*]—lead, i. e. a
leaden seal.

v. 798. *Dymingis Dale*] So in *Thersytes*, n. d.;
" Mother bryce of oxforde, and great Gyb of hynxey,
 Also mawde of thrutton, and mable of chartesey,
 And all other wytches that walke in *dymminges dale*,
 Clytteringe and clatteringe there youre pottes with
   ale."   p. 68. Roxb. ed.

v. 799. *Portyngale*] i. e. Portugal.

v. 806. *calodemonyall*] i. e. consisting of good angels.

v. 807. *cacodemonyall*] i. e. consisting of evil angels.

v. 808. *purucy*] i. e. provide.

Page 304. v. 831. *euerychone*] i. e. every one.

v. 838. *rewth*] i. e. pity.

Page 305. v. 845. *recorde*] i. e. witness, evidence.

v. 856. *set by*] i. e. valued, regarded.

v. 867. *askrye*] i. e. a shout. The verb has occurred
several times before : see notes, p. 78. v. 903. p. 88.
v. 1358. p. 144. v. 66.

Page 306. v. 877. *haute . . . base*] i. e. high . . . low.

v. 880.   *Marke me that chase*
    In the tennys play]
See the latter part of note, p. 158. v. 62.   " *Marquez
bien cette chasse.*   Heed well that passage, marke well
the point, whereof I have informed you." Cotgrave's
Dict. in v. *Chasse.*

v. 883. *a tall man*] " *Tall* or semely." *Prompt.
Parv.* ed. 1499.

v. 885. *Hay, the gye and the gan*] In one of his

copies of verses *Against Venemous Tongues*, Skelton has,

> " Nothing to write, but *hay the gy of thre*."
>
> v. 13. vol. i. 156,

where there seems to be some allusion to the dance called *hegdeguies*. In the present passage probably there is a play on words: *gye* may mean — goose; and *gan* gander.

Page 306. v. 886. *gose*] i. e. goose.

v. 887. *The waters wax wan*] Horne Tooke in his *Div. of Purley*, Part ii. p. 179. ed. 1805, citing this line from the ed. of Skelton's *Works*, 1736, thus,

> " The waters *were* wan,"

considers " wan " as the past participle of the verb " wane,"— *wand*, decreased; and he is followed by Richardson, *Dict.* in v. *Wan*. But " were " is merely a misprint of ed. 1736; and that " wan " is here an adjective expressing the colour of the water, is not to be doubted. So Skelton elsewhere;

> " For worldly shame I *wax* bothe *wanne* and bloo."
>
> *Magnyfycence*, v. 2080. vol. ii. 98.

> " The ryuers rowth, the *waters wan*."
>
> *Balett*, v. 15 vol. i. 28.

So too in Henry's *Wallace;*

> " Bot rochis heich, and *wattir* depe and *wan*."
>
> B. vii. 814. ed. Jam.

v. 888. *ban*] i. e. curse.

v. 891. *warke*] i. e. work.

v. 896. *Sem* . . . *Cam*] i. e. Shem . . . Ham.

v. 898. *cupbord*] " *Cupborde of plate*, or to sette plate vpon, *buffet*." Palsgrave, p. 211. It had a succession of " desks " or stages, on which the plate was

displayed : see the description of a magnificent enter-
tainment in Cavendish's *Life of Wolsey*, p. 195. ed.
1827, and the editor's note.

Page 307. v. 904. *alcumyn*] i. e. a sort of mixed
metal.

v. 905. *A goldsmyth youre mayre*] "A.D. 1522 . . .
Maior, Sir John Mundy, Goldsmith, Son to William
Mundy of Wycombe in Buckinghamshire." Stow's
Survey, B. v. 129. ed. 1720.

v. 908. *trotters*] " *Trotters*, shepes fete." Palsgrave,
p. 283.

v. 909. *potshordis*] i. e. potsherds.

v. 910. *shrewdly*] i. e. badly.

v. 914. *syr Trestram*] See note, p. 67. v. 634. The
name is, of course, used here for a person of rank
generally.

v. 916. *Cane*] i. e. Caen, in Normandy.

* v. 917. *wane*] i. e. wanting, not to be had.

v. 918. *royals*] ⎫
v. 919. *nobles*] ⎬ The coins so called.

v. 920. *Burgonyons*] i. e. Burgundians.

v. 928. *With, laughe and laye downe*] A punning
allusion to the game at cards so called.

v. 930. *Sprynge of Lanam*]—*Lanam*, i. e. Langham
in Essex. In the Expenses of Sir John ·Howard, first
Duke of Norfolk, we find, under the year 1463, " Item,
Apylton and *Sprynge off Lanam* owyth my mastyr, as
James Hoberd and yonge Apylton knowyth wele [a
blank left for the sum]." *Manners and Household Ex-
penses of England*, &c. p. 180. ed. Roxb. It seems
probable, however, from the early date, that the per-
son mentioned in the entry just cited was the father
(or some near relative) of the Spring noticed by Skel-

ton. But Stow certainly alludes to the clothier of our text, where he records that, during the disturbances which followed the attempt to levy money for the king's use in 1525, when the Duke of Norfolk inquired of the rebellious party in Suffolk " what was the cause of their disquiet, and who was their captaine? ... one Iohn Greene a man of fiftie yeeres olde answered, that pouertie was both cause and captaine. For the rich clothiers *Spring of Lanam* and other had giuen ouer occupying, whereby they were put from their ordinarie worke and liuing." *Annales*, p. 525. ed. 1615. Neither Hall nor Holinshed, when relating the same circumstance, make any mention of Spring.

Page 308. v. 935. *He must tax for his wull*] i. e. He must pay taxe for his wool.

v. 952. *the streytes of Marock*] i. e. the straits of Morocco.

> " Thurghout the see of Greece, unto *the straite*
> *Of Maroc.*" Chaucer's *Man of Lawes Tale*,
> v. 4884. ed. Tyr.

v. 953. *the gybbet of Baldock*] See note, p. 358. v. 75.

v. 958. *mellys*] i. e. meddles.

Page 309. v. 972. *fendys blake*] i. e. fiends black.

v. 974. *crake*] i. e. vaunt, talk bigly.

v. 975.
> *he wolde than make*
> *The deuylls to quake*]

So Roy in his satire against Wolsey, *Rede me, and be nott wrothe,* &c.;

> " Yf he be as thou hast here sayde,
> I wene the devils will be afrayde
> To have hym as a companion;
> For what with his execracions,
> And with his terrible fulminacions,
> He wolde handle theym so,

That for very drede and feare,
All the devils that be theare
Wilbe glad to let hym go."
Harl. Miscell. ix. 29. ed. Park.

Page 309. v. 978. *fyer drake*] i. e. fiery dragon.

v. 980. *Brose them on a brake*]—*Brose,* i. e. bruise, break: *brake* (which has occurred before in a different sense, see note, p. 111. v. 324) means here an engine of torture: " I Brake on *a brake* or payne banke, as men do mysdoers to confesse the trouthe." Palsgrave, p. 463. In the Tower was a celebrated *brake* known by the nick-name of the Duke of Exeter's Daughter: see the wood-cut in Steevens's note on *Measure for Measure,* — *Shakespeare* (by Malone and Boswell), ix. 44.

v. 984. *a grym syer*]—*syer,* i. e. sire, lord.

" Ryght *a grym syre* at domys day xal he be."
Coventry Mysteries,—*MS. Cott.*
Vesp. D viii. fol. 37.

v. 985. *potestolate*] Equivalent, I suppose, to—legate.

v. 986. *potestate*] " *Potestat.* A Potestat, principall Officer, chiefe Magistrate." Cotgrave's *Dict.*

v. 989. *echone*] i. e. each one.

v. 990. *trone*] i. e. throne.

Page 310. v. 996. *Folam peason*] i. e. Fulham pease.

v. 997. *geson*] i. e. scarce, rare.

* v. 1000. *herbers*] i. e. arbours.

v. 1001. *bryght and shene*] Are synonymous : yet Spenser also has ;

" Her garment was so *bright* and wondrous *sheene,*" &c.
The Faerie Queene,—*Mutabilitie,* vii. 7.

Page 310. v. 1014. *The deuyll spede whitte*] See note, p. 228. v. 1018.

v. 1016. *rechelesse*] i. e. reckless.

v. 1019. *bended*] i. e. banded. " A knotte or a *bende* of felowes." Hormanni *Vulgaria*, sig. Z viii. ed. 1530.

v. 1020. *condyscended*] i. e. agreed. See note, p. 206. v. 39.

Page 312. v. 1055. *Remordynge*] i. e. rebuking. See note, p. 146. v. 101.

v. 1056. *flytynge*] i. e. scolding, rating.

v. 1058. *dawis*] i. e. simpletons.

v. 1059. *sawis*] i. e. sayings, texts.

v. 1060. *gygawis*] i. e. gewgaws, trifles.

v. 1066. *let*] i. e. hinder, obstruct.

v. 1067. *maumet*] See note, p. 138. v. 170.

v. 1070. *crakynge*] i. e. vaunting, talking bigly.

v. 1077. *him lykys*] i. e. pleases him.

Page 313. v. 1086. *For all priuileged places, &c.*] See note. p. 360. v. 126.

v. 1094. *Saint Albons to recorde, &c.*] Wolsey, at that time Archbishop of York and Cardinal, was appointed to hold the abbacy of St. Alban's *in commendam;* and is supposed to have applied its revenues to the expensive public works in which he was then engaged, the building of his colleges at Oxford and Ipswich, &c.,—a great infraction, it was considered, of the canon law.

v. 1100. *legacy*] i. e. legatine power.

v. 1104. *ben*] i. e. be.

Page 314. v. 1113. *He is periured himselfe, &c.*] "And York [Wolsey] perceiving the obedience that Canterbury [Warham] claimed to have of York, in-

tended to provide some such means that he would
be superior in dignity to Canterbury than to be either
obedient or equal to him. Wherefore he obtained first
to be made Priest Cardinal, and *Legatus de Latere;*
unto whom the Pope sent a Cardinal's hat, with certain
bulls for his authority in that behalf." . . . . .
" Obtaining this dignity, [he] thought himself meet to
encounter with Canterbury in his high jurisdiction
before expressed; and that also he was as meet to
bear authority among the temporal powers, as among
the spiritual jurisdictions. Wherefore remembering
as well the taunts and checks before sustained of Can-
terbury, which he intended to redress, having a respect
to the advancement of worldly honour, promotion, and
great benefits, [he] found the means with the king,
that he was made Chancellor of England; and Can-
terbury thereof dismissed, who had continued in that
honourable room and office, since long before the death
of King Henry the Seventh." Cavendish's *Life of
Wolsey*, pp. 90, 92, ed. 1827. It appears, however,
from the contemporary testimonies of Sir Thomas
More and Ammonius, that this statement was founded
on false information, and that Wolsey did not employ
any unfair means to supersede Warham. The latter
had often requested permission to give up the chan-
cellorship before the king would receive his resigna-
tion. When the seals were tendered to the Cardinal,
either from affected modesty, or because he thought
the office incompatible with his other duties, he de-
clined the offer, and only accepted it after the king's
repeated solicitations. See Singer's note on Caven-
dish, *ubi supra*, and Lingard's *Hist. of Engl.* vi. 57.
ed. 8vo.

Page 314. v. 1127.

> *he setteth neuer a deale*
> *By his former othe*]

i. e. he values not a bit, regards not a bit, his former oath.

v. 1130. *pretens*] i. e. pretension, claim.

v. 1131. *equipolens*] i. e. equality of power.

v. 1137. *pore*] i. e. poor.

Page 315. v. 1151.

> *That wyll hed vs and hange vs,*
>
> .   .   .   .   .   .
>
> *And he may fange vs*]

—*fange*, i. e. catch, lay hold of. Compare Sir D. Lyndsay's *Satyre of the Three Estaitis*, Part ii. ;

> " Sum sayis ane king is cum amang us,
>   That purposis *to hede and hang us :*
>   Thare is na grace, *gif he may fang us,*
>   But on an pin."
>   *Works*, ii. 81. ed. Chalmers.

v. 1163. *Naman Sirus*] i. e. Naaman the Syrian.

> " And *Naaman Syrus* thu pourgedest of a leprye."
>   Bale's *Promyses of God*, &c. 1538. sig. E i.

v. 1167. *pocky*] So Roy in his satire against Wolsey, *Rede me, and be nott wrothe*, &c. ;

> " He had the pockes, without fayle,
>   Wherfore people on hym did rayle
>   With many obprobrious mockes."
>   *Harl. Miscell.* ix. 32. ed. Park.

This was one of the charges afterwards brought against Wolsey in parliament.

Page 316. v. 1178. *ouerthwart*] i. e. cross, perverse.

v. 1181. *Balthasor*] " Balthasar de Geurcis was

Chirurgeon to Queen Catharine of Arragon, and received letters of naturalization, dated 16 March, 13 Hen. 8. [1521–2]. See Rymer's *Collect. ined.* MS. Add. Brit. Mus. 4621. 10." Sir F. Madden's additional note on *Privy Purse Expenses of the Princess Mary,* p. 281. He is mentioned in the following letter (now for the first time printed) from Wolsey's physician, Dr. Augustine (Augustinus de Augustinis, a Venetian), to Cromwell, requiring medical assistance for the Cardinal: "Hon^do Mr Crumwell, dopo le debite raccomadatione, ui mādo el prẹsente messo a posta, qual è un mio seruitore, per pregarui si da pte de Monsr R^mo, si da parte mia, instantemēte c̄h ad ogni modo uogliati operar c̄h m^o buths [Dr. Butts] & m^o Walter [Cromer] siano qui auāti nocte, se nō ambidoi almeno uno de loro, & l'altro potra uenir dimane, pc̄h res multū urget; prudēti & amico pauca. Item uorria uolontieri parlasti a m^o Balthasar, c̄h trouasse o facesse trouare (se pho in Londra nō ce ne fusse) di bona sorte di sanguisuge seu hyrudine, accio bisognādo per Monsr R^mo antedetto fusseno preste & preparate, i. famelice etc & se p caso m^o Balthasar nō potesse o nō uolesse trouare ditte sanguisuge, & qui uenir ad administrarle (se bisognera) ui piaccia parlar a m^o Nicolas genero de m^o Marcellus, alquale ho fatto ne li tempi passati administrarle, si c̄h cū l'uno o l'altro fati le cose siano in ordine, accio poi nō si perda tempo : q̄a periculū est in mora. Aspetto ūra risposta per el p̄nte almeno in inglese ma uoi medemo dimane Monsr R^mo ad ogni modo ui aspetta. ditte preterea a li prefati doctori c̄h portino seco qualche electó uomitiuo de piu sorte cioe debile, mediocre, & forte, accio, bisognādo, se ueggia el meglio, et nō si p̄di tempo in mādar a Londra. per el mio seruitore etiā o uero p̃ un de prefatı doctorı mādati la manna da bonuisi o da qualcħ un' altro doue meglio se atrovera. Xp̃o da mal ui guardi. in Asher. 1529. ad. 19. gennaio. mādati etiā qualche granati & arācij.

a ūri cōmādi Aug.º aug^t."

MS. Cott. Tit. B i. fol. 365.

Page 316. v. 1182. wheled] i. e. whealed, wealed, or waled.

* v. 1185. It was nat heled alderbest]—alderbest, i. e. best of all,—in the best manner possible.

v. 1187. Domyngo Lomelyn, &c.] In The Privy Purse Expenses of King Henry the Eighth are several entries, relating to payments of money won by this Lombard from the King at cards and dice, amounting, in less than three years, to above 620l.: see pp. 17, 32, 33, 37, 190, 204, 205, 267, 270 of that work, edited by Sir H. Nicolas, who observes (p. 316) that Domingo " was, like Palmer and others, one of Henry's ' diverting vagabonds,' and seems to have accompanied His Majesty wherever he went, for we find that he was with him at Calais in October, 1532."

v. 1192. puskylde pocky pose]—puskylde, i. e. pustuled : pose, i. e. defluxion.

v. 1197. neder] i. e. nether, lower.

v. 1201. toke . . . warke] i. e. took . . . work.

Page 317. v. 1209. To wryght of this glorious gest, &c.] If the text be right, gest must mean—guest : so in Magnyfycence ; " thou art a fonde gest." v. 1109. vol. ii. 52. But perhaps the true reading of the passage is,

" To wryght this glorious gest
of this vayne gloryous best," in which case, *gest* would signify—story : see note, p. 122. v. 622.

Page 317. v. 1210. *best*] i. e. beast.

v. 1213. *Quia difficile est, &c.*] From Juvenal, *Sat.* i. 30.

v. 1221. *ouerse*] i. e. overlook.

v. 1224. *Omne animi vitium, &c.*] From Juvenal, *Sat.* viii. 140.

v. 1226. *defaute*] i. e. default, defect.

v. 1227. *a great astate*] i. e. a person of great estate, or rank.

Page 318. v. 1233. *fonde*] i. e. foolish.

v. 1234. *can*] i. e. know.

v. 1235. *conuenyent*] i. e. fitting.

Page 318. v. 1238. *sadnesse*] i. e. discretion. See note, p. 238. v. 1382.

v. 1239. *lack*] i. e. fault, blame.

* 1246. *it shall not skyl*] i. e. it shall not matter.

v. 1247. *byl*] i. e. writing.

v. 1248. *daucock*] See note, p. 36. v. 301.

EPITOMA, &c.

—— *Polyphemo*] In allusion to what Skelton has before said,—that the cardinal had the use of only one eye.

v. 2. *Pandulphum*] So he terms Wolsey, because Pandulph was legate from the Pope in the time of King John.

Page 319. v. 27. *Mauri*] i. e. Terentianus Maurus.

DECASTICHON, &c.

v. 1. *maris lupus*] A wretched play on words,—sea-wolf—wolf-sea—Wolsey.

Page 320. v. 8. *mulus*] See note, p. 374. v. 510.

v. 10. *Asperius nihil est misero quum surget in altum*]
From Claudian ;

> " *Asperius nihil est* humili *cum surgit in altum.*"
> *In Eutrop.* I. 181.

HOWE THE DOUTY DUKE OF ALBANY, LYKE A COW-ARDE KNYGHT, RAN AWAYE SHAMFULLY, &c.

Page 321.—— *tratlande*] i. e. prattling, idle-talking.
John duke of Albany (son of Alexander duke of
Albany, the brother of James the Third) was regent
of Scotland during the minority of James the Fifth ;
and this poem relates to his invasion of the borders in
1523; an expedition, which, according to Pinkerton,
" in its commencement only displays the regent's im-
prudence, and in its termination his total deficiency
in military talents, and even in common valour." *Hist.
of Scot.,* ii. 230.   Mr. Tytler, however, views the cha-
racter and conduct of Albany in a very different light;
and his account of the expedition (*Hist. of Scot.,* v. 166
sqq.) may be thus abridged.   Albany's army amounted
in effective numbers to about forty thousand men, not
including a large body of camp-followers.   With this
force,—his march impeded by heavy roads, the nobles
corrupted by the gold and intrigues of England, they
and their soldiers jealous of the foreign auxiliaries,
and symptoms of disorganization early appearing,—
the regent advanced as far as Melrose.   Having vainly
endeavoured to persuade his discontented army to
cross the Tweed, he encamped on its left bank, and
laid siege to Wark Castle with his foreign troops and
artillery.   There the Frenchmen manifested their

wonted courage; but the assaulting party, receiving no assistance from the Scots, and fearing that the river flooded by rain and snow would cut off their retreat, were obliged to raise the siege, and join the main body. The Earl of Surrey (see notes, p. 325. v. 769. p. 380. v. 150), who had in the mean while concentrated his troops, hearing of the attack on Wark Castle, now advanced against the enemy. At the news of his approach, the Scottish nobles being fixed in their resolution not to risk a battle, Albany retreated to Eccles, (a monastery six miles distant from Wark,) with his foreign auxiliaries and artillery; and the rest of his forces dispersed, rather with flight than retreat, amidst a tempest of snow. From Eccles Albany retired to Edinburgh, and, soon after, finally withdrew to France. His army had been assembled on the Burrow-Muir near Edinburgh towards the end of October; and its dispersion took place at the commencement of the following month.

Page 321. v. 19 *Huntley banke*] See note, p. 181. v. 149.

Page 322. v. 20. *Lowdyan*] See note, p. 175. v. 59.

v. 21. *Locryan*] See note p. 176. v. 61.

v. 22. *the ragged ray*]—*ray* seems here to be merely —array; but Skelton in his *Replycacion*, &c., has,

> " ye *dawns* all in a sute
> The heritykes *ragged ray."*   v. 168. vol. i. 239:

and see note, p. 148. v. 170.

v. 24. *Dunbar, Dunde*] See note, p. 179. v. 121.

v. 37. *With, hey, dogge, hay*] This line has occurred before, in *Elynour Rummyng*, v. 168. vol. i. 115.

v. 38. *For Syr William Lyle, &c.*] " And the seid mondaye at iij a clok at aftir none, the water of Twede being soo high that it could not be riden, the Duke sente ouer ij m¹ Frenchemen in bootis [boats] to gif assaulte to the place, who with force entred the bas courte, and by Sir William Lizle captain of the castell with c with hym were right manfully defended by the space of one houre and an half withoute suffring theym tentre the inner warde; but fynally the seid Frenche-men entred the inner warde, whiche perceiued by the seid Sir William and his company frely set vpon theym, and not onely drove theym oute of the inner warde, but alsoo oute of the vttir warde, and slewe of the seid Frenchemen x personys. And so the seid Frenche-men wente ouer the water," &c. Letter from Surrey to Henry the Eighth,—*MS. Cott. Calig. B.* vi. fol. 304. Mr. Tytler says that the assaulting party left " three hundred slain, of which the greater number were Frenchmen." *Hist. of Scot.*, v. 169.

v. 45. *lacke*] i. e. blame, reproach.

Page 323. v. 52. *reculed*] i. e. recoiled, retreated.

v. 55. *That my lorde amrell, &c.*]—*amrell*, i. e. ad-miral,—Surrey.

v. 63. *With sainct Cutberdes banner*] An earlier passage of the letter just cited is as follows. " At whiche tyme I being at Holy Island, vij myles from Berwike, was aduertised of the same [Albany's attack on Wark Castle] at v a clok at night the seid sondaye; and incontynente sente lettres to my lord cardynallis company, my lord of Northumbreland, my lord of Westmereland at Sainte Cutbertes baner lying at Anwike and thereaboutes, and in likewise to my lord Dacre and other lordes and gentilmen lying abrode in the contre to mete me at Barmer woode v myles from Werk on mondaye, whoo soo dede."

Page 323. v. 68. *crake*] i. e. vaunt.

v. 73. *ascry*] i. e. call out against, raise a shout against — assail; see notes, p. 78. v. 903. p. 88. v. 1358, &c.

v. 78. *stoutty*] i. e. stout.

Page 324. v. 91. *But ye meane a thyng, &c.*] That Albany aimed at the destruction of James v. was a popular rumour, but, according to Mr. Tytler, entirely without foundation.

v. 101. *cast*] i. e. contrivance, stratagem.

Page 325. v. 110. *beyght*] i. e., perhaps, (not bait, but) noose. *Beight, bight*, or *bought*, is any thing bent, folded: in Markham's *Masterpiece* (as Stevenson observes, Additions to Boucher's *Gloss.* in v.) it is used both to express a noose formed of a rope, and the bent or arched part of a horse's neck. In Hormanni *Vulgaria* we find " *Boughtes.* . . . Chartæ complicatæ." Sig. Q iii. ed. 1530.

v. 115. *recrayd*] i. e. recreant.

v. 120. *puaunt*] i. e. stinking.

v. 126. *Vnhaply vred*] See note, p. 197. v. 95.

v. 128. *discured*] i. e. discovered.

v. 132. *echone*] i. e. each one.

v. 135. *flery*] i. e. fleer.

Page 326. v. 146. *Mell nat*] i. e. Meddle not.

v. 152. *byrne*] i. e. burn.

v. 155. *at ylke mennes hecke*] i. e. at each man's hatch, door.

v. 156. *fynde*] i. e. fiend.

v. 159. *shake thy dogge, hay*] See note, p. 189. v. 28.

v. 161.   *We set nat a flye*
            By, &c.]
i. e. We value not a fly, care not a fly for.

Page 326. v. 163. *prane*] i. e. prawn.

v. 164. *drane*] i. e. drone. See note, p. 183. v. 172

v. 165. *We set nat a myght*] So Chaucer ;

"I nolde *setten* at his sorow *a mite.*"
Troilus and Creseide, B iii.— *Workes*,
fol. 161. ed. 1602.

v. 167. *proude palyarde*] See note, p. 370. v. 427.

Page 327. v. 168. *skyrgaliarde*] See note, p. 177. v. 101.

v. 171. *coystrowne*] See note on title of poem, p. 11.

v. 172. *dagswayne*] See note, p. 254, v. 2195. I know not if the word was ever used as a term of reproach by any writer except Skelton.

v. 182. *mell*] i. e. meddle.

v. 189.　　*Right inconuenyently*
　　　　　Ye rage and ye raue,
　　　　　And your worshyp depraue]

—*inconuenyently*, i. e. unsuitably, unbecomingly : *your worshyp depraue*, i. e. debase, degrade, lower your dignity. " I am also aduertised that he [Albany] is so passionate that and he bee aparte amongis his familiers and doth here any thing contrarius to his myende and pleasure, his accustumed maner is too take his bonet sodenly of his hed and to throwe it in the fire, and no man dare take it oute but let it to bee brent. My lord Dacre doth affirme that at his last being in Scotland he ded borne aboue a dosyn bonettes aftir that maner." Letter from Lord Surrey to Wolsey,— *MS. Cott., Calig. B* vi. fol. 316.

v. 192. *Duke Hamylcar*] ⎫ —*Duke*, i. e. leader, lord.
v. 195. *Duke Hasdruball*] ⎬ So Lydgate ;
　　　　　" *Duke* whylom of Cartage
　　　　Called *Amylchar.*"
Fall of Prynces, B. v. leaf cxxvi. ed. Wayland.

" *Duke Hasdrubal*, whome bokes magnify."

Ibid. B. ii. leaf xlv.

Page 328. v. 198. *condicions*] i. e. qualities. See note, p. 132. v. 12.

v. 209. *Howe ye wyll beres bynde*]—*beres*, i. e. bears, Compare;

" With mede men may *bynde berys*."

Coventry Mysteries,—MS. Cott. Vesp.
D viii. fol. 195.

" Som man is strong *berys for to bynde*."

Lydgate's verses *Against Self-love*, &c.—
MS. Harl. 2255. fol. 10.

" That with the strenth of my hand
　　Beres may bynd."

The Droichis Part of the Play, attributed
to Dunbar,—*Poems*, ii. 37. ed. Laing.

"Makynge the people to beleve he coulde *bynde bears*."

Bale's *Kynge Johan*, p. 72. ed. Camd.

v. 210. *the deuill downe dynge*]—*dynge*, i. e. knock. See note, p. 255. v. 2210.

v. 227. *entrusar*] i. e. intruder.

" But an *intrusour*, one called Julyan."

Lydgate's *Fall of Prynces*, B. viii.
leaf ii. ed. Wayland.

Page 329. v. 230. *to*] i. e. too.

v. 237. *lorde amrell*] i. e. lord admiral (Surrey).

v. 240. *marciall shoure*] See note, p. 179. v. 133.

v. 243. *derayne*] i. e. contest.

v. 248. *keteryng*] i. e. caterane, marauder. See note, p. 177. v. 83.

v. 251. *The fynde of hell mot sterue the*] i. e. May

the fiend of hell cause thee to die, destroy thee.   (To *sterue* in our old writers is common in the sense of —die, perish).

Page 329. v. 255. *Caried in a cage, &c.*] In no historian can I find any allusion to the strange vehicle here mentioned.

v. 257. *mawment*] See note, p. 138. v. 170.

Page 330. v. 268. *warke*] i. e. work.

* v. 270.   *Therin, lyke a royle,*
                 Sir Dunkan, ye dared]

Compare ;

> " By your reuellous riding on euery *royle*, ·
> Welny euery day a new mare or a moyle."
> > Heywood's *Dialogue*, &c. sig. H 4,—
> > *Workes*, ed. 1598.

" *Nulla in tam magno est corpore mica salis*, There is not one crum or droppe of good fashion in al that great *royls* bodye.   For Catullus ther speaketh of a certaine mayden that was called Quintia," &c.   Udall's *Flowers, or Eloquent Phrases of the Latine speach,*" &c. sig. G 5. ed. 1581.   Grose gives " *Roil* or *royle*, a big ungainly slamakin, a great awkward blowze or hoyden."   *Prov. Gloss.*:—*Sir Dunkan* is a Scottish name used here at random by Skelton, as he elsewhere uses other Scottish names, see note, p. 179. v. 121: *dared* [lurked, lay hid], see note, p. 237. v. 1358; and compare ; " *Daren* or preuyly ben hyd. Latito." *Prompt. Parv.* ed. 1499.

> " Vnder freshe floures sote and fayre to se,
> The serpent *dareth* with his couert poyson."
> > Lydgate's *Fall of Prynces*, B. iv.
> > leaf cvii. ed. Wayland.

> " the snayl goth lowe doun,
> *Daryth* in his shelle."
>> Poem by Lydgate (entitled in the Cata-
>> logue, *Advices for people to keep a*
>> *guard over their tongues,*—*MS. Harl.*
>> 2255. fol. 133.

Page 330. v. 274. *sely*] i. e. silly, simple, harmless.

v. 282. *It made no great fors*] i. e. It was no great
matter, it mattered not greatly.

* v. 285. *a gon stone*] i. e. gun stone, ball. See note.
p. 321. v. 629.

v. 287. *sir Topias*] See note, p. 127. v. 40.

v. 288. *Bas*] The *Bass* is an island, or rather rock,
of immense height in the Firth of Forth, about a mile
distant from the south shore.

v. 290. [*l*]*as*] I may just notice, in support of this
reading, that " a lusty *lasse* " occurs in our author's
Magnyfycence, v. 1577. vol. ii. 73.

v. 292. *I shrewe*] i. e. I beshrew, curse.

—— *lugges*] i. e. ears.

v. 293. *munpynnys*] Compare ;

> " Syrs, let us cryb furst for oone thyng or oder,
>> That thise wordes be purst, and let us go foder
>>> Our *mompyns.*"
>>>> *Prima Pastorum,*—*Towneley*
>>>> *Mysteries*, p. 89,

(a passage which the writer of the *Gloss.* altogether
misunderstands), and ;

> " Thy *mone pynnes* bene lyche olde yuory,
>> Here are stumpes feble and her are none," &c.
>>> Lydgate, *The prohemy of a mariage*, &c.—
>>> *MS. Harl.* 372. fol. 45.

Munpynnys is, I apprehend, mouth-pins, teeth. Ray gives " The *Munne*, the Mouth." *Coll. of Engl. Words*, &c.—Preface, p. x. ed. 1768 : and Jamieson has " *Munds*. The mouth."—" *Muns*. The hollow behind the jaw-bone." *Et. Dict. of Scot. Lang*. and *Suppl*.

Page 330. v. 293. *crag*] i. e. neck, throat.

v. 295. *hag*] See note, p. 21. v. 19.

v. 296. *sir Wrig wrag*] ⎫
v. 297. *sir Dalyrag*] ⎬ See note, p. 139. v. 186.

Page 331. v. 298. *mellyng*] i. e. meddling.

v. 301. *huddypeke*] See note, p. 232. v. 1176.

v. 303. *a farly freke*] i. e. a strange fellow : see notes, p. 32. v. 187 ; p. 124. v. 15.

* v. 304. *an horne keke*] A term which I am unable to explain. [" *Hornkecke*, a fysshe lyke a mackerell." Palsgrave, p. 232. " Garfysche, or *hornkeke* " (green-back). *Prompt. Parv*. Here used as a term of contempt].

v. 308. *swerde*] i. e. sword.

v. 309. *the Lyon White*] i. e. the Earl of Surrey. See note, p. 179. v. 135.

v. 316. *render the*] i. e. consign thee.

v. 317. *the flingande fende*] i. e. the flinging-fiend. So in Ingelend's *Disobedient Child*, n. d. ;

" *The flyinge and* [sic] *fiende* go with my wyfe."

Sig. F ii.

Northern readers at least need not be informed that to *fling* means—to throw out the legs;

" Sumtyme, in dansing, feirelie I *flang*."

Sir D. Lyndsay's *Epistill* before his *Dreme*,—
Works, i. 187. ed. Chalmers.

Page 332. v. 319. *borde*] i. e. jest.

v. 322. *parbrake*] i. e. vomit.

Page 332. v. 323. *auauns*] i. e. vaunts. " The brag-ing *avaunts* of the Spaniards be so accalmed," &c. *Letter of Wolsey,*—Burnet's *Hist. of the Reform.*, iii. P. ii. 9. ed. 1816.

v. 324. *wordes enbosed*] i. e. swollen, big words.

v. 329. *lewde*] i. e. evil, vile.

v. 330. *Sir Dunkan*] See note on v. 270. p. 417.

—— *in the deuill waye*] See note, p. 280. v. 672.

v. 336. *lurdayne*] See note, p. 213. v. 423.

v. 341. *varry*] i. e. fall at variance, contend.

v. 344. *stownde*] i. e. moment.

Page 333. v. 348. *ryn*] i. e. run.

v. 353. *defoyle*] i. e. defile.

v. 360. *welc*] i. e. well.

v. 366. *bace*] i. e. low.

v. 375. *cordylar*] i. e cordelier,—a Franciscan friar, whose cincture is a *cord*.

v. 377. *to*] i. e. too.

Page 334. v. 380. *daucockes*] i. e. simpletons.

v. 381. *reme*] i. e. realm.

v. 382. *Ge heme*] Scottice for—Go home (as before in *Why come ye nat to Courte*, v, 123. vol. ii. 280.)

v. 383. *fonde*] i. e. foolish.

v. 386. *mate you with chekmate*] In allusion to the king's being put in *check* at the game of chess. And see note, p. 380. v. 158.

v. 389. *pype in a quibyble*] The word *quibyble*, as far as I am aware, occurs only in Skelton. Chaucer has a well-known passage,

> " And playen songes on a small ribible ;
> Therto he song somtime a loud *quinible*."

The Milleres Tale, v. 3331, where Tyrwhitt (appar-ently against the context) supposes *quinible* to be an instrument: and I may notice that Forby gives " *Why-bibble*, a whimsy; idle fancy; silly scruple, &c." *Voc. of East Anglia.*

Page 334. v. 398. *faytes*] i. e. facts, doings.

v. 399. *me dresse*] i. e. address, apply myself.

v. 406. *auaunce*] i. e. advance.

Page 335. v. 410. *nobles*] i. e. noblesse, nobleness.

v. 417. *rechelesse*] i. e. reckless.

v. 418. *a lunatyke ouerage*] See note, p. 376. v. 39.

* v. 420. *ennewde*] i. e. embellished. See note, p. 76. v. 775.

v. 431. *Lyke vnto Hercules*] Barclay goes still farther in a compliment to the same monarch;

" *He passeth Hercules* in manhode and courage."
                    The Ship of Fooles, fol. 205. ed. 1570.

v. 436. *foy*] i. e. faith.

Page 336. v. 439. *Scipiades*] i. e. Scipio.

v. 442. *Duke Iosue*]—*Duke*, i. e. leader, lord. So Hawes;

" And in lyke wyse *duke Iosue* the gente," &c.
                    The Pastime of Pleasure, sig. c ii. ed. 1555.

v. 448. *animosite*] i. e. bravery.

v. 457. *to*] i. e. too.

v. 459. *losels*] i. e. good-for-nothing fellows, scoundrels.

v. 461. *astate*] i. e. estate, high dignity.

Page 337. v. 468. *domage*] i. e. damage.

v. 470. *rydes or goos*] See note, p. 51. v. 186.

v. 475. *a knappishe sorte*] " *Knappish.* Proterve, pervers, fascheux." Cotgrave's *Dict.* " *Knappish.* Tart, testy, snappish." Jamieson's *Et. Dict. of Scot. Lang.*: *sorte*, i. e. set.

Page 337. v. 477. *enbosed*] i. e. covered with foam. See note, p. 301. v. 24.

v. 478. *dawes*] i. e. simpletons.

v. 479. *fende*] i. e. fiend.

v. 487. *hart blode*] i. e. heart-blood.

v. 488. *gode*] i. e. good,—goods.

* v. 494. *faytour*] i. e. villain. See note, p. 149. v. 2.

v. 495. *recrayed*] i. e. recreant.

Page 338. v. 500. *rede* . . . *loke*] i. e. advise . . . look.

v. 506. *Sainct George to borowe*] i. e. St. George being my surety or pledge : the expression is common in our early poetry.

v. 508. *quayre*] i. e. quire,—pamphlet, book.

—— *Lenuoy*] Concerning this second *L'envoy*, which, I believe, does not belong to the poem against Albany, see *Account of Skelton*, &c.

Page 339. v. 9. *ammas*] i. e. amice: see note, p. 63. v. 560.

——*Ie foy enterment, &c*] i. e. Je fie entièrement, &c.

Page 340. v. 3. *stede*] i. e. place.

* Page 341. v. 22. *chare*] i. e. drive out or away. " *Charyn*' a-way, cachyn' a-way. *Abigo.*" — *Prompt. Parv.*

* v. 27. *wrote*] i. e. grub or root up.

—— *Rosary*] i. e. Rose-bush.

* v. 38. *ouer all*] i. e. everywhere.

* v. 39. *face*] i. e. outface.

v. 46. *paves*] i. e. shield (properly, a large shield covering the body).

v. 54. *sad*] i. e. grave—discreet.

INDEX TO THE NOTES.

[The figures, except in a few cases specially noted, indicate the pages of the Third Volume only.]

Printed in Great Britain by
Amazon.co.uk, Ltd.,
Marston Gate.